PRODUCTION REPORT 3: ALIEN N
HE COMES FROM TENTEKE (THUMPULON),
A PLANET .... AY,
.... HEAD
....
.... A
S............................... ORK,
.... MS
D............................... E, THE
DEBUT SONG OF ICHIRO TOBA (AN ENKA
SINGER WHO SINGS MAINLY ABOUT THE
OCEAN AND FISHING). HE SAYS HE WANTS
TO GO BACK TO HIS HOME PLANET SOON,
BUT I'M NOT LETTING HIM.

—YOSHIHIRO TOGASHI, 1992

Born in 1966, Yoshihiro Togashi won
the prestigious Tezuka Award for new
manga artists at the age of 20. He
debuted in Japan's WEEKLY SHONEN JUMP
magazine in 1988 with the romantic
comedy manga *Tende Showaru
Cupid.* His hit comic *YuYu Hakusho*
ran in WEEKLY SHONEN JUMP from 1990
to 1994. Togashi's other manga include
*I'm Not Afraid of Wolves!, Level
E,* and *Hunter x Hunter. Hunter x
Hunter* is also available through
VIZ Media.

YUYU HAKUSHO VOL. 8
The SHONEN JUMP Graphic Novel Edition

This graphic novel contains material that was originally published in English in **SHONEN JUMP** #31-34.

STORY AND ART BY
YOSHIHIRO TOGASHI

English Adaptation/Gary Leach
Translation/Lillian Olsen
Touch-up Art & Lettering/Alan Toh
Graphics & Cover Design/Courtney Utt
Editor/Michelle Pangilinan

Managing Editor/Elizabeth Kawasaki
Director of Production/Noboru Watanabe
Vice President of Publishing/Alvin Lu
Vice President & Editor in Chief/ Yumi Hoashi
Sr. Director of Acquisitions/Rika Inouye
Vice President of Sales & Marketing/Liza Coppola
Publisher/Hyoe Narita

Printed in the U.S.A.

Published by VIZ Media, LLC
P.O. Box 77010
San Francisco, CA 94107

SHONEN JUMP Graphic Novel Edition
10 9 8 7 6 5 4 3 2 1
First printing, September 2005

www.viz.com

PARENTAL ADVISORY
YUYU HAKUSHO is rated T for Teen and is recommended for ages 13 and up. This volume contains fantasy violence.

SHONEN JUMP GRAPHIC NOVEL

HAKUSHO ™

Vol.8

Open Your Eyes!!

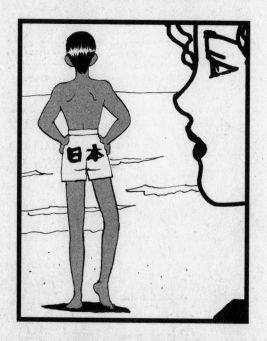

STORY AND ART BY
YOSHIHIRO TOGASHI

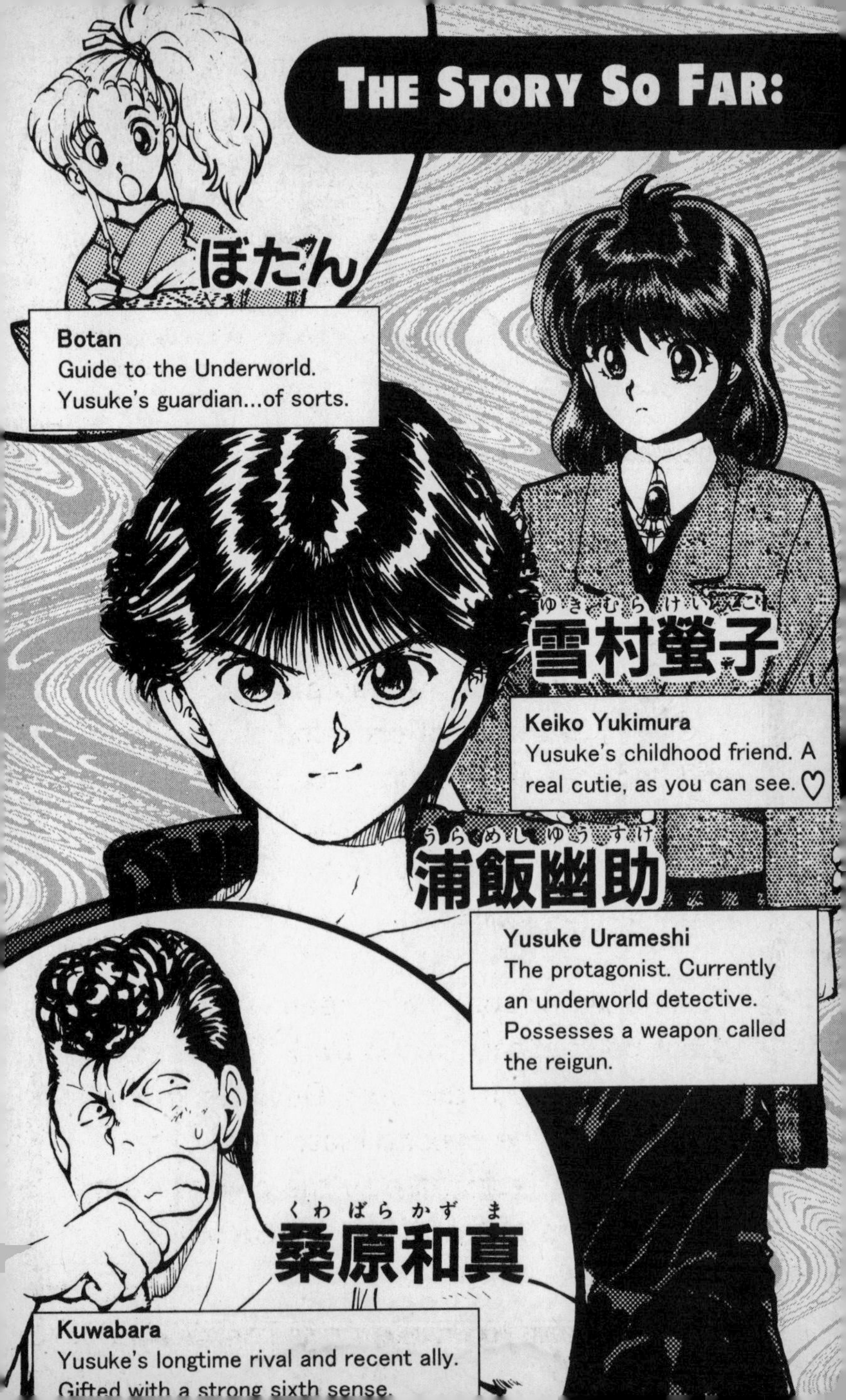

THE STORY SO FAR:
ぼたん
Botan
Guide to the Underworld.
Yusuke's guardian...of sorts.
雪村螢子
Keiko Yukimura
Yusuke's childhood friend. A real cutie, as you can see. ♡
うらめしゆうすけ
浦飯幽助
Yusuke Urameshi
The protagonist. Currently an underworld detective. Possesses a weapon called the reigun.
くわばらかずま
桑原和真
Kuwabara
Yusuke's longtime rival and recent ally.
Gifted with a strong sixth sense.

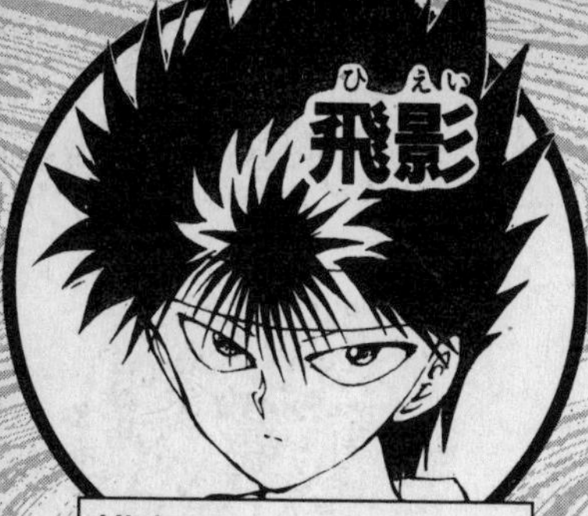
飛影

Hiei
A thief with abilities enhanced by the evil eye.

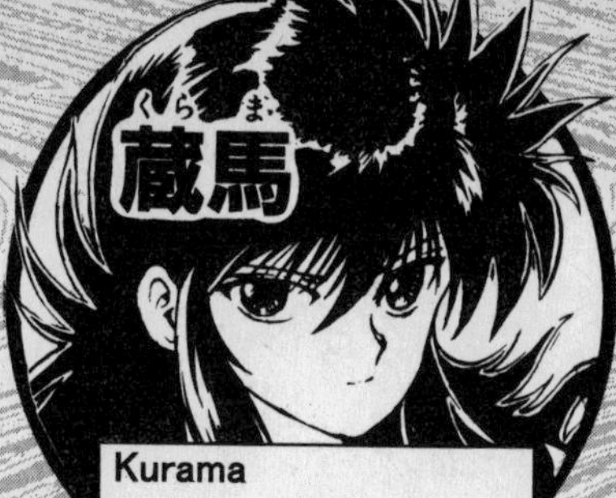
蔵馬

Kurama
A former fox demon. Suppresses his demonic powers in order to live in a human society.

This is the story of the hapless Yusuke Urameshi, killed by a car while trying to save a child. As a ghost, he was put through a number of ordeals by King Enma and had to earn his way back to life. He now works as an Underworld Detective, and all sorts of demons would be thrilled to see him die once again.

Yusuke and friends have been entered as guest competitors in the Dark Tournament, barely edging out the Jolly Devil Six in their first match. The second match has been even tougher going due to the evil machinations of Dr. Ichigaki. What will happen now...?!

YU YU HAKUSHO VOLUME 8 OPEN YOUR EYES!!

CONTENTS

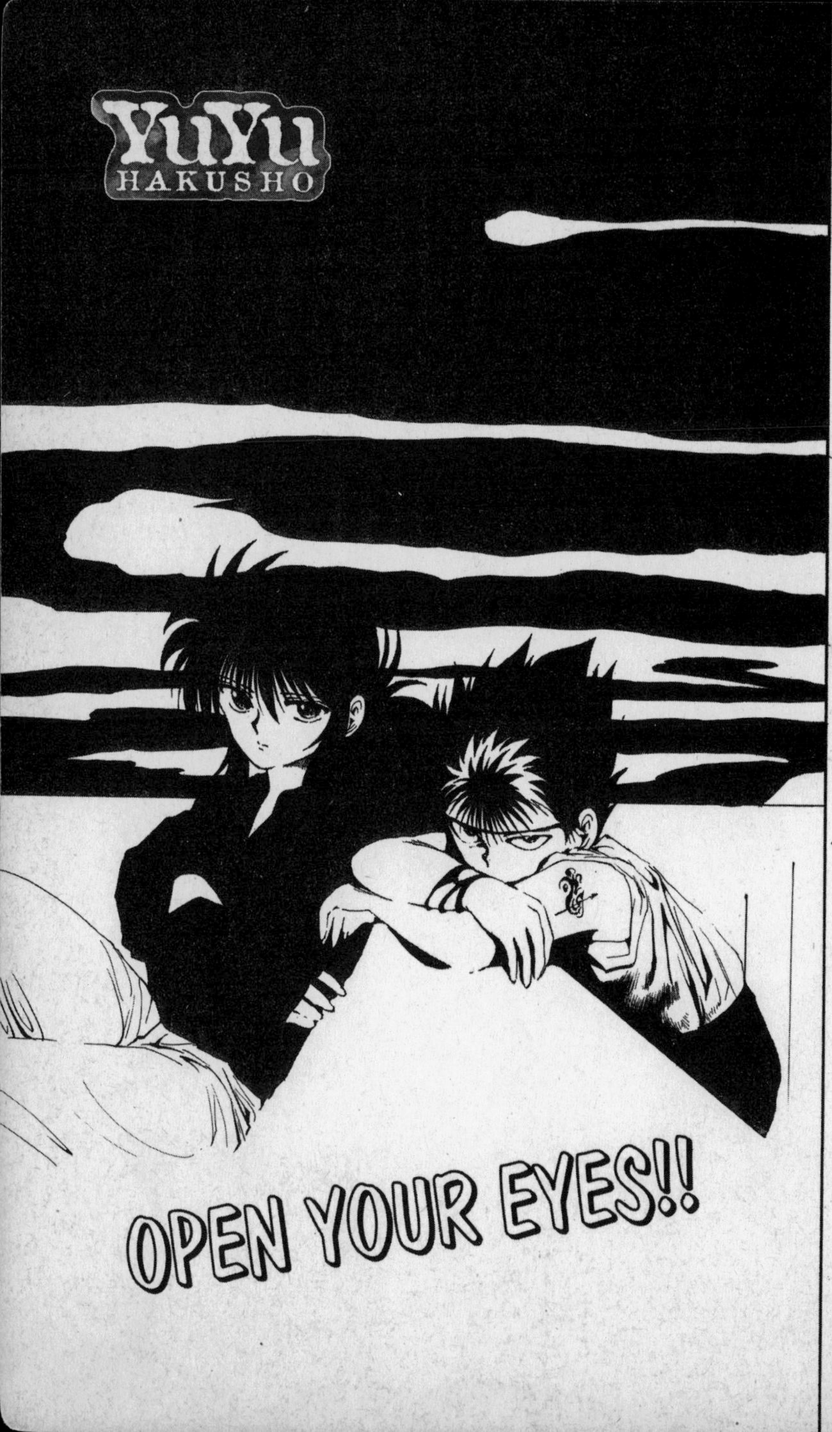
YuYu HAKUSHO
OPEN YOUR EYES!!

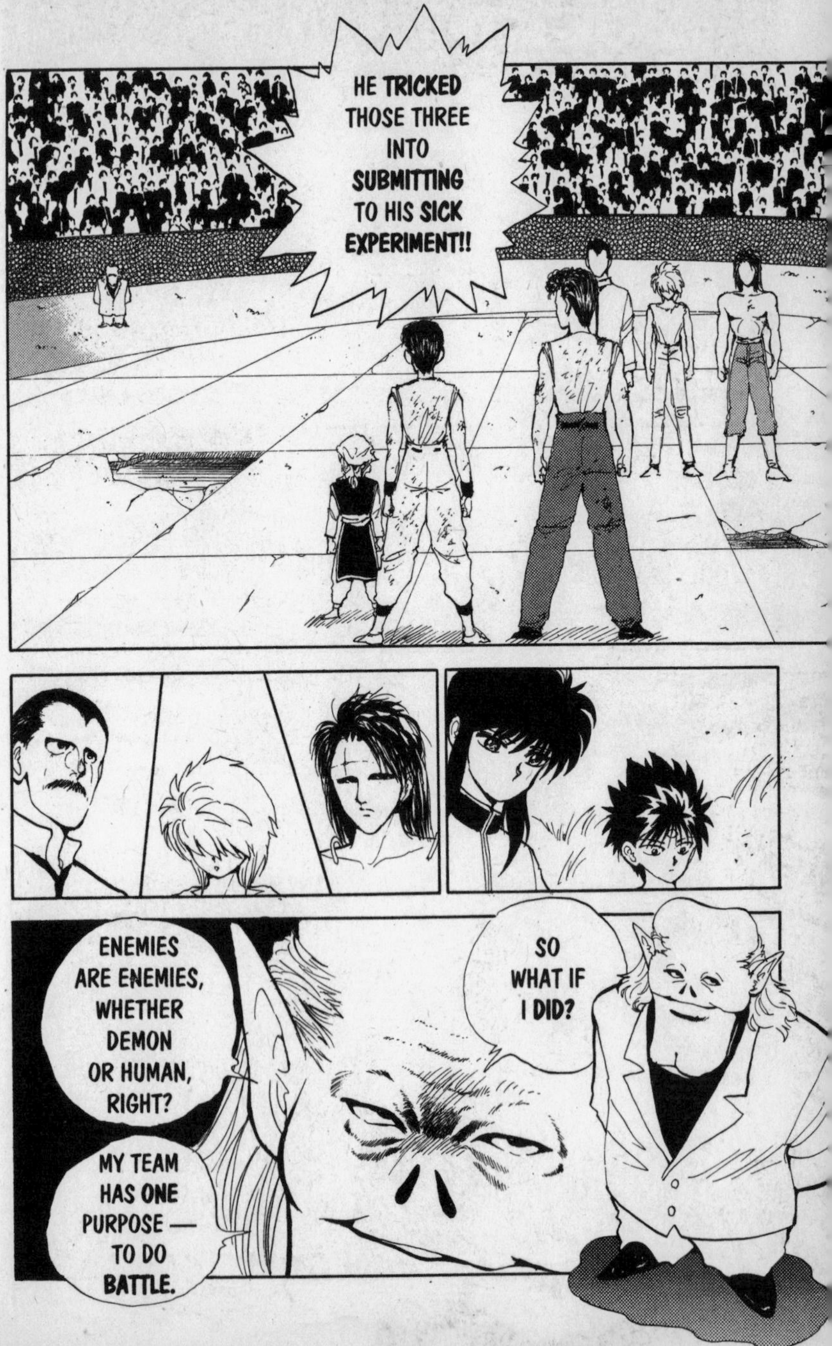
HE TRICKED THOSE THREE INTO SUBMITTING TO HIS SICK EXPERIMENT!!
SO WHAT IF I DID?
ENEMIES ARE ENEMIES, WHETHER DEMON OR HUMAN, RIGHT?
MY TEAM HAS ONE PURPOSE — TO DO BATTLE.

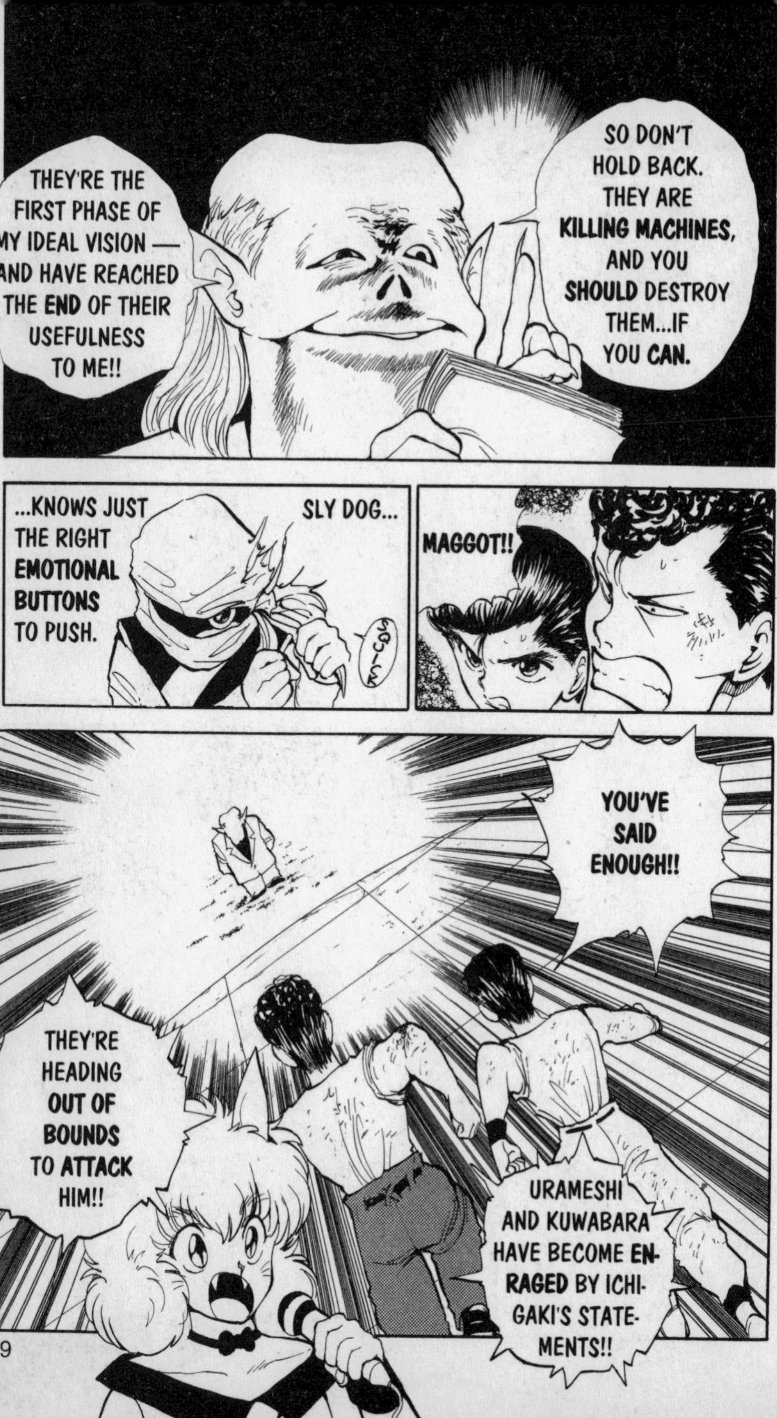
SO DON'T HOLD BACK. THEY ARE KILLING MACHINES, AND YOU SHOULD DESTROY THEM...IF YOU CAN.
THEY'RE THE FIRST PHASE OF MY IDEAL VISION — AND HAVE REACHED THE END OF THEIR USEFULNESS TO ME!!
MAGGOT!!
SLY DOG...
...KNOWS JUST THE RIGHT EMOTIONAL BUTTONS TO PUSH.
SQUICK
YOU'VE SAID ENOUGH!!
THEY'RE HEADING OUT OF BOUNDS TO ATTACK HIM!!
URAMESHI AND KUWABARA HAVE BECOME ENRAGED BY ICHIGAKI'S STATEMENTS!!

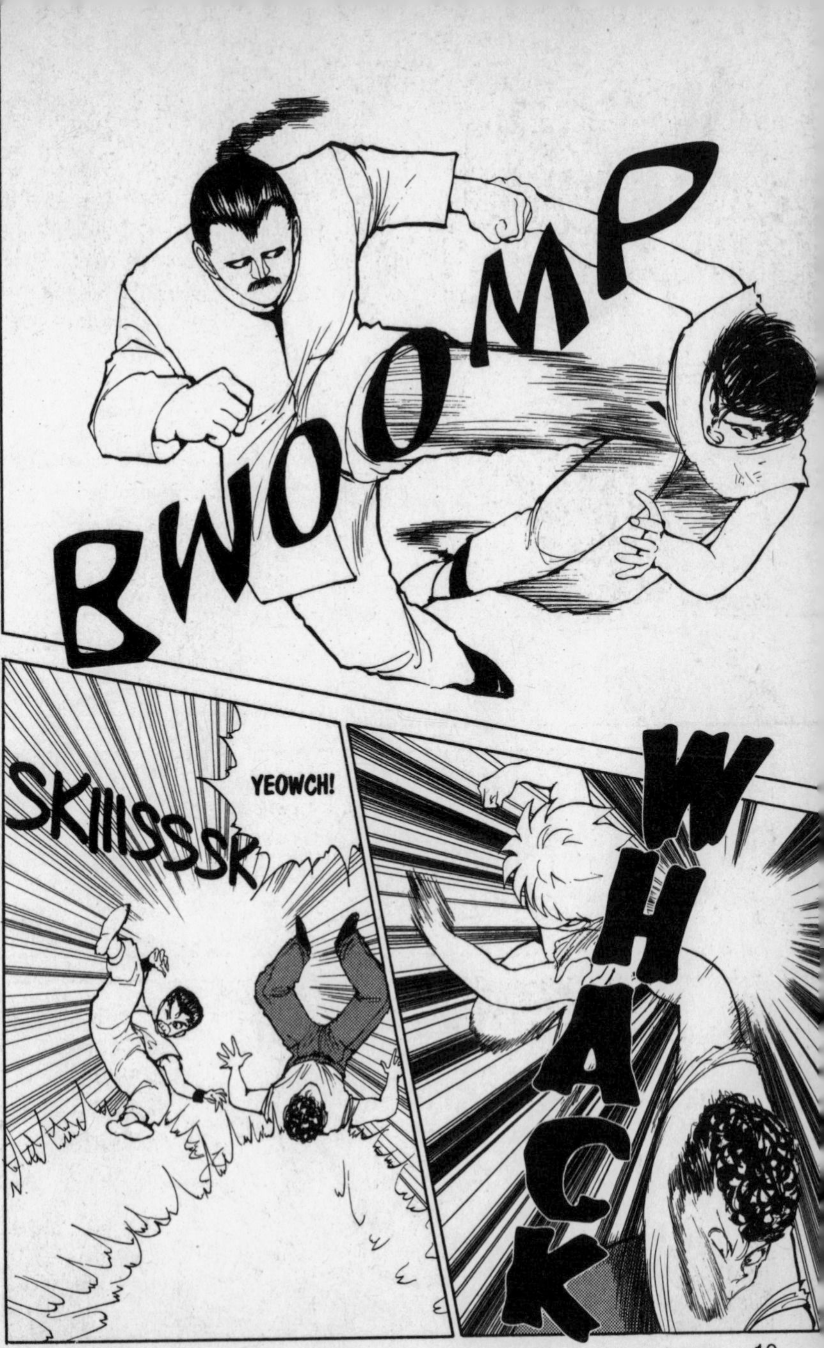
BWOOMP
WHACK
YEOWCH!
SKIIISSSK

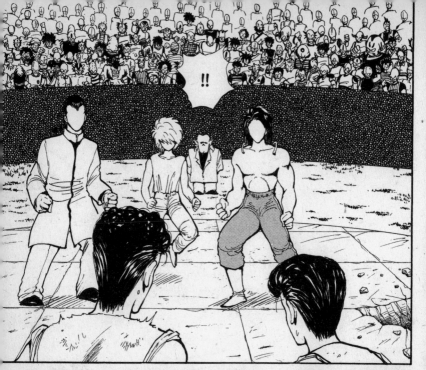

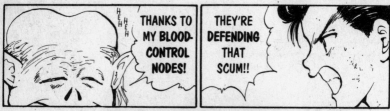

!!
THEY'RE DEFENDING THAT SCUM!!
HEH HEH
THANKS TO MY BLOOD-CONTROL NODES!
THEY FUNCTION AS SECOND BRAINS AND HEARTS — DOMINATING THE HOSTS!!
AND THEY ARE PERMANENT. REMOVE THEM, AND THE HOSTS DIE!

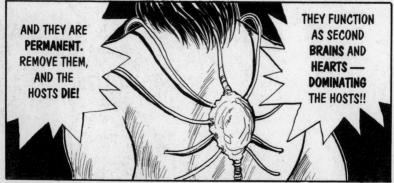

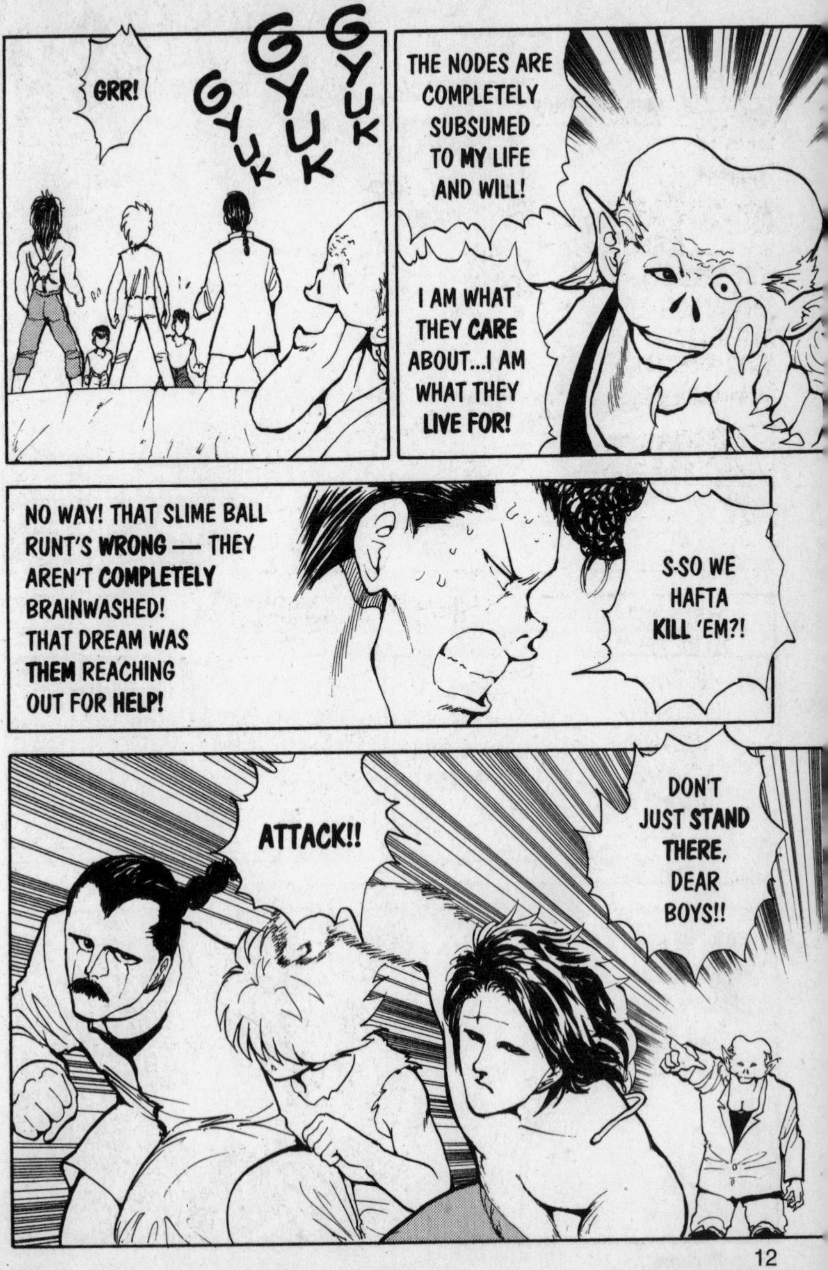
THE NODES ARE COMPLETELY SUBSUMED TO MY LIFE AND WILL!
I AM WHAT THEY CARE ABOUT...I AM WHAT THEY LIVE FOR!
GYUK
GYUK
GYUK
GRR!
S-SO WE HAFTA KILL 'EM?!
NO WAY! THAT SLIME BALL RUNT'S WRONG — THEY AREN'T COMPLETELY BRAINWASHED! THAT DREAM WAS THEM REACHING OUT FOR HELP!
DON'T JUST STAND THERE, DEAR BOYS!!
ATTACK!!

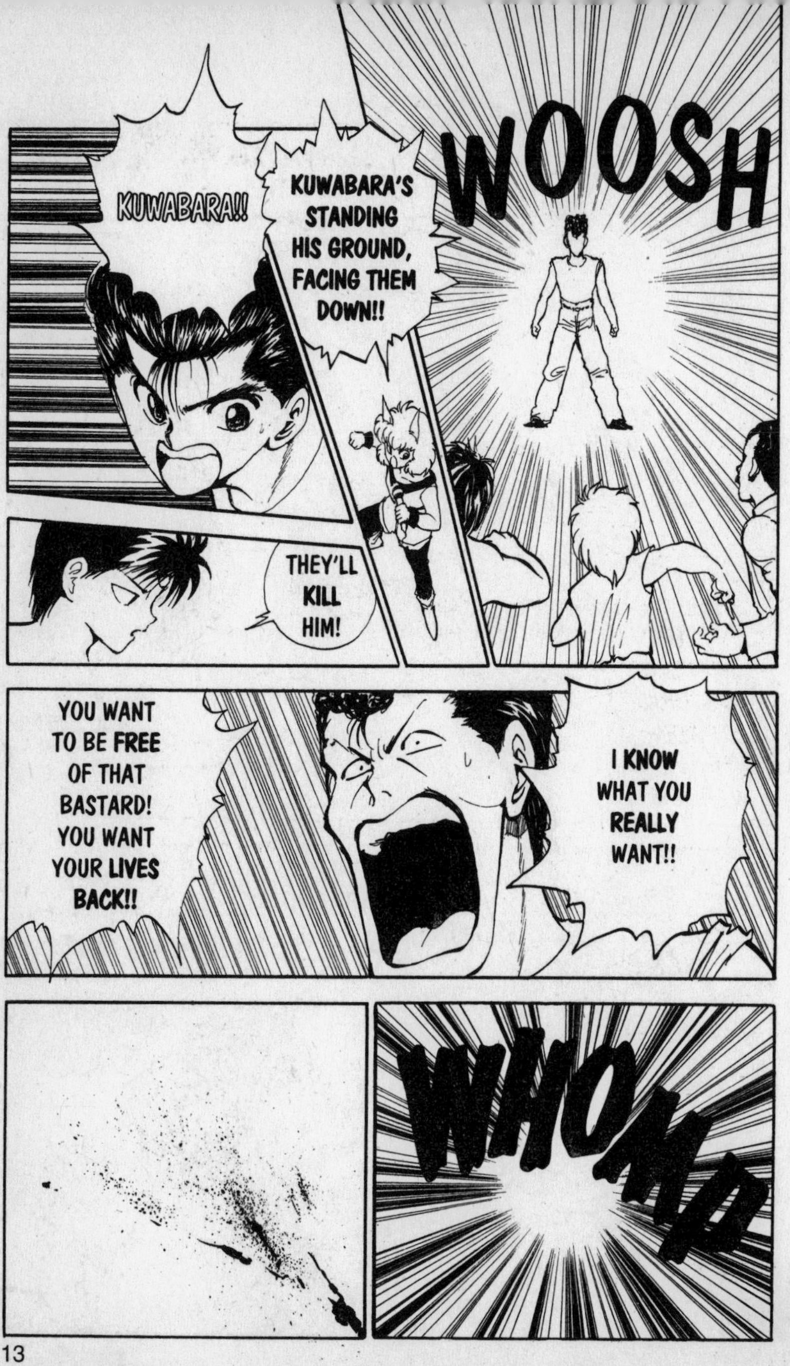
WOOSH
KUWABARA'S STANDING HIS GROUND, FACING THEM DOWN!!
KUWABARA!!
THEY'LL KILL HIM!
I KNOW WHAT YOU REALLY WANT!!
YOU WANT TO BE FREE OF THAT BASTARD! YOU WANT YOUR LIVES BACK!!
WHOMP

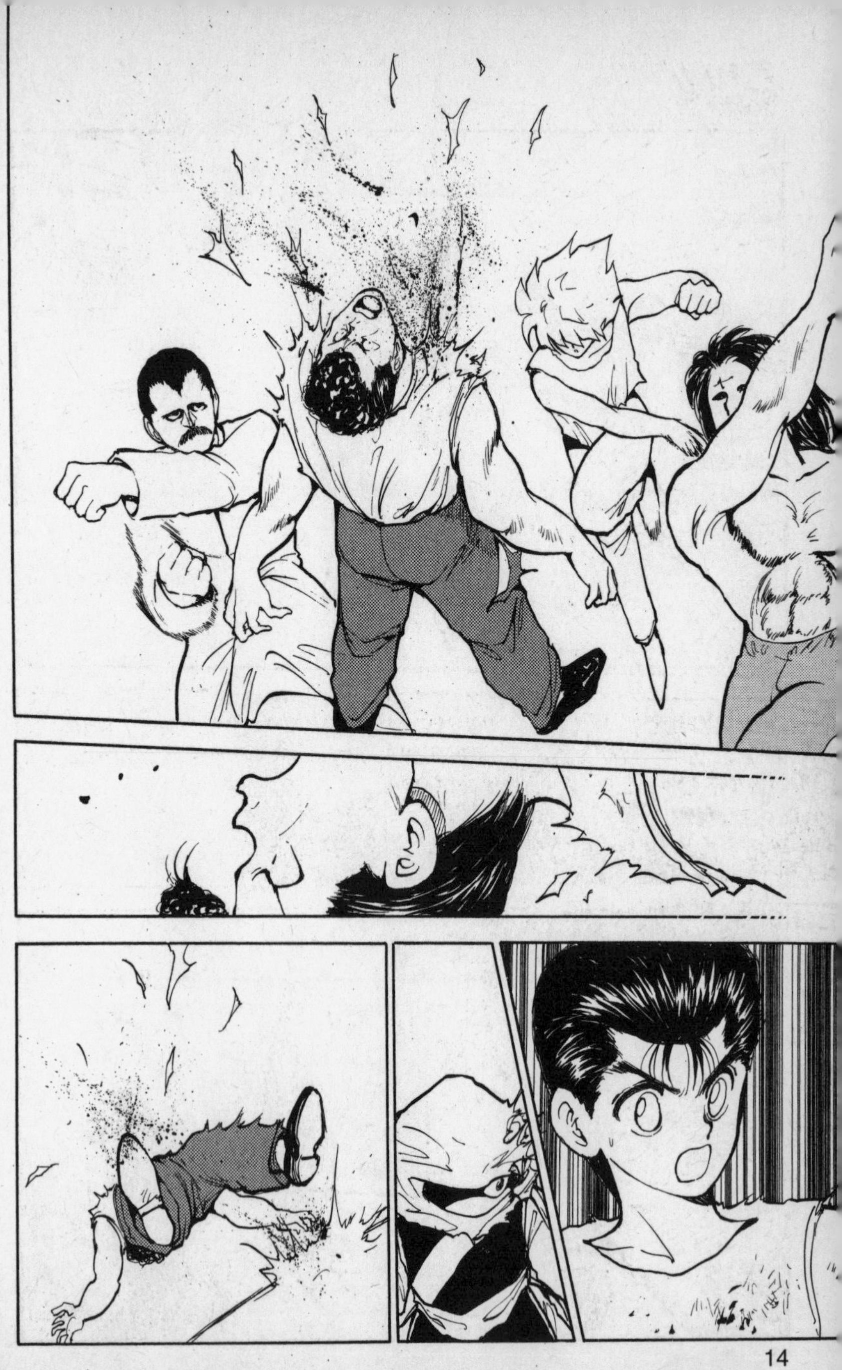

READ THIS WAY

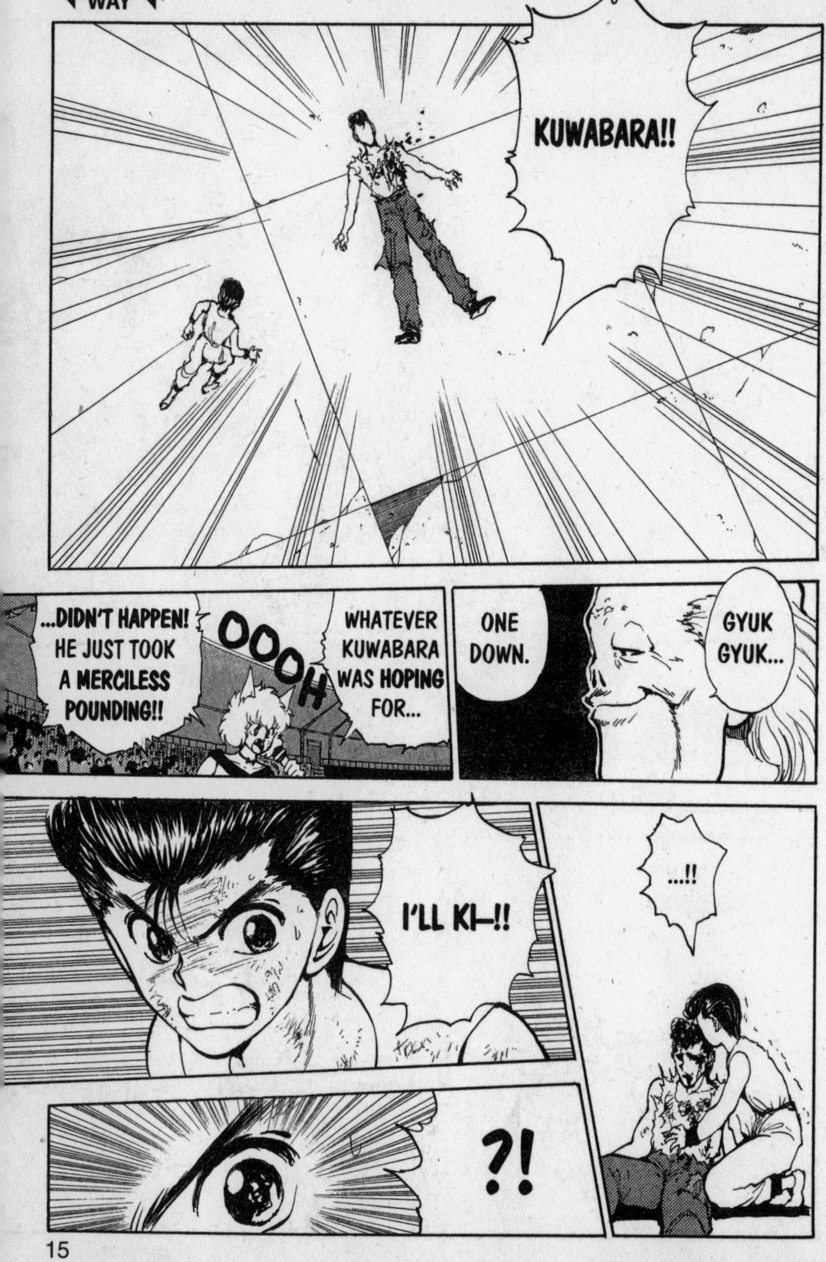

KUWABARA!!
GYUK GYUK...
ONE DOWN.
WHATEVER KUWABARA WAS HOPING FOR...
...DIDN'T HAPPEN! HE JUST TOOK A MERCILESS POUNDING!!
OOOH
...!!
I'LL KI—!!
?!

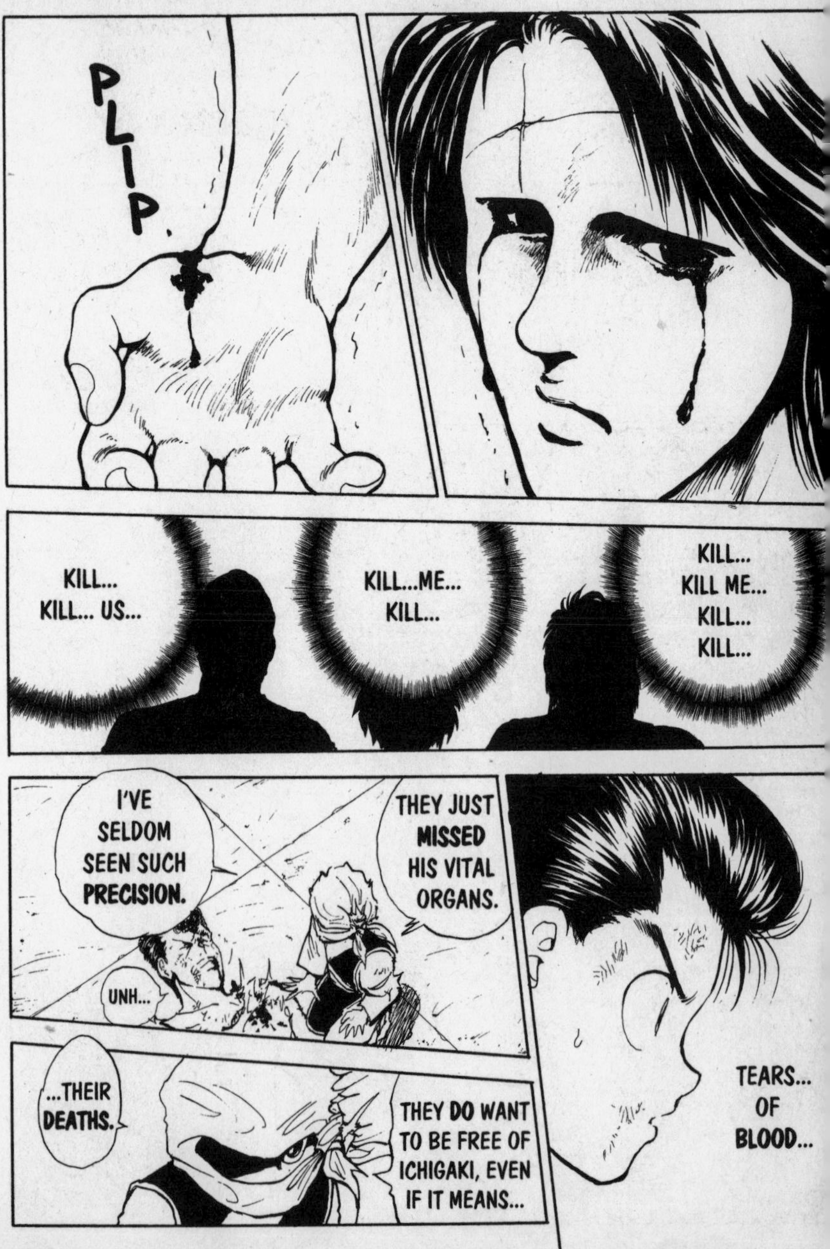
PLIP
KILL... KILL ME... KILL... KILL...
KILL...ME... KILL...
KILL... KILL... US...
TEARS... OF BLOOD...
THEY JUST MISSED HIS VITAL ORGANS.
I'VE SELDOM SEEN SUCH PRECISION.
UNH...
THEY DO WANT TO BE FREE OF ICHIGAKI, EVEN IF IT MEANS...
...THEIR DEATHS.

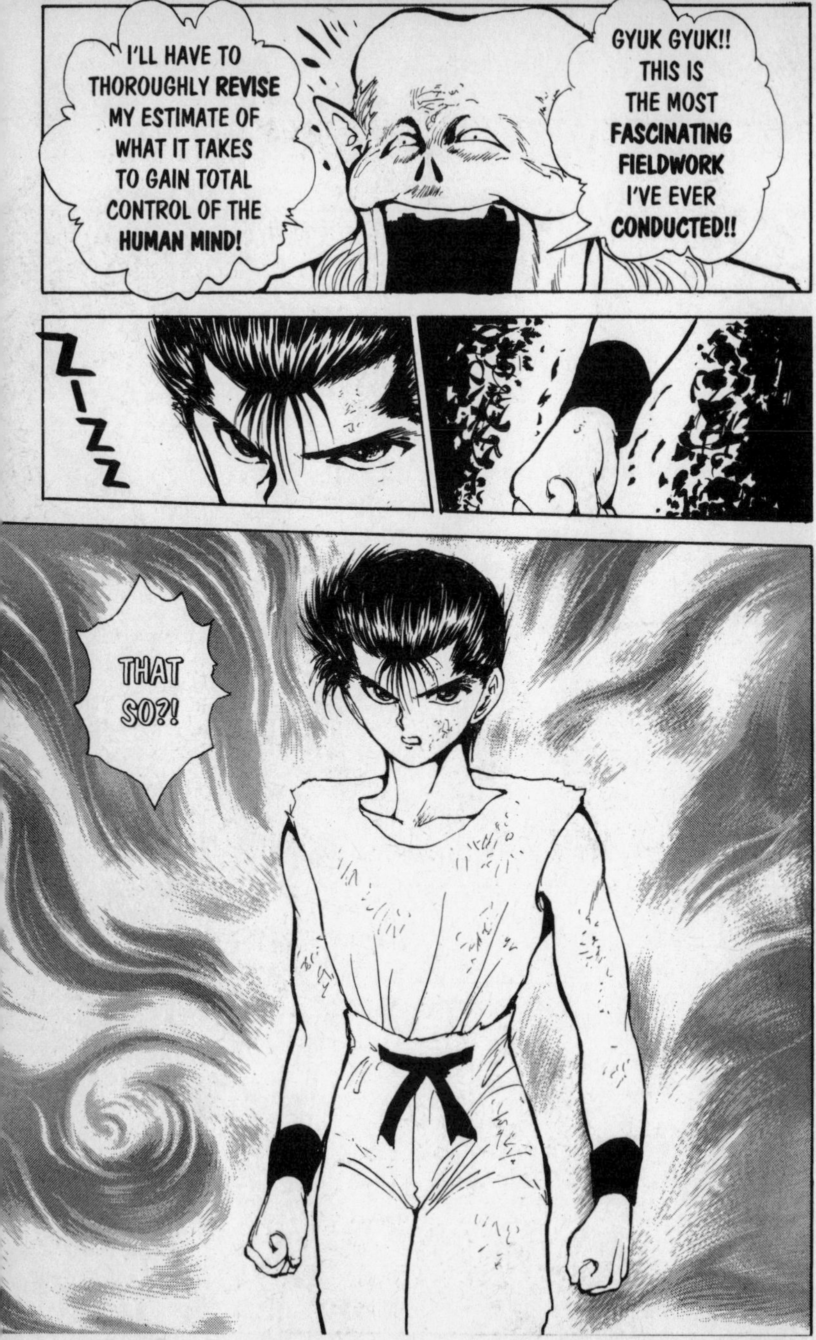
GYUK GYUK!! THIS IS THE MOST FASCINATING FIELDWORK I'VE EVER CONDUCTED!!
I'LL HAVE TO THOROUGHLY REVISE MY ESTIMATE OF WHAT IT TAKES TO GAIN TOTAL CONTROL OF THE HUMAN MIND!
ZIZZ
THAT SO?!

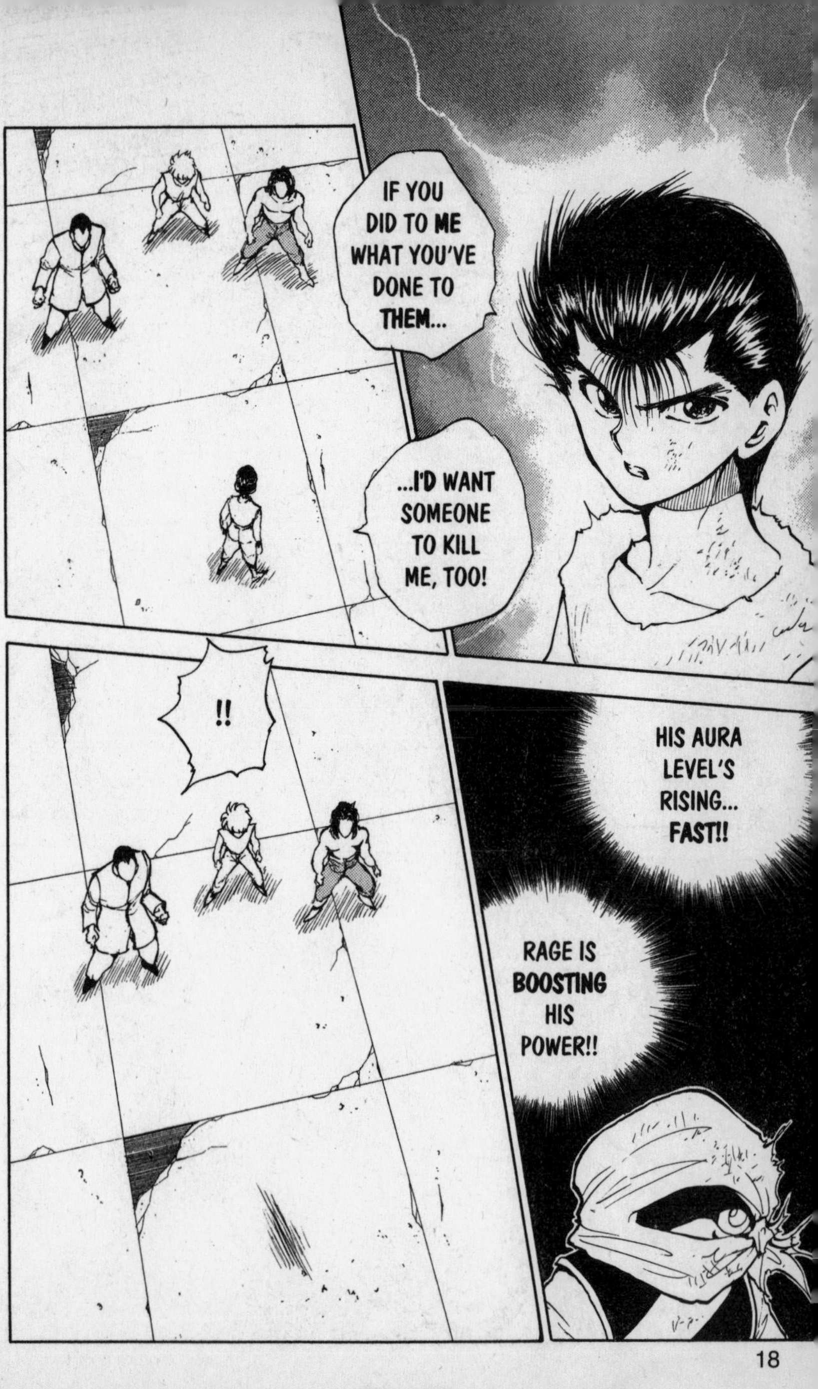
IF YOU DID TO ME WHAT YOU'VE DONE TO THEM...
...I'D WANT SOMEONE TO KILL ME, TOO!
HIS AURA LEVEL'S RISING... FAST!!
RAGE IS BOOSTING HIS POWER!!
!!

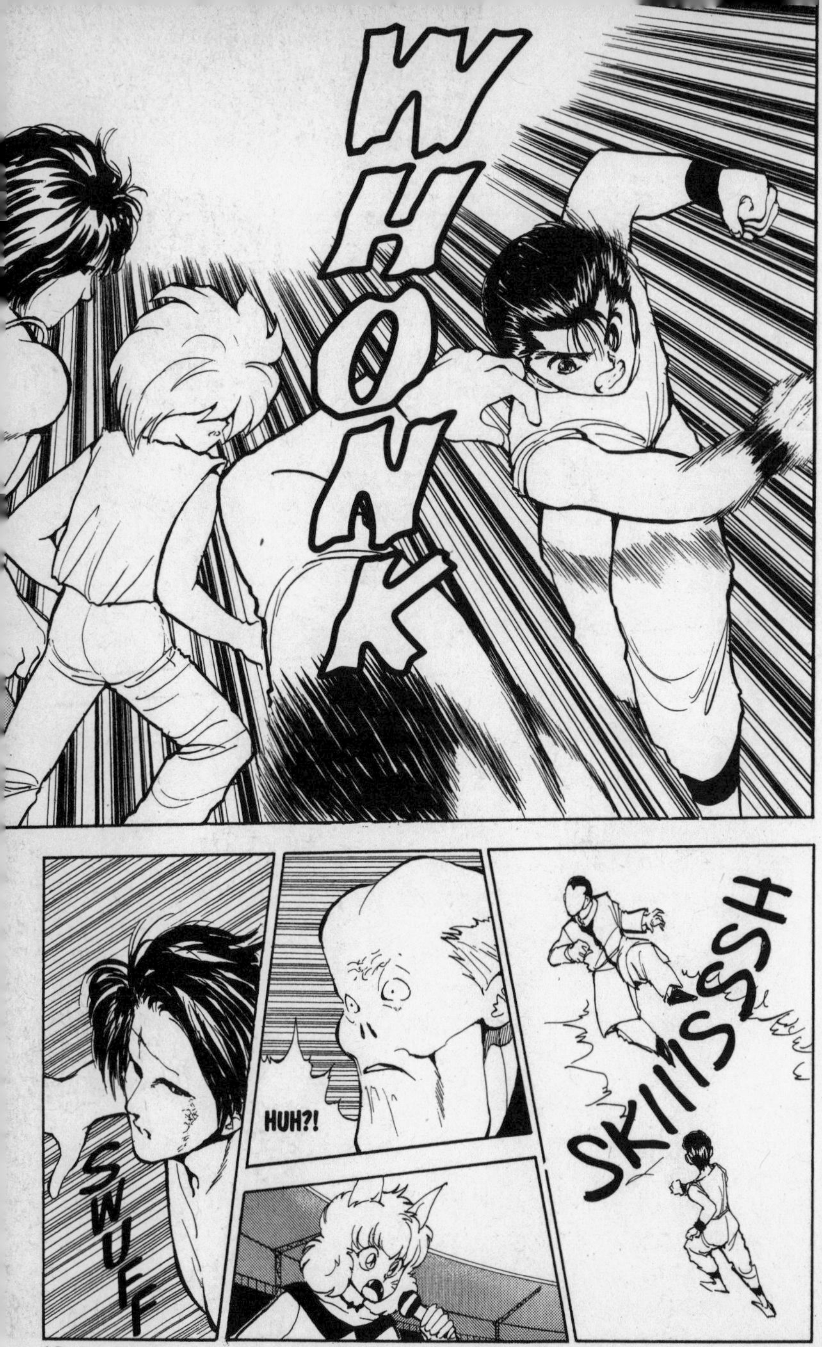
WHONK
SKIIISSSH
HUH?!
SWUFF

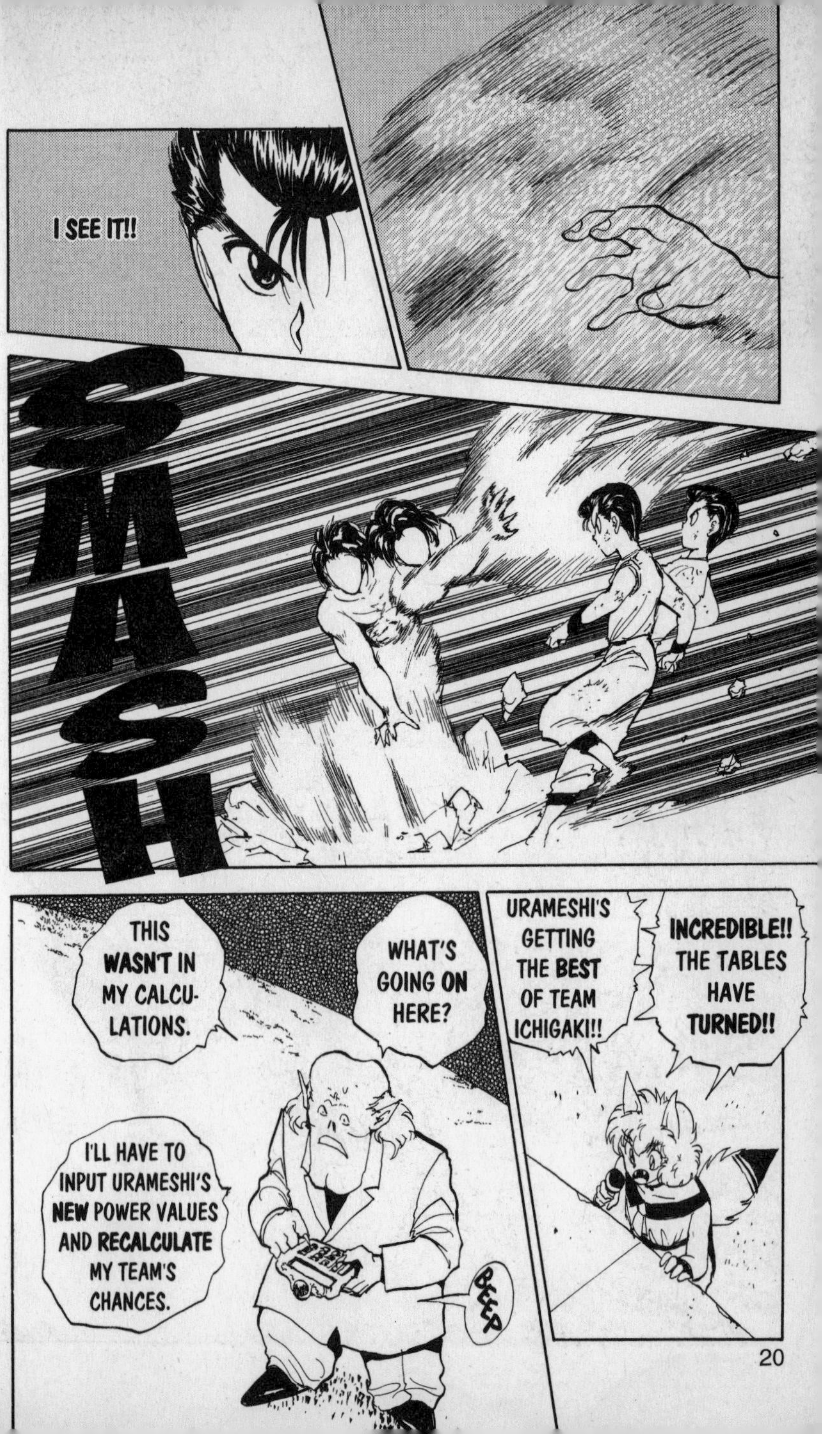
I SEE IT!!
SMASH
INCREDIBLE!! THE TABLES HAVE TURNED!!
URAMESHI'S GETTING THE BEST OF TEAM ICHIGAKI!!!
WHAT'S GOING ON HERE?
THIS WASN'T IN MY CALCULATIONS.
I'LL HAVE TO INPUT URAMESHI'S NEW POWER VALUES AND RECALCULATE MY TEAM'S CHANCES.
BEEEP

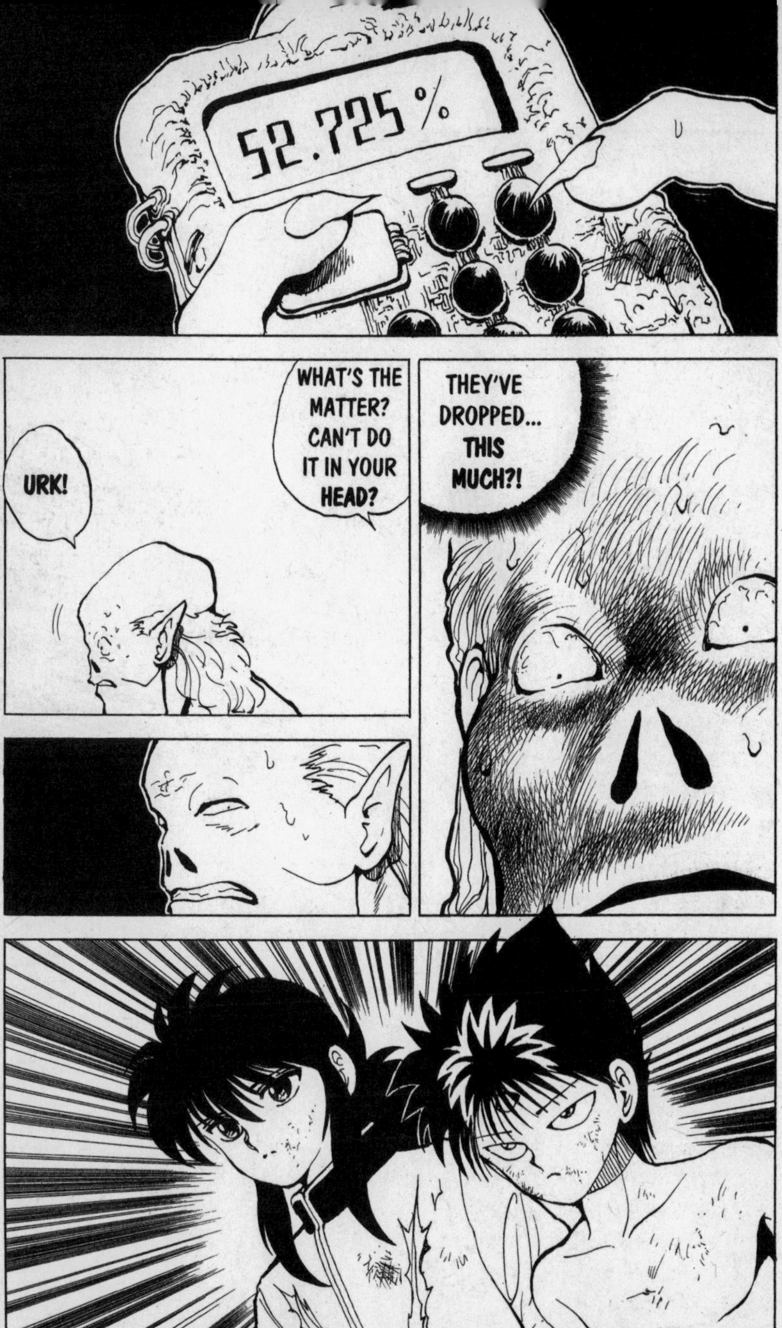
52.725 %
THEY'VE DROPPED... THIS MUCH?!
WHAT'S THE MATTER? CAN'T DO IT IN YOUR HEAD?
URK!

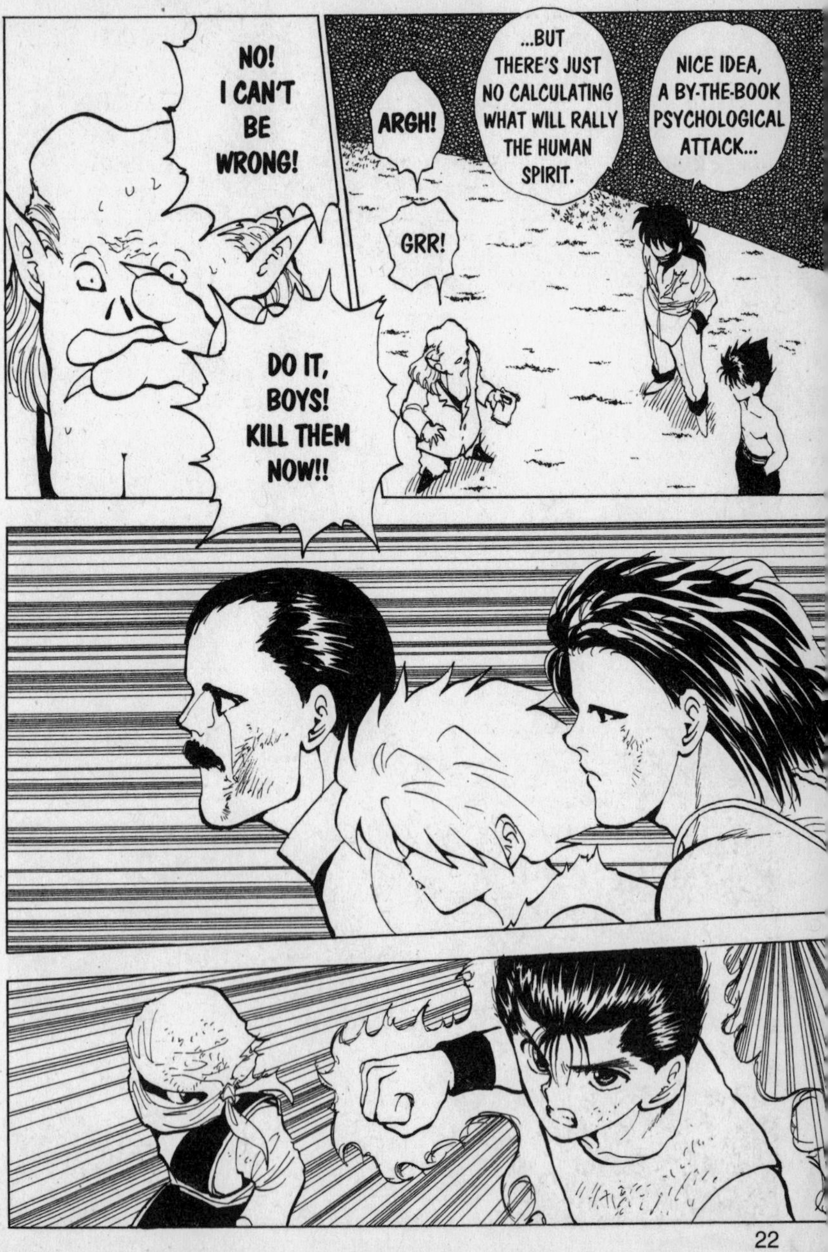
NICE IDEA, A BY-THE-BOOK PSYCHOLOGICAL ATTACK...
...BUT THERE'S JUST NO CALCULATING WHAT WILL RALLY THE HUMAN SPIRIT.
ARGH!
GRR!
NO! I CAN'T BE WRONG!
DO IT, BOYS! KILL THEM NOW!!

READ THIS WAY

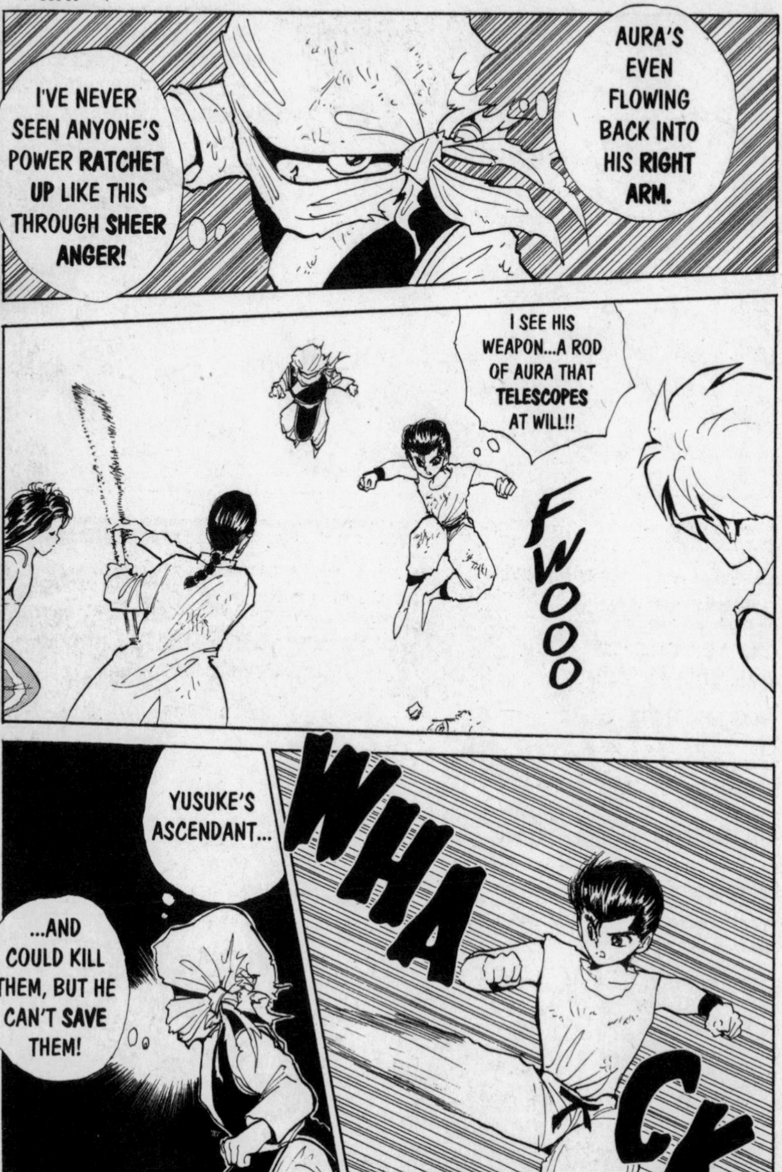

AURA'S EVEN FLOWING BACK INTO HIS RIGHT ARM.
I'VE NEVER SEEN ANYONE'S POWER RATCHET UP LIKE THIS THROUGH SHEER ANGER!
I SEE HIS WEAPON...A ROD OF AURA THAT TELESCOPES AT WILL!!
FWOOOO
WHACK
YUSUKE'S ASCENDANT...
...AND COULD KILL THEM, BUT HE CAN'T SAVE THEM!

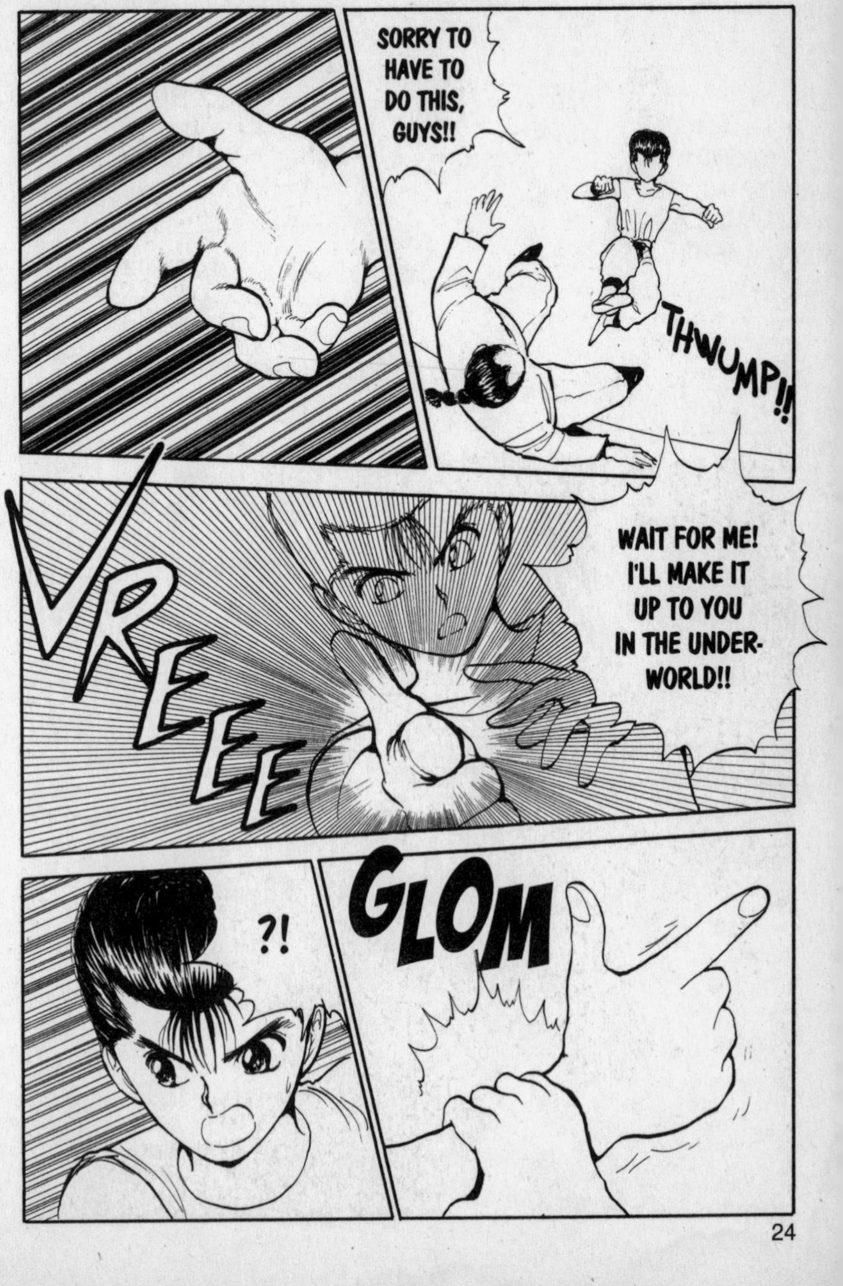
SORRY TO HAVE TO DO THIS, GUYS!!
THWUMP!!
WAIT FOR ME! I'LL MAKE IT UP TO YOU IN THE UNDER-WORLD!!
VREEE
GLOM
?!

READ THIS WAY

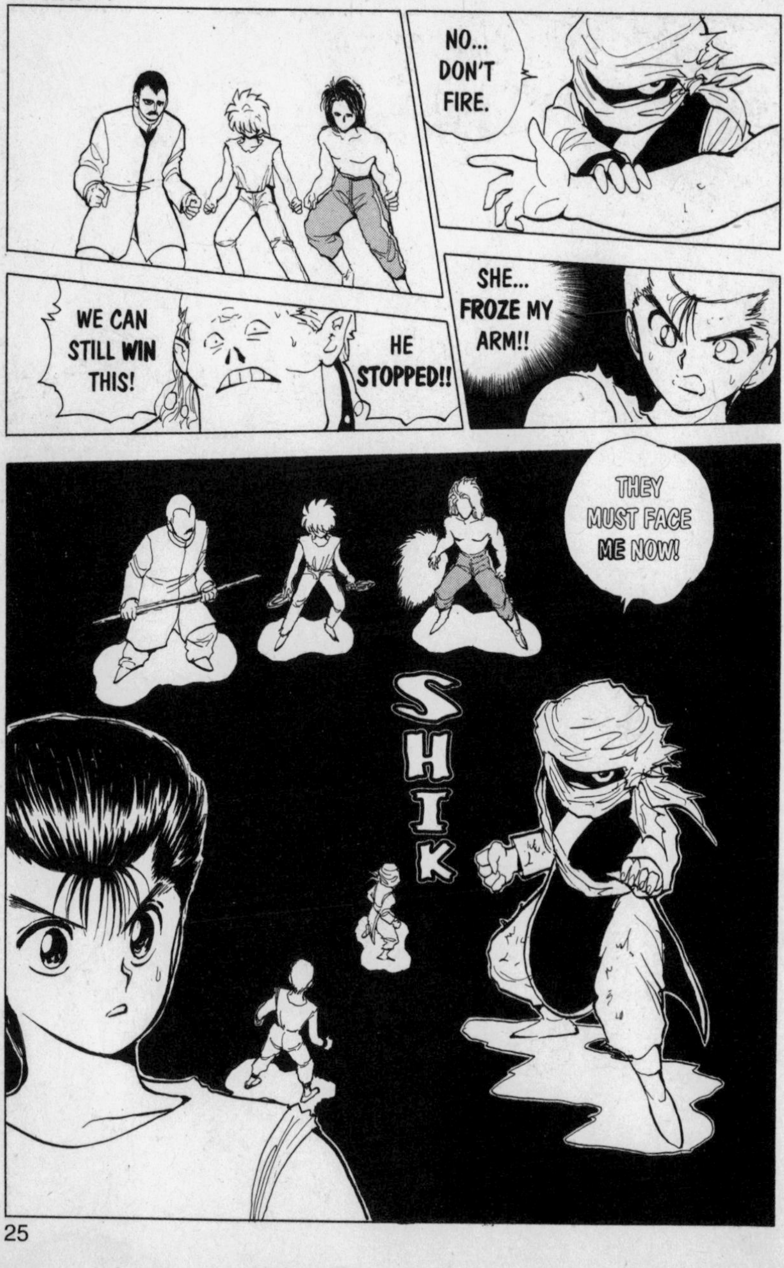
NO... DON'T FIRE.
SHE... FROZE MY ARM!!
HE STOPPED!!
WE CAN STILL WIN THIS!
THEY MUST FACE ME NOW!
SHIK

YUYU THEREAFTER

(FROM "HER FIRST CHRISTMAS")

"ISN'T IT A NICE DAY, KANA?"

"YEAH, IT IS."

"....."

"....."

"GOSH, IT REALLY IS A NICE DAY, ISN'T IT?"

"YEAH, IT IS."

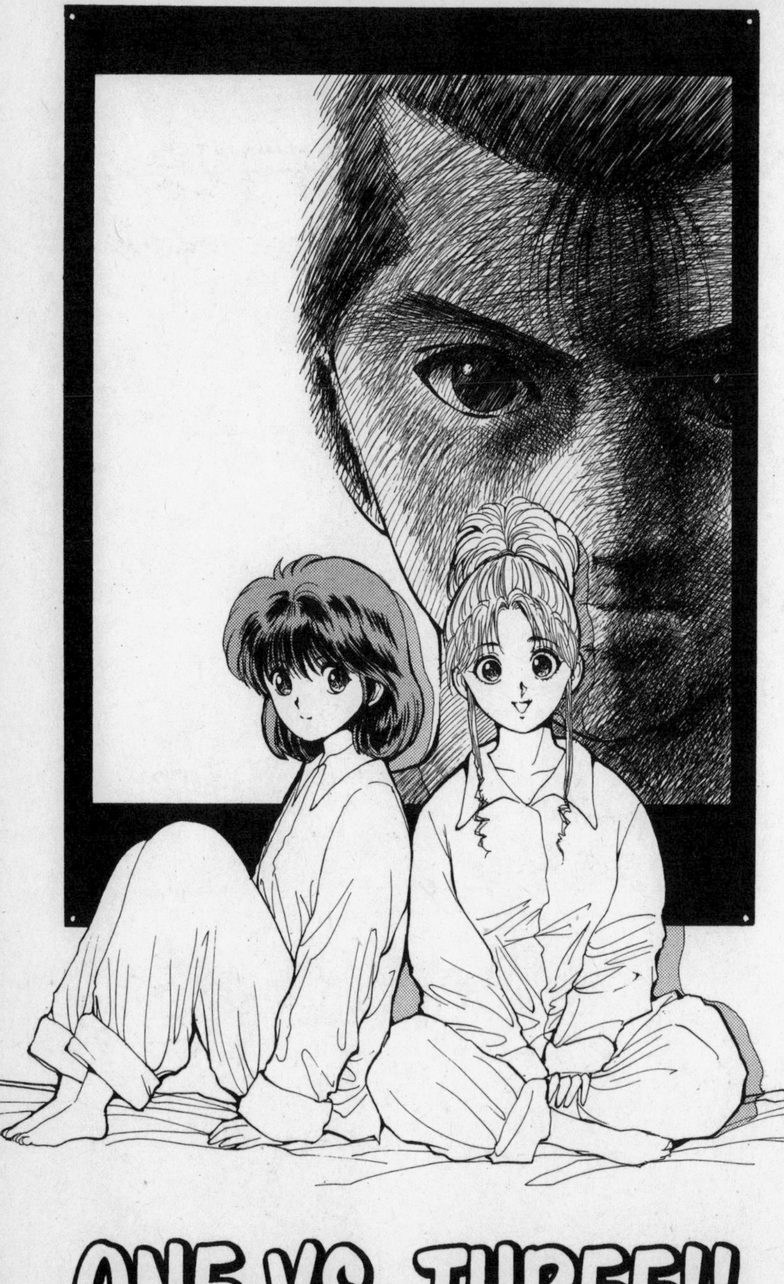

ONE VS. THREE!!

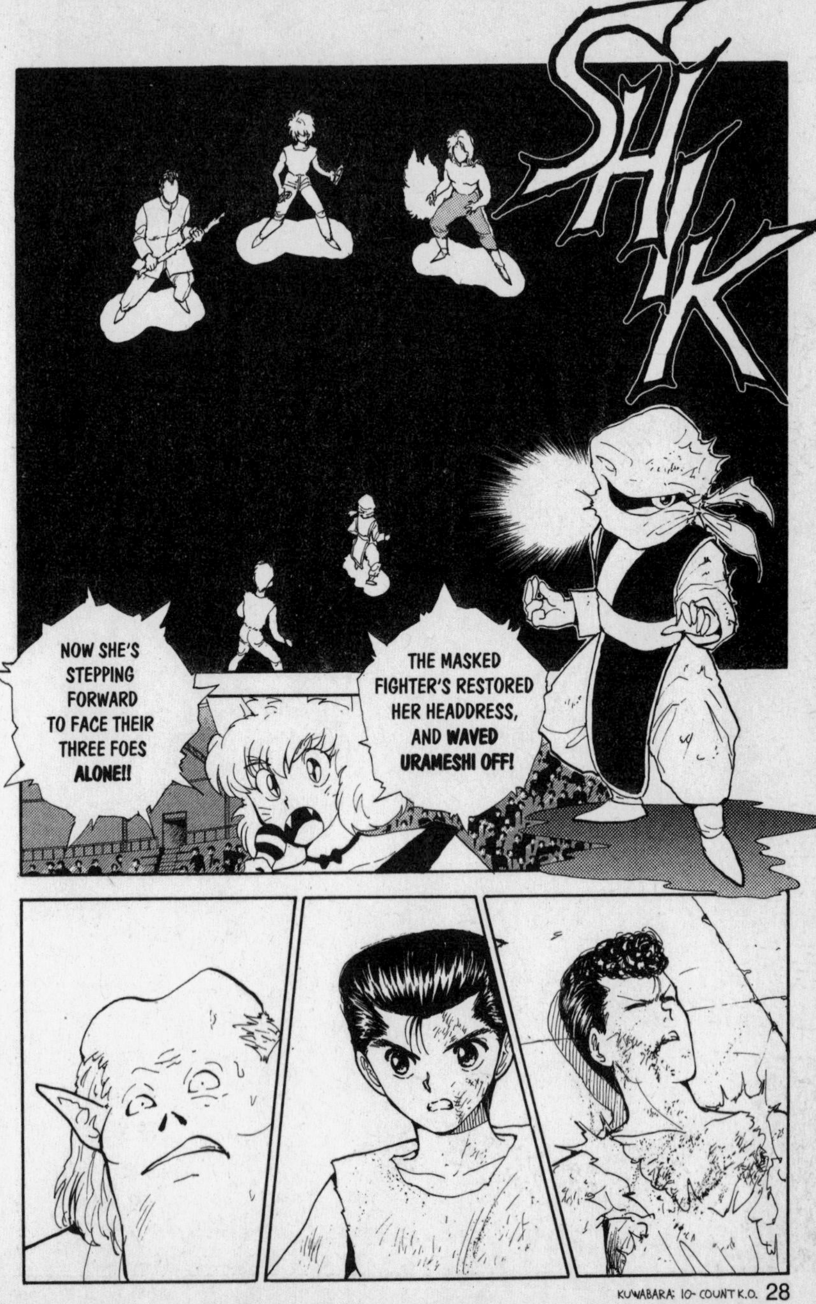
SHIK
THE MASKED FIGHTER'S RESTORED HER HEADDRESS, AND WAVED URAMESHI OFF!
NOW SHE'S STEPPING FORWARD TO FACE THEIR THREE FOES ALONE!!

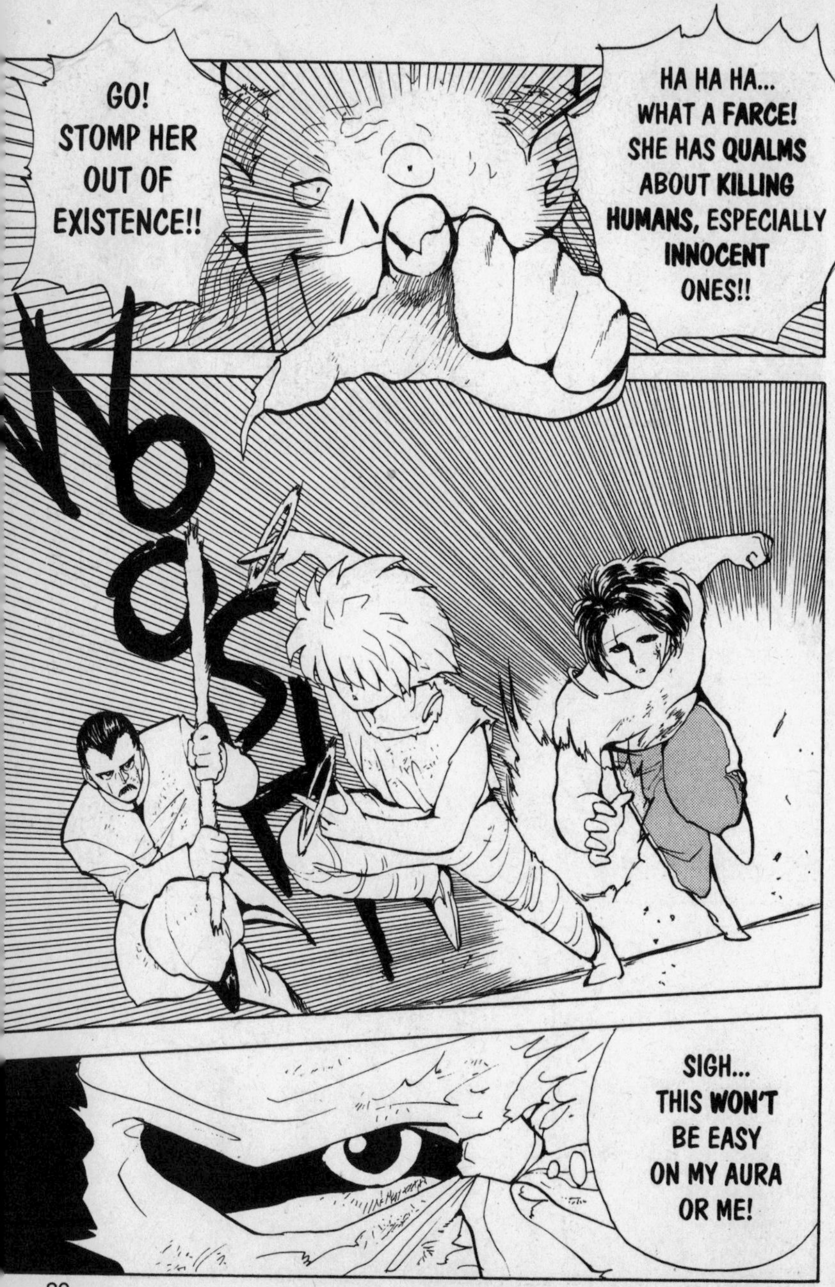
HA HA HA... WHAT A FARCE! SHE HAS QUALMS ABOUT KILLING HUMANS, ESPECIALLY INNOCENT ONES!!
GO! STOMP HER OUT OF EXISTENCE!!
WOOSH
SIGH... THIS WON'T BE EASY ON MY AURA OR ME!

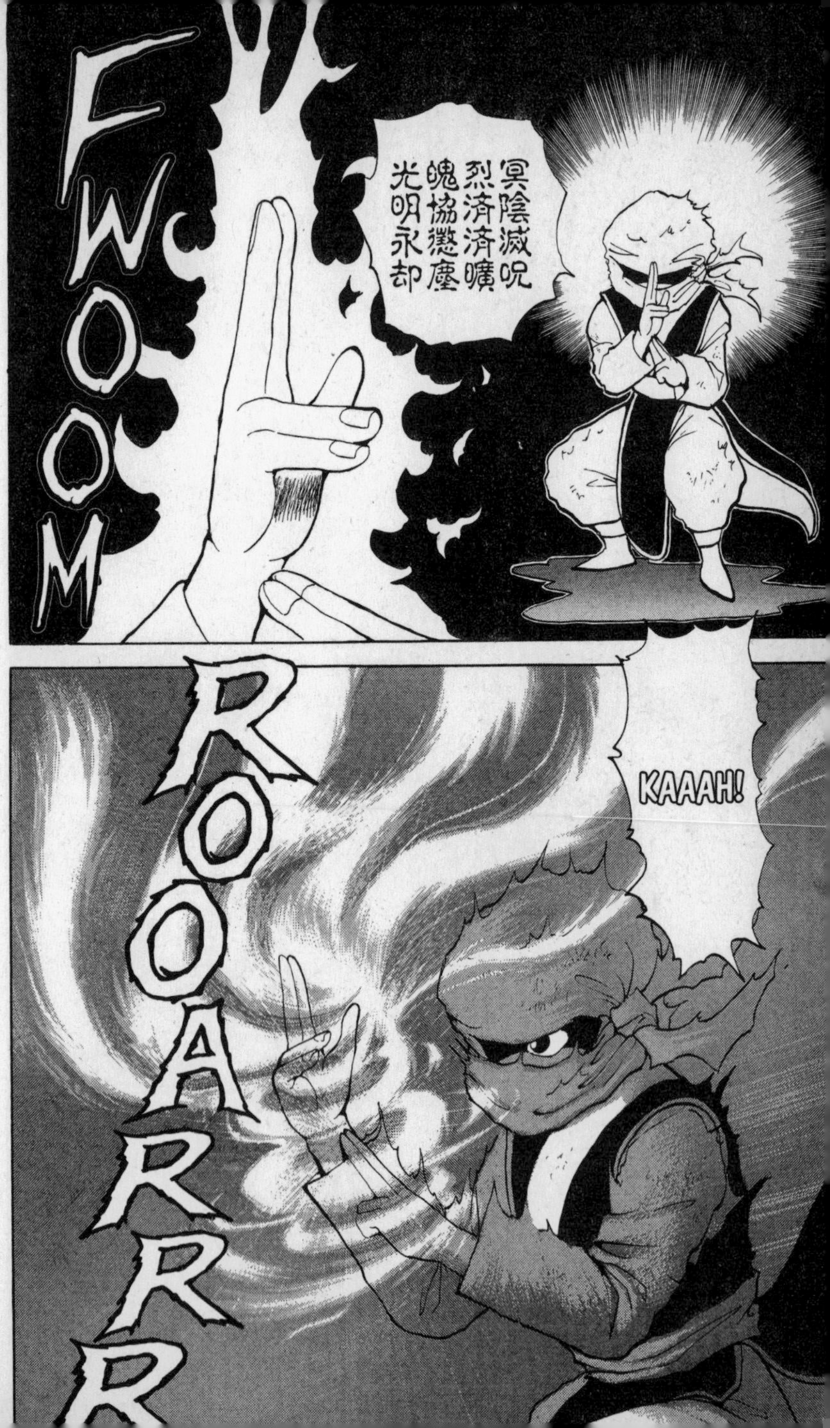
冥陰滅呪
烈済済曠
魄協懲塵
光明永却
FWOOM
KAAAH!
ROOOARRR

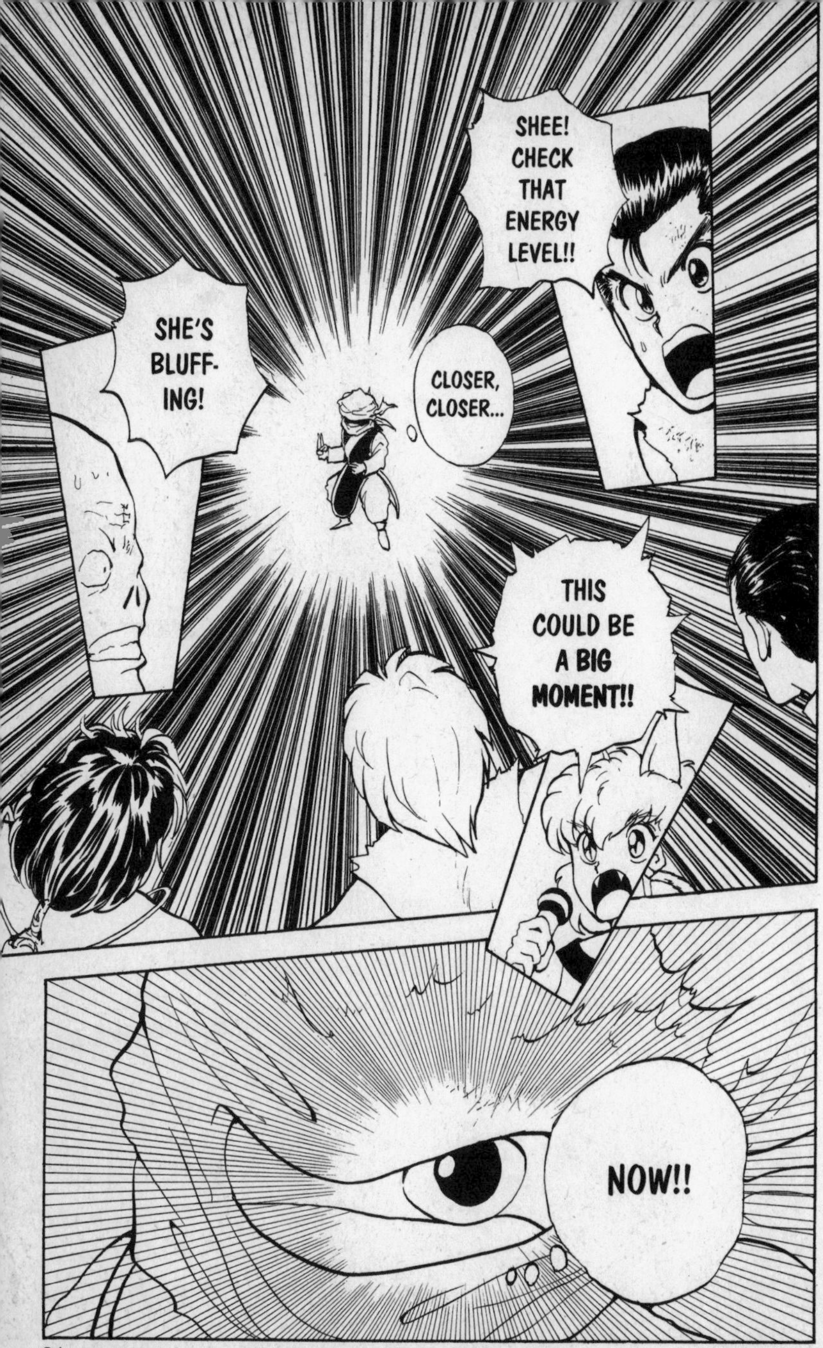
SHEE! CHECK THAT ENERGY LEVEL!!
CLOSER, CLOSER...
SHE'S BLUFF-ING!
THIS COULD BE A BIG MOMENT!!
NOW!!

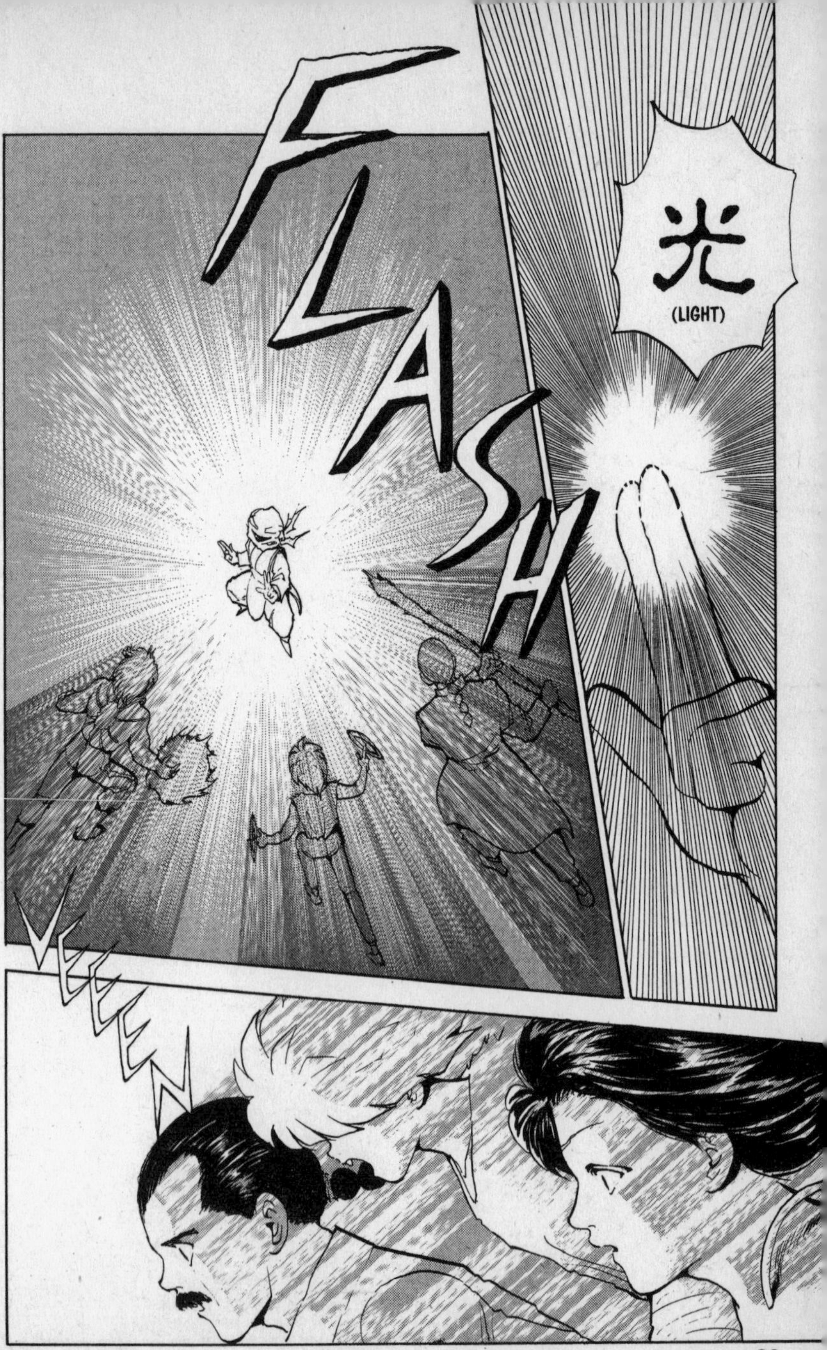
光
(LIGHT)
FLASH
VEEEN

READ THIS WAY

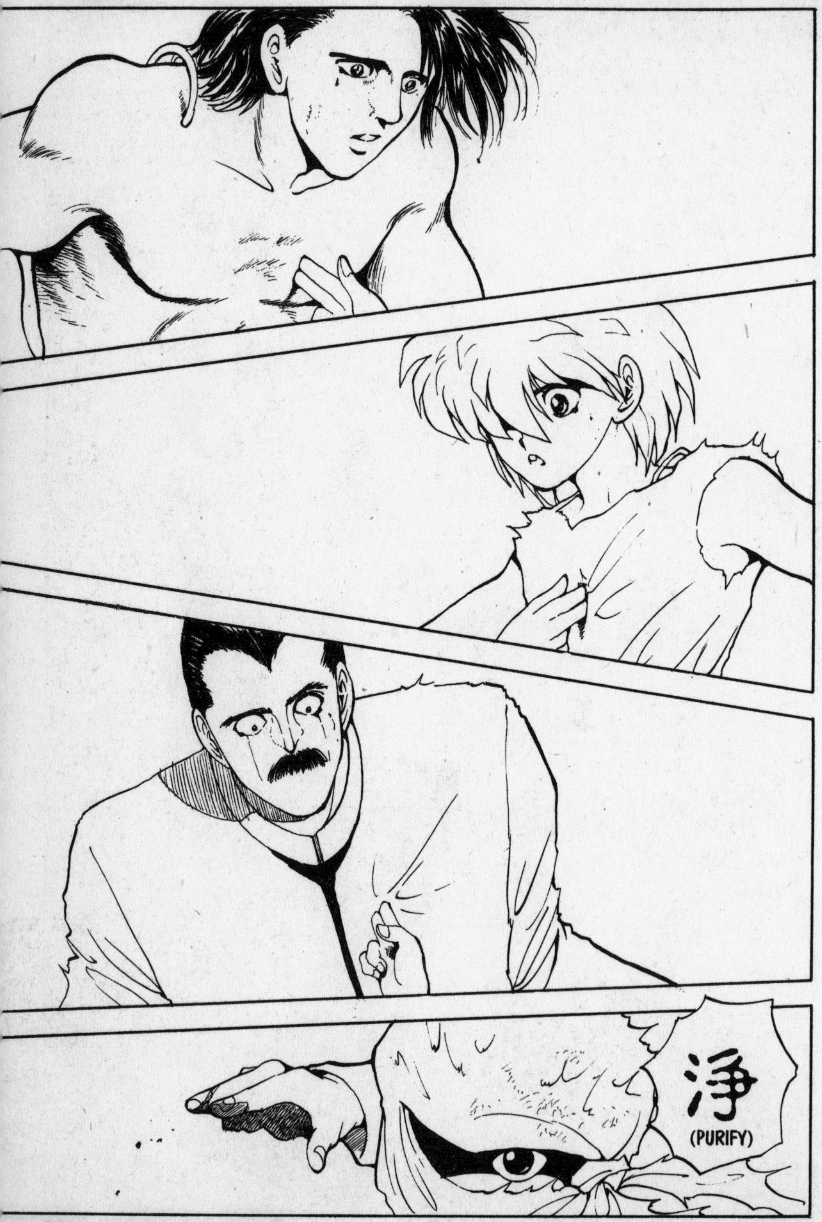

浄
(PURIFY)

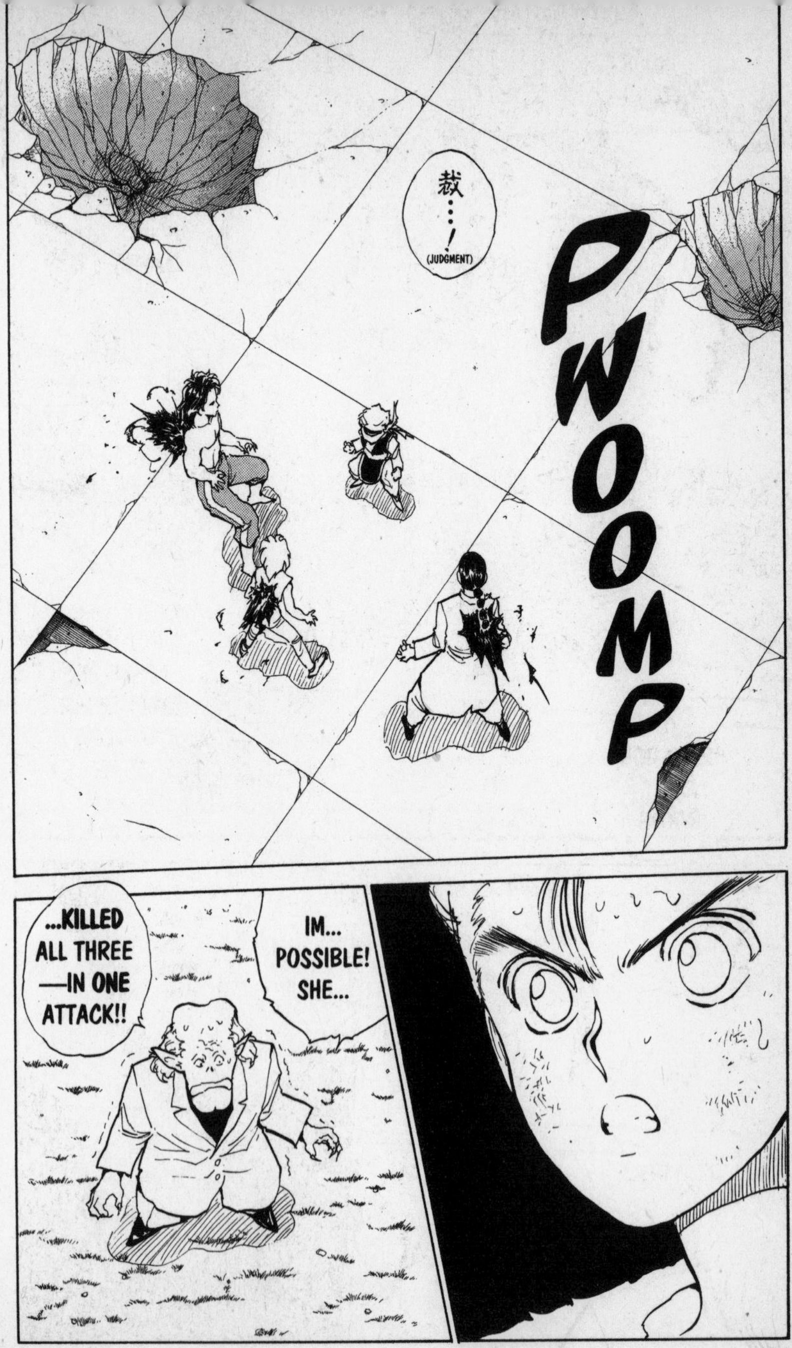

PWOOMP
裁…!
(JUDGMENT)
IM... POSSIBLE! SHE...
...KILLED ALL THREE —IN ONE ATTACK!!

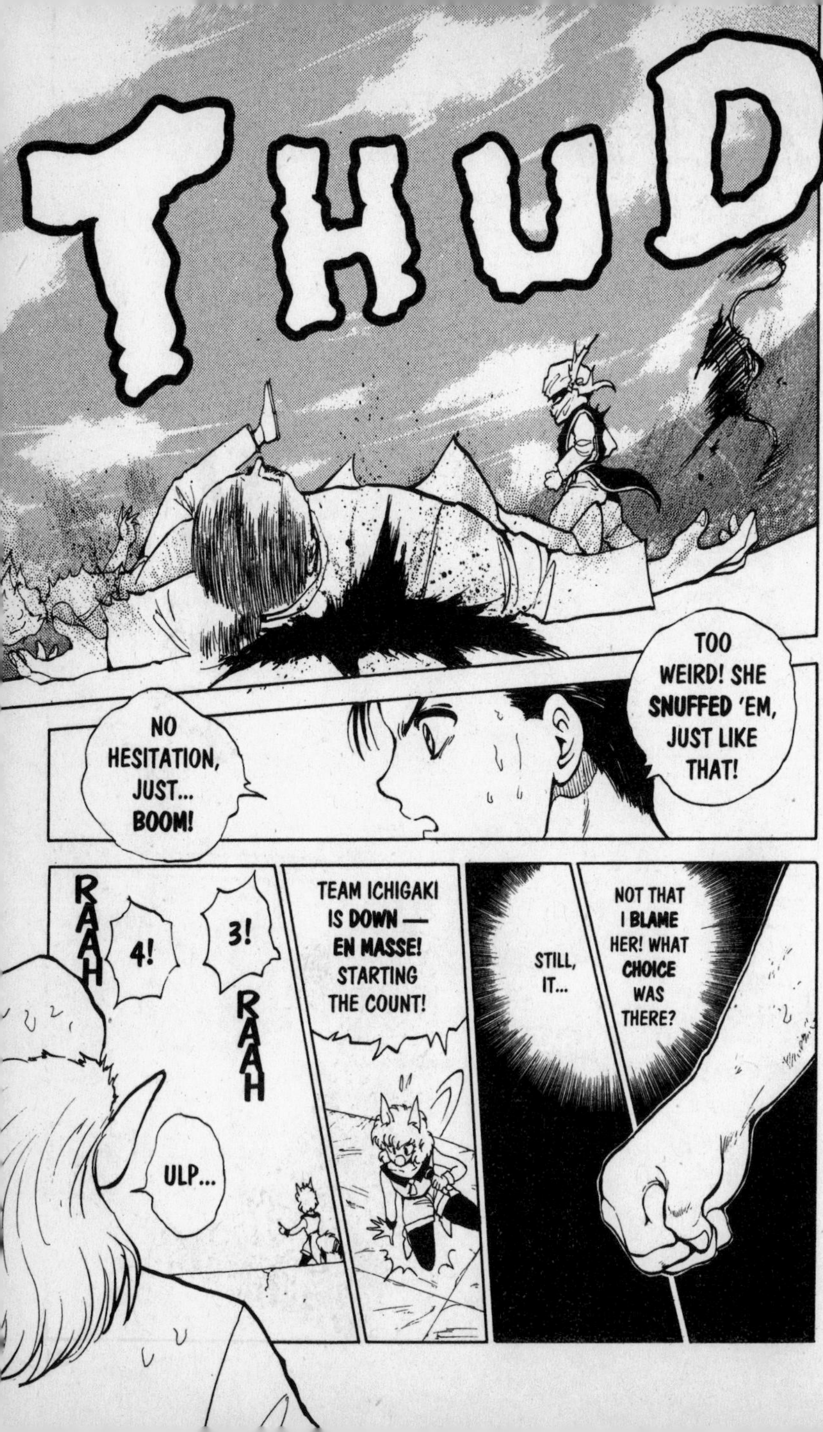
THUD
TOO WEIRD! SHE SNUFFED 'EM, JUST LIKE THAT!
NO HESITATION, JUST... BOOM!
NOT THAT I BLAME HER! WHAT CHOICE WAS THERE?
STILL, IT...
TEAM ICHIGAKI IS DOWN — EN MASSE! STARTING THE COUNT!
3!
RAAH
4!
RAAH
ULP...

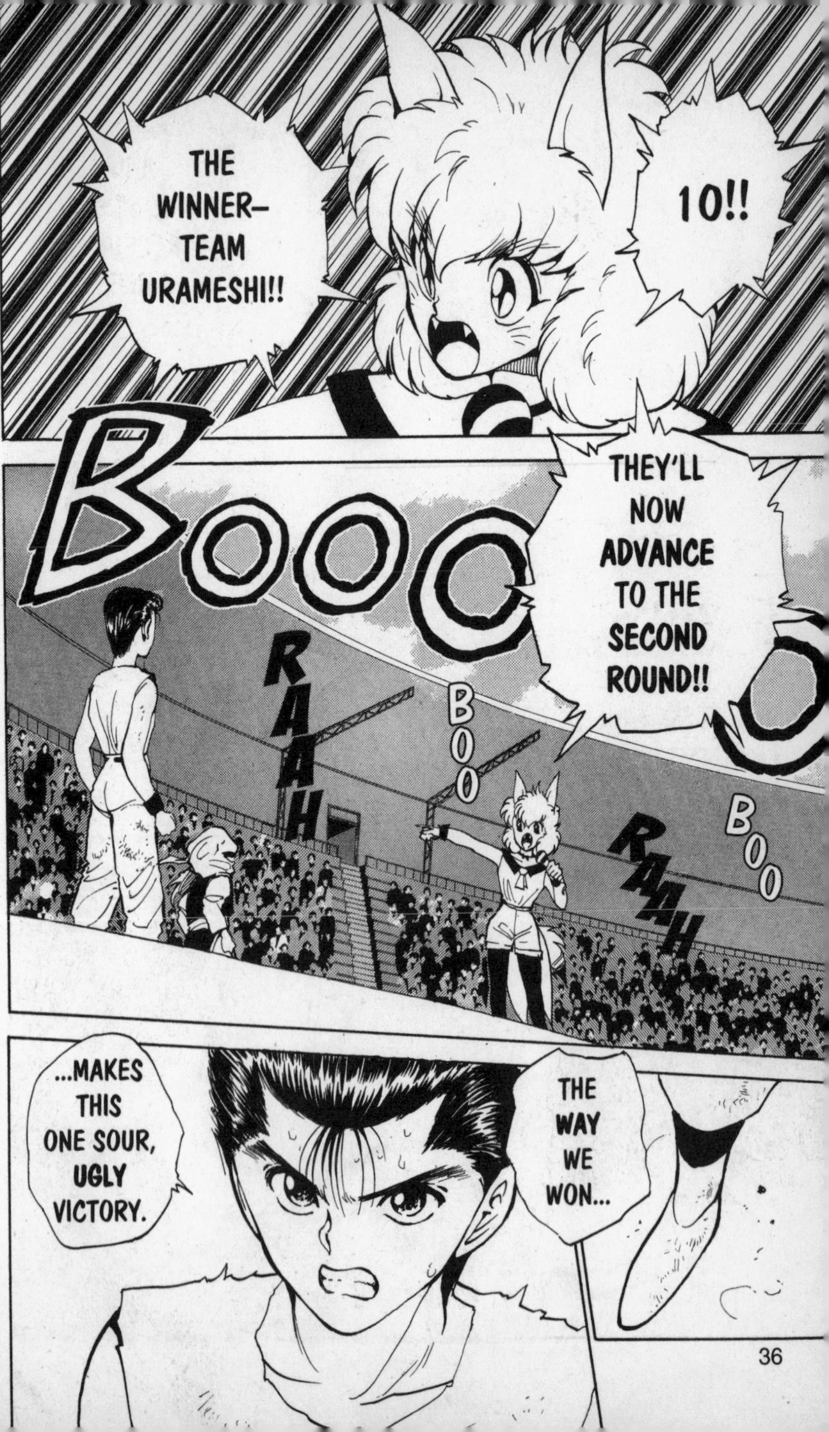
10!!
THE WINNER— TEAM URAMESHI!!
THEY'LL NOW ADVANCE TO THE SECOND ROUND!!
BOOOO
BOO BOO
RAAH RAAH
BOO BOO
THE WAY WE WON...
...MAKES THIS ONE SOUR, UGLY VICTORY.

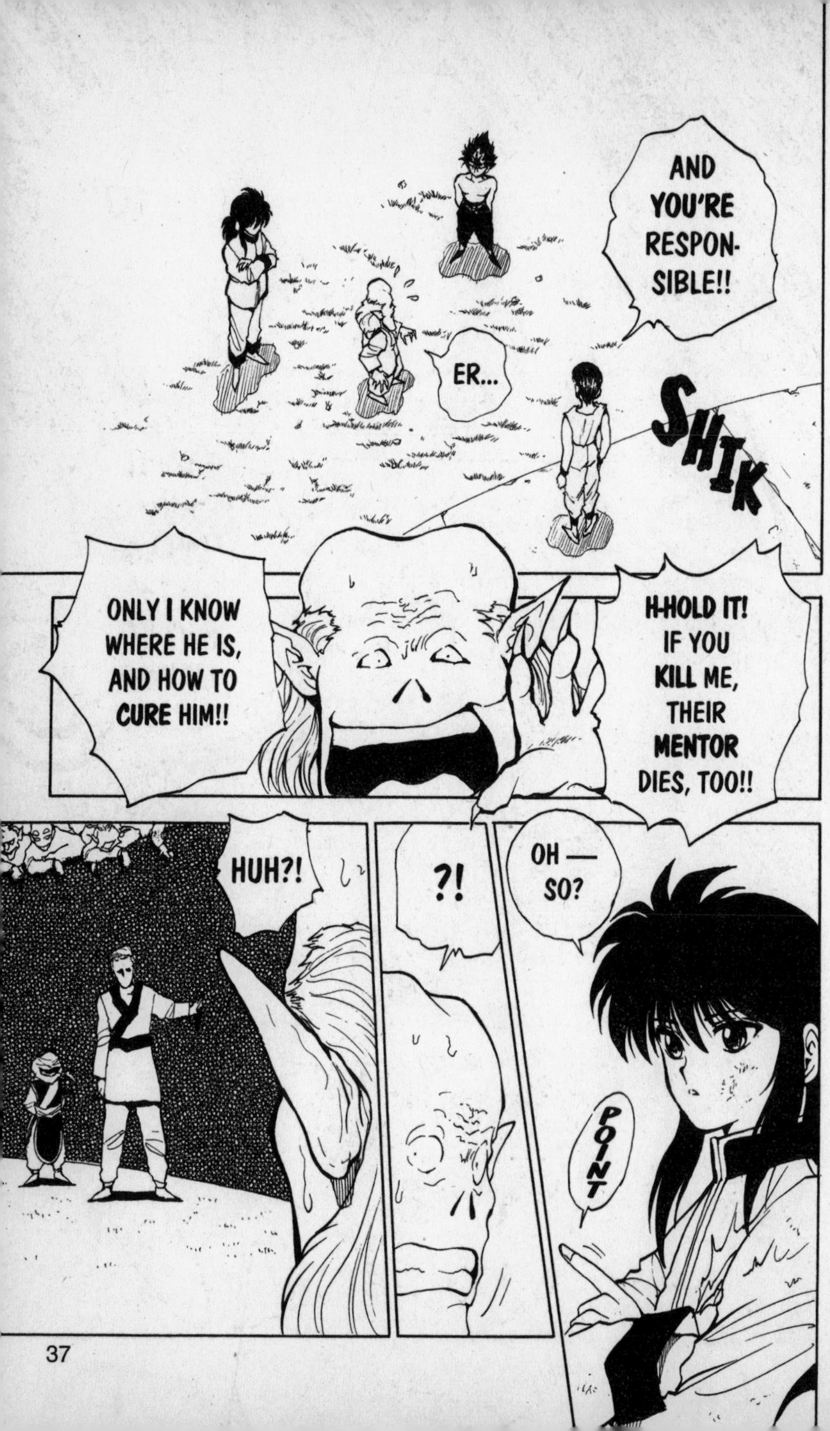

AND YOU'RE RESPON-SIBLE!!
SHIK
ER...
H-HOLD IT! IF YOU KILL ME, THEIR MENTOR DIES, TOO!!
ONLY I KNOW WHERE HE IS, AND HOW TO CURE HIM!!
OH — SO?
POINT
?!
HUH?!

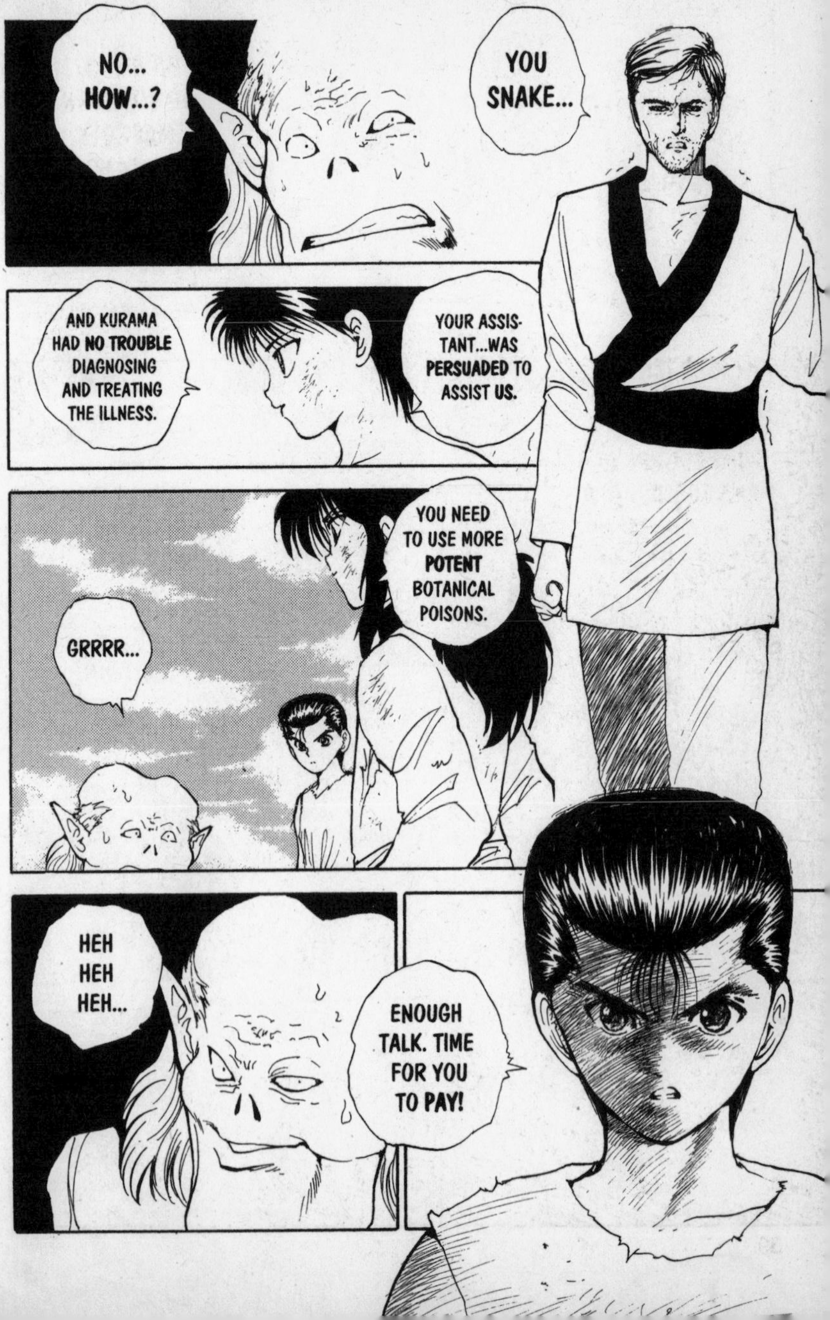
YOU SNAKE...
NO... HOW...?
YOUR ASSIS-TANT...WAS PERSUADED TO ASSIST US.
AND KURAMA HAD NO TROUBLE DIAGNOSING AND TREATING THE ILLNESS.
YOU NEED TO USE MORE POTENT BOTANICAL POISONS.
GRRRR...
HEH HEH HEH...
ENOUGH TALK. TIME FOR YOU TO PAY!

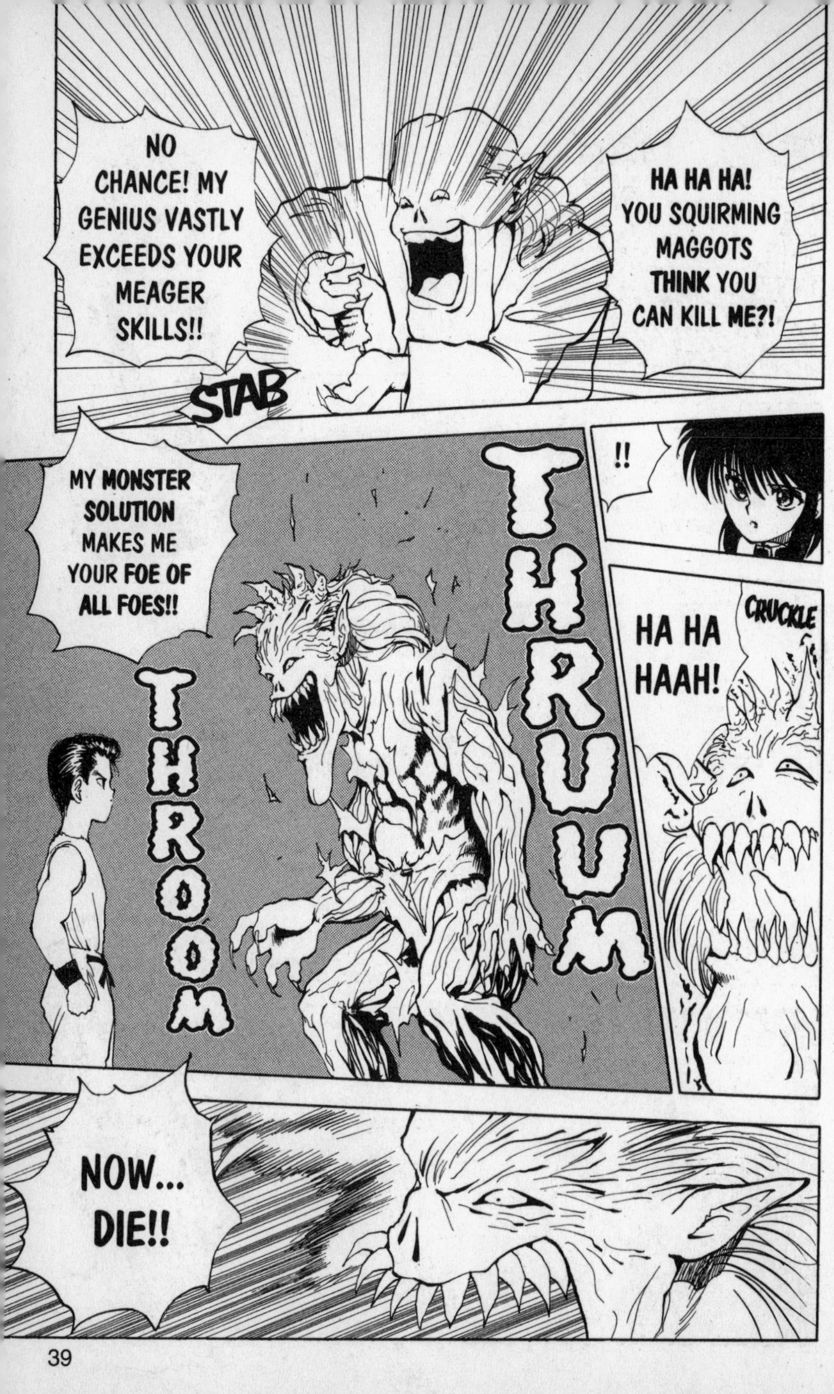
HA HA HA! YOU SQUIRMING MAGGOTS THINK YOU CAN KILL ME?!
NO CHANCE! MY GENIUS VASTLY EXCEEDS YOUR MEAGER SKILLS!!
STAB
!!
CRUCKLE
HA HA HAAH!
THRUUM
MY MONSTER SOLUTION MAKES ME YOUR FOE OF ALL FOES!!
THROOM
NOW... DIE!!

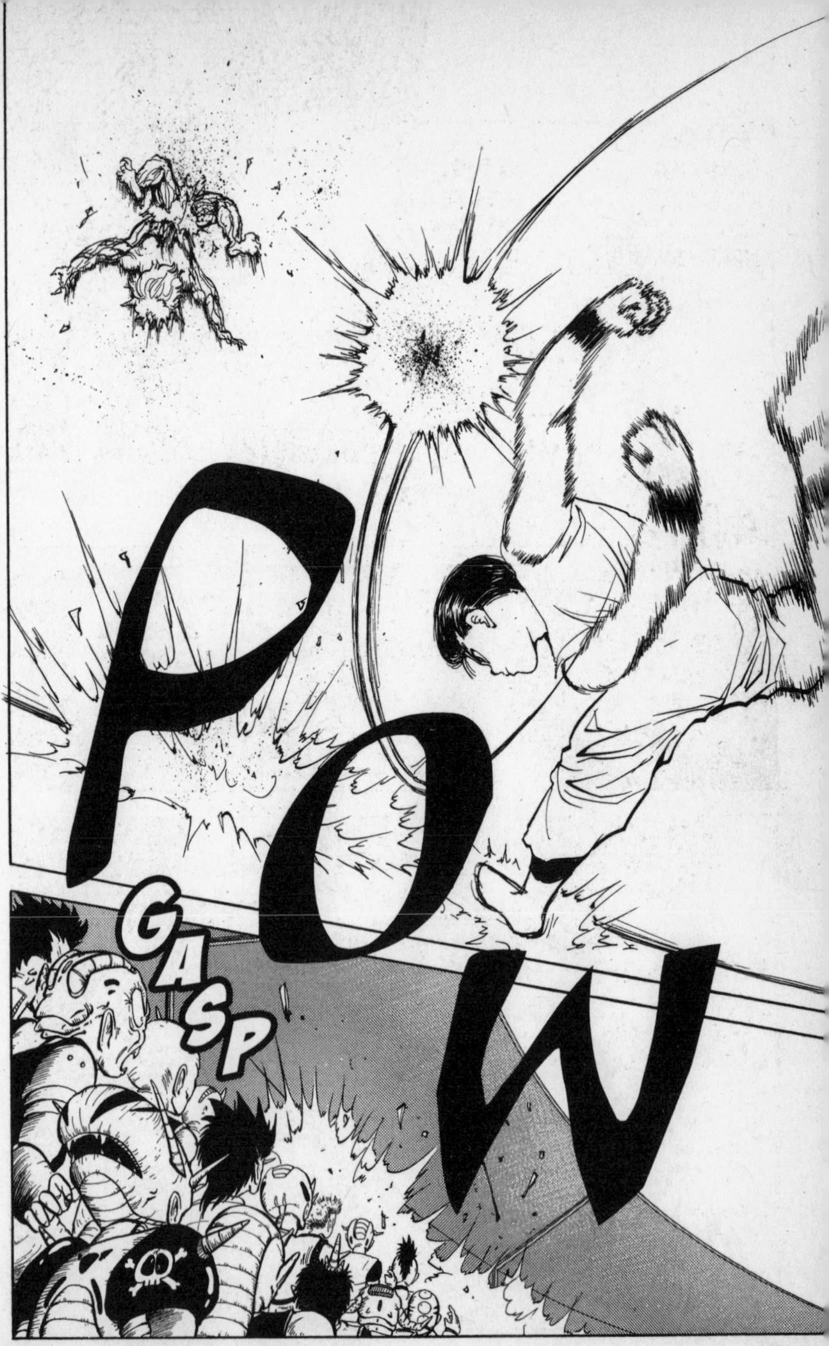
POW
GASP

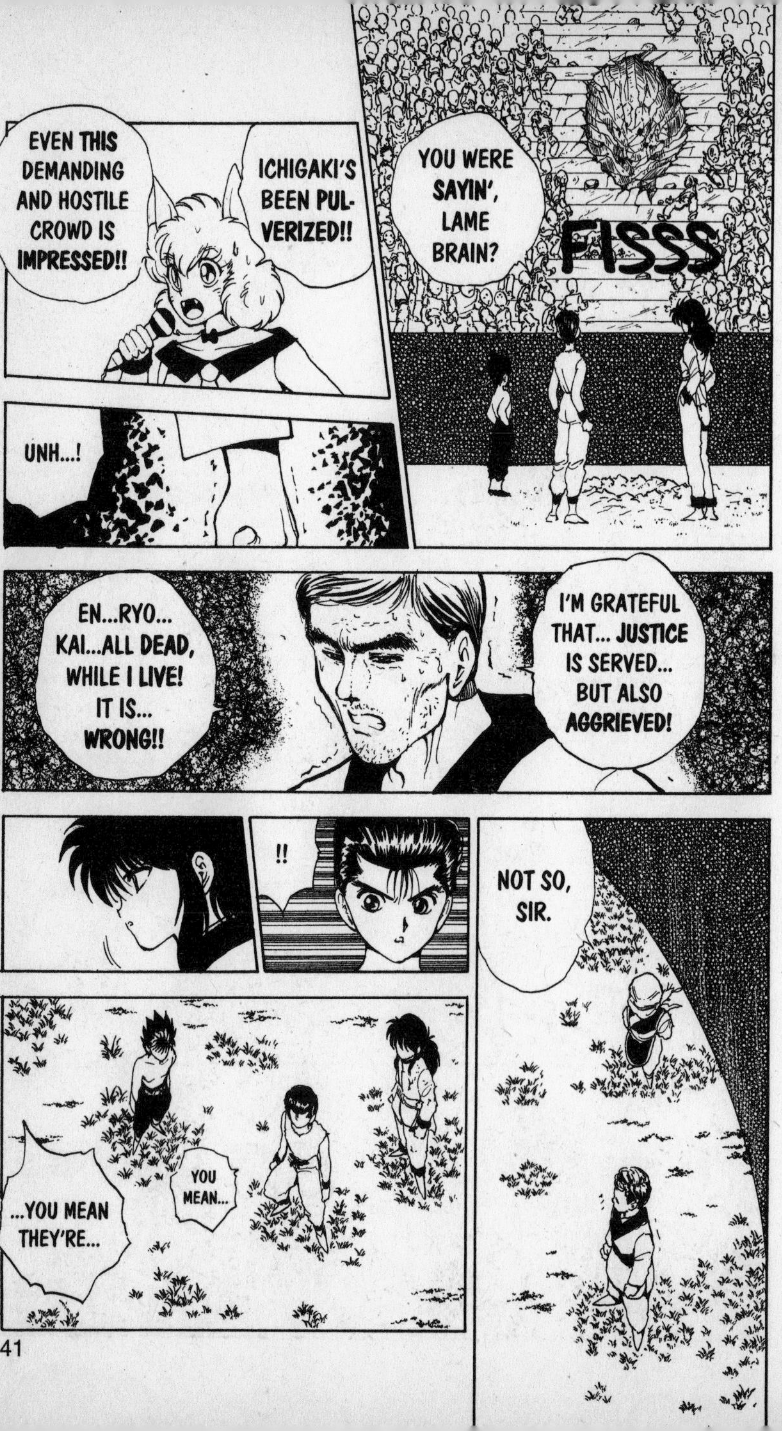

YOU WERE SAYIN', LAME BRAIN?
FISSS
ICHIGAKI'S BEEN PUL-VERIZED!!
EVEN THIS DEMANDING AND HOSTILE CROWD IS IMPRESSED!!
UNH...!
I'M GRATEFUL THAT... JUSTICE IS SERVED... BUT ALSO AGGRIEVED!
EN...RYO... KAI...ALL DEAD, WHILE I LIVE! IT IS... WRONG!!
NOT SO, SIR.
!!
YOU MEAN...
...YOU MEAN THEY'RE...

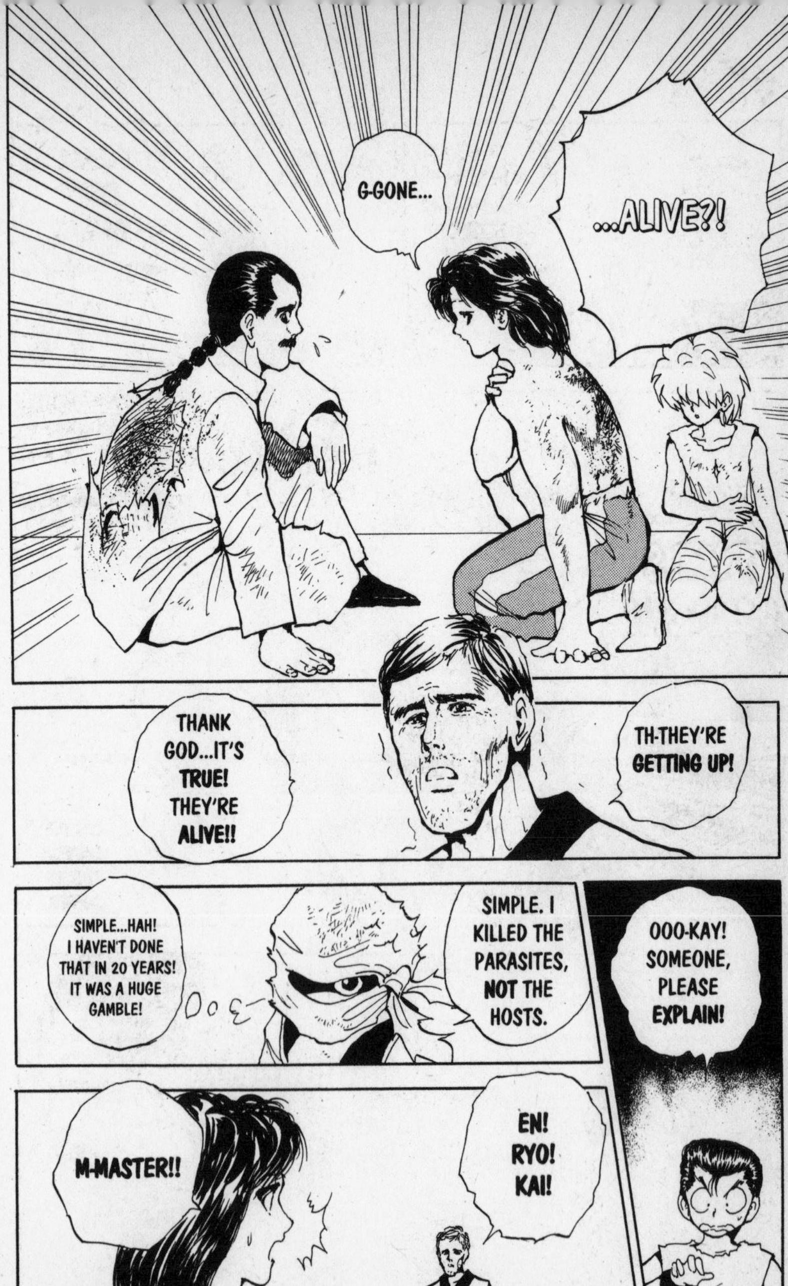
G-GONE...
...ALIVE?!
TH-THEY'RE GETTING UP!
THANK GOD...IT'S TRUE! THEY'RE ALIVE!!
OOO-KAY! SOMEONE, PLEASE EXPLAIN!
SIMPLE. I KILLED THE PARASITES, NOT THE HOSTS.
SIMPLE...HAH! I HAVEN'T DONE THAT IN 20 YEARS! IT WAS A HUGE GAMBLE!
EN! RYO! KAI!
M-MASTER!!

READ THIS WAY

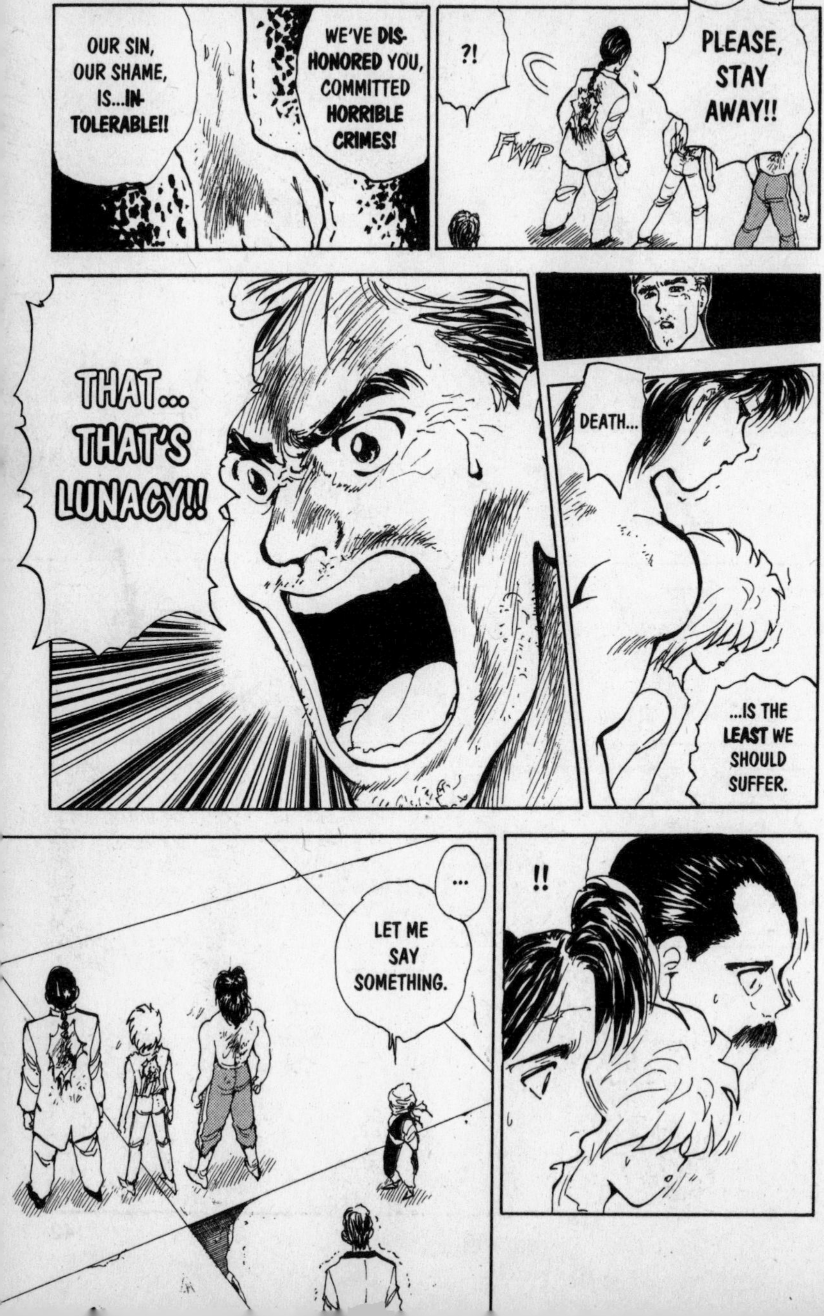

PLEASE, STAY AWAY!!
?!
FWIP
WE'VE DIS-HONORED YOU, COMMITTED HORRIBLE CRIMES!
OUR SIN, OUR SHAME, IS...IN-TOLERABLE!!
DEATH...
...IS THE LEAST WE SHOULD SUFFER.
THAT... THAT'S LUNACY!!
!!
...
LET ME SAY SOMETHING.

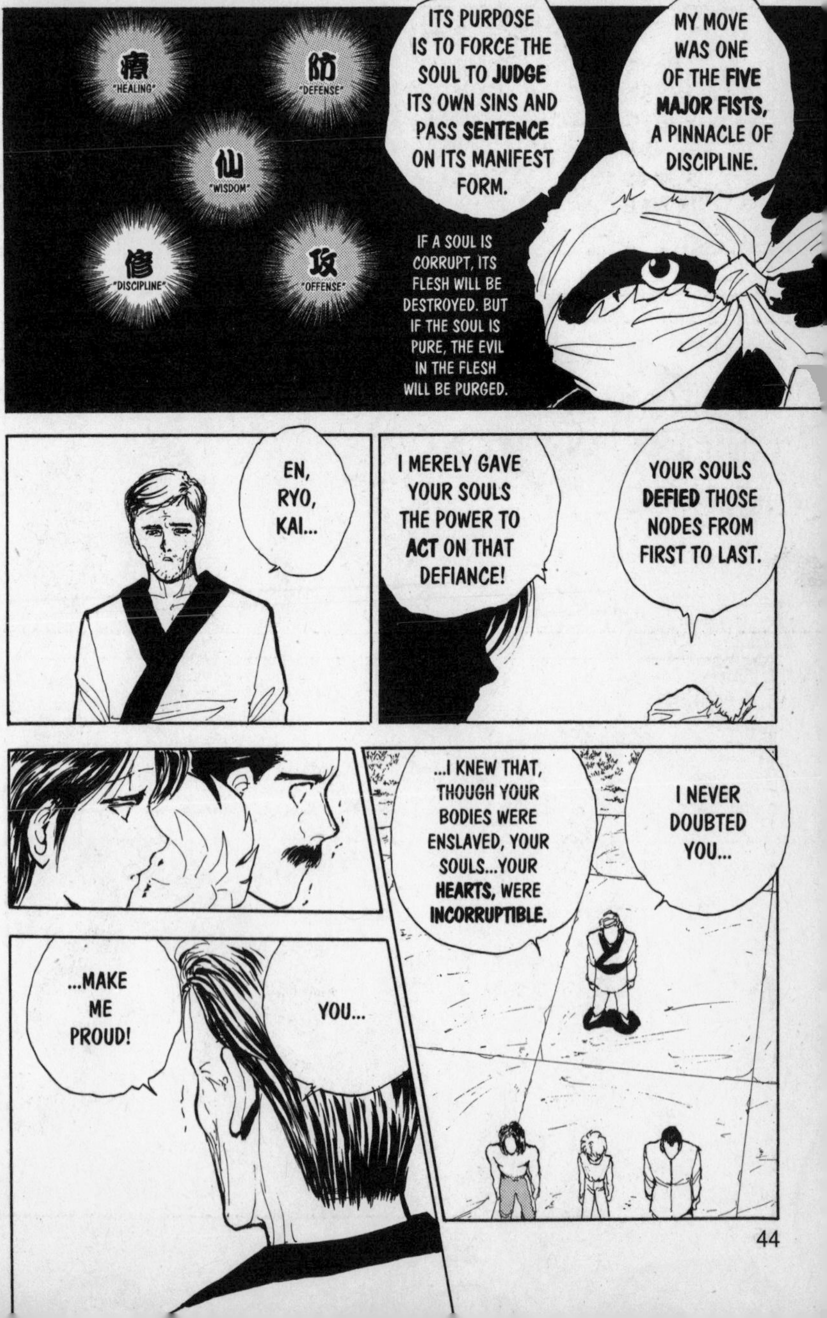
MY MOVE WAS ONE OF THE FIVE MAJOR FISTS, A PINNACLE OF DISCIPLINE.
ITS PURPOSE IS TO FORCE THE SOUL TO JUDGE ITS OWN SINS AND PASS SENTENCE ON ITS MANIFEST FORM.
IF A SOUL IS CORRUPT, ITS FLESH WILL BE DESTROYED. BUT IF THE SOUL IS PURE, THE EVIL IN THE FLESH WILL BE PURGED.
防 "DEFENSE"
療 "HEALING"
仙 "WISDOM"
攻 "OFFENSE"
修 "DISCIPLINE"
YOUR SOULS DEFIED THOSE NODES FROM FIRST TO LAST.
I MERELY GAVE YOUR SOULS THE POWER TO ACT ON THAT DEFIANCE!
EN, RYO, KAI...
I NEVER DOUBTED YOU...
...I KNEW THAT, THOUGH YOUR BODIES WERE ENSLAVED, YOUR SOULS...YOUR HEARTS, WERE INCORRUPTIBLE.
YOU...
...MAKE ME PROUD!

READ THIS WAY

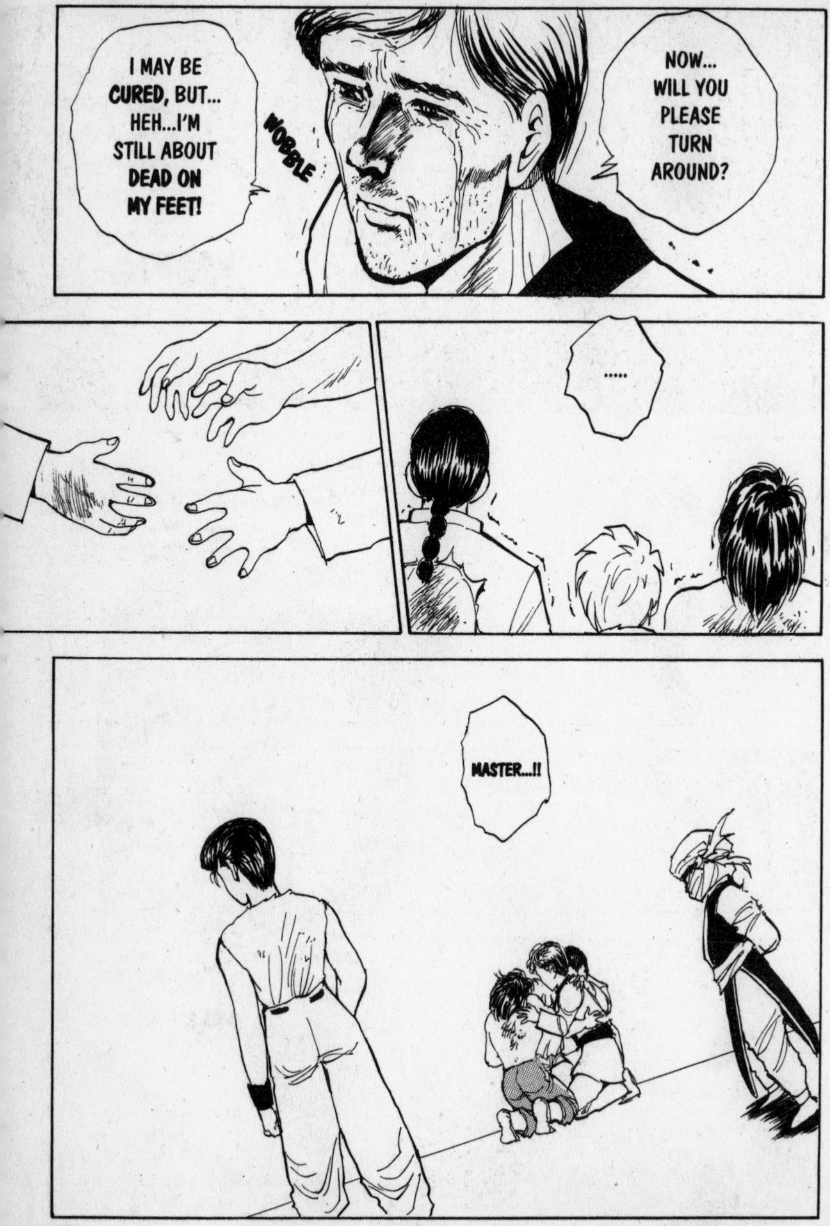
NOW... WILL YOU PLEASE TURN AROUND?
I MAY BE CURED, BUT... HEH...I'M STILL ABOUT DEAD ON MY FEET!
WOBBLE
.....
MASTER...!!

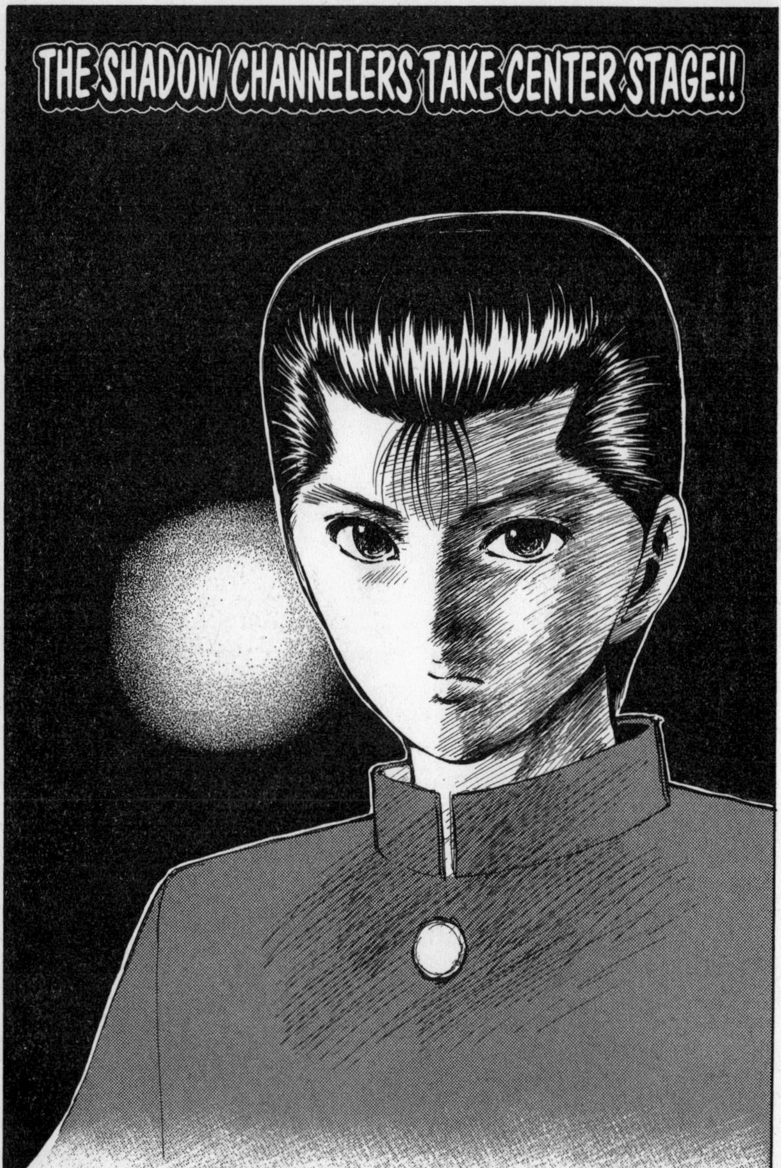
THE SHADOW CHANNELERS TAKE CENTER STAGE!!

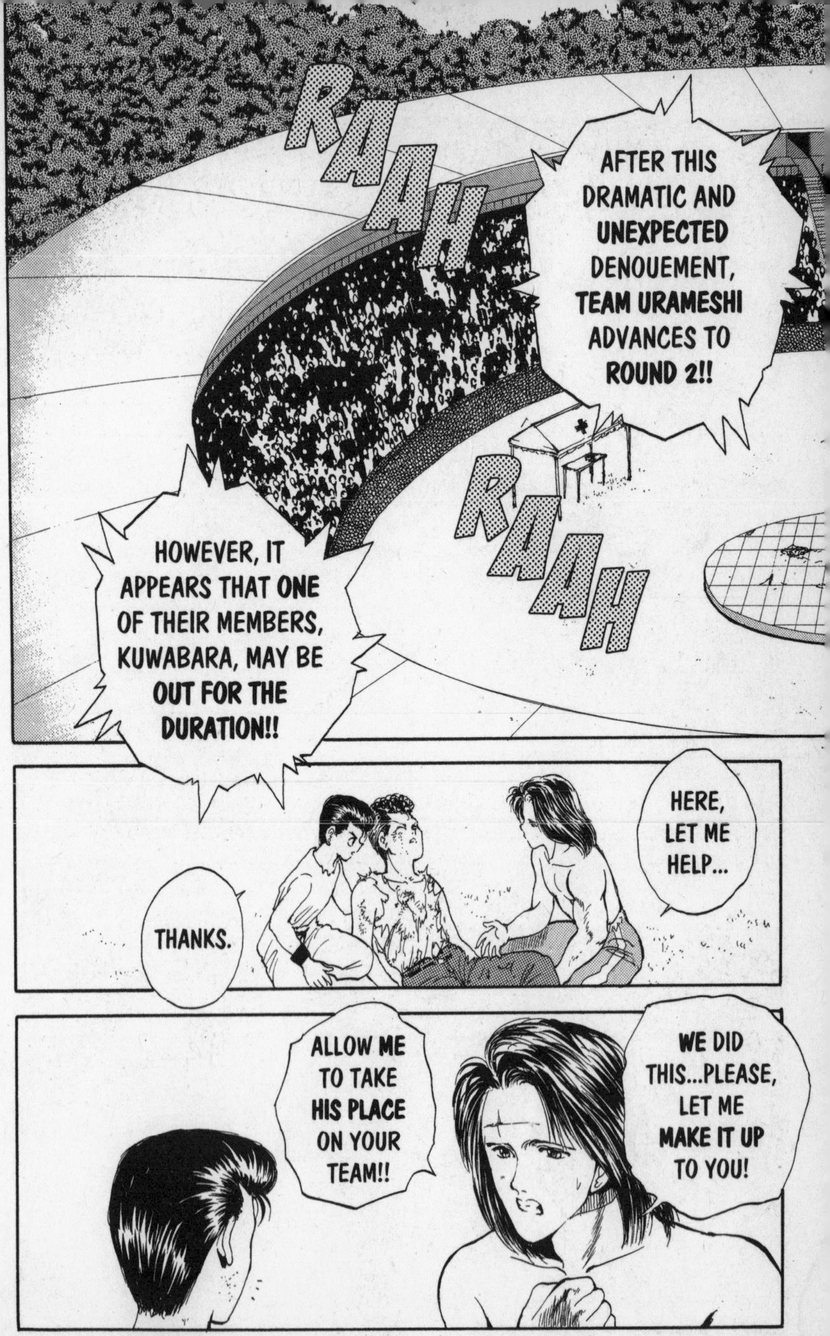
AFTER THIS DRAMATIC AND UNEXPECTED DENOUEMENT, TEAM URAMESHI ADVANCES TO ROUND 2!!
RAAH
RAAAH
HOWEVER, IT APPEARS THAT ONE OF THEIR MEMBERS, KUWABARA, MAY BE OUT FOR THE DURATION!!
HERE, LET ME HELP...
THANKS.
WE DID THIS...PLEASE, LET ME MAKE IT UP TO YOU!
ALLOW ME TO TAKE HIS PLACE ON YOUR TEAM!!

READ THIS WAY

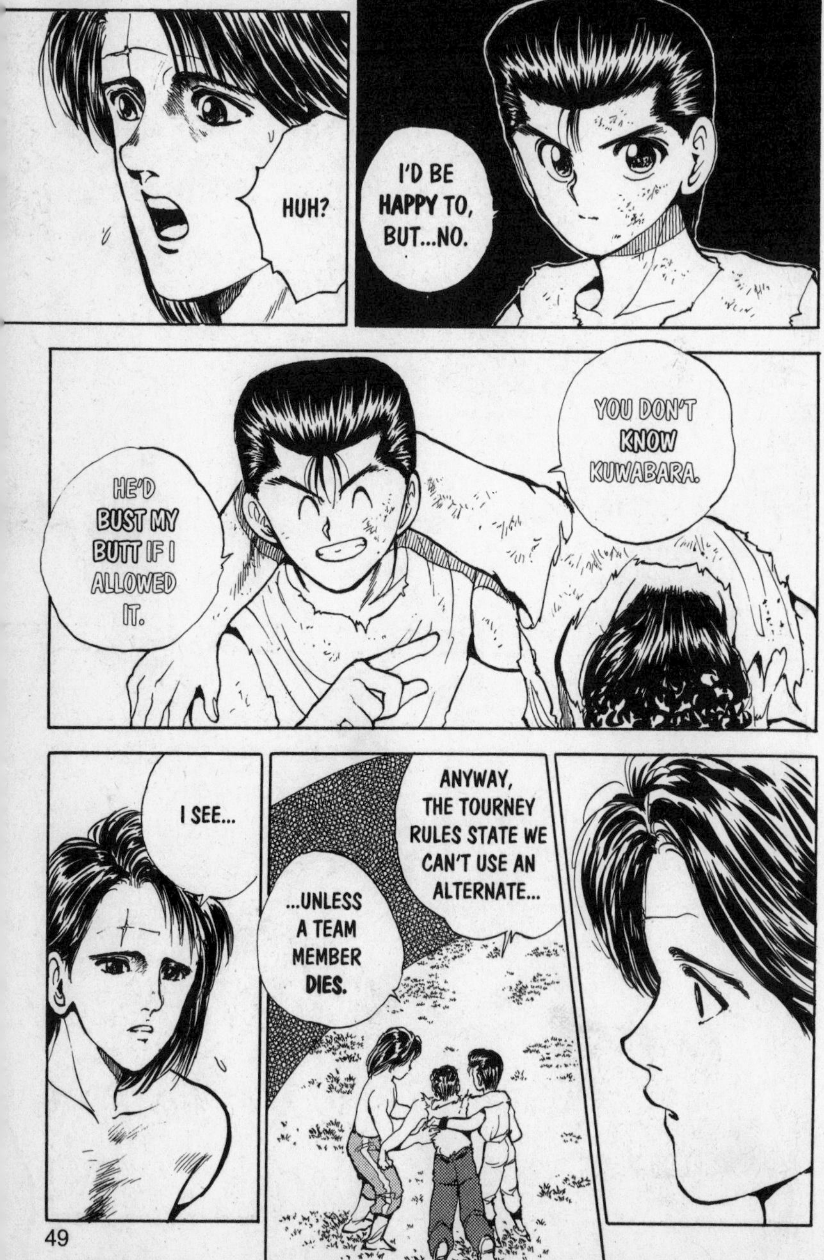

I'D BE HAPPY TO, BUT...NO.
HUH?
YOU DON'T KNOW KUWABARA.
HE'D BUST MY BUTT IF I ALLOWED IT.
ANYWAY, THE TOURNEY RULES STATE WE CAN'T USE AN ALTERNATE...
...UNLESS A TEAM MEMBER DIES.
I SEE...

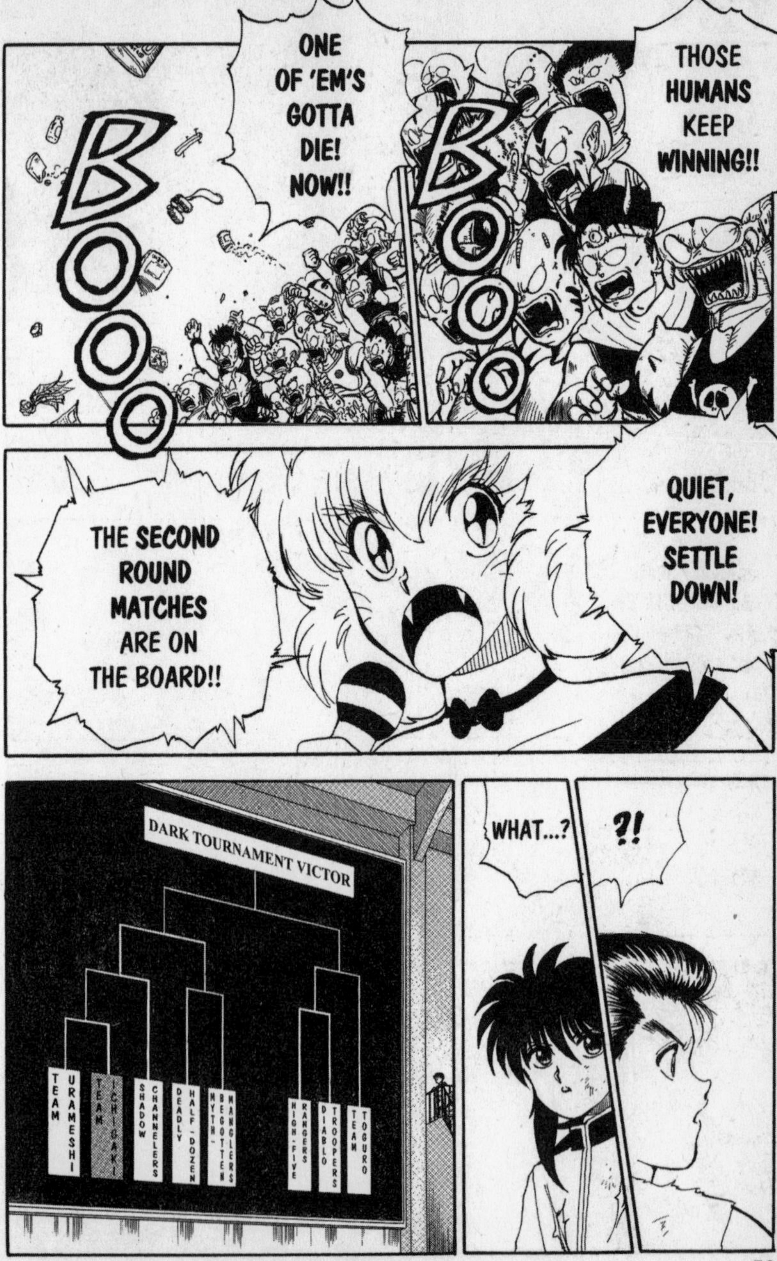
THOSE HUMANS KEEP WINNING!!
ONE OF 'EM'S GOTTA DIE! NOW!!
BOOOOO
BOOOO
QUIET, EVERYONE! SETTLE DOWN!
THE SECOND ROUND MATCHES ARE ON THE BOARD!!
DARK TOURNAMENT VICTOR
TEAM URAMESHI
TEAM ICHIGAKI
SHADOW CHANNELERS
DEADLY HALF-DOZEN
MYTH-BEGOTTEN MANGLERS
HIGH-FIVE RANGERS
DIABLO TROOPERS
TEAM TOGURO
WHAT...?
?!

READ THIS WAY

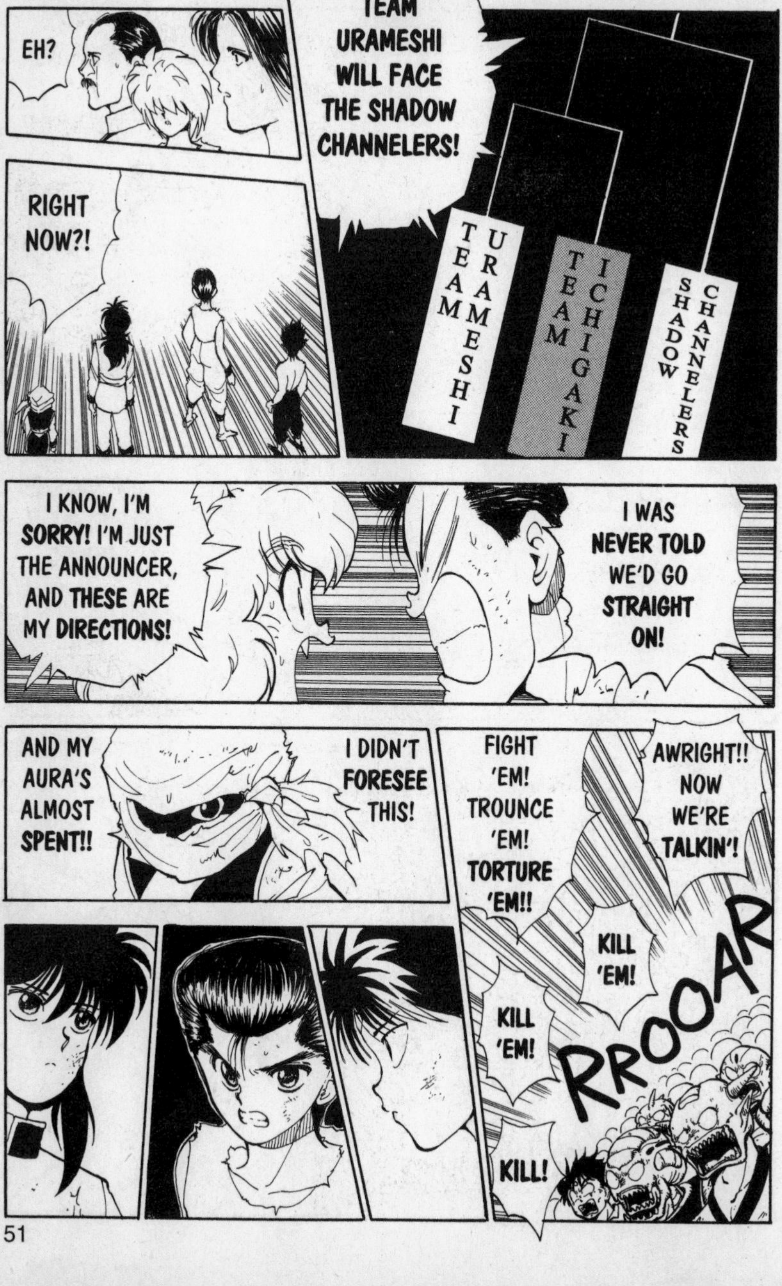

TEAM URAMESHI WILL FACE THE SHADOW CHANNELERS!
SHADOW CHANNELERS
TEAM ICHIGAKI
TEAM URAMESHI
EH?
RIGHT NOW?!
I WAS NEVER TOLD WE'D GO STRAIGHT ON!
I KNOW, I'M SORRY! I'M JUST THE ANNOUNCER, AND THESE ARE MY DIRECTIONS!
AWRIGHT!! NOW WE'RE TALKIN'!
FIGHT 'EM! TROUNCE 'EM! TORTURE 'EM!!
RROOAR
KILL 'EM!
KILL 'EM!
KILL!
I DIDN'T FORESEE THIS!
AND MY AURA'S ALMOST SPENT!!

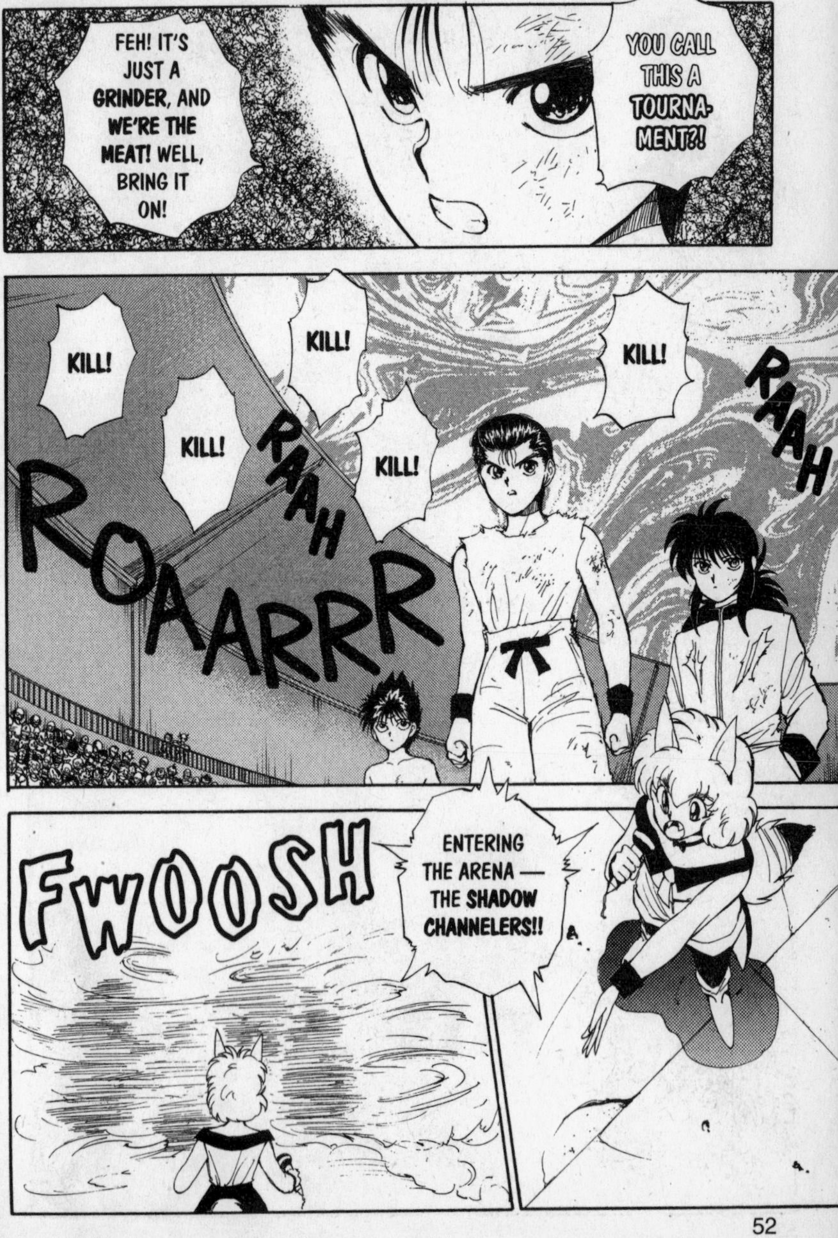
YOU CALL THIS A TOURNA-MENT?!
FEH! IT'S JUST A GRINDER, AND WE'RE THE MEAT! WELL, BRING IT ON!
RAAAH
KILL!
KILL!
KILL!
KILL!
RAAAH
KILL!
ROAARRR
ENTERING THE ARENA — THE SHADOW CHANNELERS!!
FWOOSH

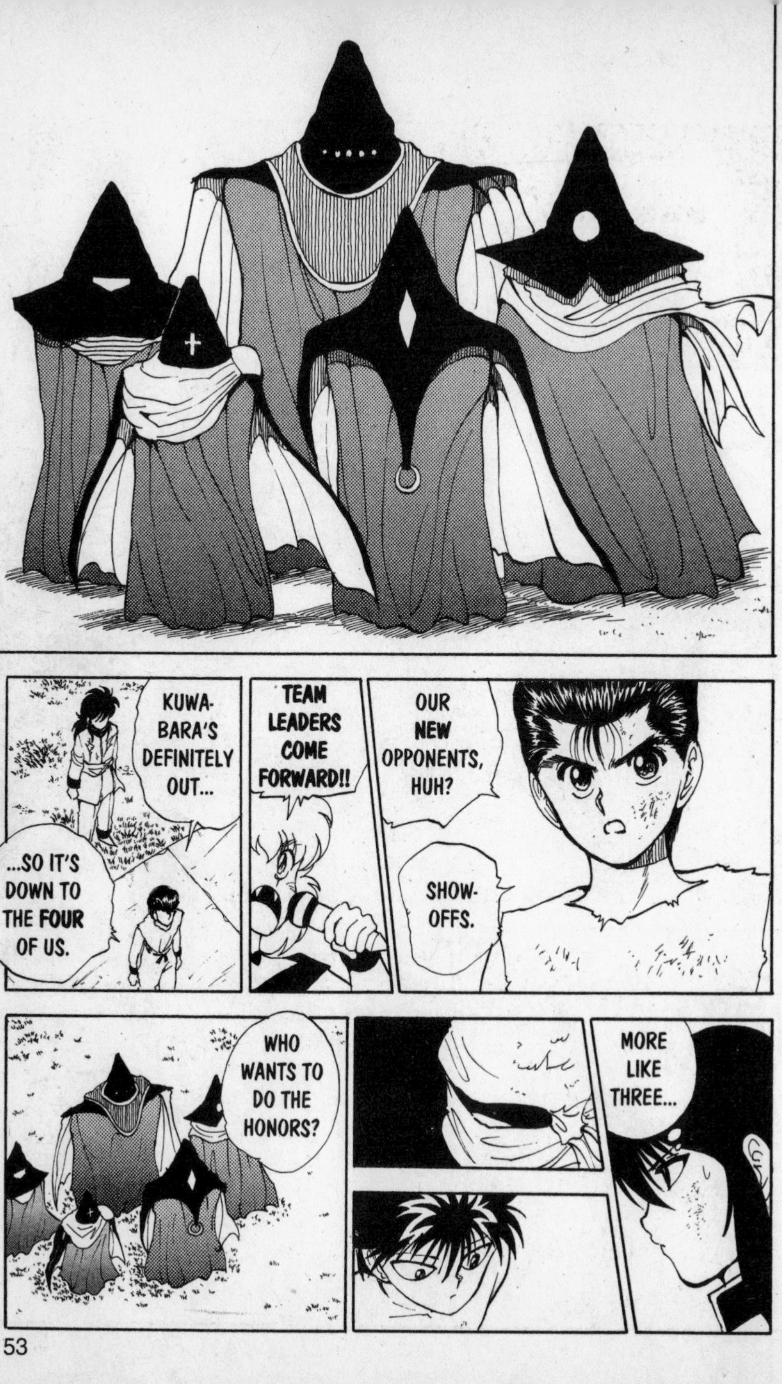
OUR NEW OPPONENTS, HUH?
SHOW-OFFS.
TEAM LEADERS COME FORWARD!!
KUWA-BARA'S DEFINITELY OUT...
...SO IT'S DOWN TO THE FOUR OF US.
MORE LIKE THREE...
WHO WANTS TO DO THE HONORS?

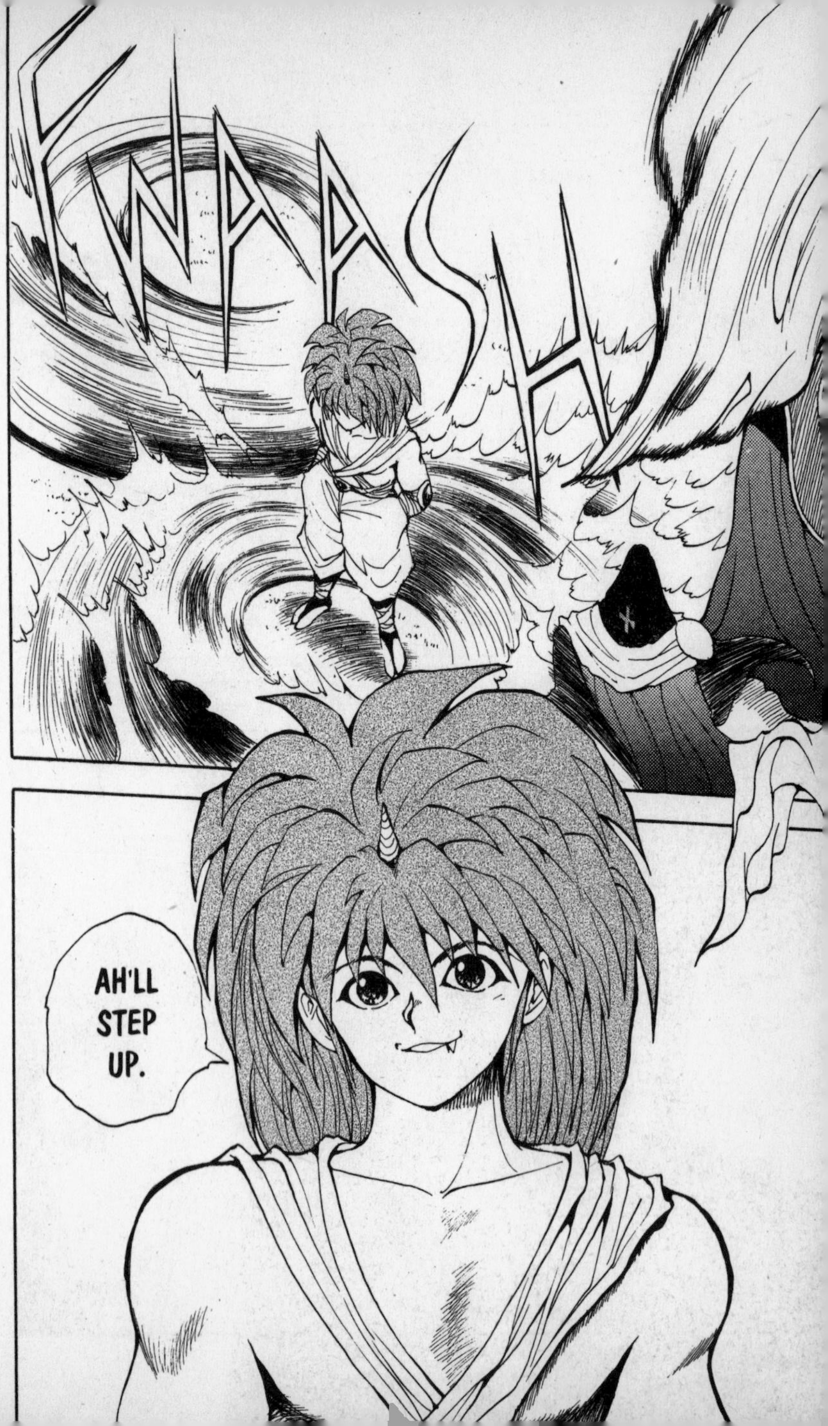
KWASH
AH'LL STEP UP.

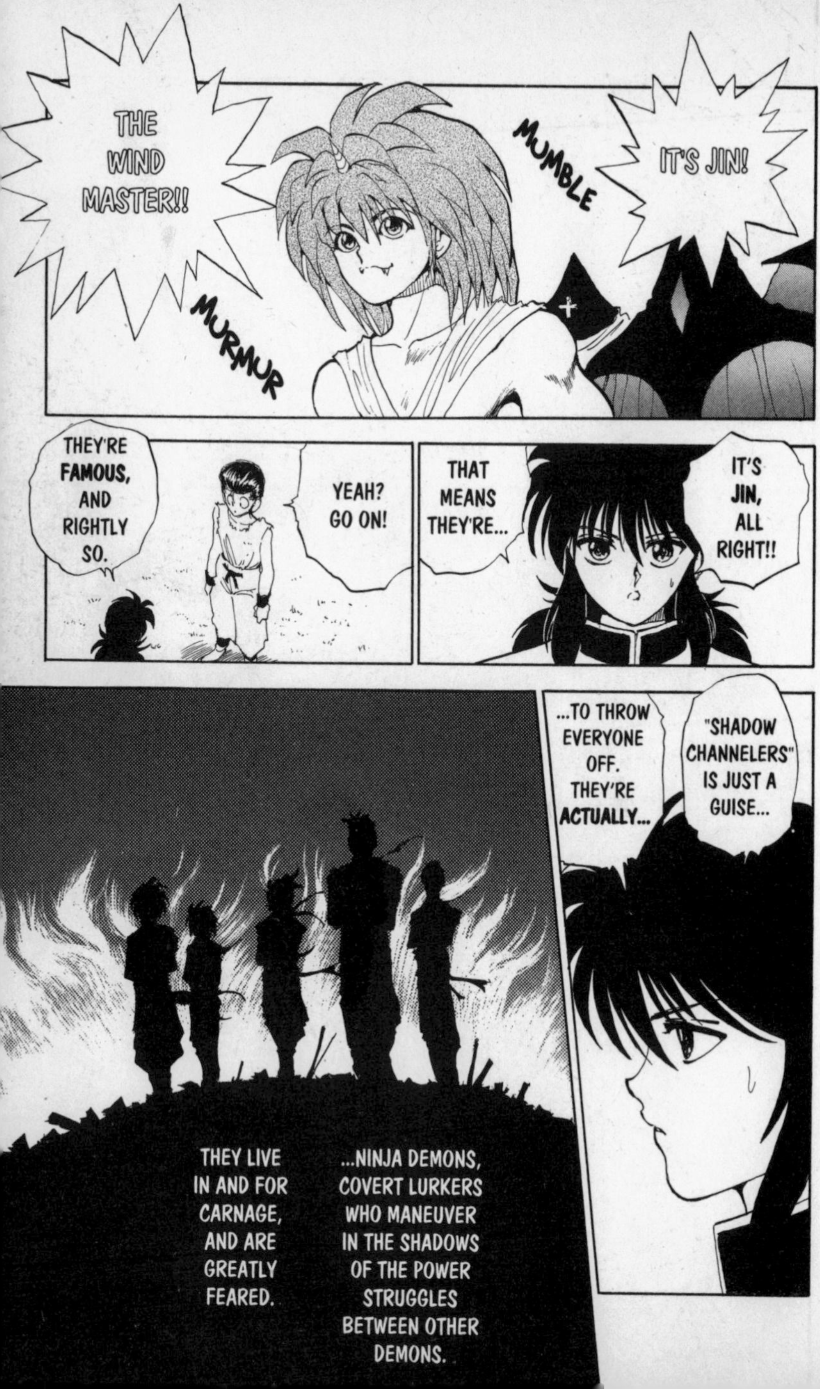
IT'S JIN!
MUMBLE
THE WIND MASTER!!
MURMUR
IT'S JIN, ALL RIGHT!!
THAT MEANS THEY'RE...
YEAH? GO ON!
THEY'RE FAMOUS, AND RIGHTLY SO.
"SHADOW CHANNELERS" IS JUST A GUISE...
...TO THROW EVERYONE OFF. THEY'RE ACTUALLY...
...NINJA DEMONS, COVERT LURKERS WHO MANEUVER IN THE SHADOWS OF THE POWER STRUGGLES BETWEEN OTHER DEMONS.
THEY LIVE IN AND FOR CARNAGE, AND ARE GREATLY FEARED.

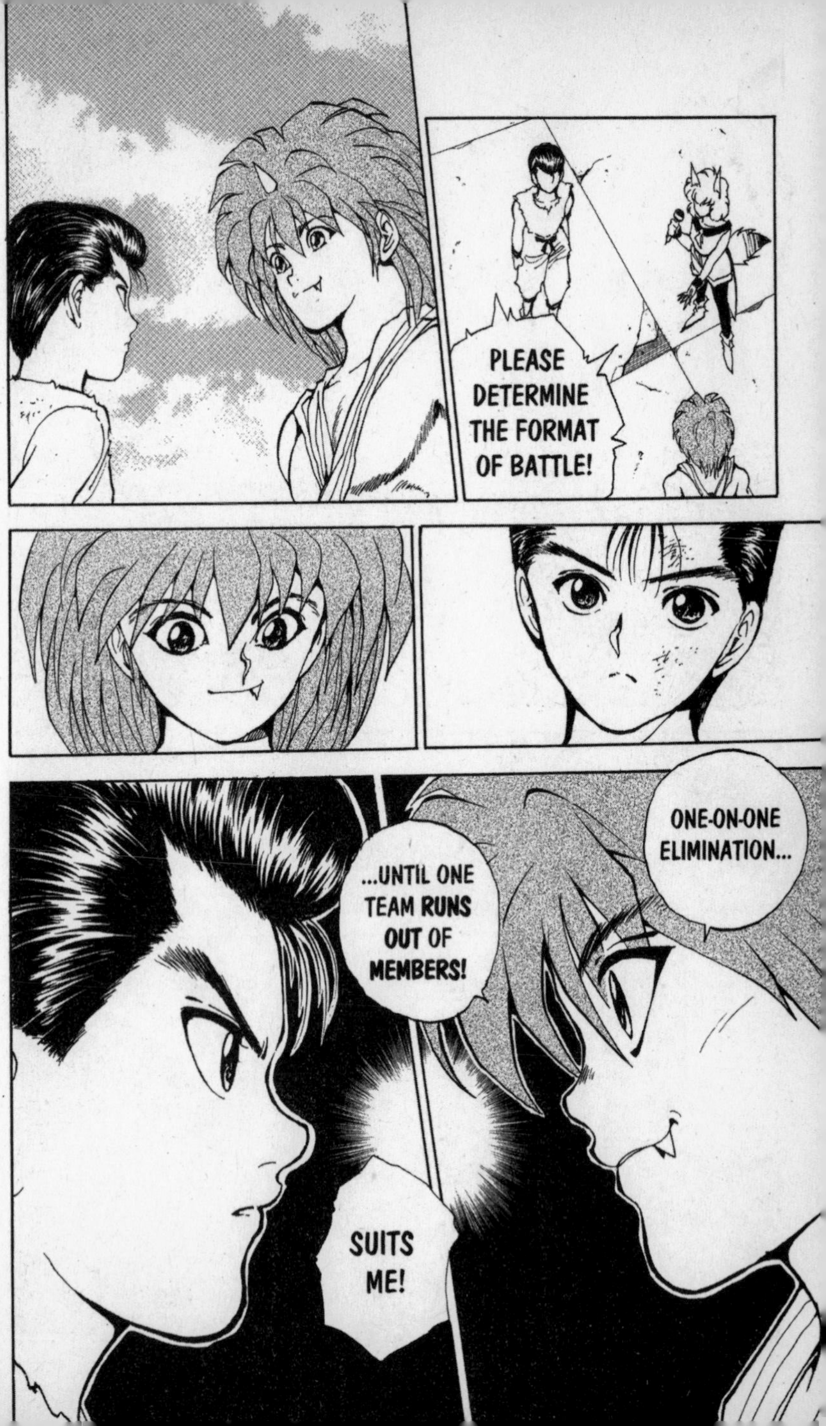

PLEASE DETERMINE THE FORMAT OF BATTLE!
ONE-ON-ONE ELIMINATION...
...UNTIL ONE TEAM RUNS OUT OF MEMBERS!
SUITS ME!

THE TEAMS HAVE CHOSEN ONE-ON-ONE ELIMINATION!

YAH, BRING A HALE BREEZE WIT' YAH.

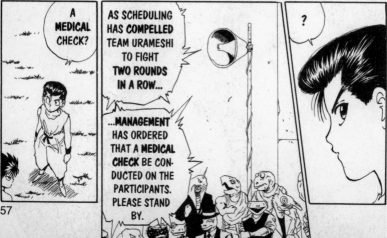

A MEDICAL CHECK?

AS SCHEDULING HAS COMPELLED TEAM URAMESHI TO FIGHT TWO ROUNDS IN A ROW...

...MANAGEMENT HAS ORDERED THAT A MEDICAL CHECK BE CONDUCTED ON THE PARTICIPANTS. PLEASE STAND BY.

?

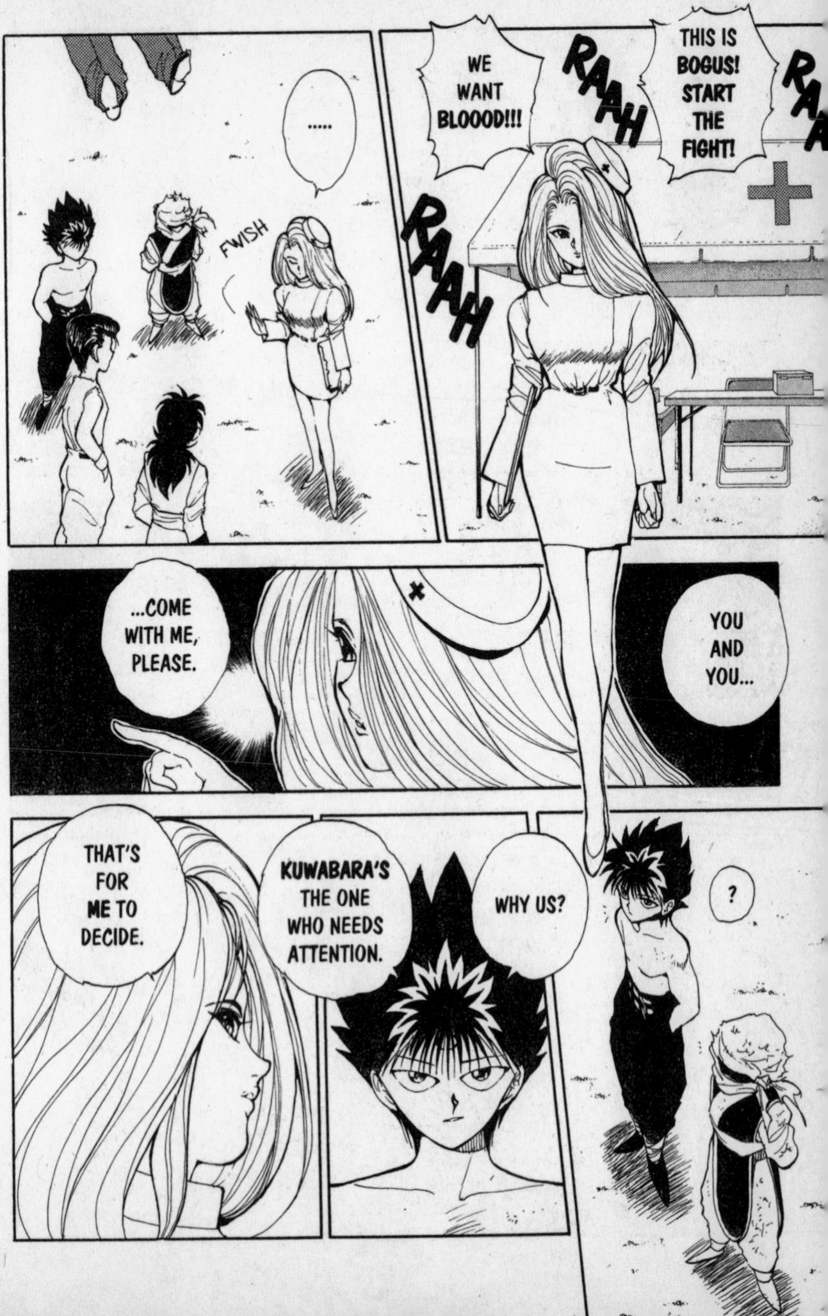
RAAAH
THIS IS BOGUS! START THE FIGHT!
WE WANT BLOOOD!!!
RAAAH
FWISH
......
YOU AND YOU...
...COME WITH ME, PLEASE.
?
WHY US?
KUWABARA'S THE ONE WHO NEEDS ATTENTION.
THAT'S FOR ME TO DECIDE.

READ THIS WAY

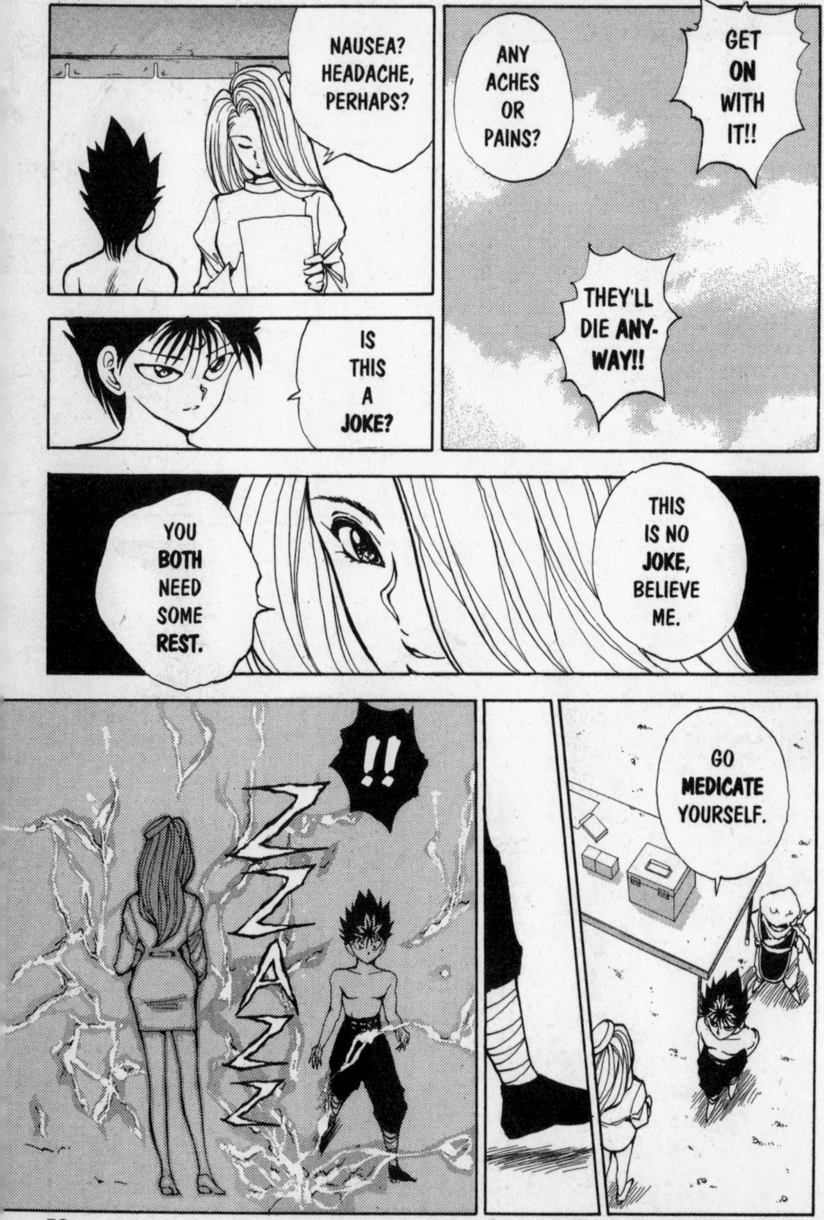

GET ON WITH IT!!
ANY ACHES OR PAINS?
THEY'LL DIE ANYWAY!!
NAUSEA? HEADACHE, PERHAPS?
IS THIS A JOKE?
THIS IS NO JOKE, BELIEVE ME.
YOU BOTH NEED SOME REST.
GO MEDICATE YOURSELF.
!!
ZZAZZ

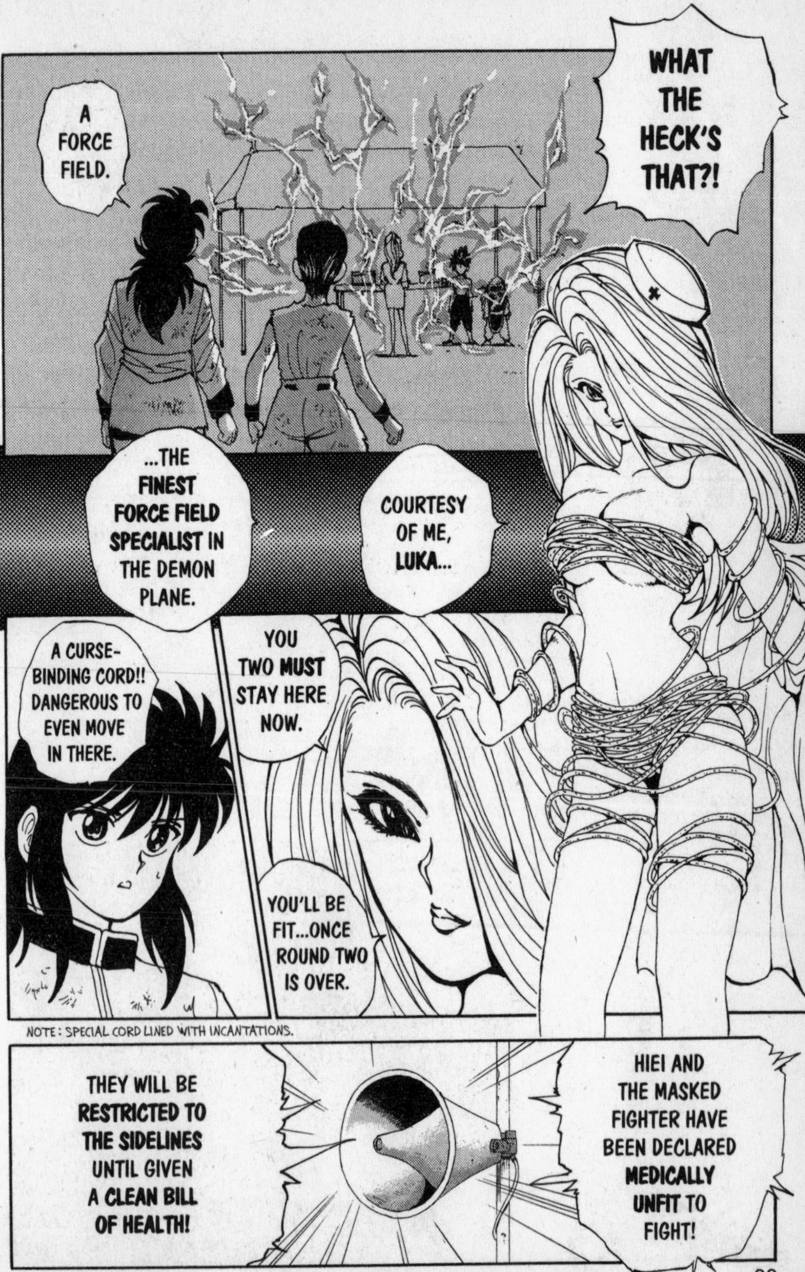

WHAT THE HECK'S THAT?!
A FORCE FIELD.
COURTESY OF ME, LUKA...
...THE FINEST FORCE FIELD SPECIALIST IN THE DEMON PLANE.
A CURSE-BINDING CORD!! DANGEROUS TO EVEN MOVE IN THERE.
YOU TWO MUST STAY HERE NOW.
YOU'LL BE FIT...ONCE ROUND TWO IS OVER.
NOTE: SPECIAL CORD LINED WITH INCANTATIONS.
HIEI AND THE MASKED FIGHTER HAVE BEEN DECLARED MEDICALLY UNFIT TO FIGHT!
THEY WILL BE RESTRICTED TO THE SIDELINES UNTIL GIVEN A CLEAN BILL OF HEALTH!

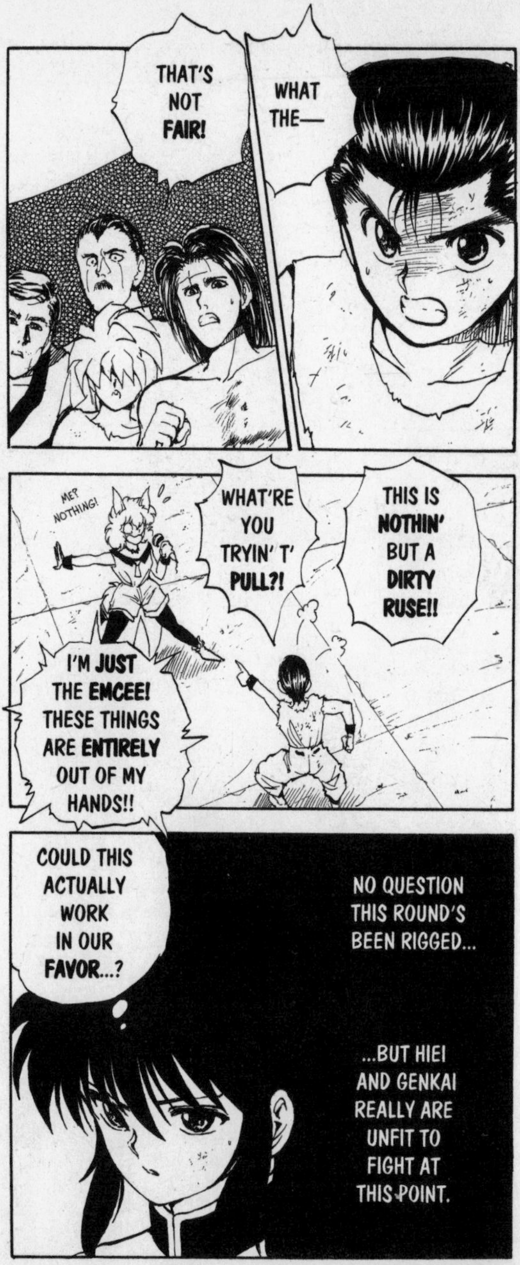
WHAT THE—
THAT'S NOT FAIR!
THIS IS NOTHIN' BUT A DIRTY RUSE!!
WHAT'RE YOU TRYIN' T' PULL?!
ME? NOTHING!
I'M JUST THE EMCEE! THESE THINGS ARE ENTIRELY OUT OF MY HANDS!!
NO QUESTION THIS ROUND'S BEEN RIGGED...
...BUT HIEI AND GENKAI REALLY ARE UNFIT TO FIGHT AT THIS POINT.
COULD THIS ACTUALLY WORK IN OUR FAVOR...?

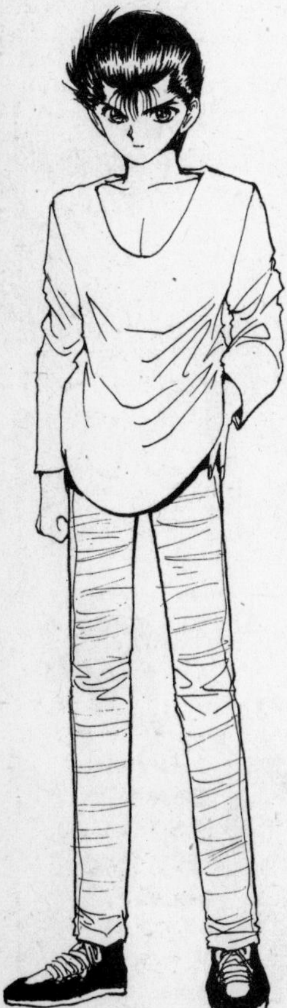

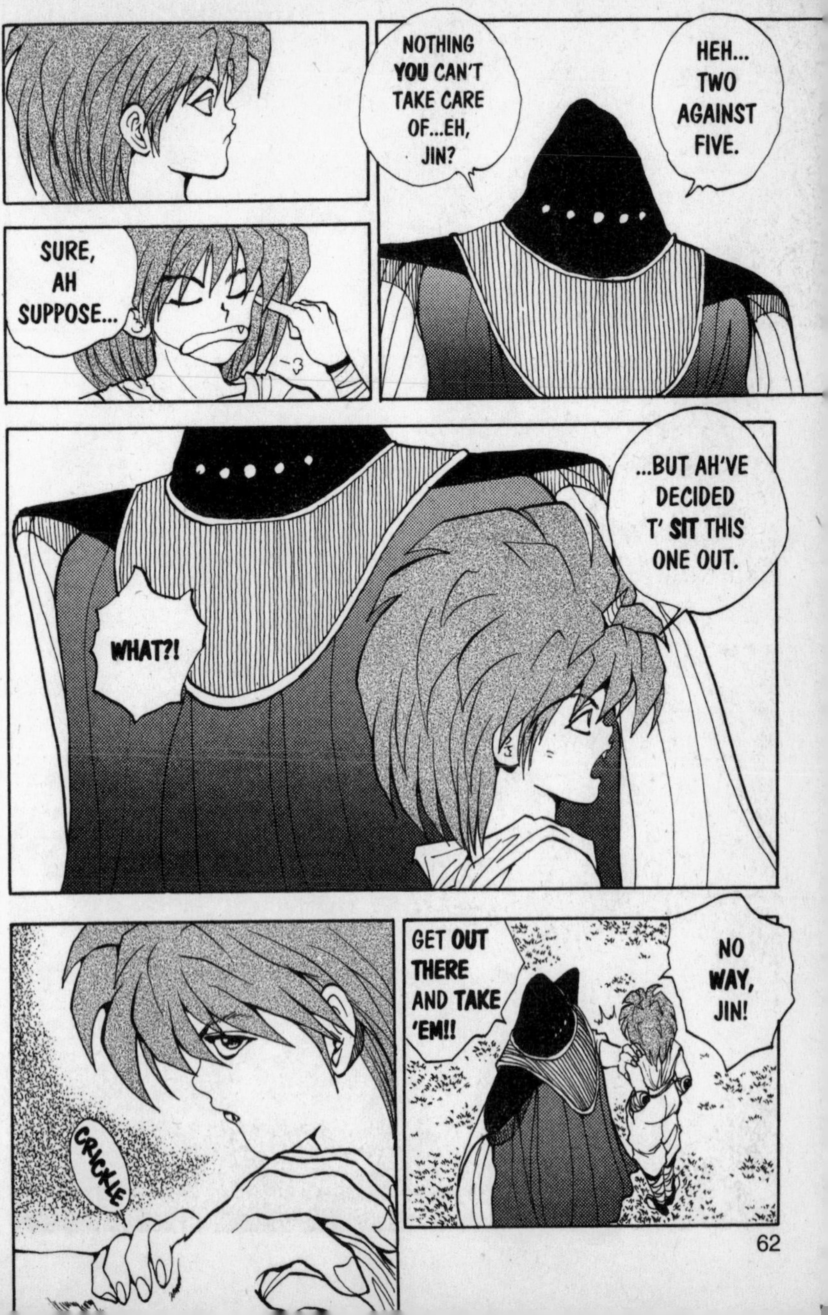
HEH... TWO AGAINST FIVE.
NOTHING YOU CAN'T TAKE CARE OF...EH, JIN?
SURE, AH SUPPOSE...
...BUT AH'VE DECIDED T' SIT THIS ONE OUT.
WHAT?!
NO WAY, JIN!
GET OUT THERE AND TAKE 'EM!!
CRICKLE

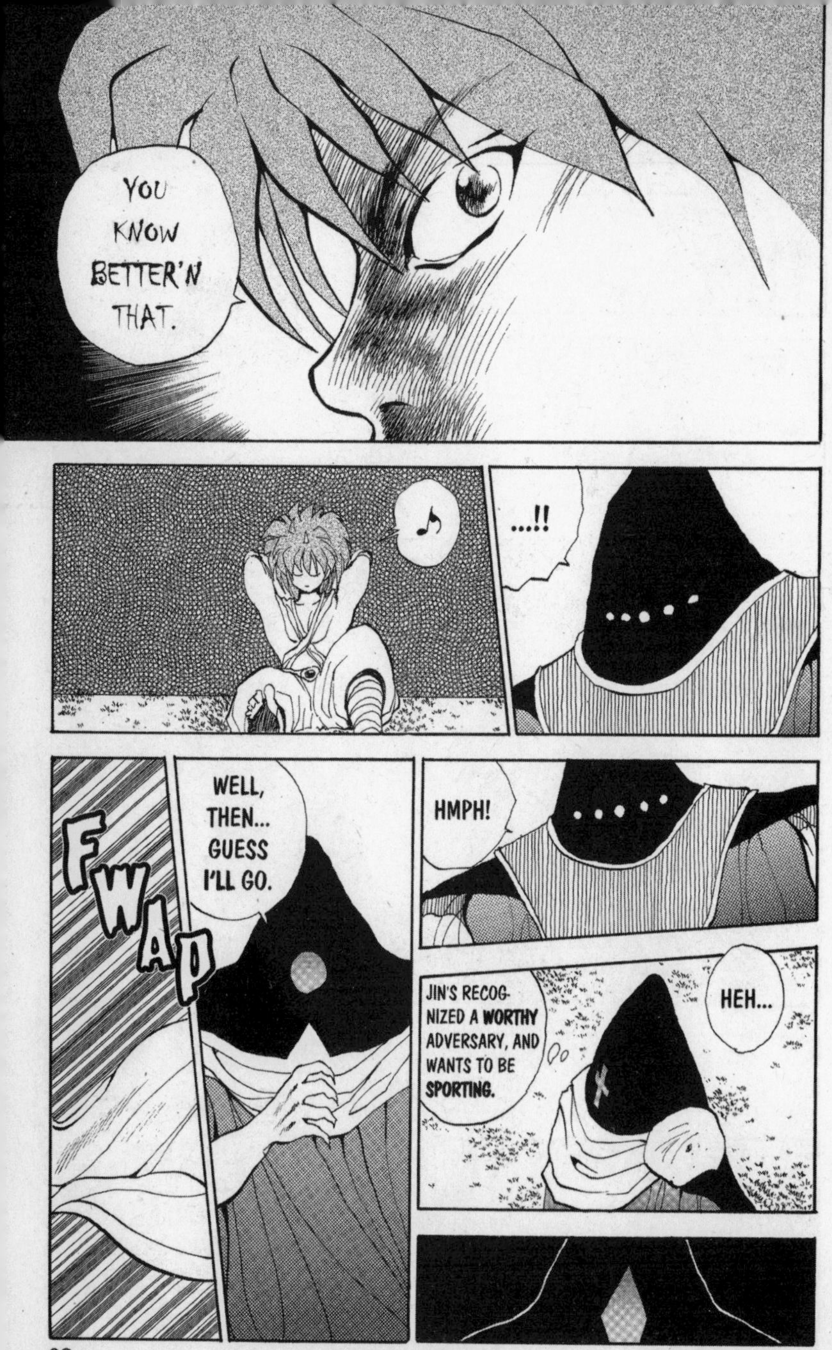
YOU KNOW BETTER'N THAT.
...!!
♪
HMPH!
HEH...
JIN'S RECOGNIZED A **WORTHY** ADVERSARY, AND WANTS TO BE **SPORTING.**
WELL, THEN... GUESS I'LL GO.
FWAP

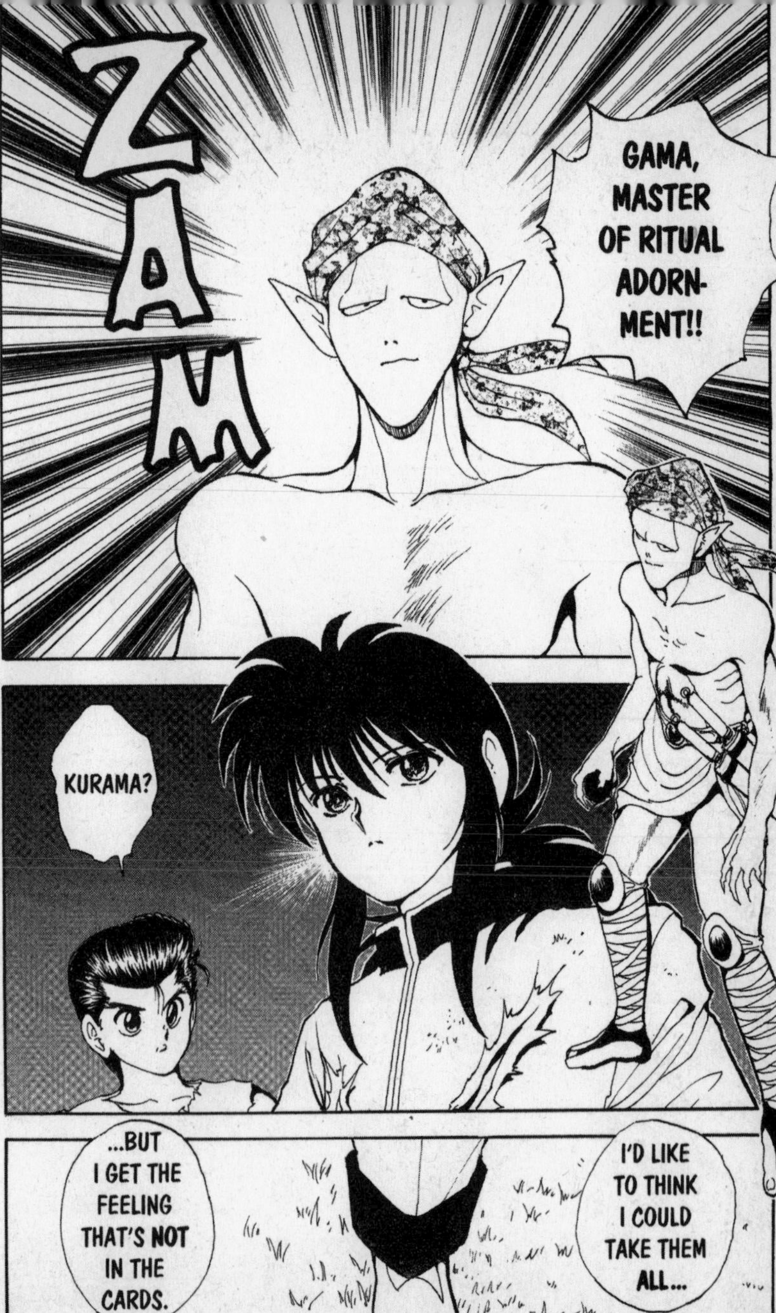
GAMA, MASTER OF RITUAL ADORN-MENT!!
ZAM
KURAMA?
I'D LIKE TO THINK I COULD TAKE THEM ALL...
...BUT I GET THE FEELING THAT'S NOT IN THE CARDS.

READ THIS WAY

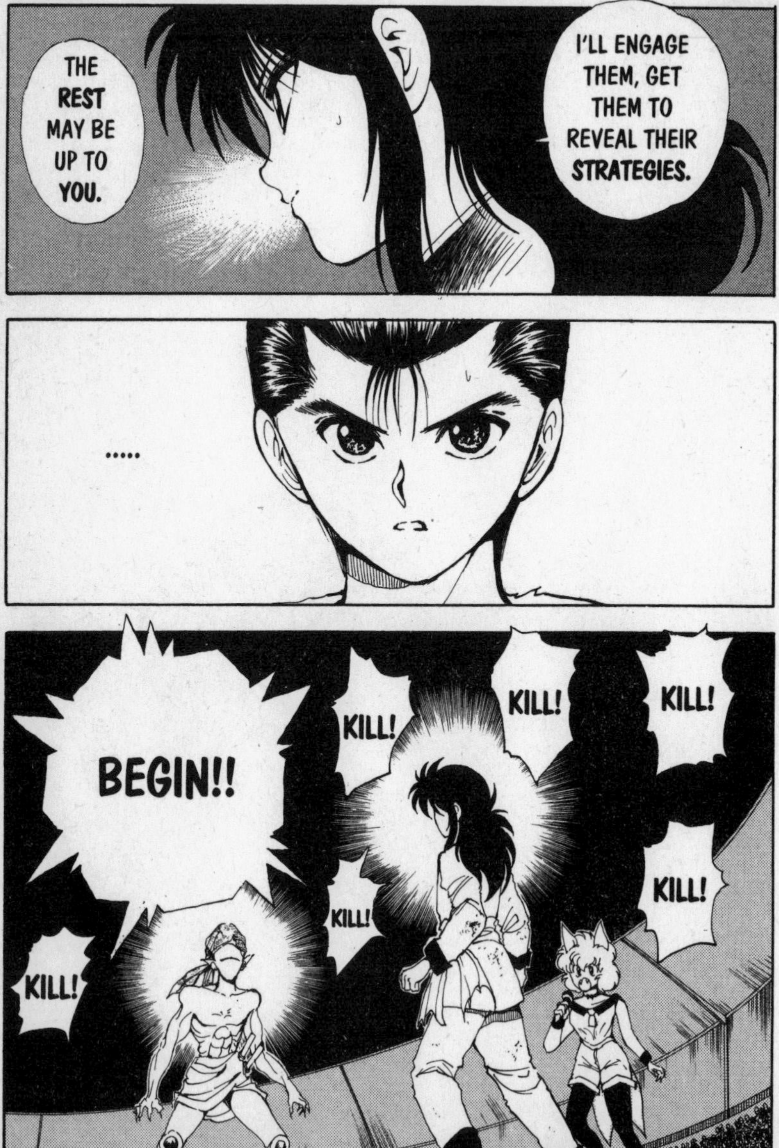
I'LL ENGAGE THEM, GET THEM TO REVEAL THEIR **STRATEGIES.**
THE **REST** MAY BE UP TO YOU.
.....
KILL!
KILL!
KILL!
KILL!
BEGIN!!
KILL!
KILL!

GAMA: RITUAL BODY ART MASTER!!

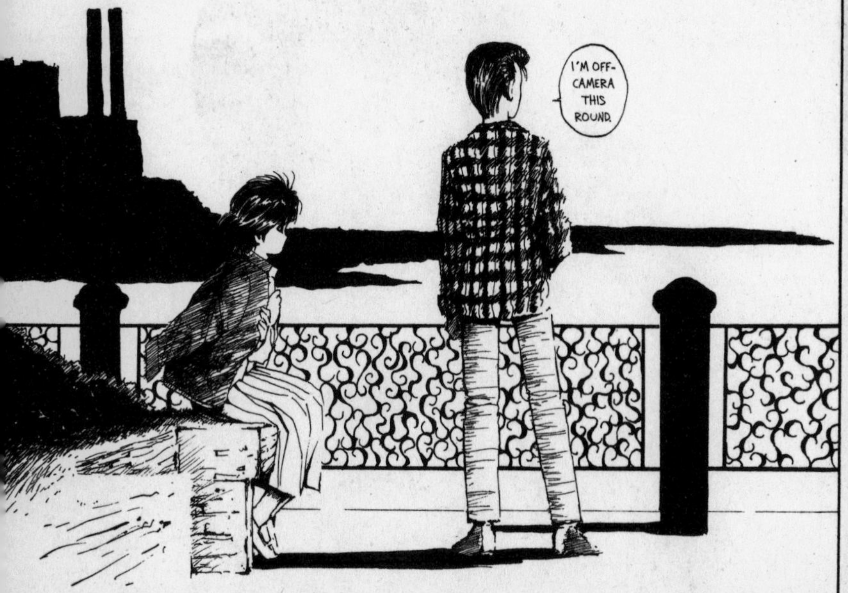
I'M OFF-CAMERA THIS ROUND.

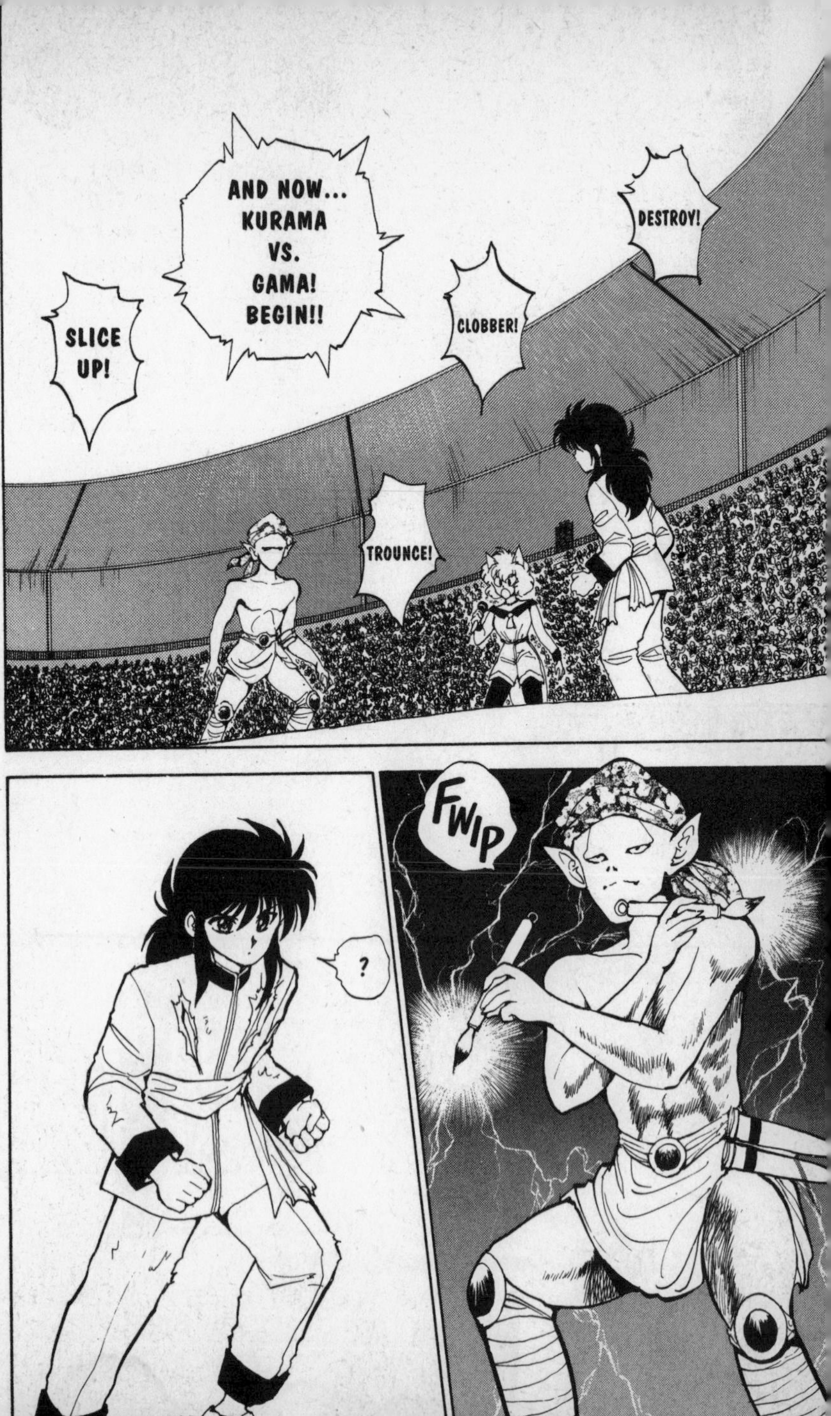
DESTROY!
CLOBBER!
AND NOW... KURAMA VS. GAMA! BEGIN!!
SLICE UP!
TROUNCE!
FWIP
?

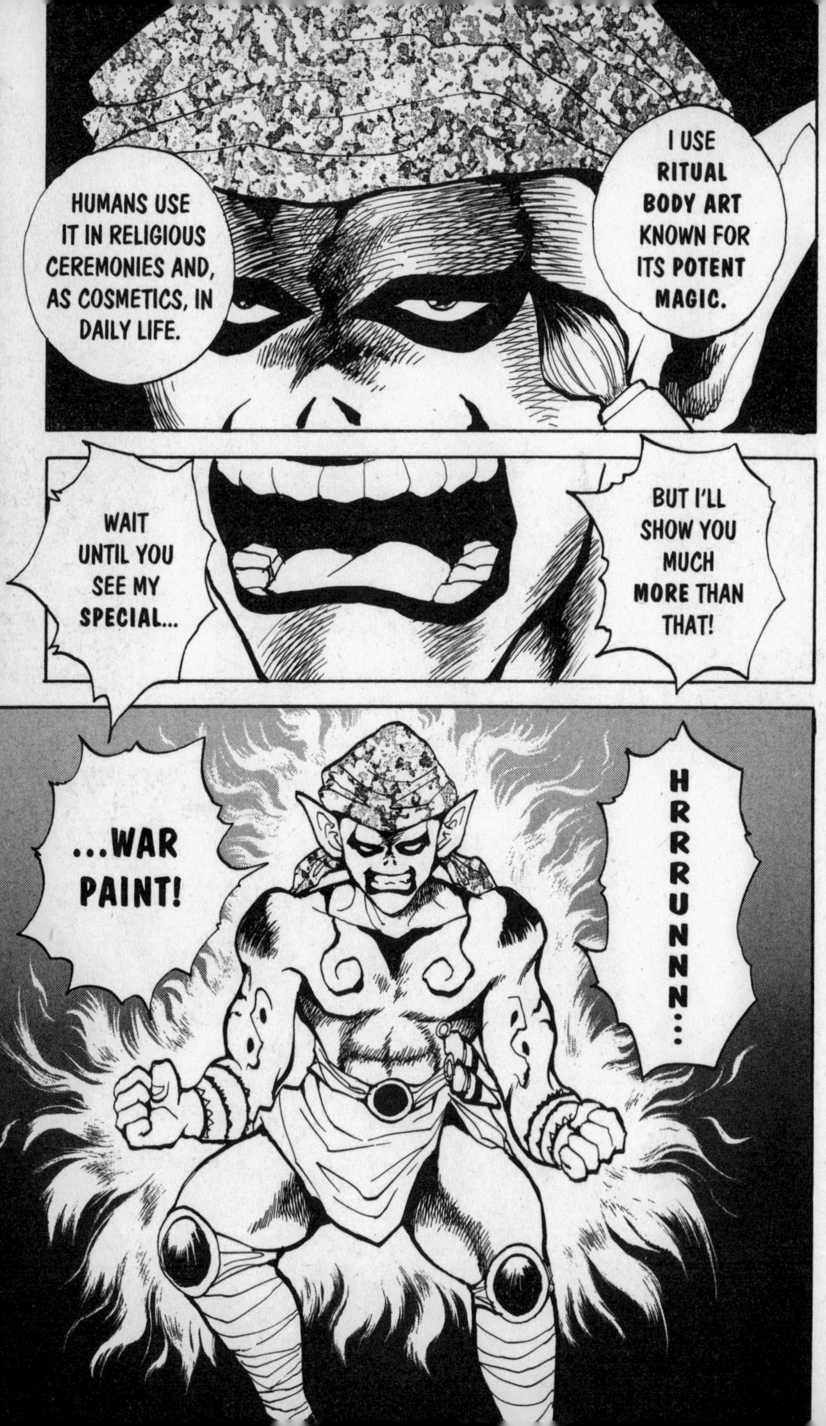
I USE RITUAL BODY ART KNOWN FOR ITS POTENT MAGIC.
HUMANS USE IT IN RELIGIOUS CEREMONIES AND, AS COSMETICS, IN DAILY LIFE.
BUT I'LL SHOW YOU MUCH MORE THAN THAT!
WAIT UNTIL YOU SEE MY SPECIAL...
HRRRUNNN...
...WAR PAINT!

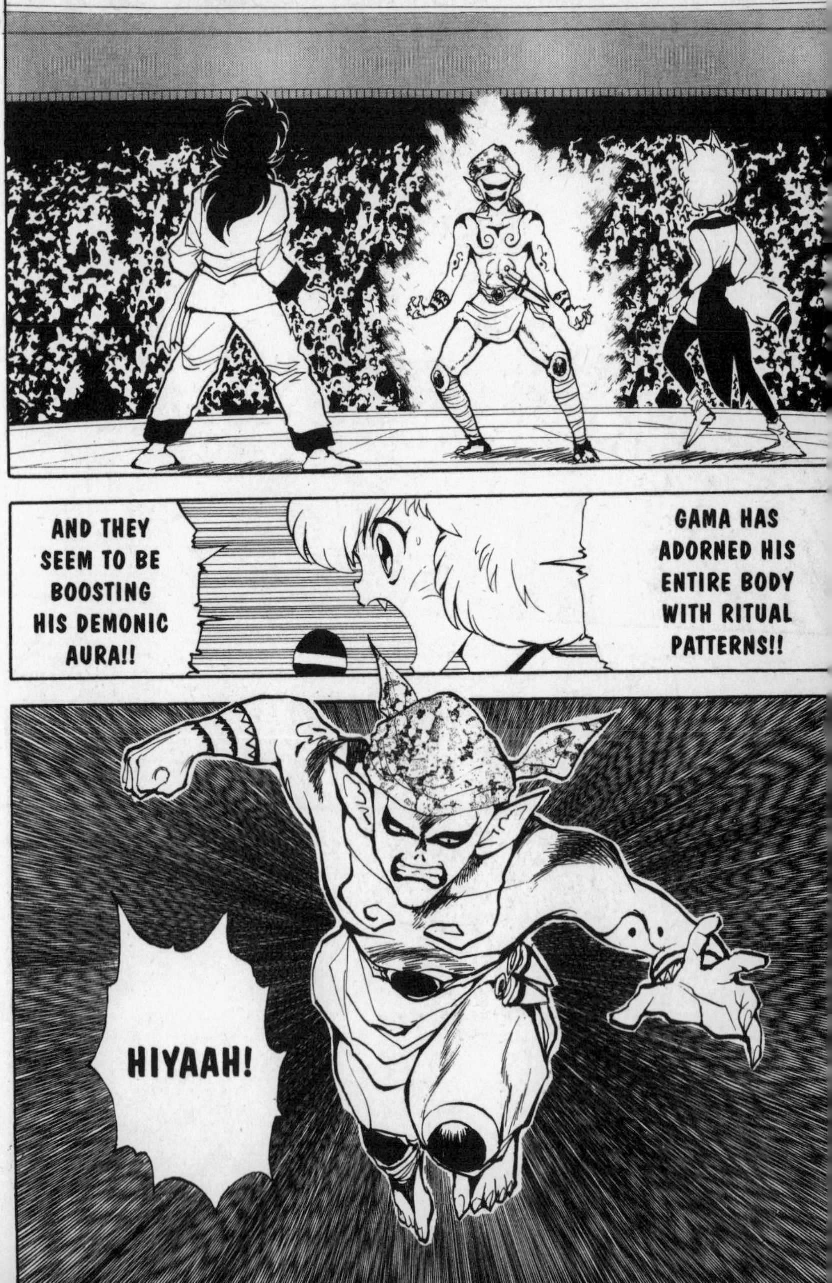
GAMA HAS ADORNED HIS ENTIRE BODY WITH RITUAL PATTERNS!!
AND THEY SEEM TO BE BOOSTING HIS DEMONIC AURA!!
HIYAAH!

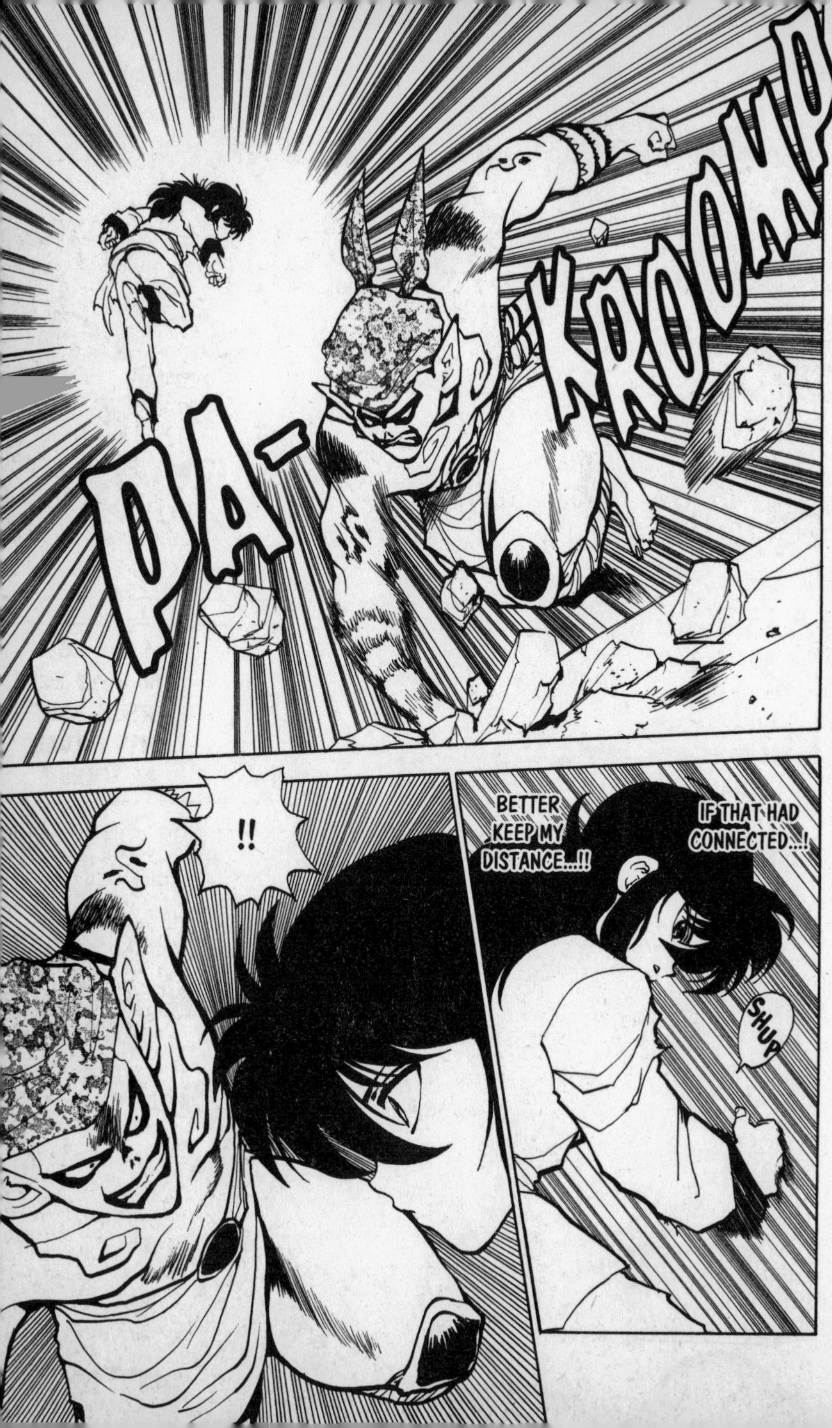
PA-KROOOM
IF THAT HAD CONNECTED...!
BETTER KEEP MY DISTANCE...!!
SHUP
!!

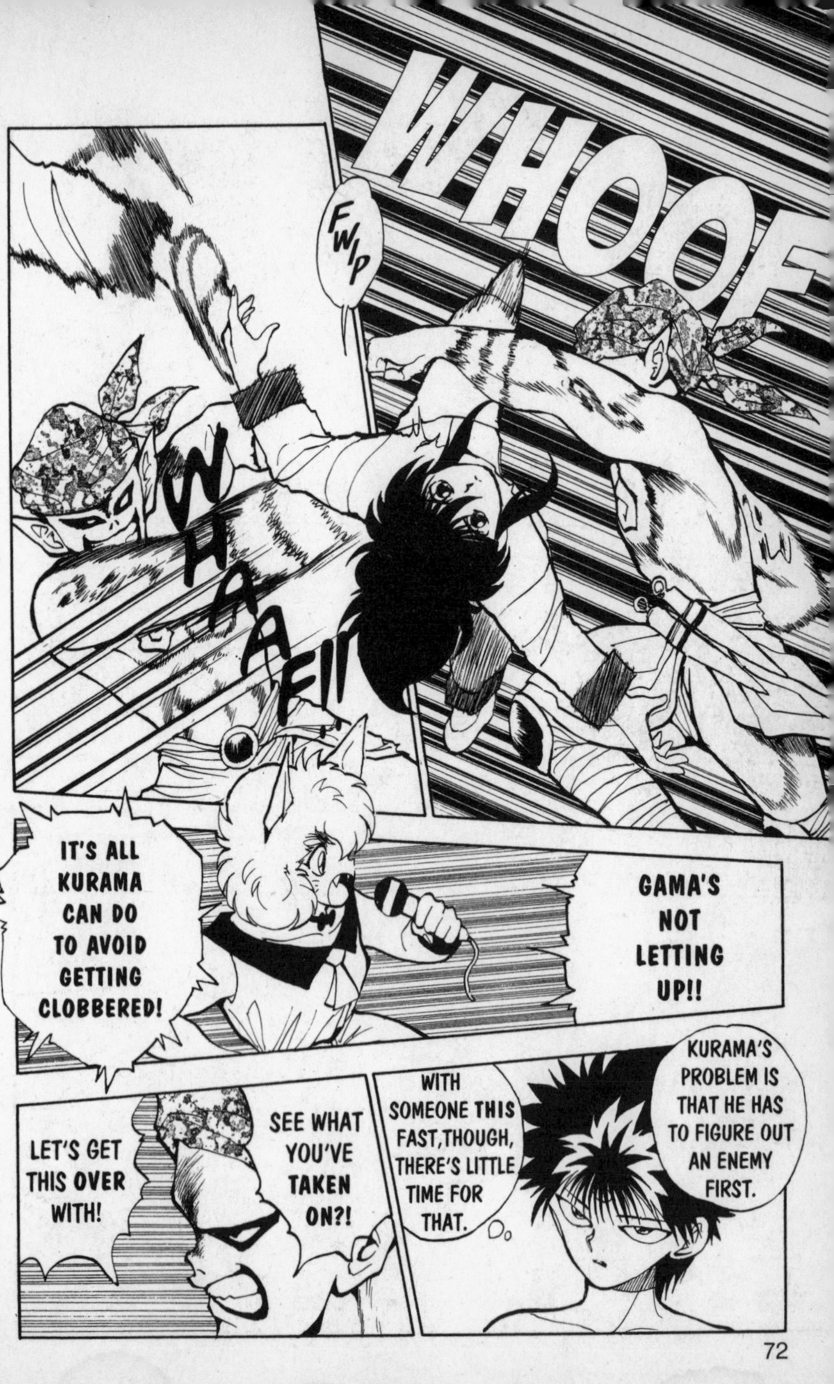

WHOOF
FWIP
WHAAF!!
GAMA'S NOT LETTING UP!!
IT'S ALL KURAMA CAN DO TO AVOID GETTING CLOBBERED!
KURAMA'S PROBLEM IS THAT HE HAS TO FIGURE OUT AN ENEMY FIRST.
WITH SOMEONE THIS FAST, THOUGH, THERE'S LITTLE TIME FOR THAT.
SEE WHAT YOU'VE TAKEN ON?!
LET'S GET THIS OVER WITH!

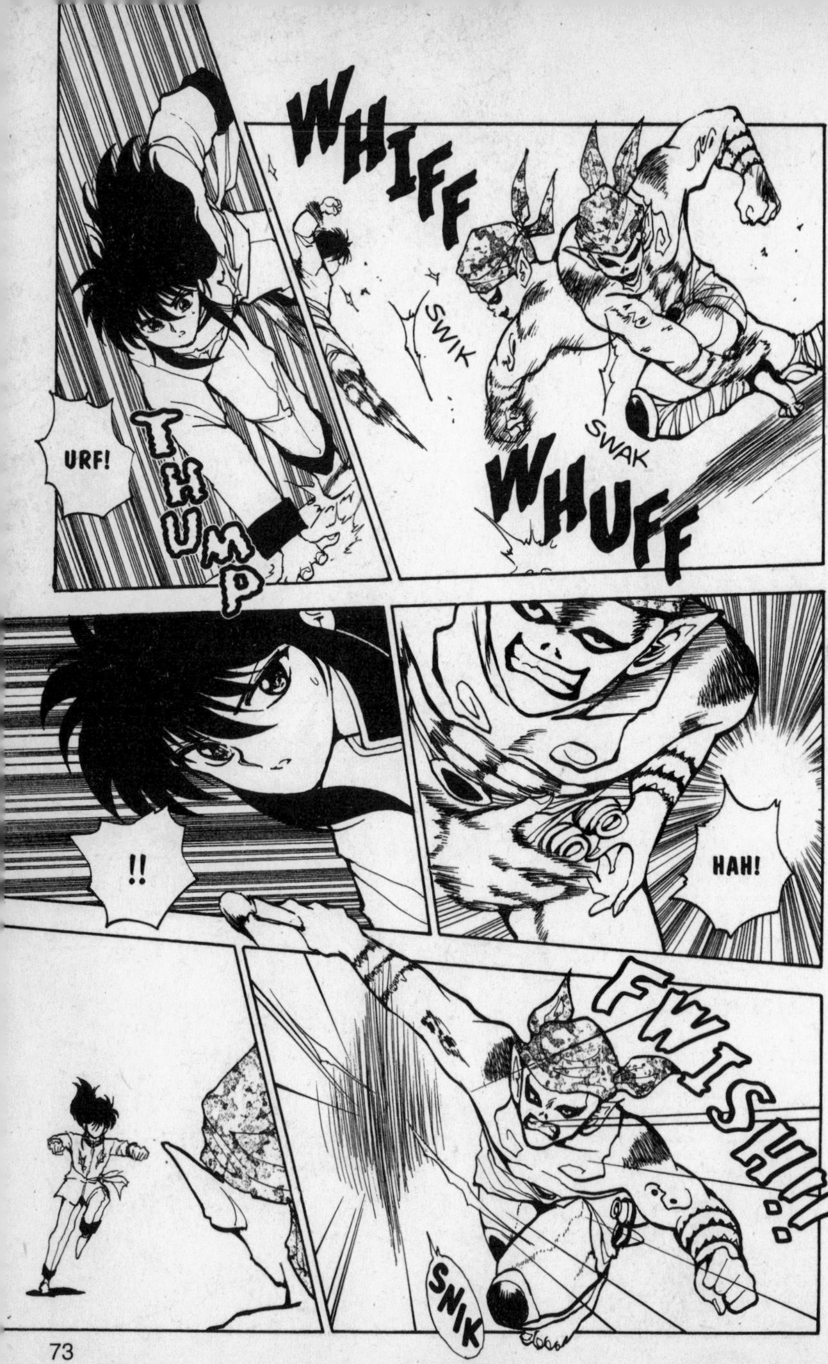

WHIFF
SWIK
SWAK
WHUFF
URF!
THUMP
HAH!
!!
FWISHH!!
SNIK

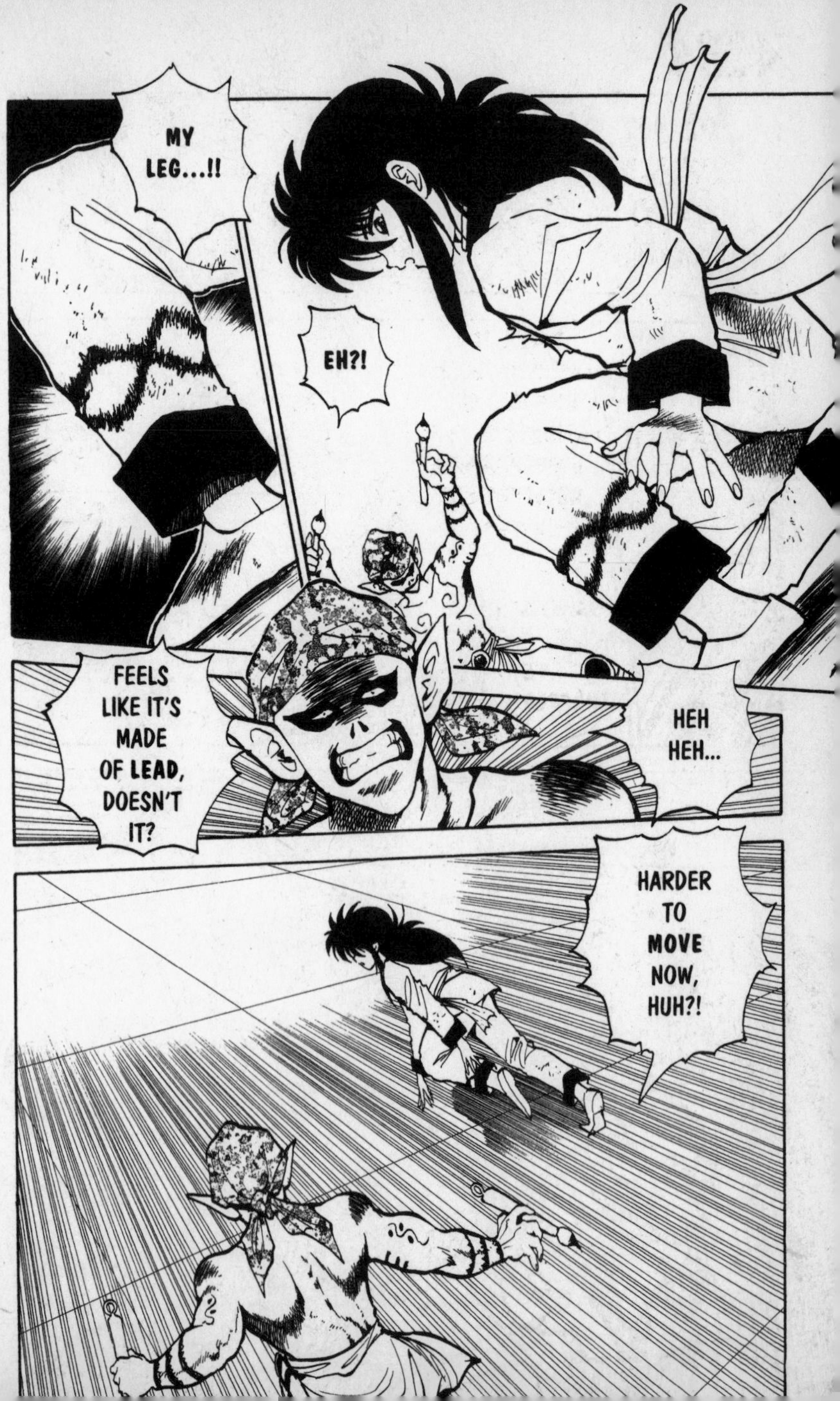
EH?!
MY LEG...!!
HEH HEH...
FEELS LIKE IT'S MADE OF LEAD, DOESN'T IT?
HARDER TO MOVE NOW, HUH?!

READ THIS WAY

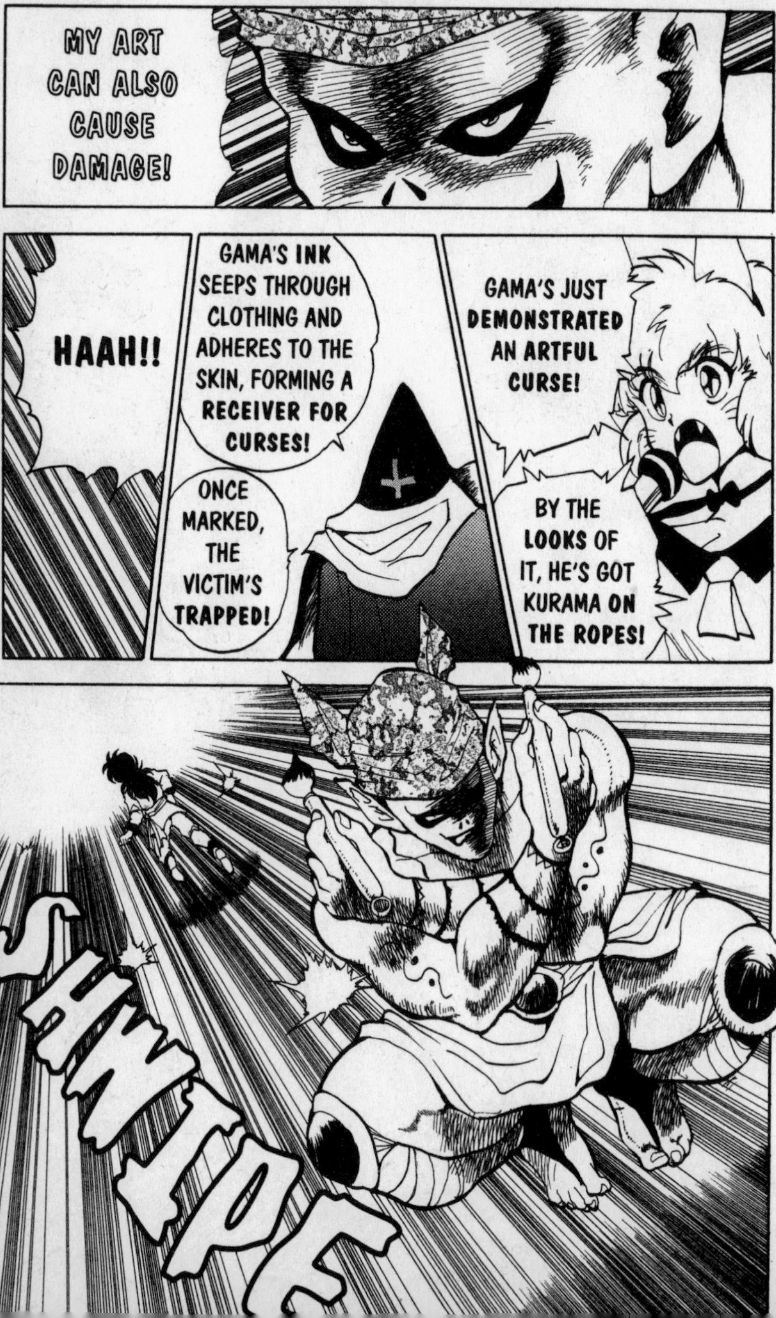
MY ART CAN ALSO CAUSE DAMAGE!
GAMA'S JUST DEMONSTRATED AN ARTFUL CURSE!
BY THE LOOKS OF IT, HE'S GOT KURAMA ON THE ROPES!
GAMA'S INK SEEPS THROUGH CLOTHING AND ADHERES TO THE SKIN, FORMING A RECEIVER FOR CURSES!
ONCE MARKED, THE VICTIM'S TRAPPED!
HAAH!!
SHWIP

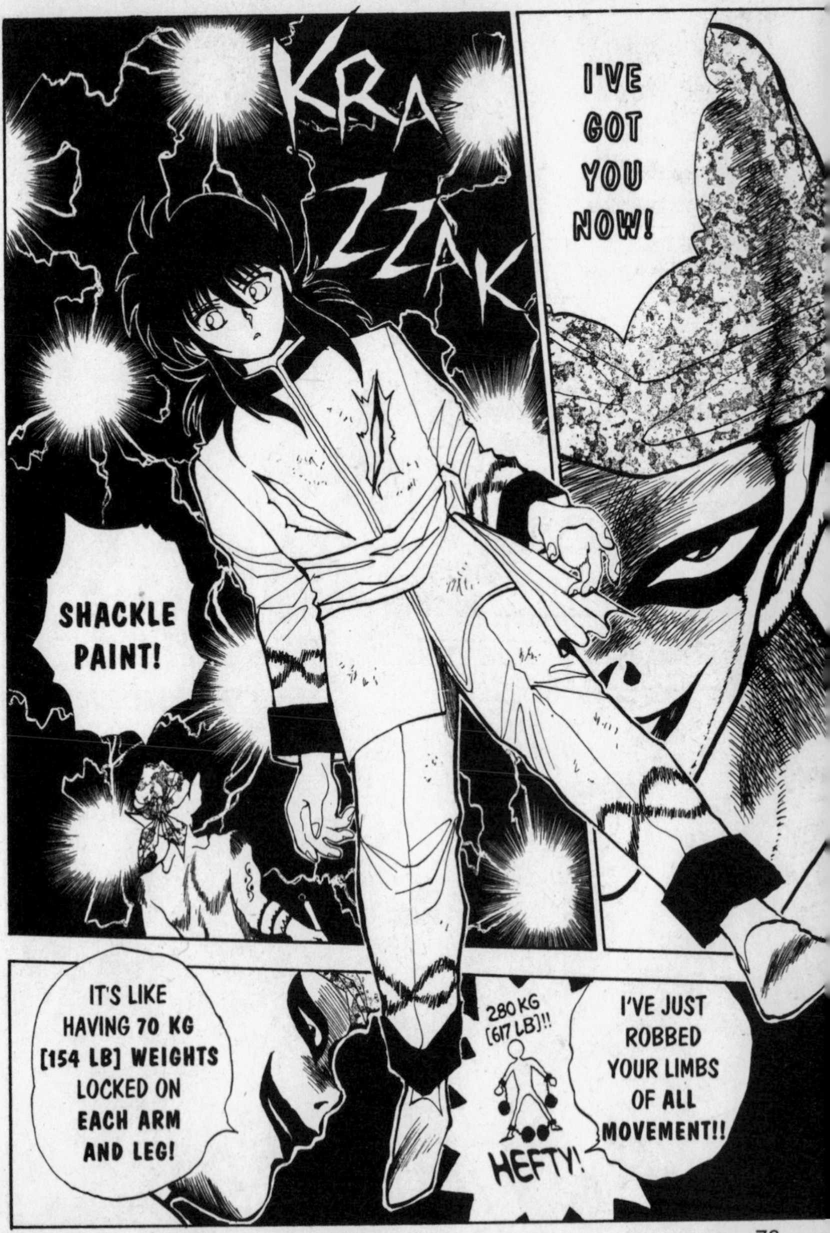
I'VE GOT YOU NOW!
KRAZZAK
SHACKLE PAINT!
I'VE JUST ROBBED YOUR LIMBS OF ALL MOVEMENT!!
280 KG [617 LB]!!
HEFTY!
IT'S LIKE HAVING 70 KG [154 LB] WEIGHTS LOCKED ON EACH ARM AND LEG!

READ THIS WAY

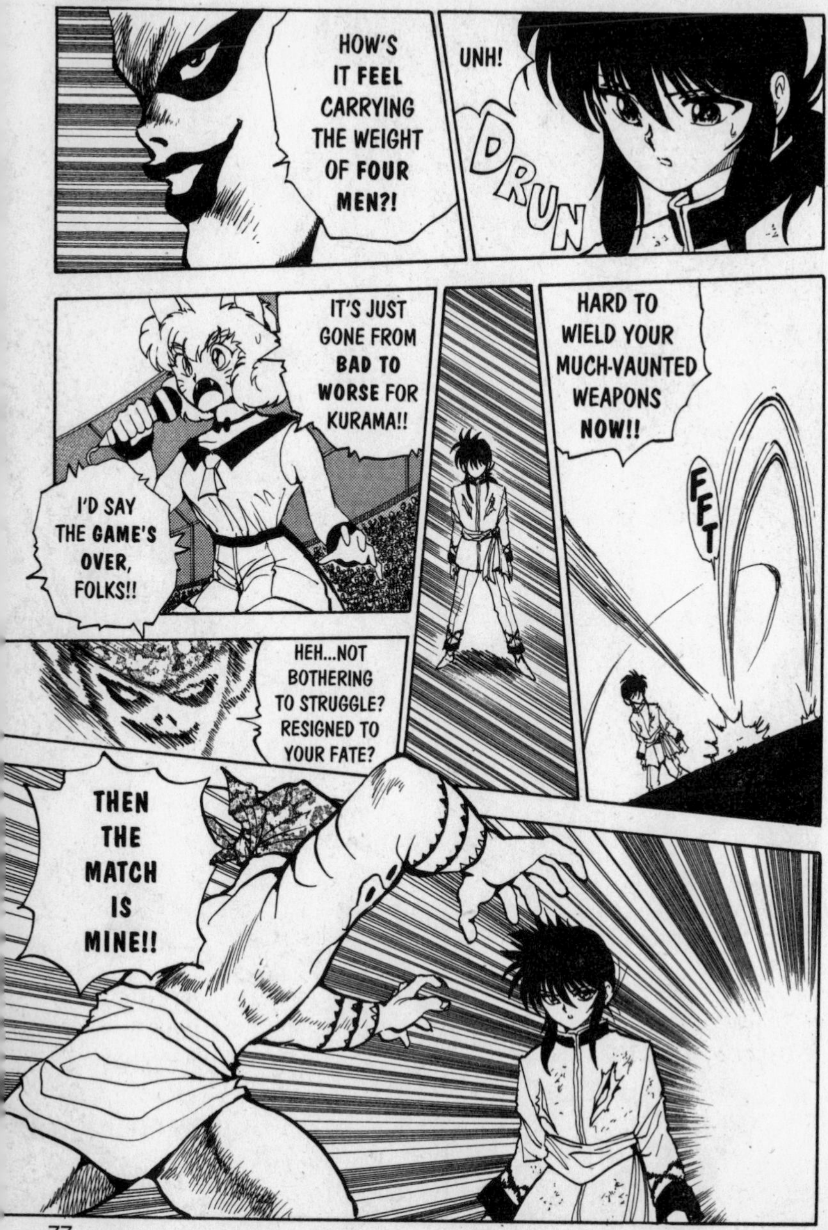
UNH!
DRUN
HOW'S IT FEEL CARRYING THE WEIGHT OF FOUR MEN?!
HARD TO WIELD YOUR MUCH-VAUNTED WEAPONS NOW!!
FFT
IT'S JUST GONE FROM BAD TO WORSE FOR KURAMA!!
I'D SAY THE GAME'S OVER, FOLKS!!
HEH...NOT BOTHERING TO STRUGGLE? RESIGNED TO YOUR FATE?
THEN THE MATCH IS MINE!!

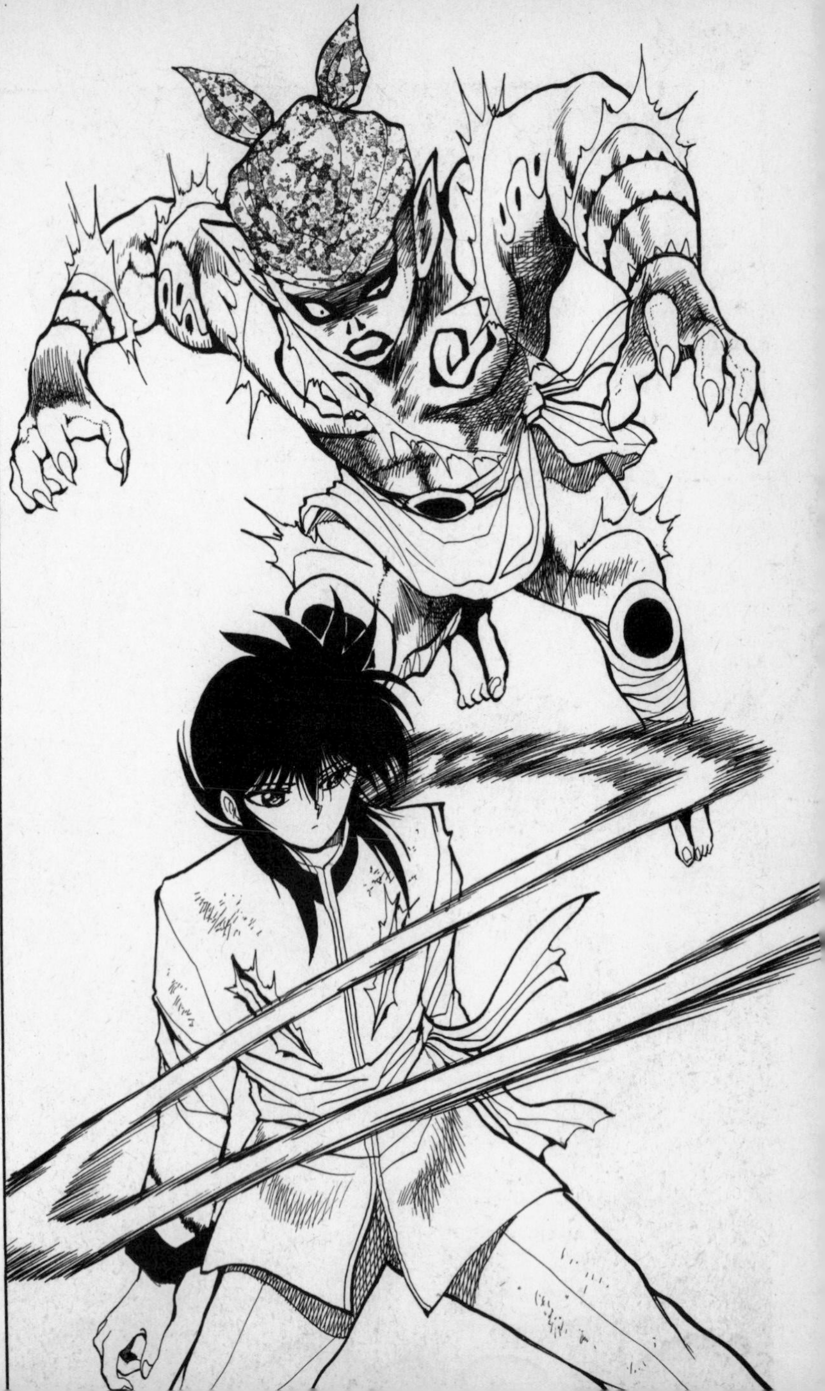

READ THIS WAY

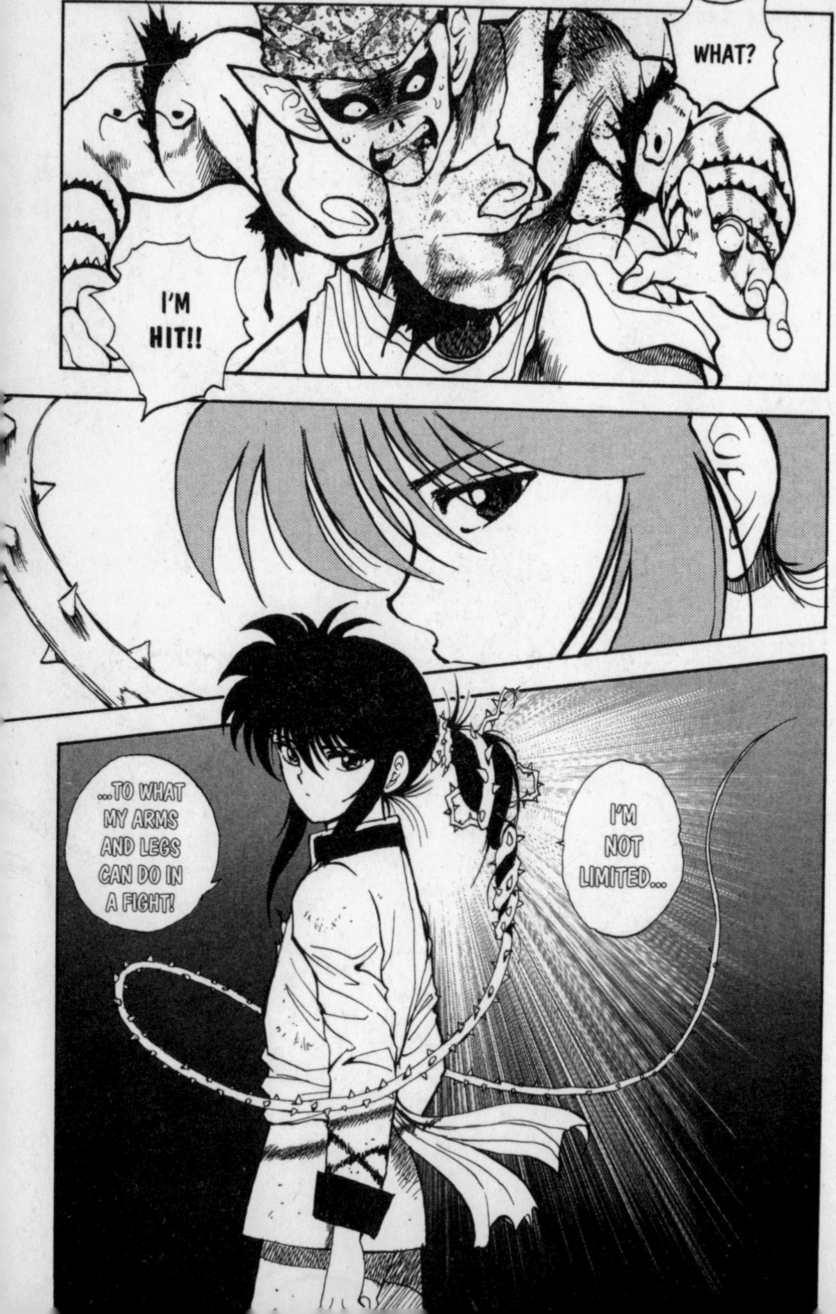
WHAT?
I'M HIT!!
I'M NOT LIMITED...
...TO WHAT MY ARMS AND LEGS CAN DO IN A FIGHT!

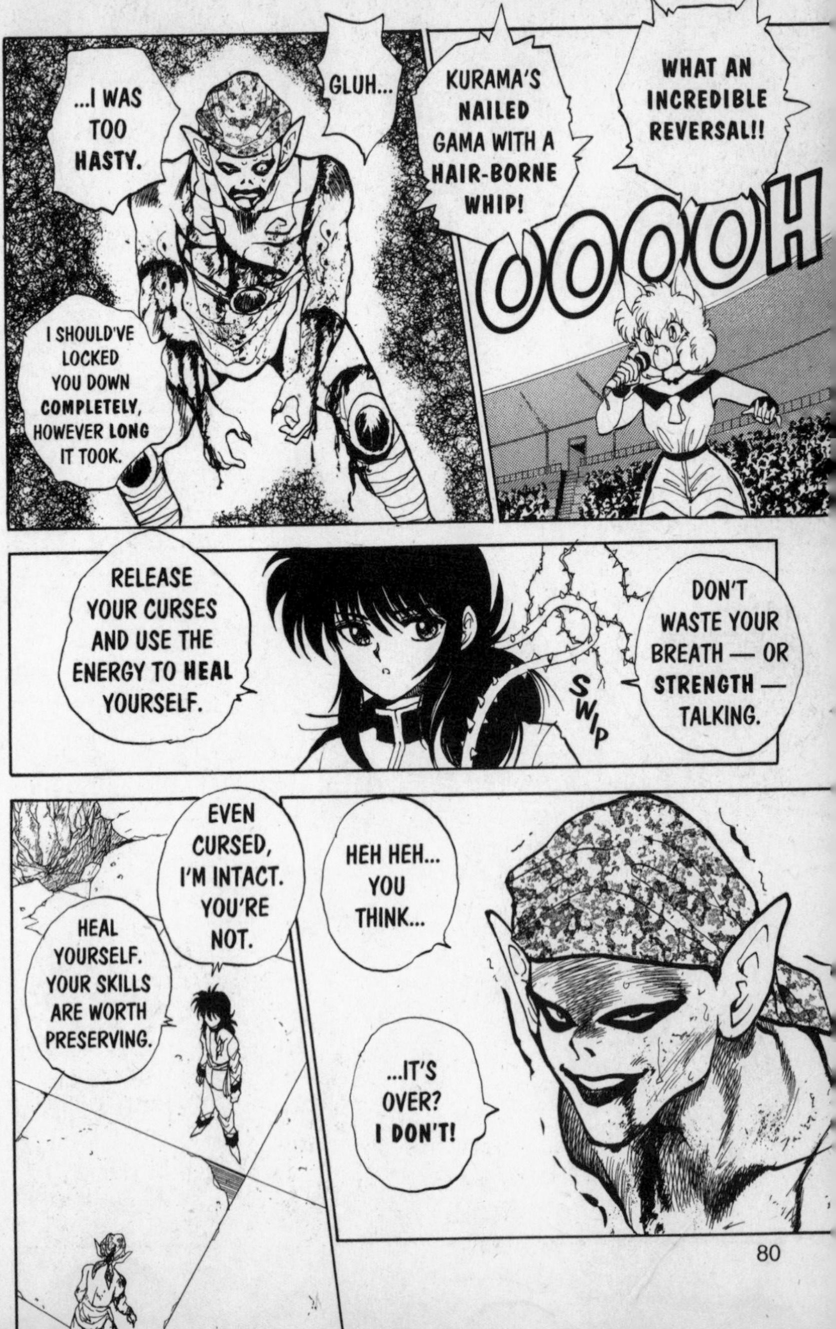
WHAT AN INCREDIBLE REVERSAL!!
KURAMA'S NAILED GAMA WITH A HAIR-BORNE WHIP!
OOOOOH
GLUH...
...I WAS TOO HASTY.
I SHOULD'VE LOCKED YOU DOWN COMPLETELY, HOWEVER LONG IT TOOK.
DON'T WASTE YOUR BREATH — OR STRENGTH — TALKING.
SWIP
RELEASE YOUR CURSES AND USE THE ENERGY TO HEAL YOURSELF.
HEH HEH... YOU THINK...
...IT'S OVER? I DON'T!
EVEN CURSED, I'M INTACT. YOU'RE NOT.
HEAL YOURSELF. YOUR SKILLS ARE WORTH PRESERVING.

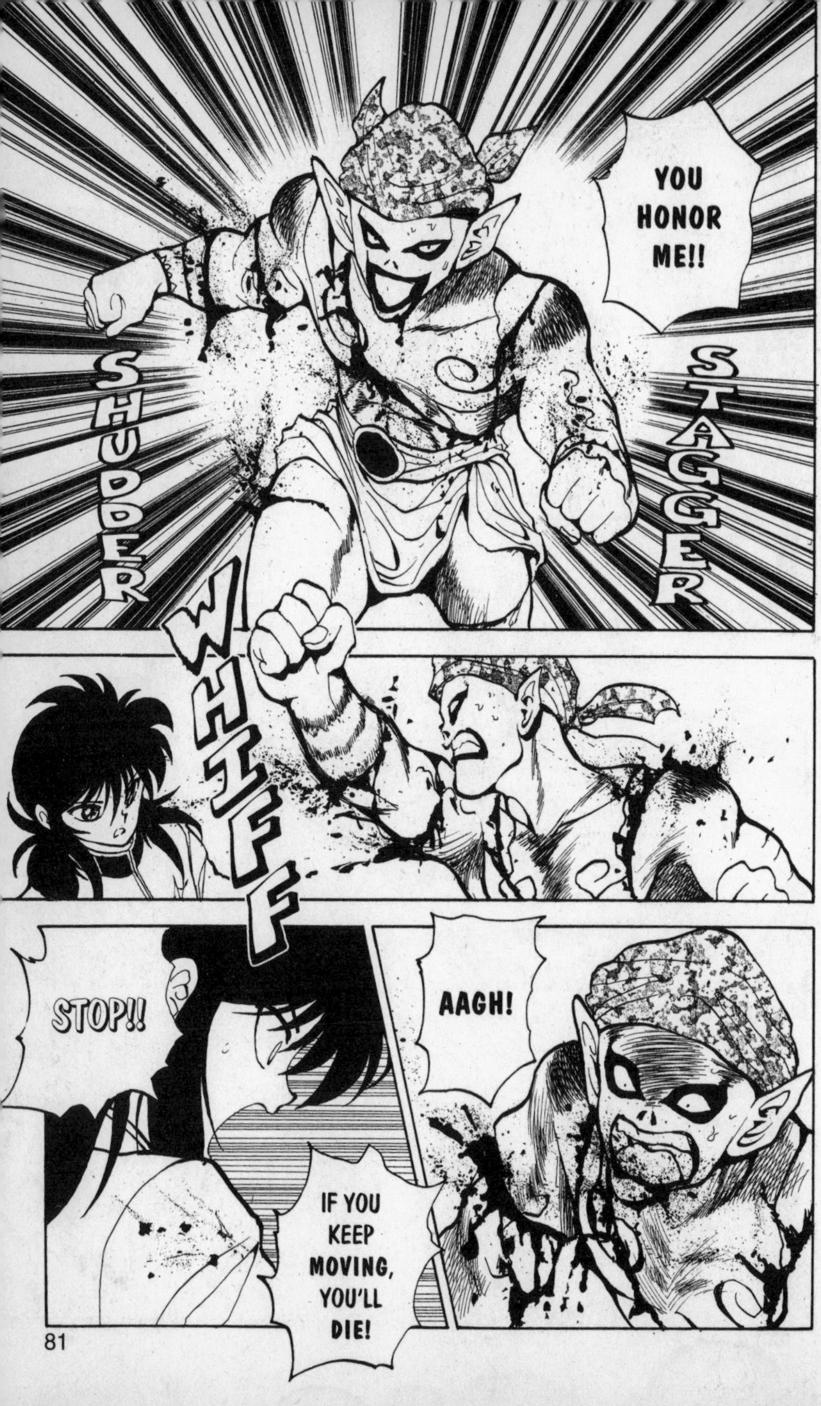
YOU HONOR ME!!
STAGGER
SHUDDER
WHIFF
AAGH!
STOP!!
IF YOU KEEP MOVING, YOU'LL DIE!

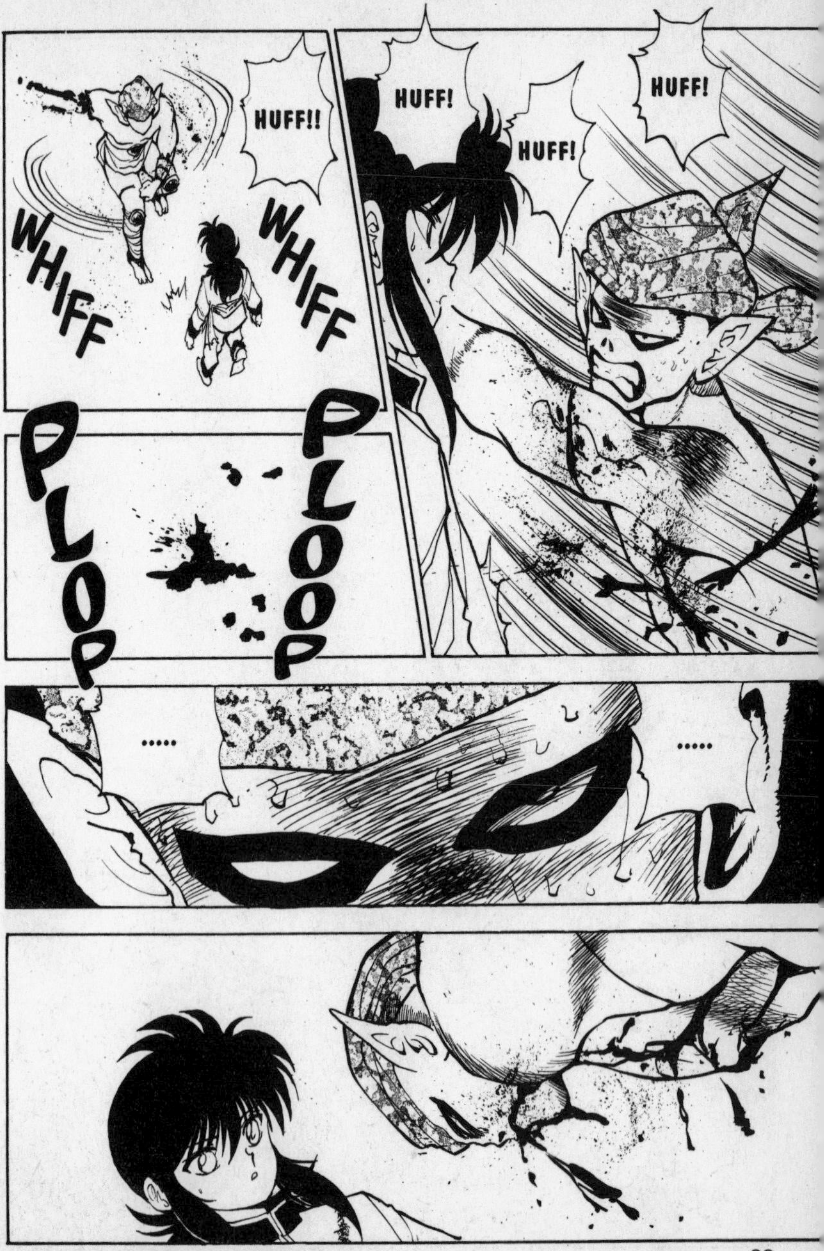
HUFF!
HUFF!
HUFF!
HUFF!!
WHIFF
WHIFF
PLOOP
PLOP
.....
.....

READ THIS WAY

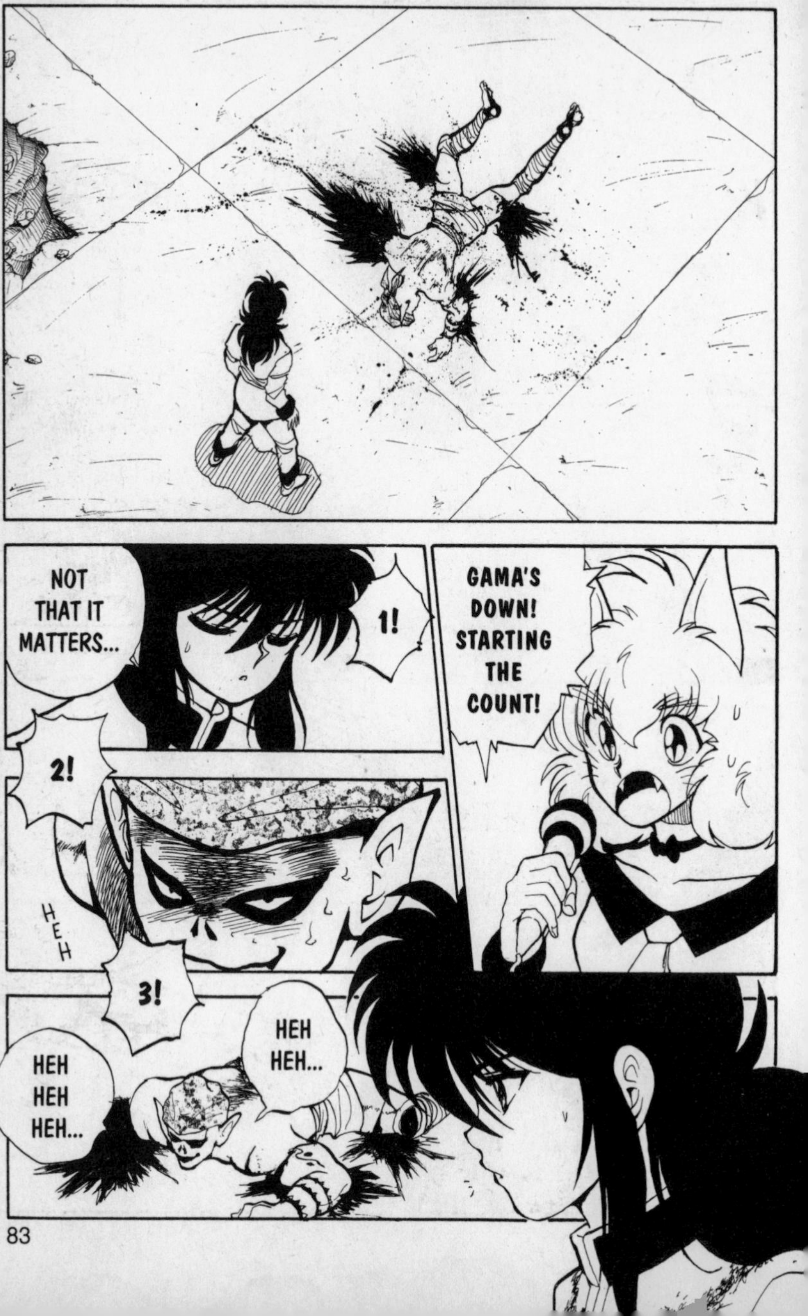
GAMA'S DOWN! STARTING THE COUNT!
1!
NOT THAT IT MATTERS...
2!
HEH
HEH
3!
HEH HEH...
HEH HEH HEH...

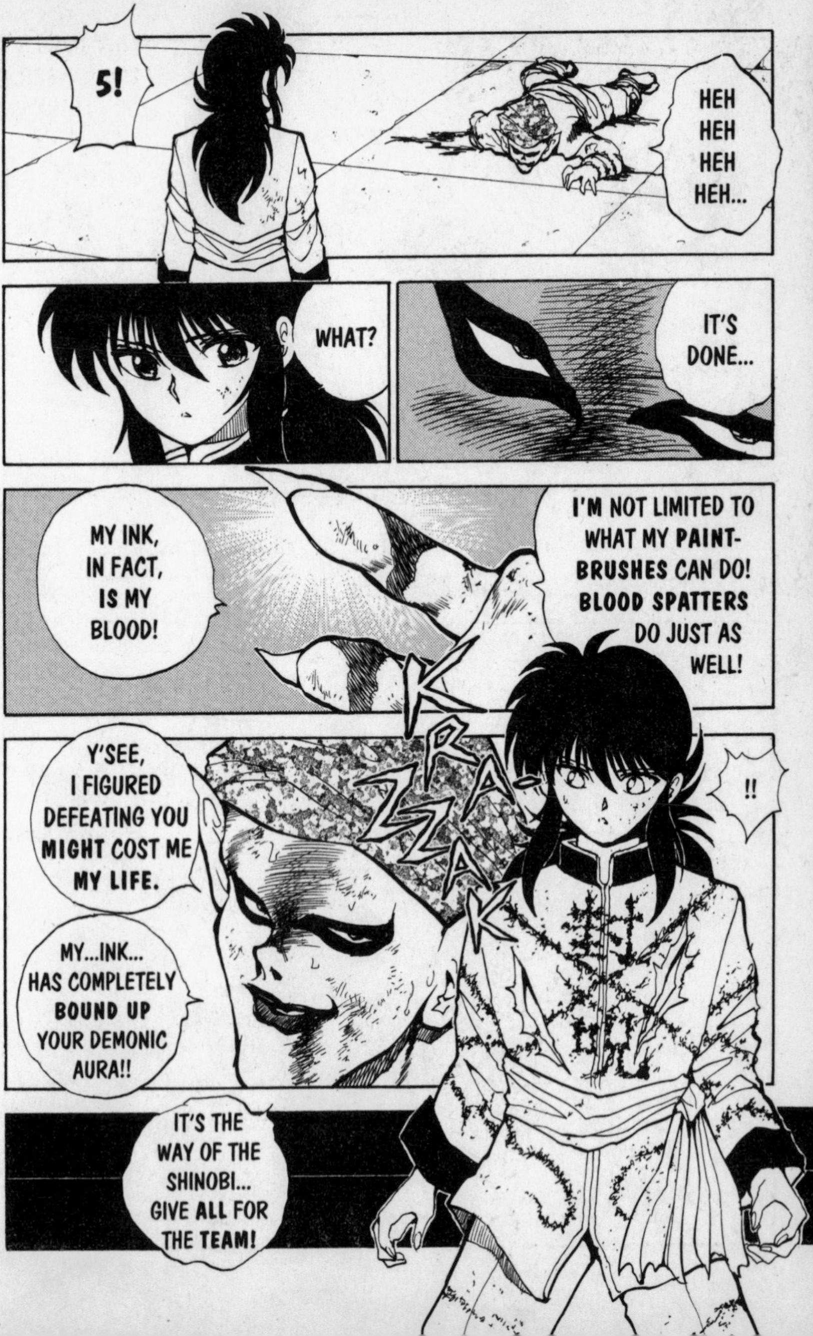

HEH HEH HEH HEH...
5!
IT'S DONE...
WHAT?
I'M NOT LIMITED TO WHAT MY PAINT-BRUSHES CAN DO! BLOOD SPATTERS DO JUST AS WELL!
MY INK, IN FACT, IS MY BLOOD!
!!
KRAZAK
Y'SEE, I FIGURED DEFEATING YOU MIGHT COST ME MY LIFE.
MY...INK... HAS COMPLETELY BOUND UP YOUR DEMONIC AURA!!
IT'S THE WAY OF THE SHINOBI... GIVE ALL FOR THE TEAM!

READ THIS WAY

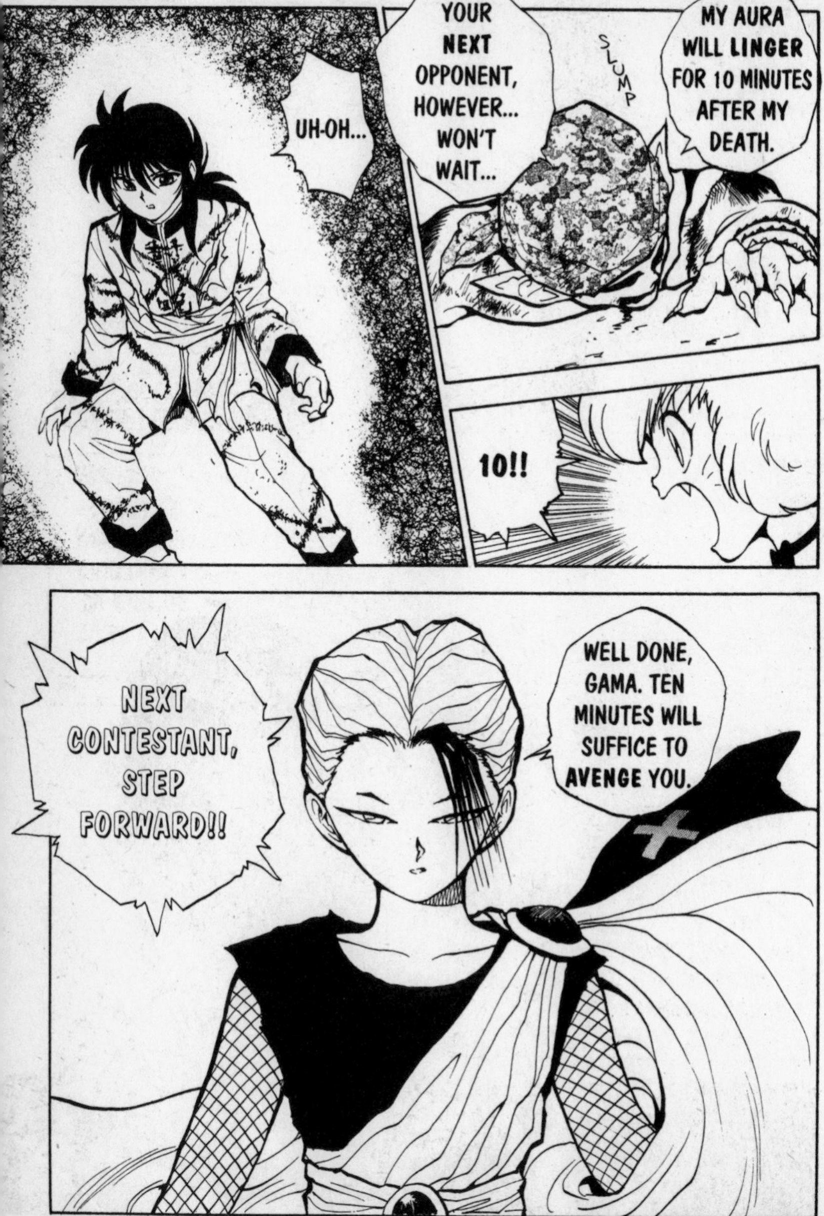
MY AURA WILL LINGER FOR 10 MINUTES AFTER MY DEATH.
SLUMP
YOUR NEXT OPPONENT, HOWEVER... WON'T WAIT...
10!!
UH-OH...
WELL DONE, GAMA. TEN MINUTES WILL SUFFICE TO AVENGE YOU.
NEXT CONTESTANT, STEP FORWARD!!

TOYA: ICE MASTER!!

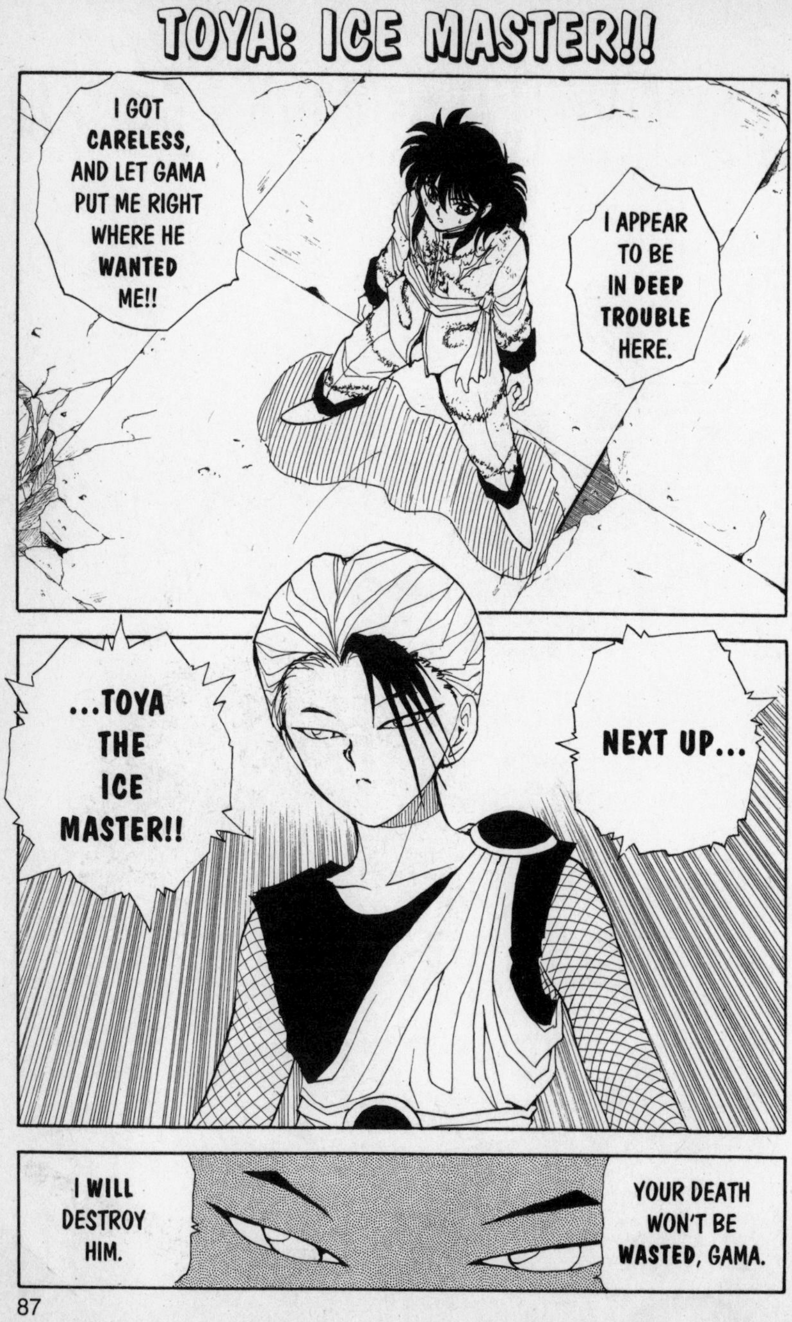
I APPEAR TO BE IN DEEP TROUBLE HERE.
I GOT CARELESS, AND LET GAMA PUT ME RIGHT WHERE HE WANTED ME!!
NEXT UP...
...TOYA THE ICE MASTER!!
YOUR DEATH WON'T BE WASTED, GAMA.
I WILL DESTROY HIM.

TOYA: ICE MASTER!!

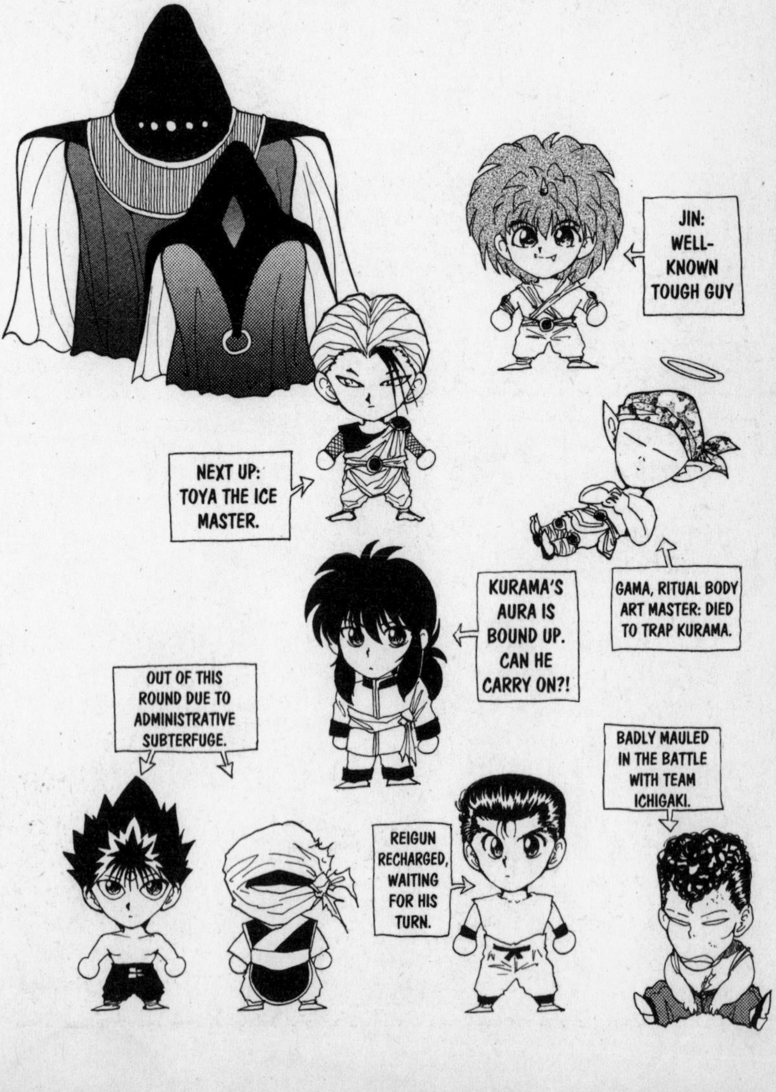
JIN: WELL-KNOWN TOUGH GUY
NEXT UP: TOYA THE ICE MASTER.
GAMA, RITUAL BODY ART MASTER: DIED TO TRAP KURAMA.
KURAMA'S AURA IS BOUND UP. CAN HE CARRY ON?!
BADLY MAULED IN THE BATTLE WITH TEAM ICHIGAKI.
REIGUN RECHARGED, WAITING FOR HIS TURN.
OUT OF THIS ROUND DUE TO ADMINISTRATIVE SUBTERFUGE.

READ THIS WAY

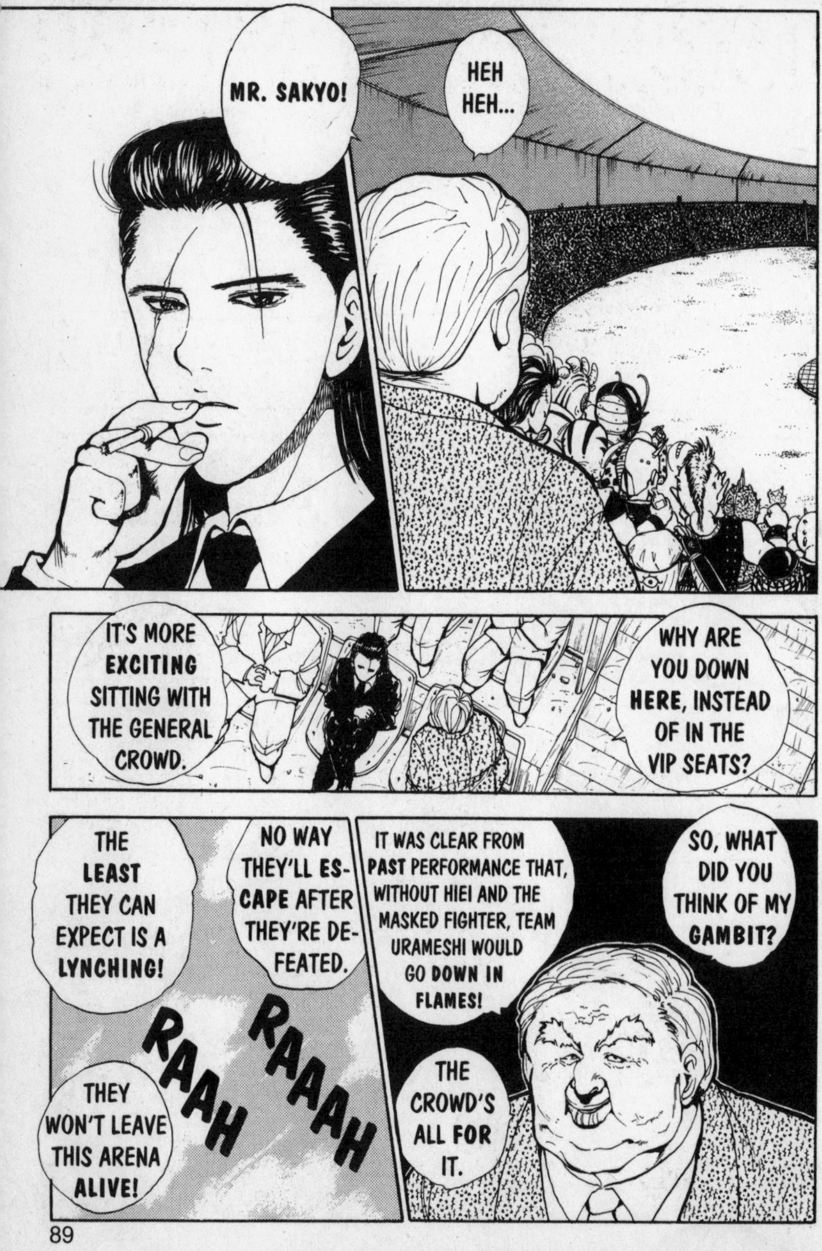
HEH HEH...
MR. SAKYO!
WHY ARE YOU DOWN HERE, INSTEAD OF IN THE VIP SEATS?
IT'S MORE EXCITING SITTING WITH THE GENERAL CROWD.
SO, WHAT DID YOU THINK OF MY GAMBIT?
IT WAS CLEAR FROM PAST PERFORMANCE THAT, WITHOUT HIEI AND THE MASKED FIGHTER, TEAM URAMESHI WOULD GO DOWN IN FLAMES!
THE CROWD'S ALL FOR IT.
NO WAY THEY'LL ES-CAPE AFTER THEY'RE DE-FEATED.
THE LEAST THEY CAN EXPECT IS A LYNCHING!
RAAAAH
RAAAH
THEY WON'T LEAVE THIS ARENA ALIVE!

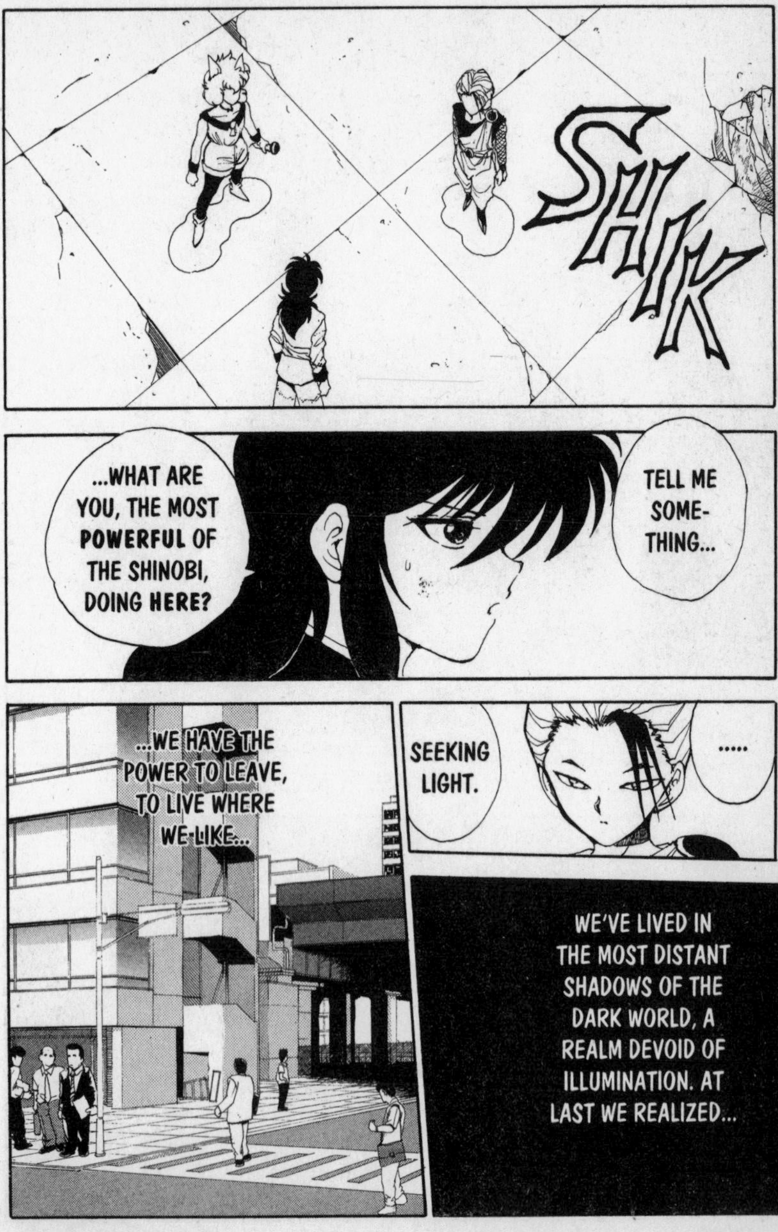
SHIK
TELL ME SOME-THING...
...WHAT ARE YOU, THE MOST **POWERFUL** OF THE SHINOBI, DOING **HERE**?
.....
SEEKING LIGHT.
WE'VE LIVED IN THE MOST DISTANT SHADOWS OF THE DARK WORLD, A REALM DEVOID OF ILLUMINATION. AT LAST WE REALIZED...
...WE HAVE THE POWER TO LEAVE, TO LIVE WHERE WE LIKE...

READ THIS WAY

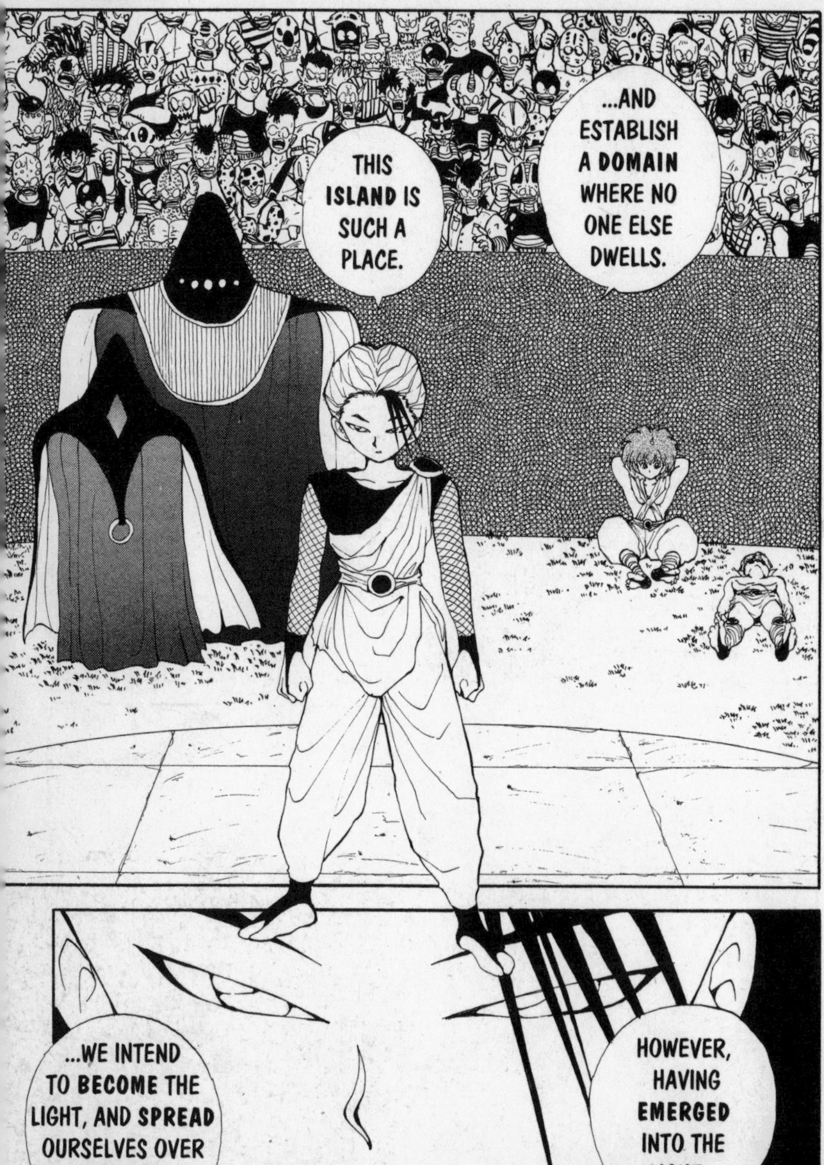
...AND ESTABLISH A DOMAIN WHERE NO ONE ELSE DWELLS.
THIS ISLAND IS SUCH A PLACE.
HOWEVER, HAVING EMERGED INTO THE LIGHT...
...WE INTEND TO BECOME THE LIGHT, AND SPREAD OURSELVES OVER THE ENTIRE WORLD.

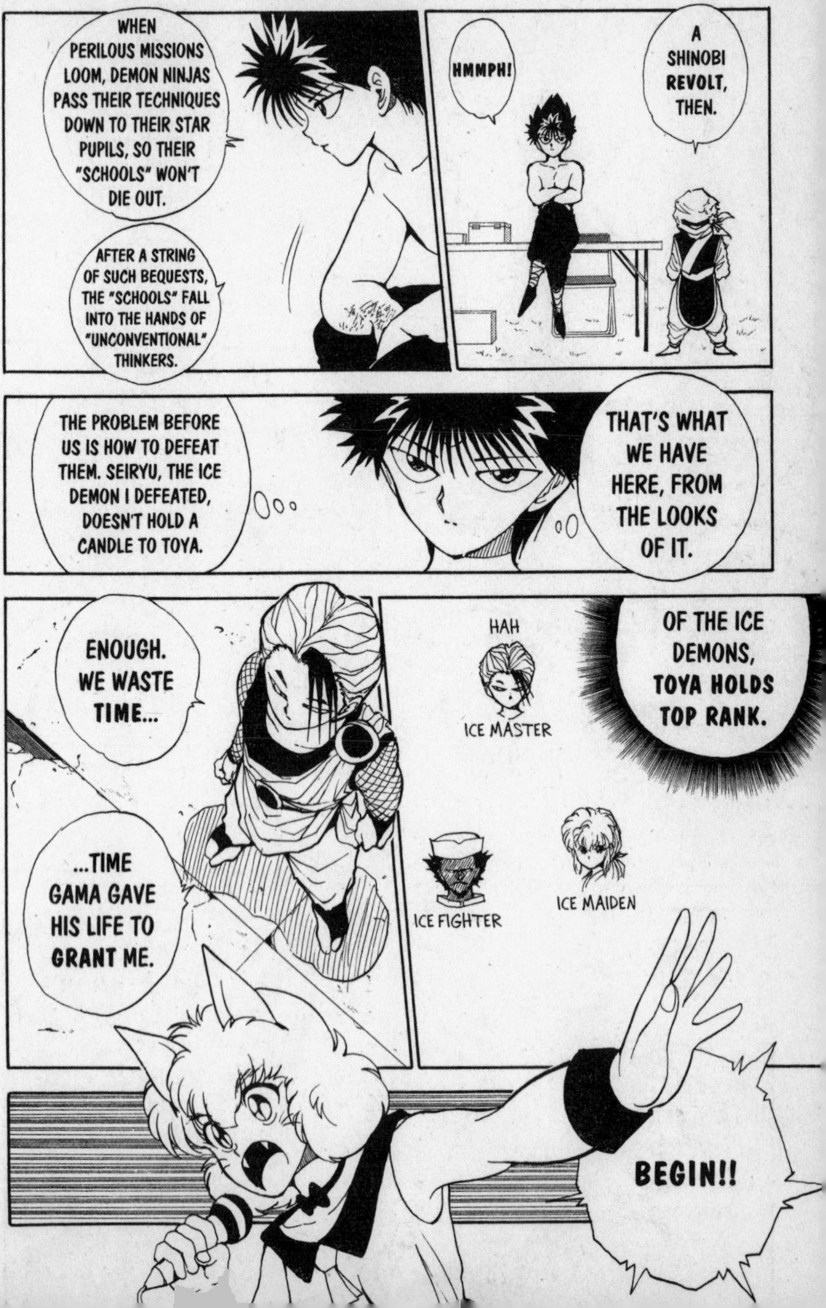
A SHINOBI REVOLT, THEN.
HMMPH!
WHEN PERILOUS MISSIONS LOOM, DEMON NINJAS PASS THEIR TECHNIQUES DOWN TO THEIR STAR PUPILS, SO THEIR "SCHOOLS" WON'T DIE OUT.
AFTER A STRING OF SUCH BEQUESTS, THE "SCHOOLS" FALL INTO THE HANDS OF "UNCONVENTIONAL" THINKERS.
THAT'S WHAT WE HAVE HERE, FROM THE LOOKS OF IT.
THE PROBLEM BEFORE US IS HOW TO DEFEAT THEM. SEIRYU, THE ICE DEMON I DEFEATED, DOESN'T HOLD A CANDLE TO TOYA.
OF THE ICE DEMONS, TOYA HOLDS TOP RANK.
HAH
ICE MASTER
ICE MAIDEN
ICE FIGHTER
ENOUGH. WE WASTE TIME...
...TIME GAMA GAVE HIS LIFE TO GRANT ME.
BEGIN!!

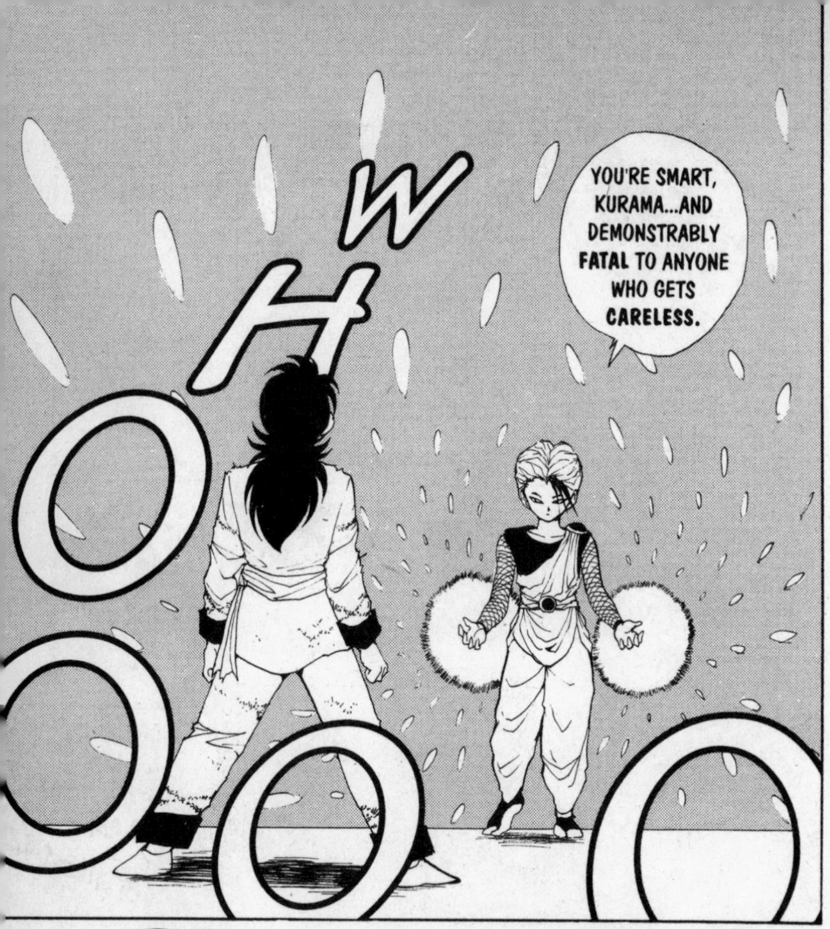
WHOOOOO
YOU'RE SMART, KURAMA...AND DEMONSTRABLY FATAL TO ANYONE WHO GETS CARELESS.
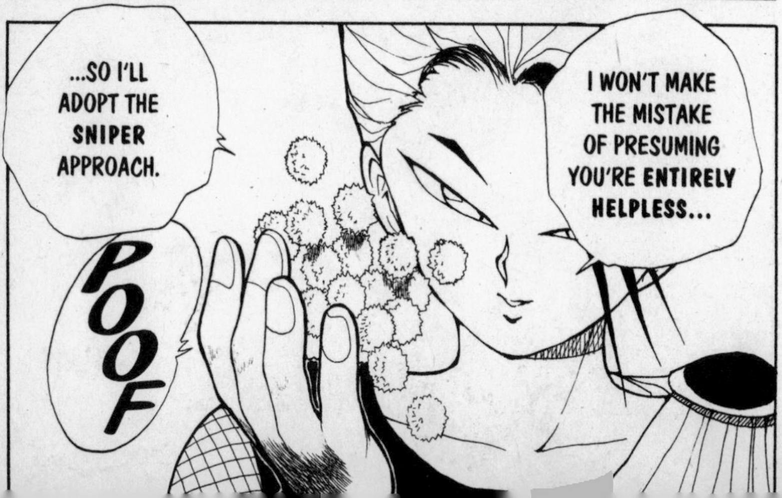
I WON'T MAKE THE MISTAKE OF PRESUMING YOU'RE ENTIRELY HELPLESS...
...SO I'LL ADOPT THE SNIPER APPROACH.
POOF

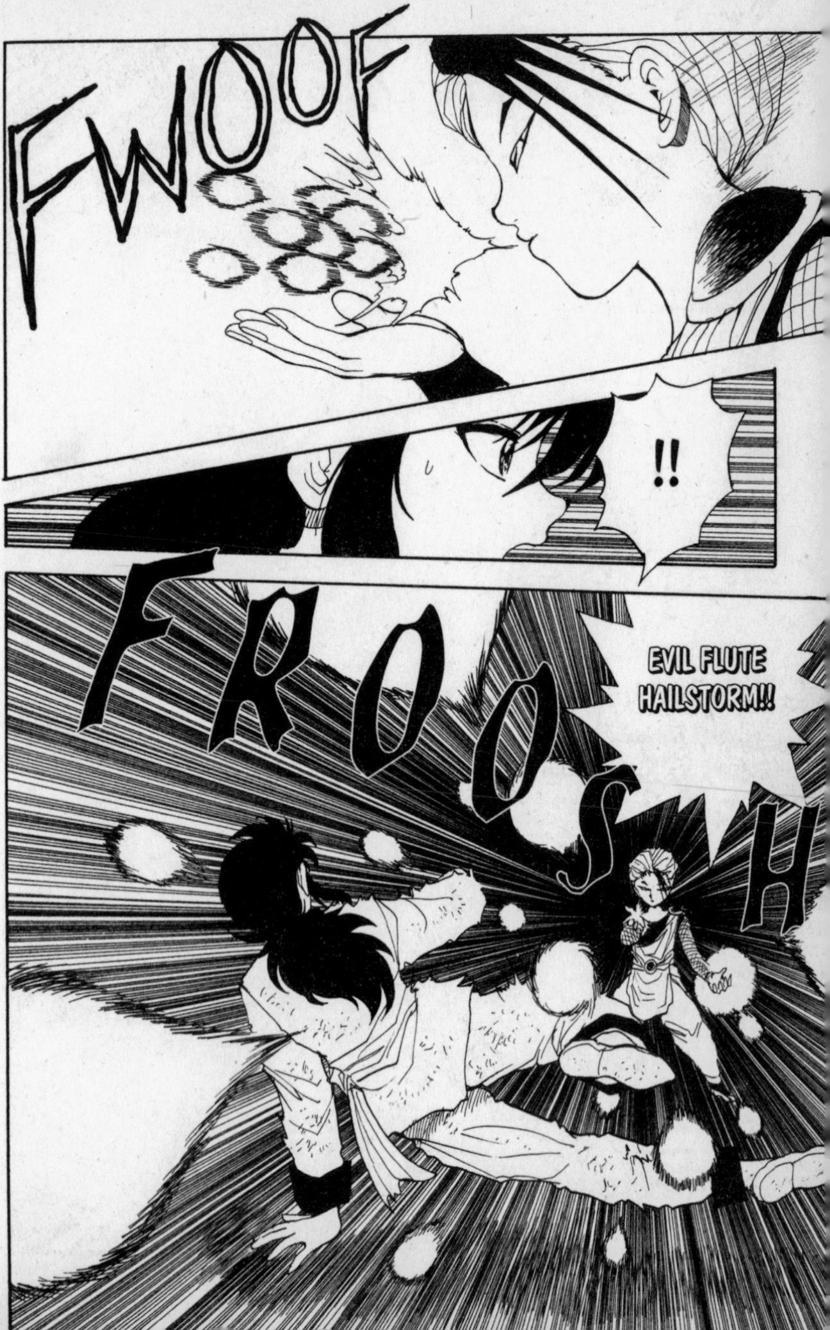
FWOOF
!!
FROOSH
EVIL FLUTE HAILSTORM!!

READ THIS WAY

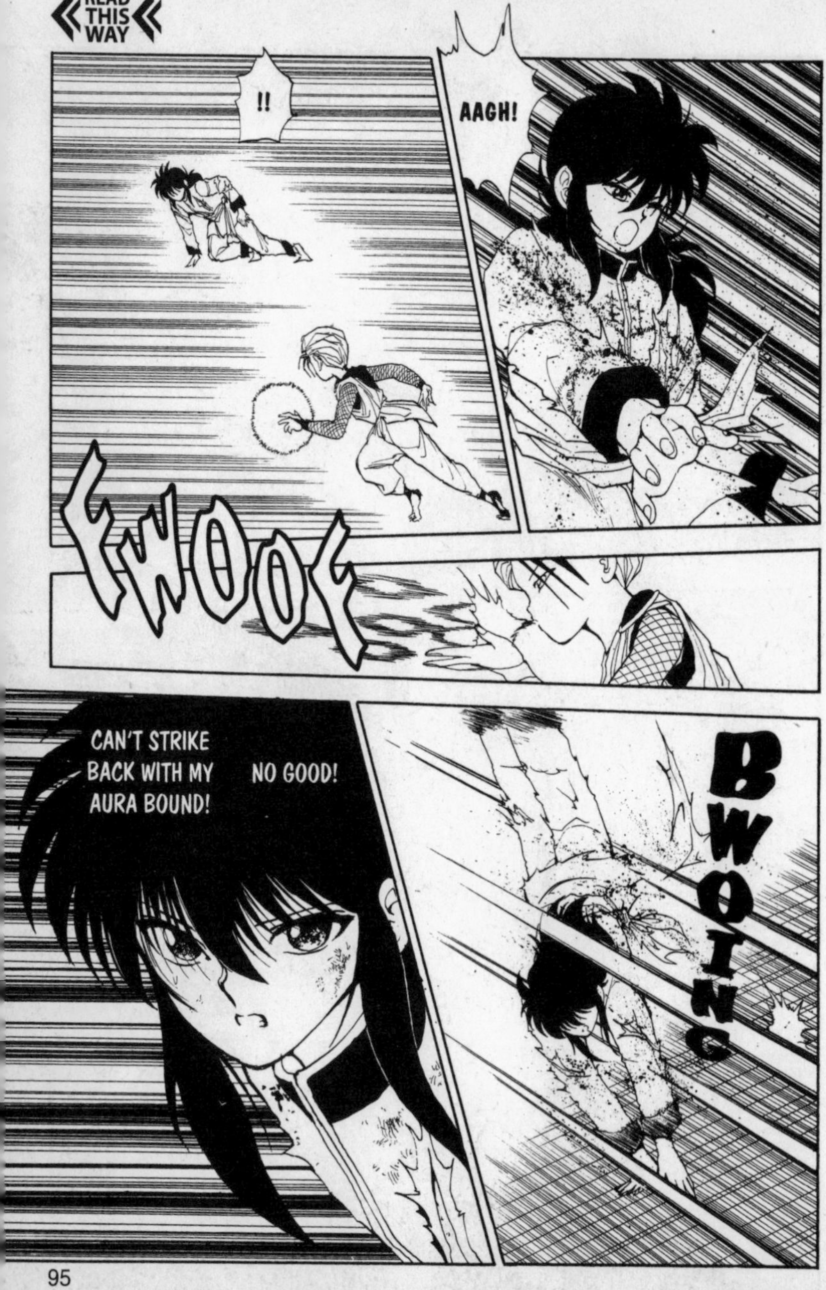

AAGH!
!!
FWOOF
BWOING
NO GOOD!
CAN'T STRIKE BACK WITH MY AURA BOUND!

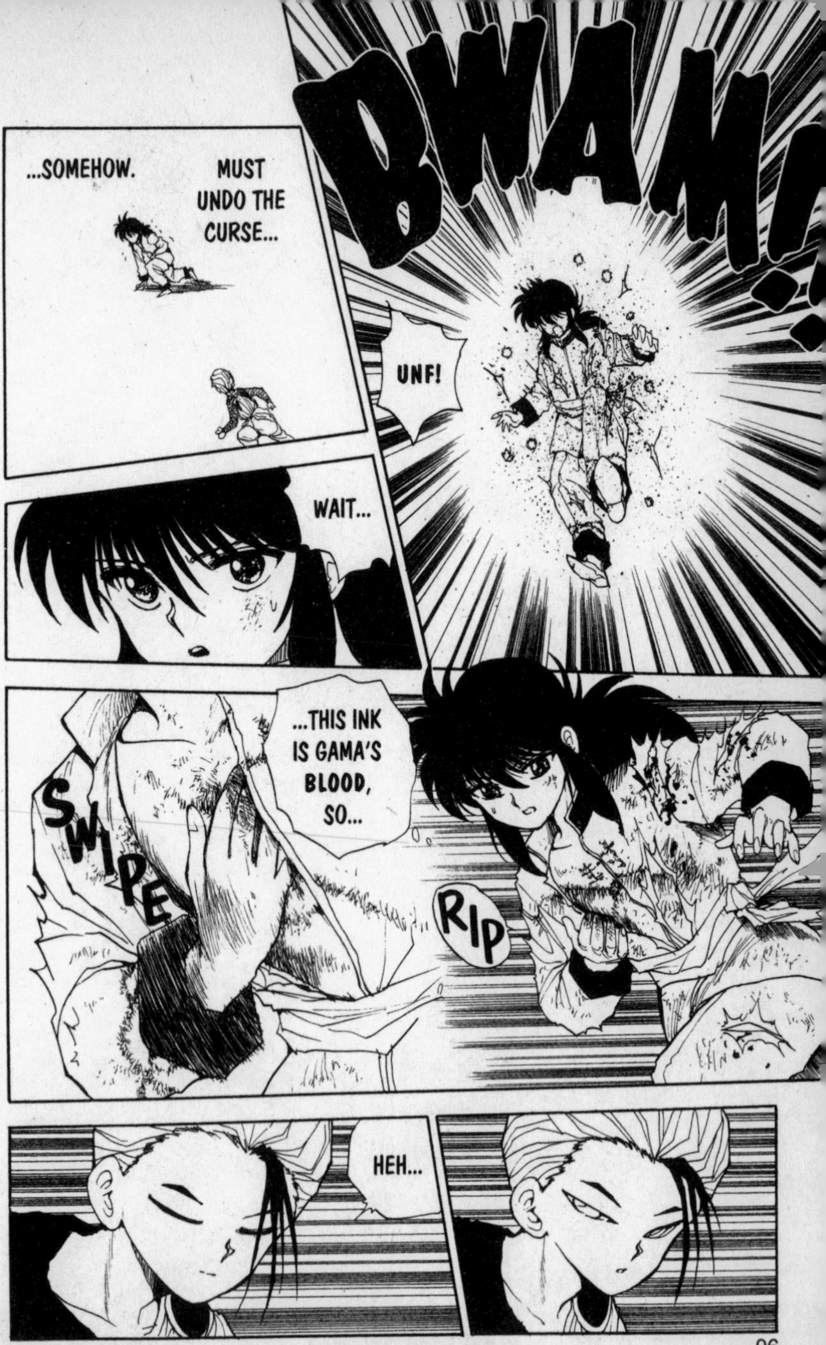
BWAM!!
UNF!
MUST UNDO THE CURSE...
...SOMEHOW.
WAIT...
...THIS INK IS GAMA'S BLOOD, SO...
RIP
SWIPE
HEH...

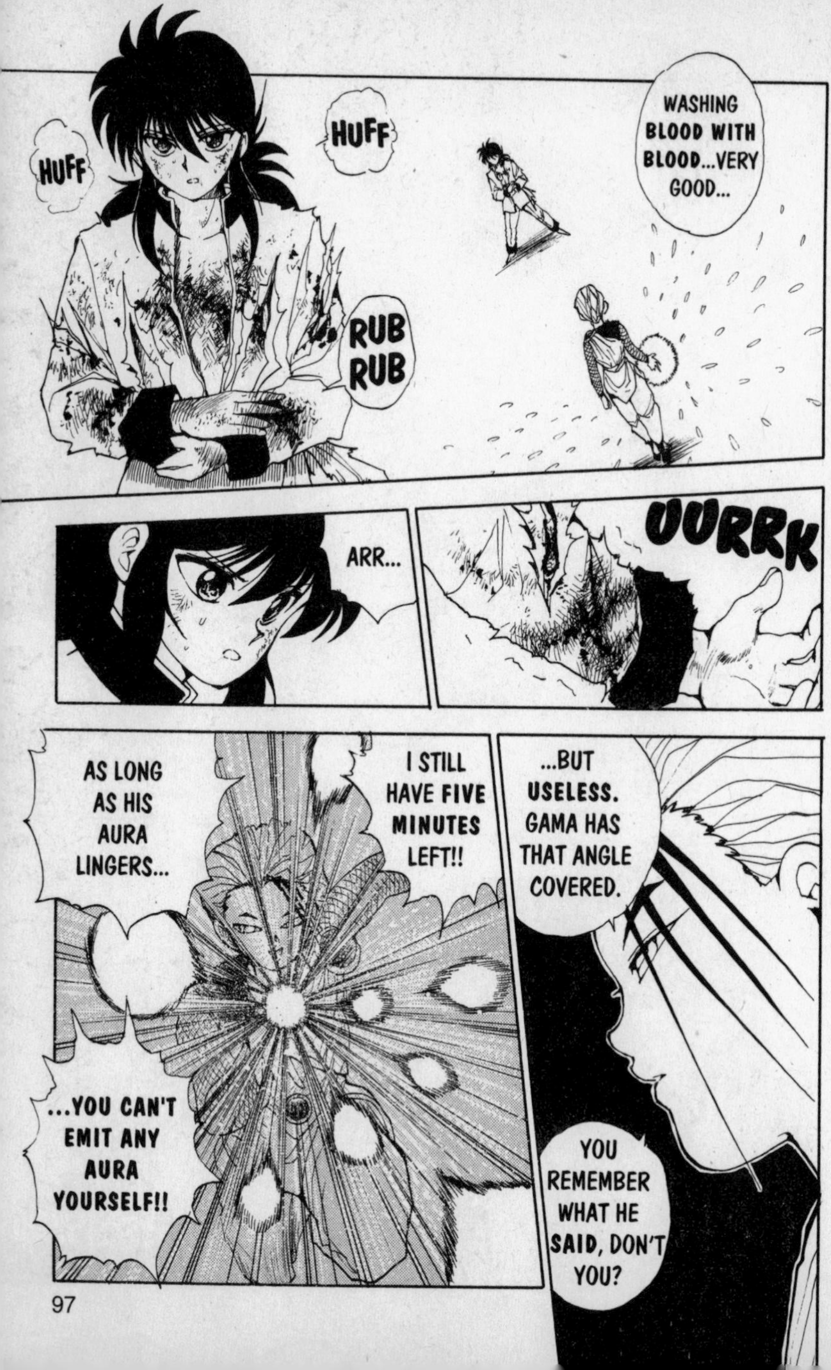
WASHING BLOOD WITH BLOOD...VERY GOOD...
HUFF
HUFF
RUB RUB
UURRK
ARR...
...BUT USELESS. GAMA HAS THAT ANGLE COVERED.
YOU REMEMBER WHAT HE SAID, DON'T YOU?
I STILL HAVE FIVE MINUTES LEFT!!
AS LONG AS HIS AURA LINGERS...
...YOU CAN'T EMIT ANY AURA YOURSELF!!

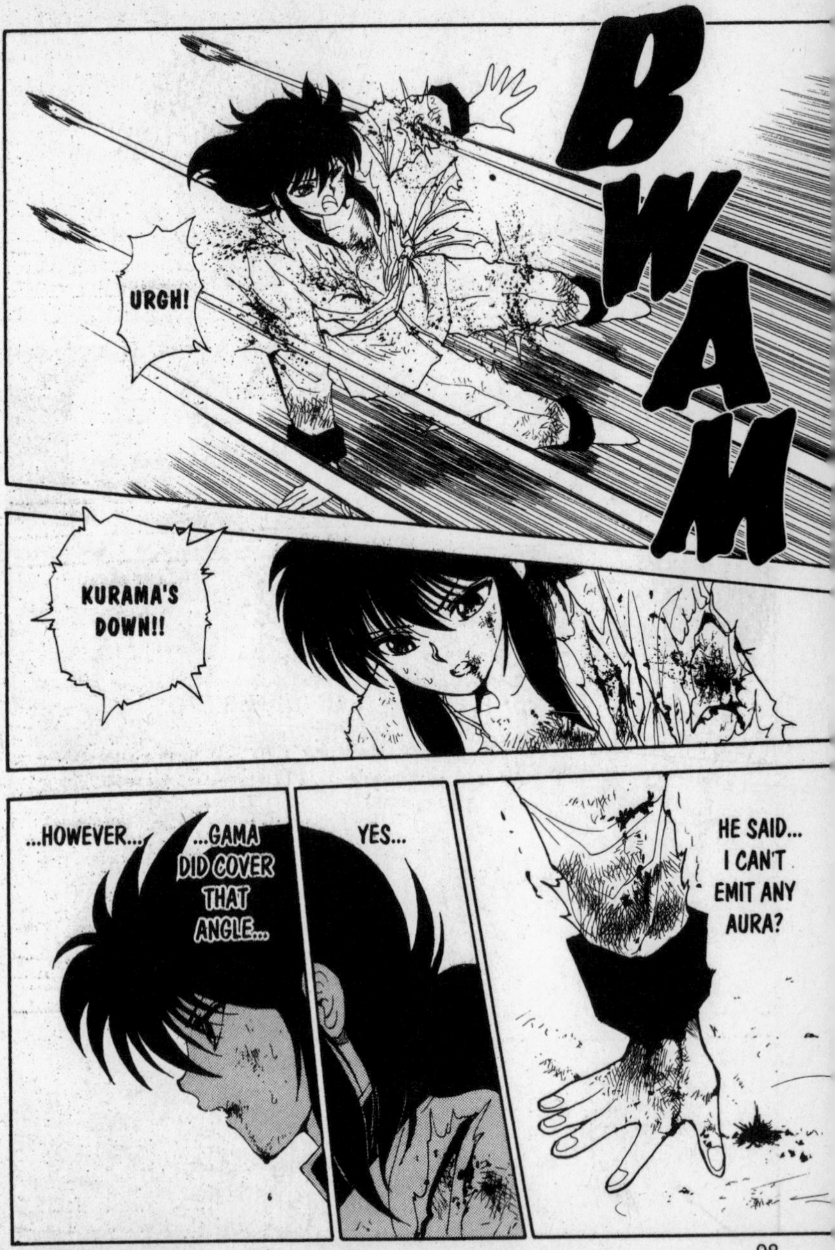
BWAM
URGH!
KURAMA'S DOWN!!
HE SAID... I CAN'T EMIT ANY AURA?
YES...
...GAMA DID COVER THAT ANGLE...
...HOWEVER...

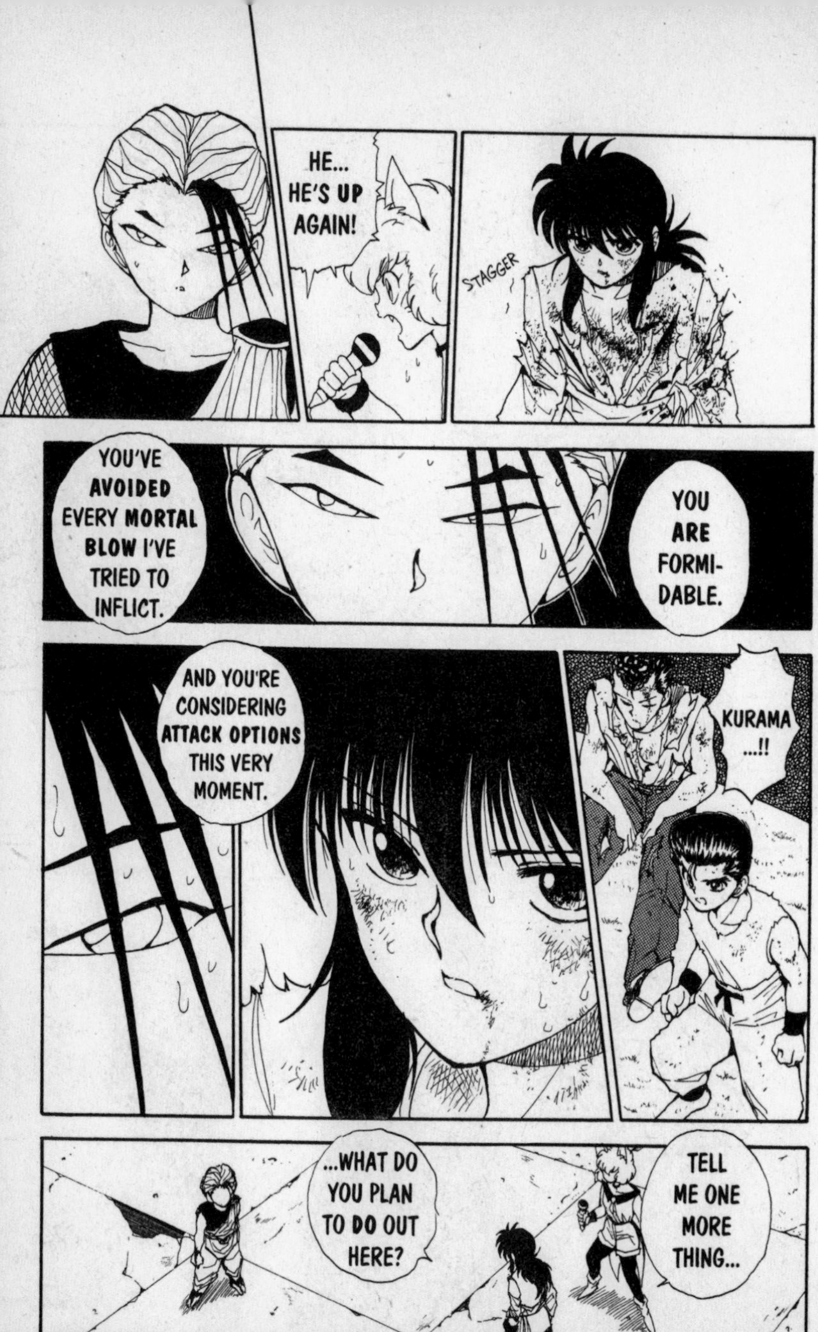
STAGGER
HE... HE'S UP AGAIN!
YOU ARE FORMI-DABLE.
YOU'VE AVOIDED EVERY MORTAL BLOW I'VE TRIED TO INFLICT.
KURAMA ...!!
AND YOU'RE CONSIDERING ATTACK OPTIONS THIS VERY MOMENT.
TELL ME ONE MORE THING...
...WHAT DO YOU PLAN TO DO OUT HERE?

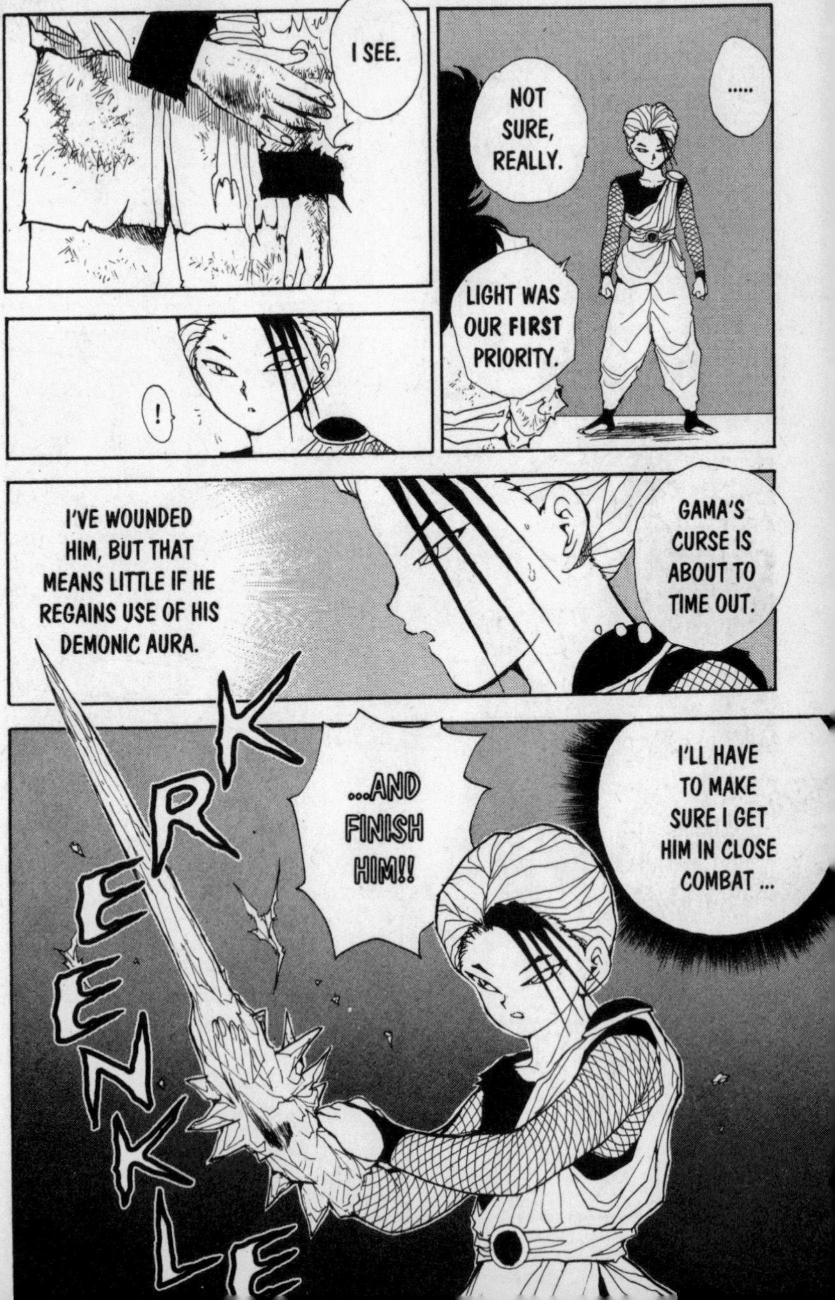
.....
NOT SURE, REALLY.
LIGHT WAS OUR FIRST PRIORITY.
I SEE.
!
GAMA'S CURSE IS ABOUT TO TIME OUT.
I'VE WOUNDED HIM, BUT THAT MEANS LITTLE IF HE REGAINS USE OF HIS DEMONIC AURA.
I'LL HAVE TO MAKE SURE I GET HIM IN CLOSE COMBAT ...
...AND FINISH HIM!!
KREENKLE

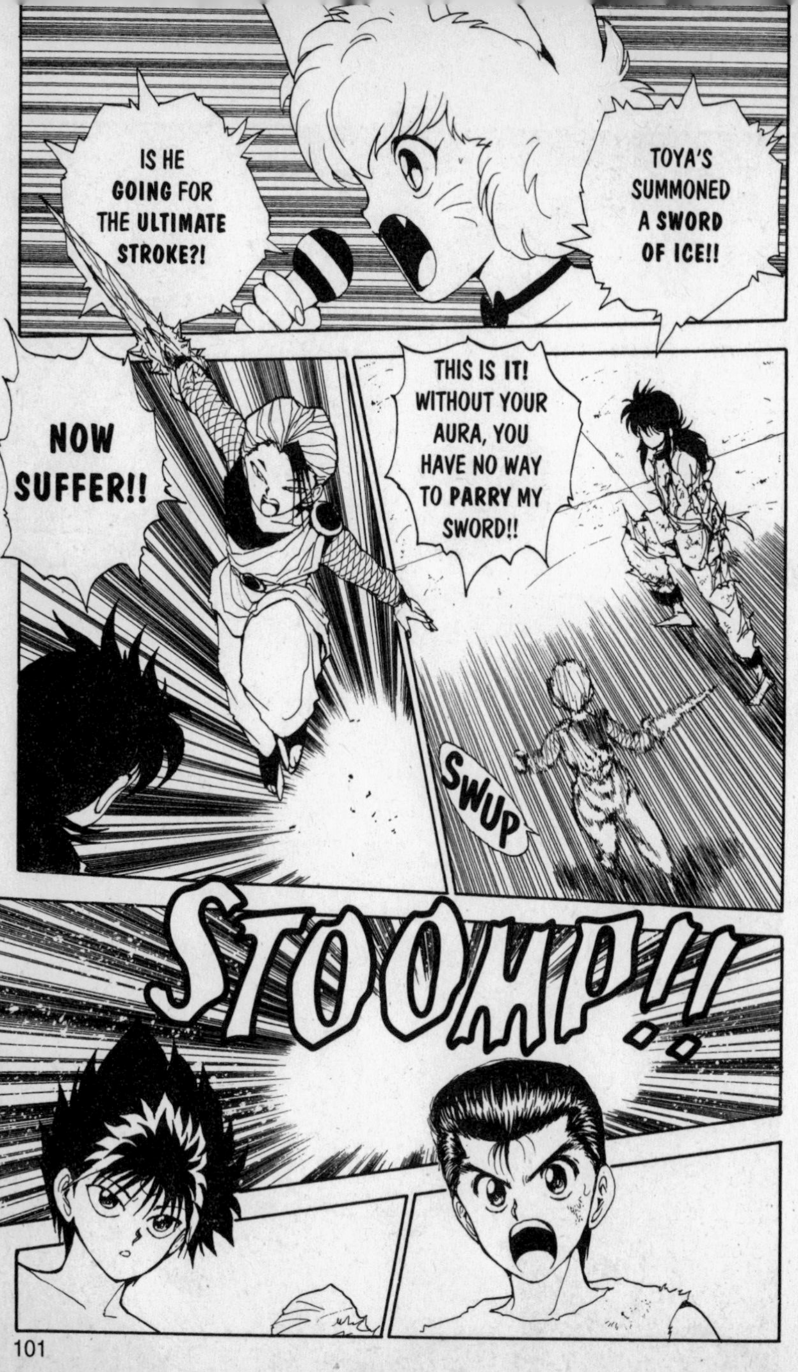

TOYA'S SUMMONED A SWORD OF ICE!!
IS HE GOING FOR THE ULTIMATE STROKE?!
THIS IS IT! WITHOUT YOUR AURA, YOU HAVE NO WAY TO PARRY MY SWORD!!
SWUP
NOW SUFFER!!
STOOMP!!

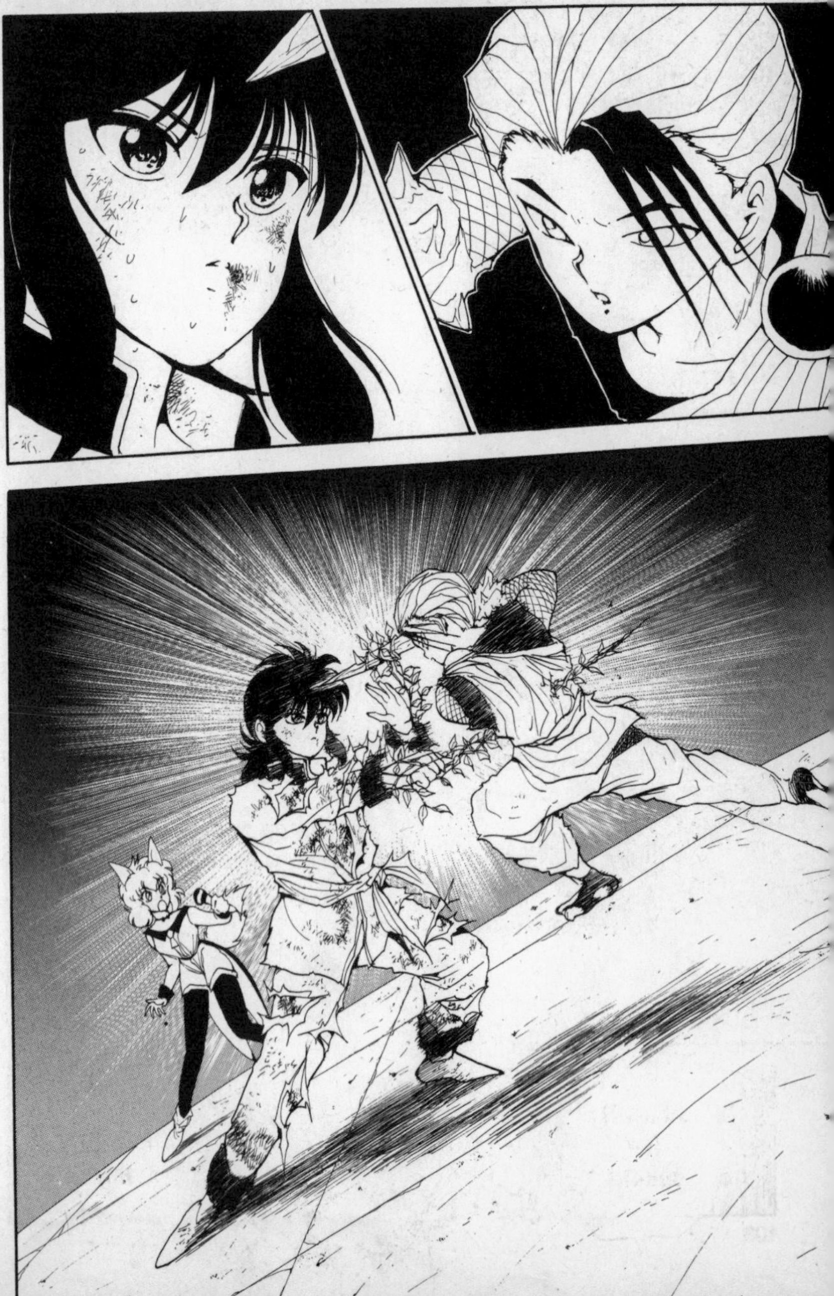

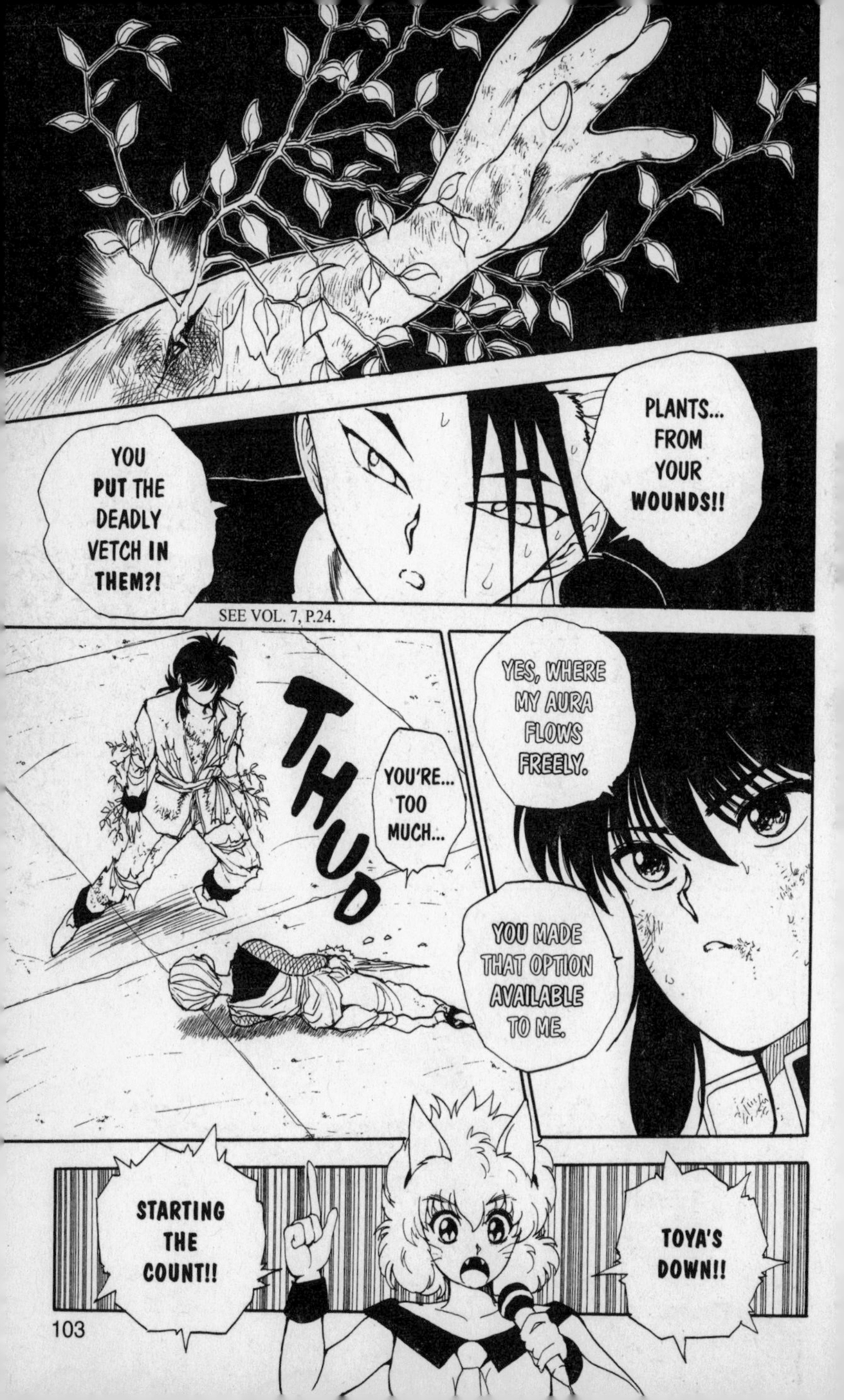
PLANTS... FROM YOUR WOUNDS!!
YOU PUT THE DEADLY VETCH IN THEM?!
SEE VOL. 7, P.24.
YES, WHERE MY AURA FLOWS FREELY.
YOU MADE THAT OPTION AVAILABLE TO ME.
YOU'RE... TOO MUCH...
THUD
TOYA'S DOWN!!
STARTING THE COUNT!!

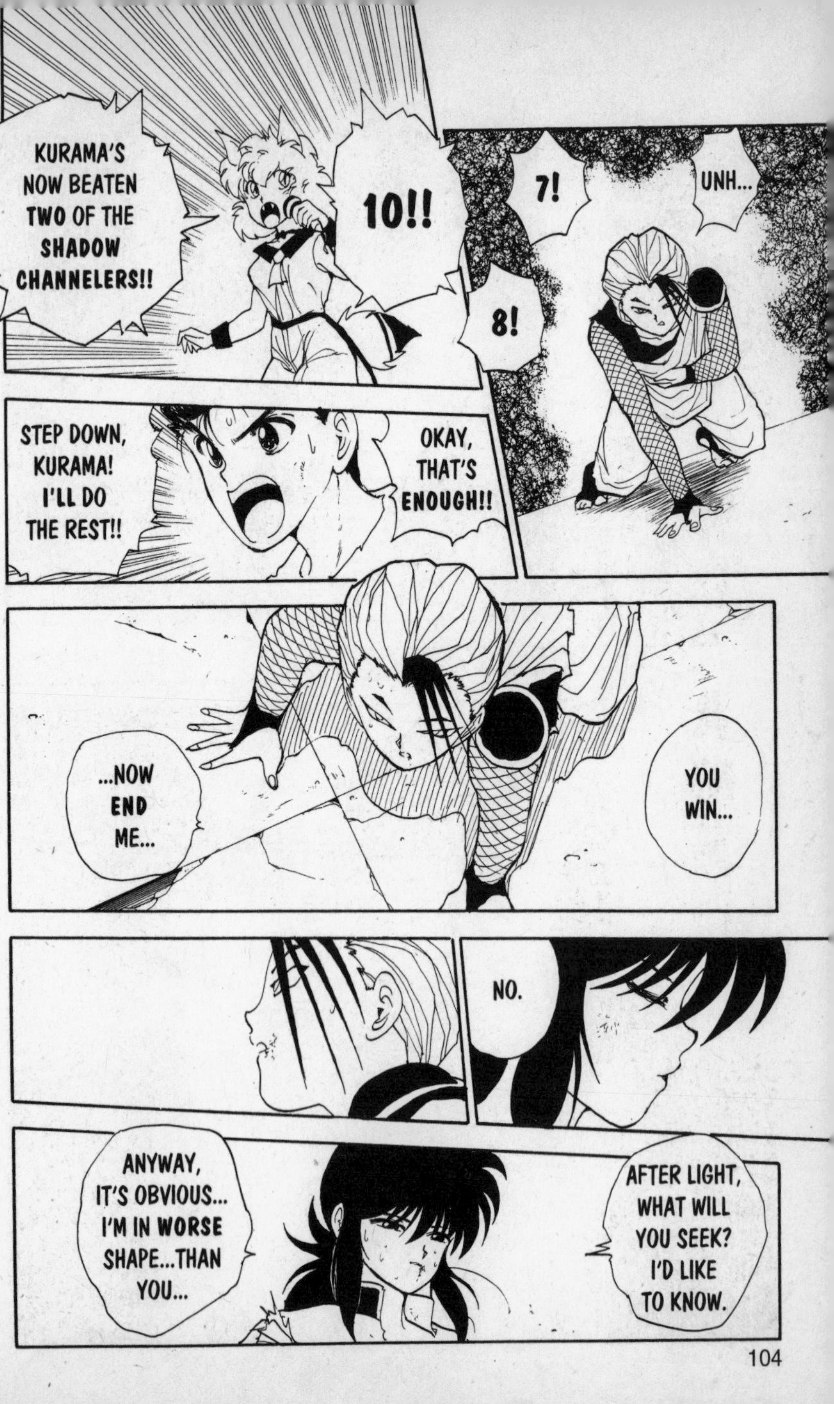
UNH...
7!
8!
10!!
KURAMA'S NOW BEATEN TWO OF THE SHADOW CHANNELERS!!
OKAY, THAT'S ENOUGH!!
STEP DOWN, KURAMA! I'LL DO THE REST!!
YOU WIN...
...NOW END ME...
NO.
AFTER LIGHT, WHAT WILL YOU SEEK? I'D LIKE TO KNOW.
ANYWAY, IT'S OBVIOUS... I'M IN WORSE SHAPE...THAN YOU...

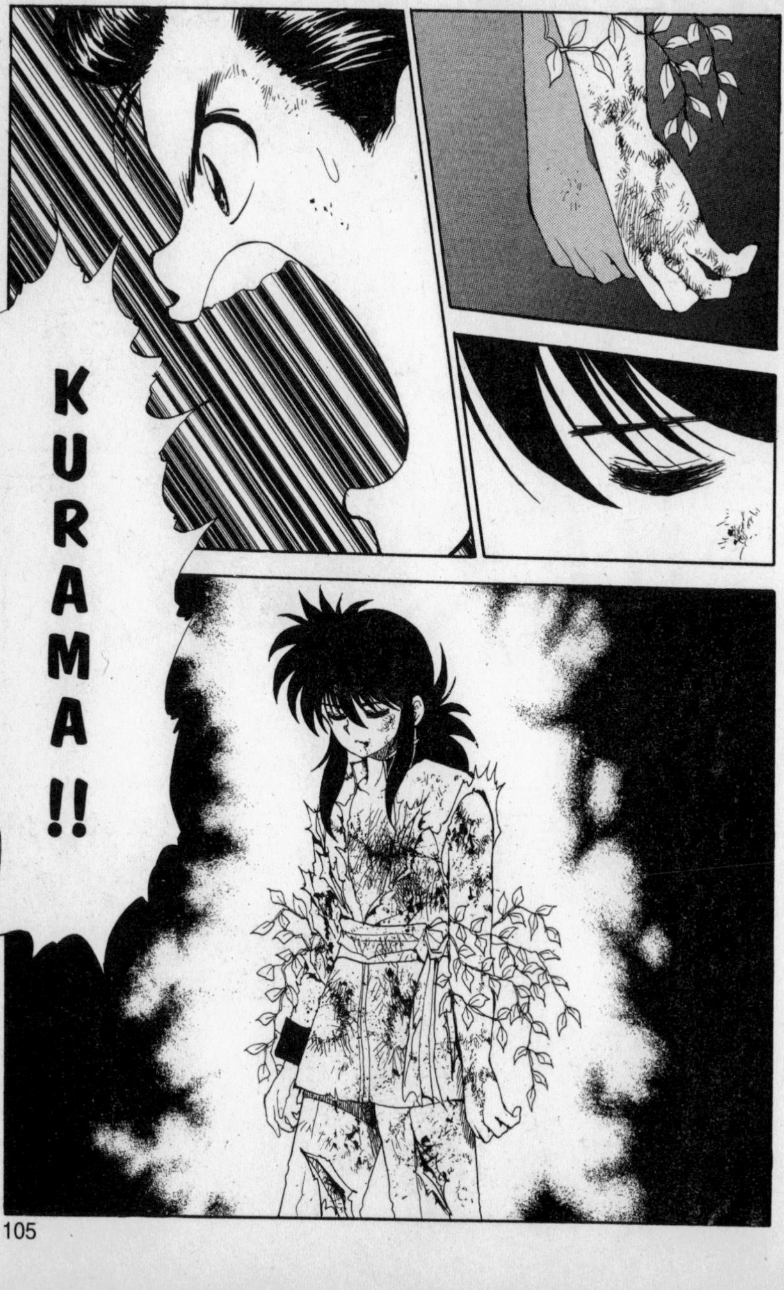
KURAMA!!

A BATTLE ALL ALONE

YUYU

HAKUSHO

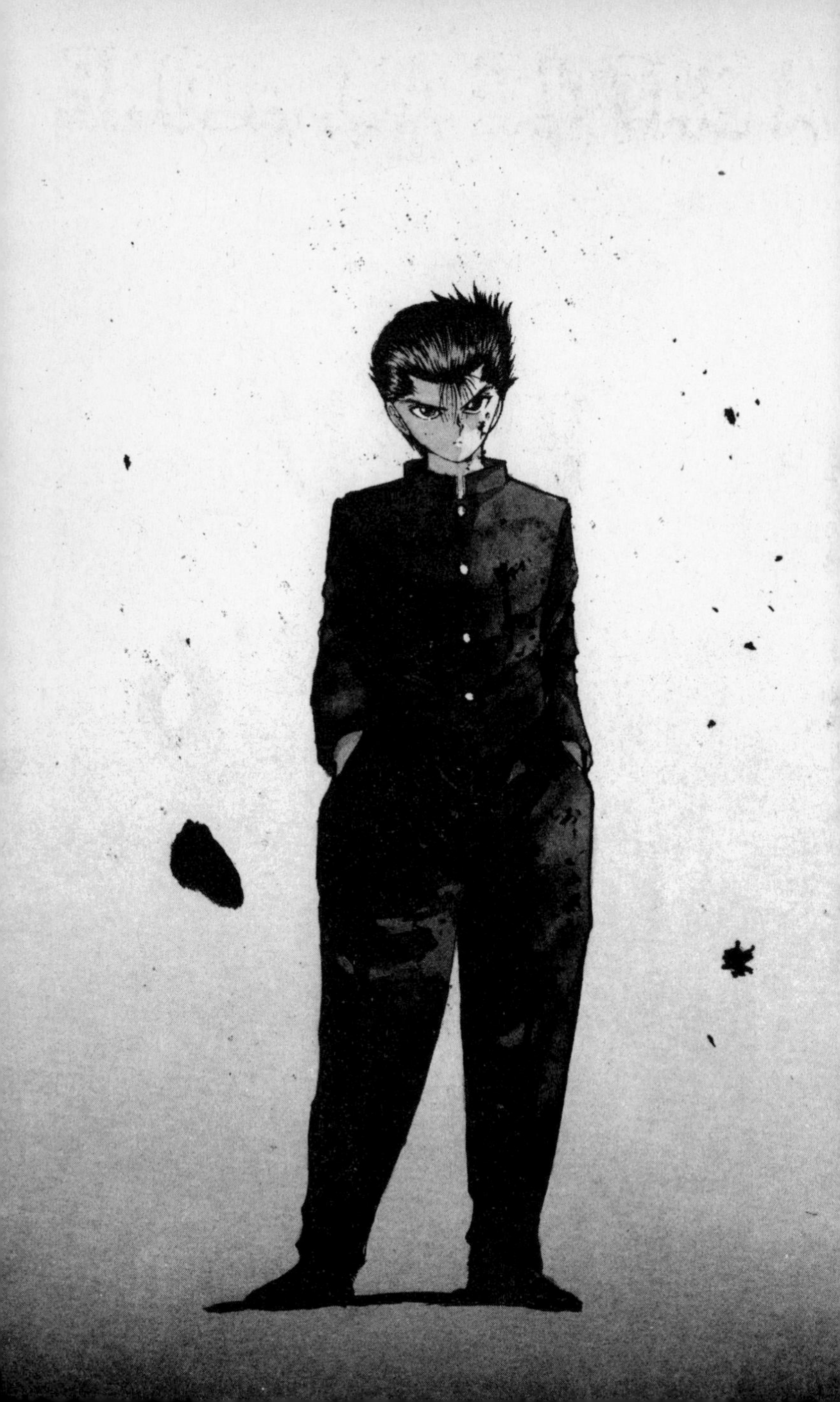

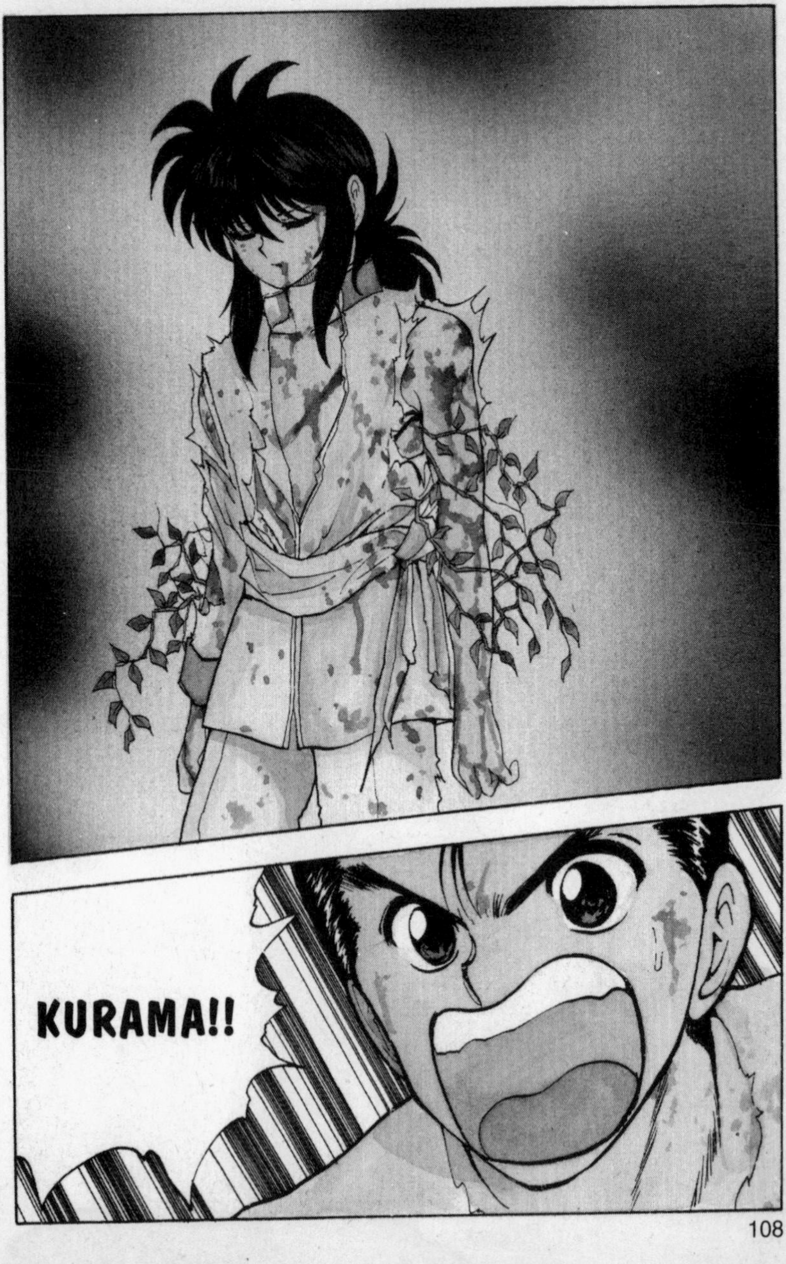
KURAMA!!

READ THIS WAY

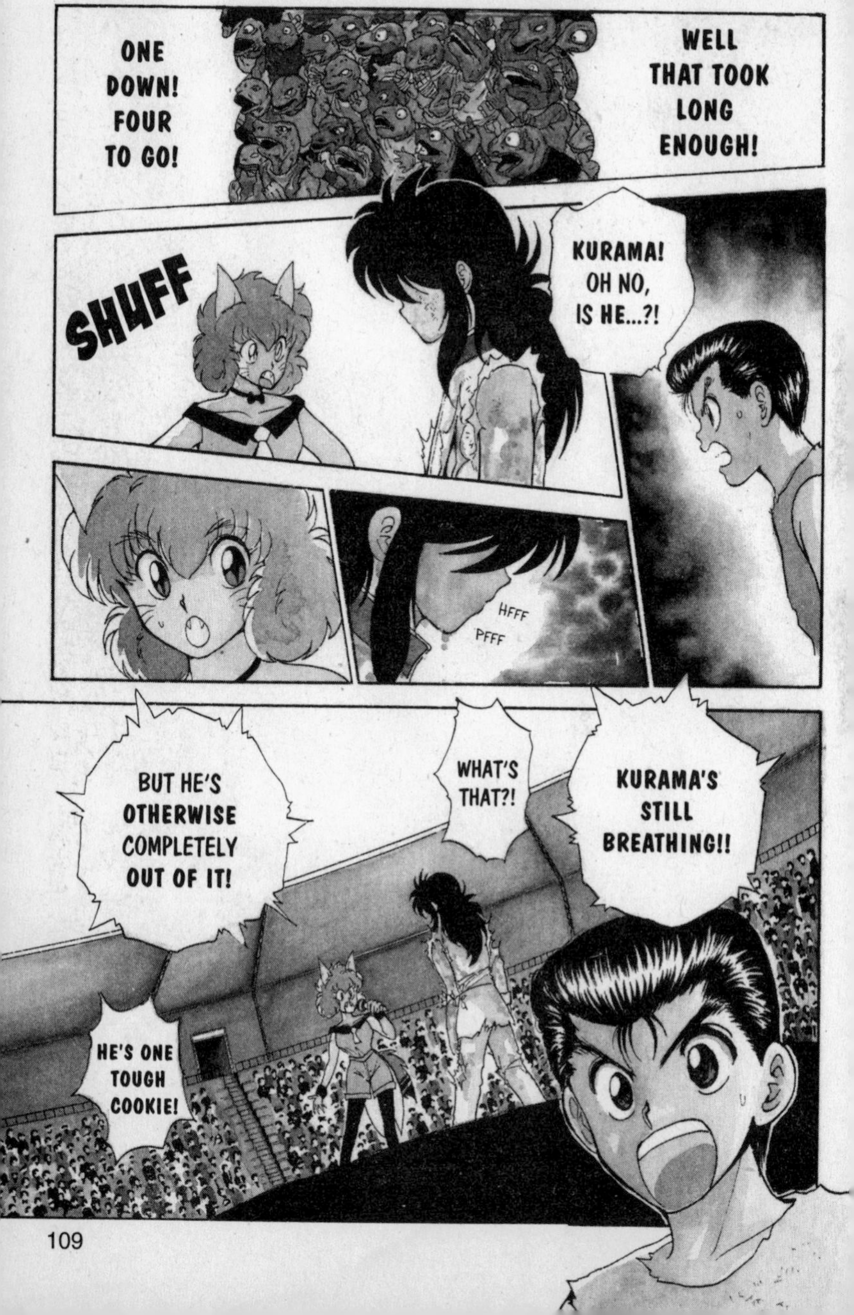

WELL THAT TOOK LONG ENOUGH!
ONE DOWN! FOUR TO GO!
KURAMA! OH NO, IS HE...?!
SHUFF
HFFF PFFF
KURAMA'S STILL BREATHING!!
WHAT'S THAT?!
BUT HE'S OTHERWISE COMPLETELY OUT OF IT!
HE'S ONE TOUGH COOKIE!

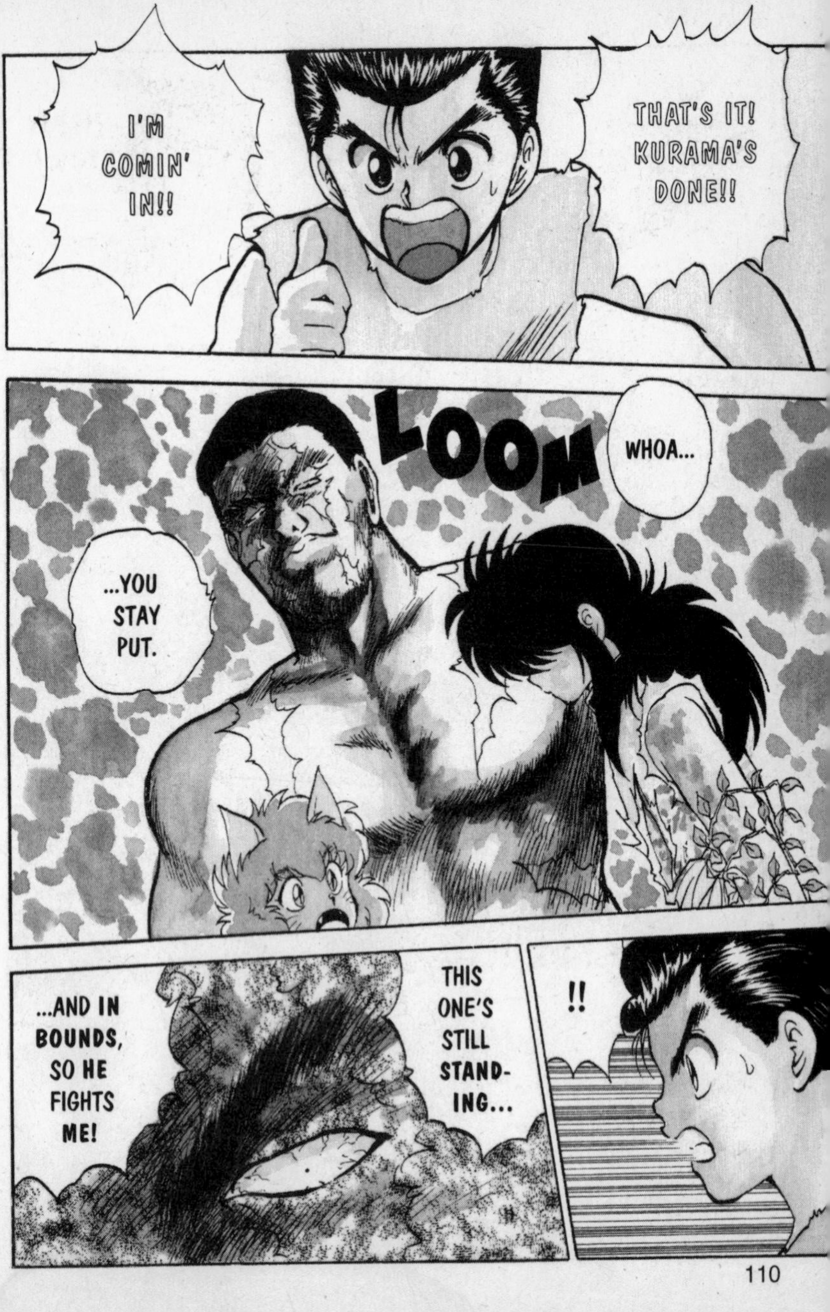
THAT'S IT! KURAMA'S DONE!!
I'M COMIN' IN!!
LOOM
WHOA...
...YOU STAY PUT.
!!
THIS ONE'S STILL STAND-ING...
...AND IN BOUNDS, SO HE FIGHTS ME!

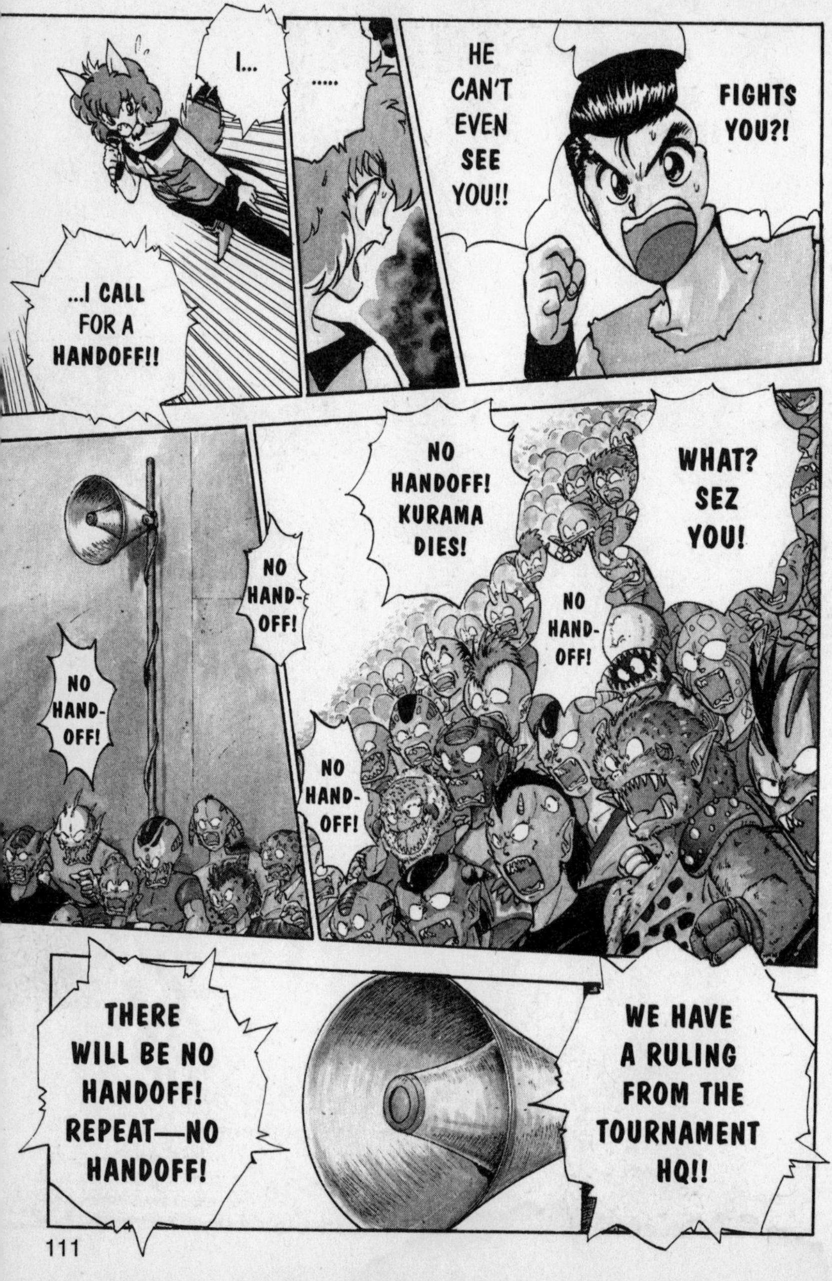
FIGHTS YOU?!
HE CAN'T EVEN SEE YOU!!
.....
I...
...I CALL FOR A HANDOFF!!
WHAT? SEZ YOU!
NO HANDOFF! KURAMA DIES!
NO HAND-OFF!
NO HAND-OFF!
NO HAND-OFF!
NO HAND-OFF!
WE HAVE A RULING FROM THE TOURNAMENT HQ!!
THERE WILL BE NO HANDOFF! REPEAT—NO HANDOFF!

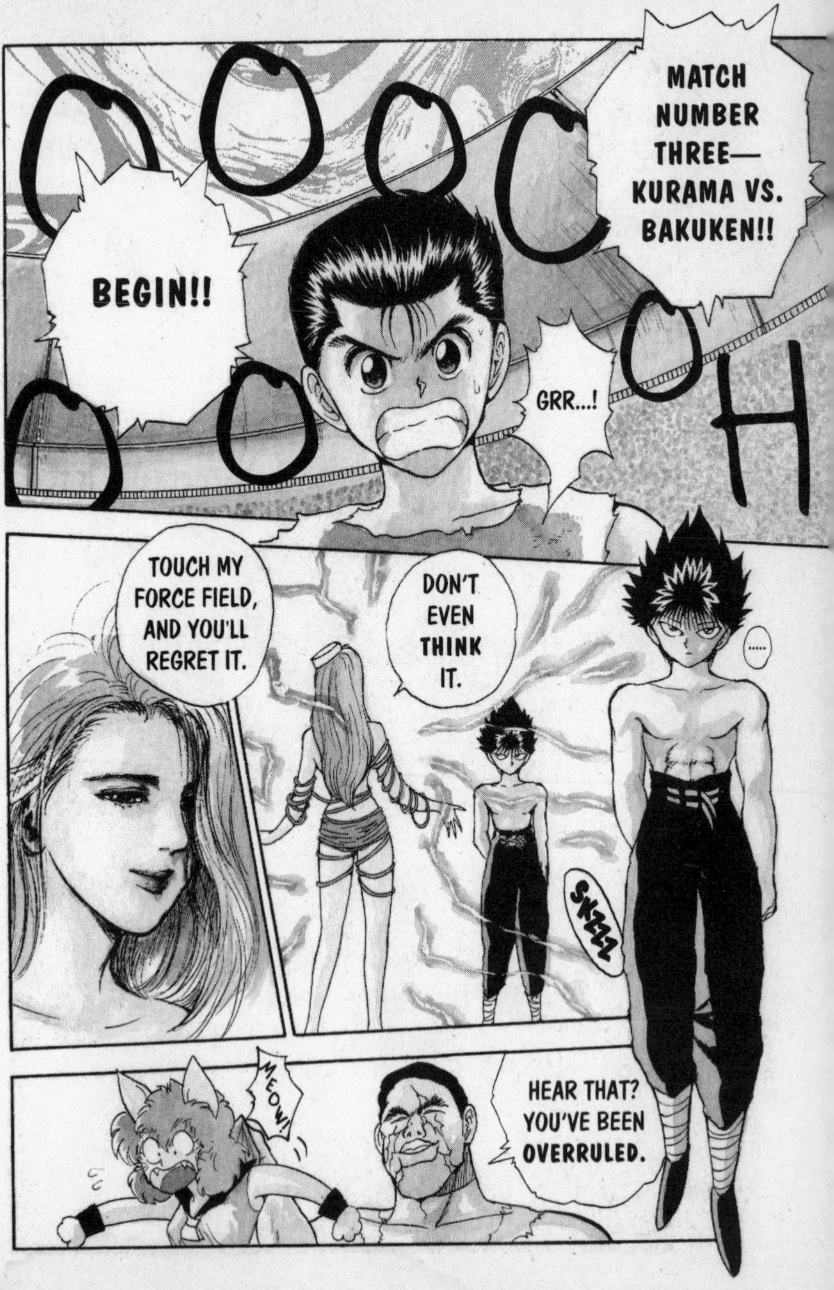
MATCH NUMBER THREE— KURAMA VS. BAKUKEN!!
OOOOOOOH
BEGIN!!
GRR...!
......
DON'T EVEN THINK IT.
SKZZZ
TOUCH MY FORCE FIELD, AND YOU'LL REGRET IT.
HEAR THAT? YOU'VE BEEN OVERRULED.
MEOW!

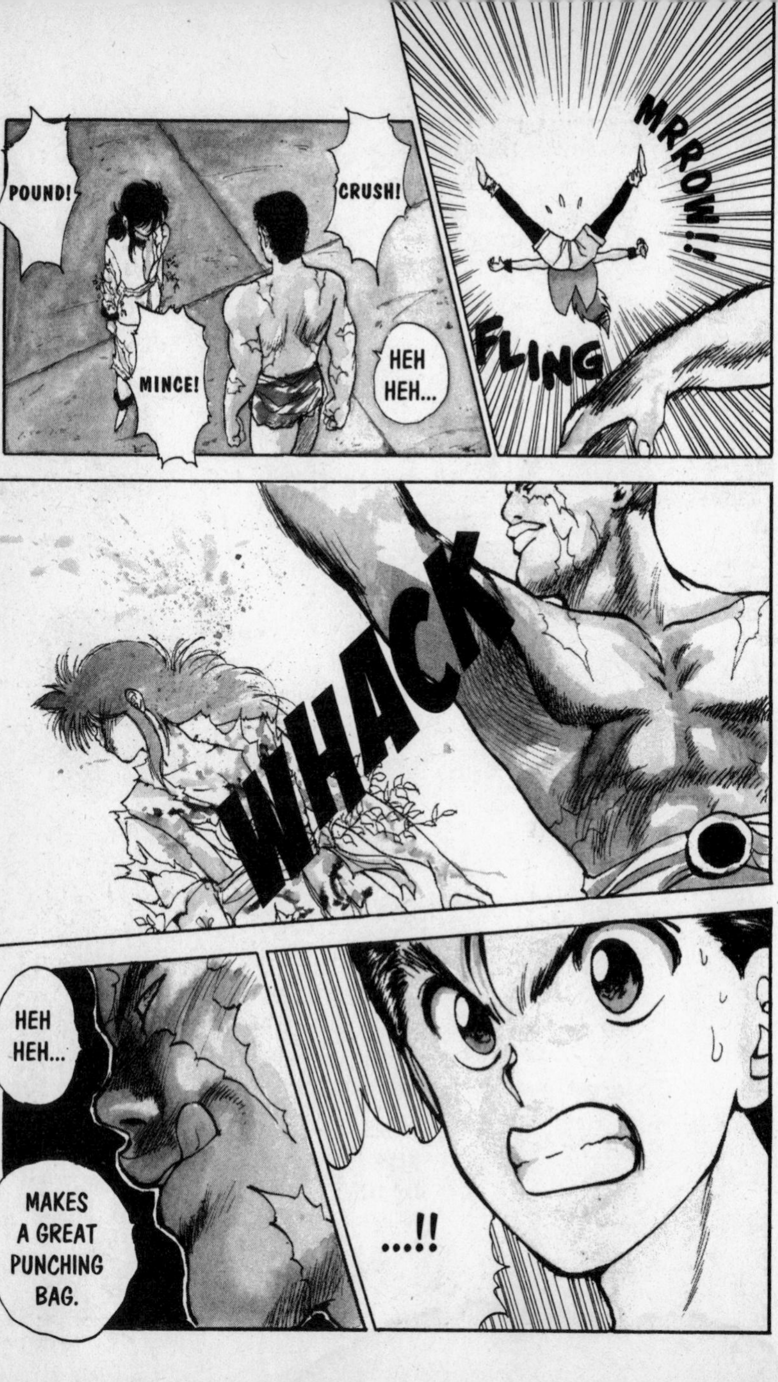
MRROW!!
FLING
CRUSH!
POUND!
HEH HEH...
MINCE!
WHACK
...!!
HEH HEH...
MAKES A GREAT PUNCHING BAG.

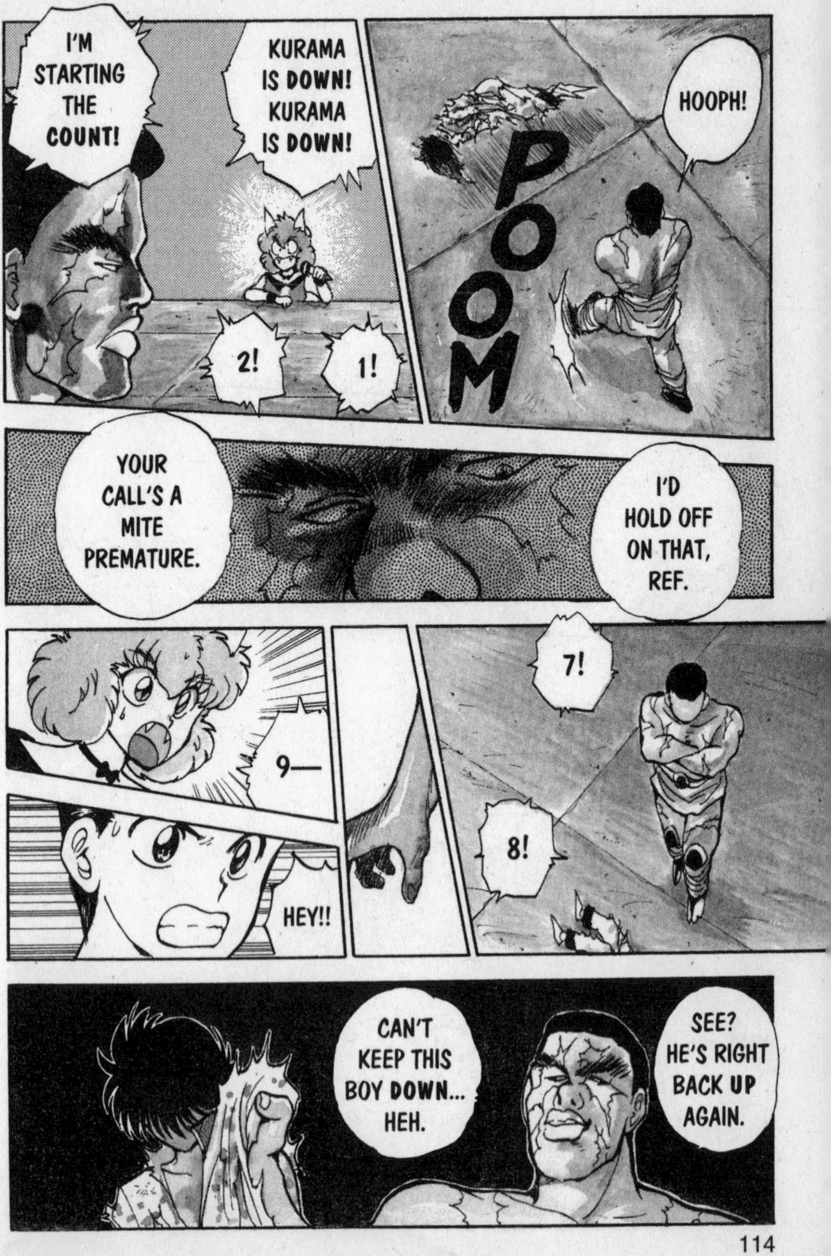
HOOPH!
POOM
KURAMA IS DOWN! KURAMA IS DOWN!
I'M STARTING THE COUNT!
1!
2!
I'D HOLD OFF ON THAT, REF.
YOUR CALL'S A MITE PREMATURE.
7!
8!
9—
HEY!!
SEE? HE'S RIGHT BACK UP AGAIN.
CAN'T KEEP THIS BOY DOWN... HEH.

READ THIS WAY

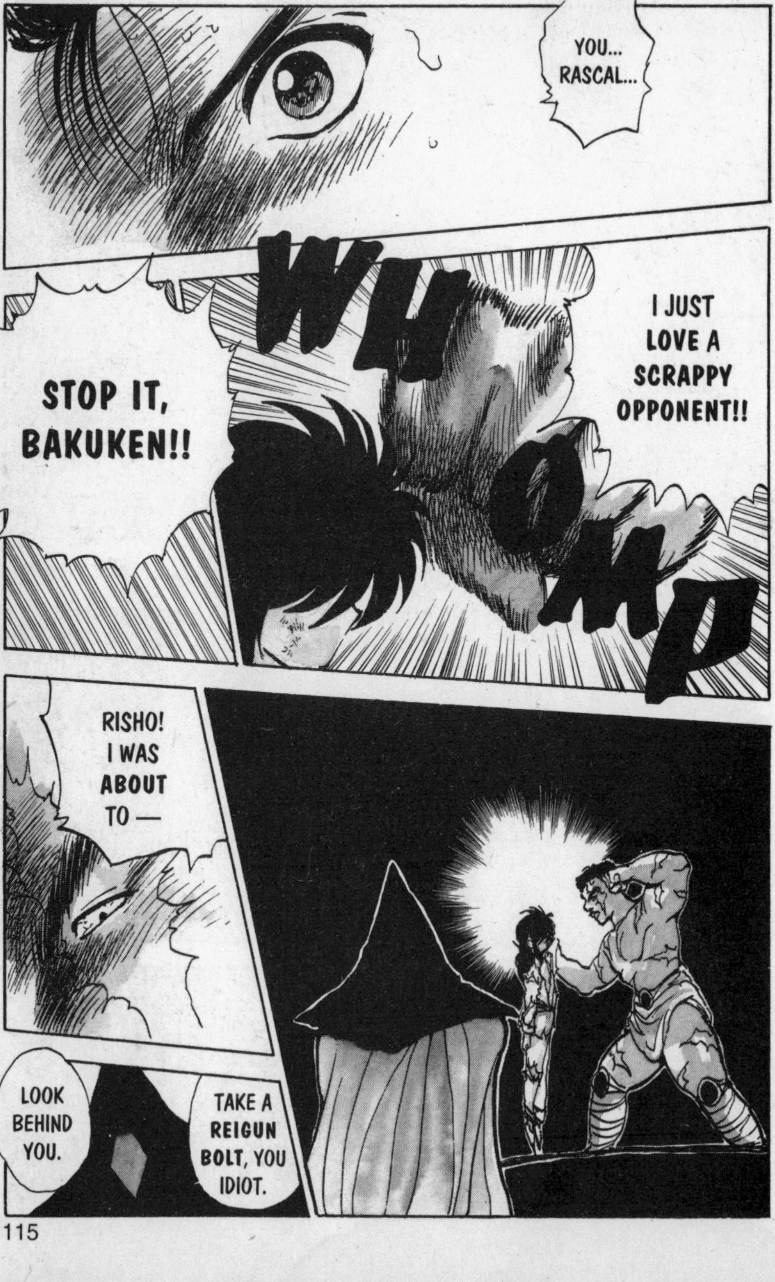
YOU... RASCAL...
I JUST LOVE A SCRAPPY OPPONENT!!
WHOMP
STOP IT, BAKUKEN!!
RISHO! I WAS ABOUT TO —
TAKE A REIGUN BOLT, YOU IDIOT.
LOOK BEHIND YOU.

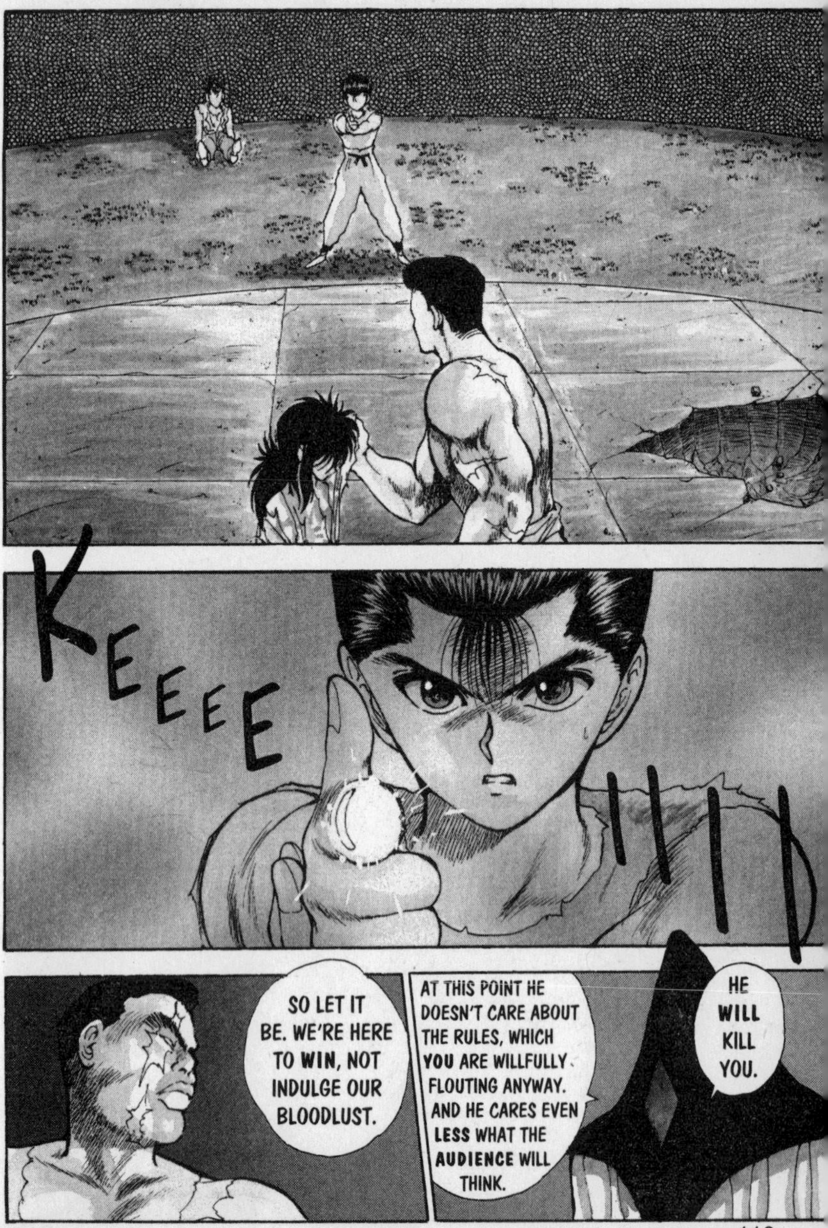
KEEEE
HE **WILL** KILL YOU.
AT THIS POINT HE DOESN'T CARE ABOUT THE RULES, WHICH **YOU** ARE WILLFULLY FLOUTING ANYWAY. AND HE CARES EVEN **LESS** WHAT THE **AUDIENCE** WILL THINK.
SO LET IT BE. WE'RE HERE TO **WIN**, NOT INDULGE OUR BLOODLUST.

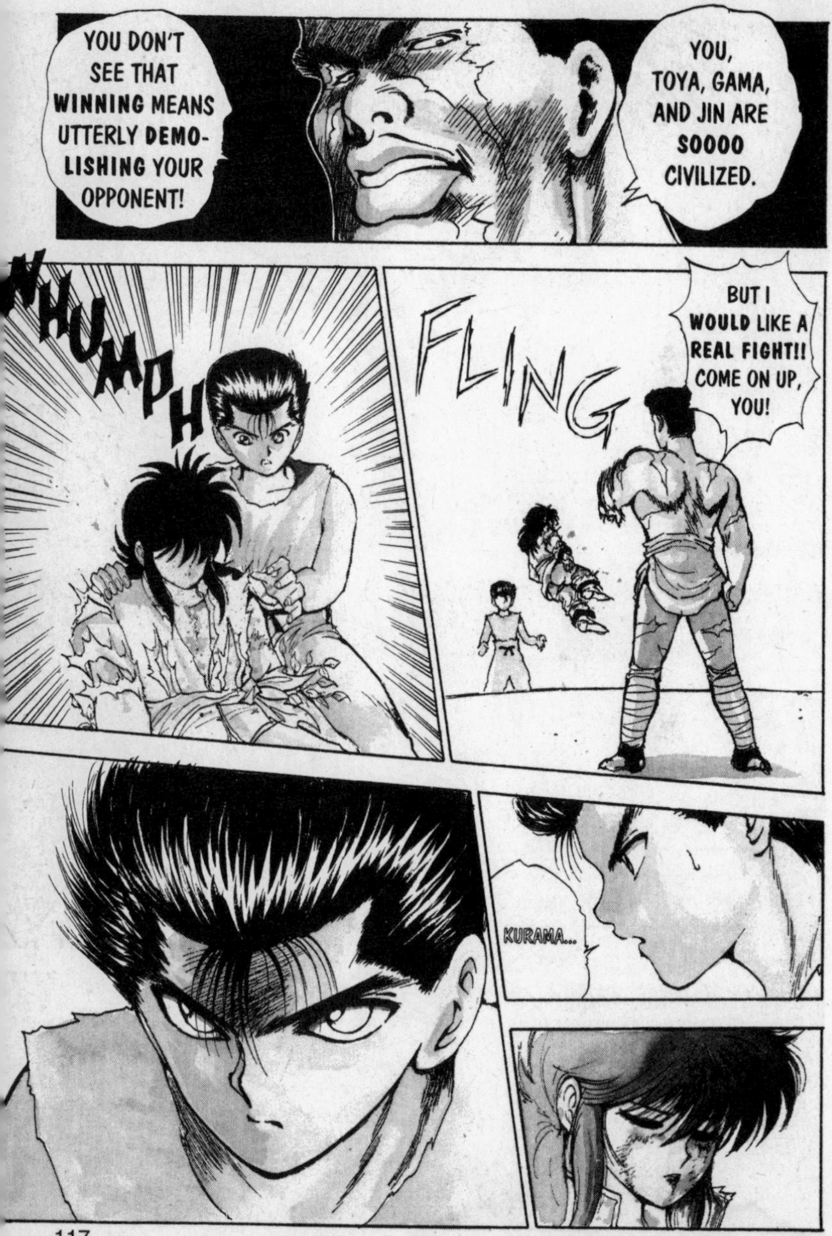
YOU, TOYA, GAMA, AND JIN ARE SOOOO CIVILIZED.
YOU DON'T SEE THAT WINNING MEANS UTTERLY DEMOLISHING YOUR OPPONENT!
FLING
BUT I WOULD LIKE A REAL FIGHT!! COME ON UP, YOU!
WHUMPH
KURAMA...

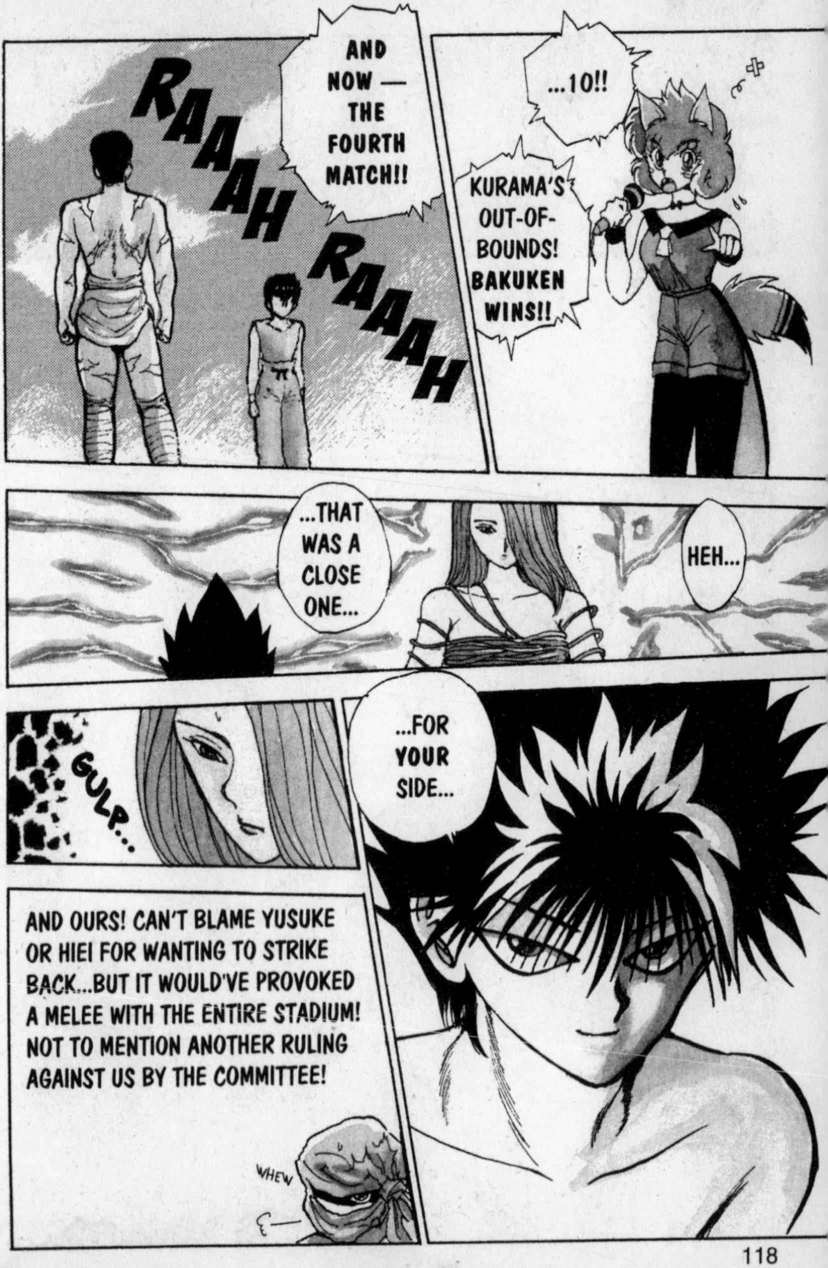
...10!!
KURAMA'S OUT-OF-BOUNDS! BAKUKEN WINS!!
AND NOW — THE FOURTH MATCH!!
RAAAAH RAAAAH
HEH...
...THAT WAS A CLOSE ONE...
...FOR YOUR SIDE...
GULP...
AND OURS! CAN'T BLAME YUSUKE OR HIEI FOR WANTING TO STRIKE BACK...BUT IT WOULD'VE PROVOKED A MELEE WITH THE ENTIRE STADIUM! NOT TO MENTION ANOTHER RULING AGAINST US BY THE COMMITTEE!
WHEW

READ THIS WAY

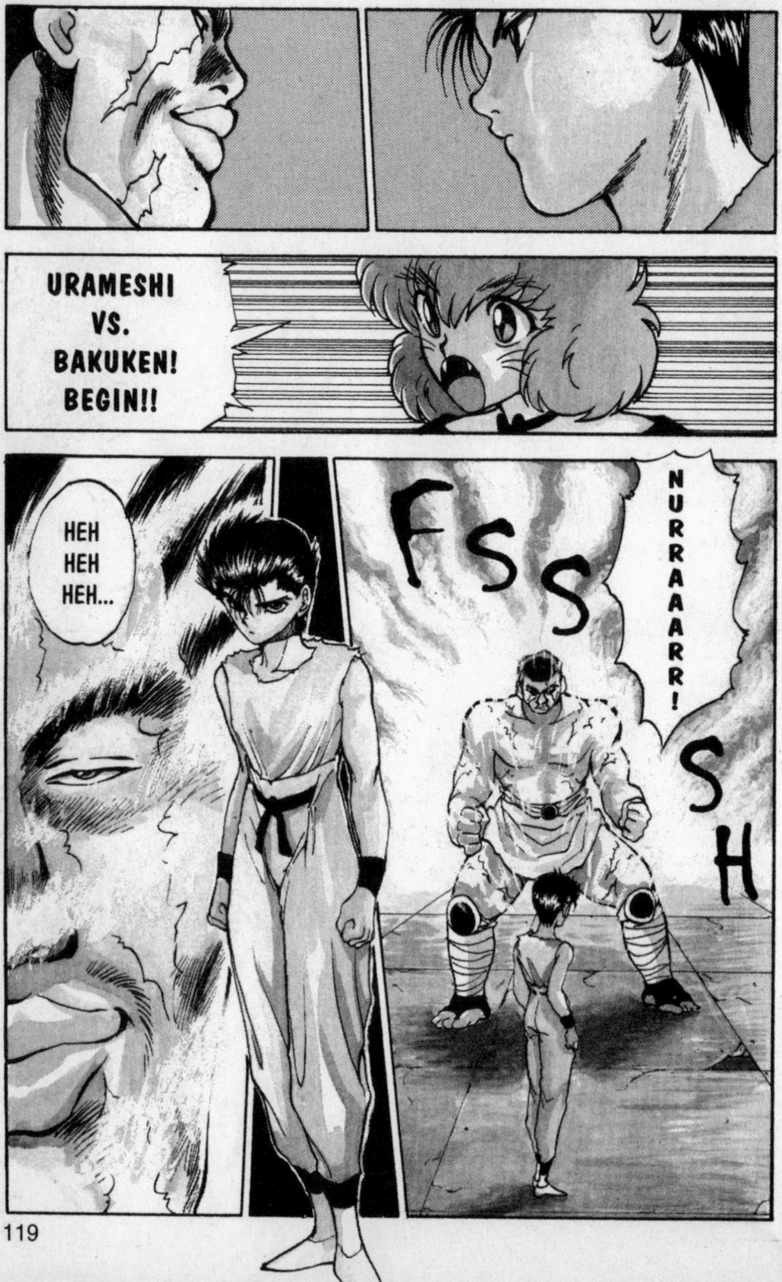
URAMESHI VS. BAKUKEN! BEGIN!!
FSSSSH
NURRAAAARR!
HEH HEH HEH...

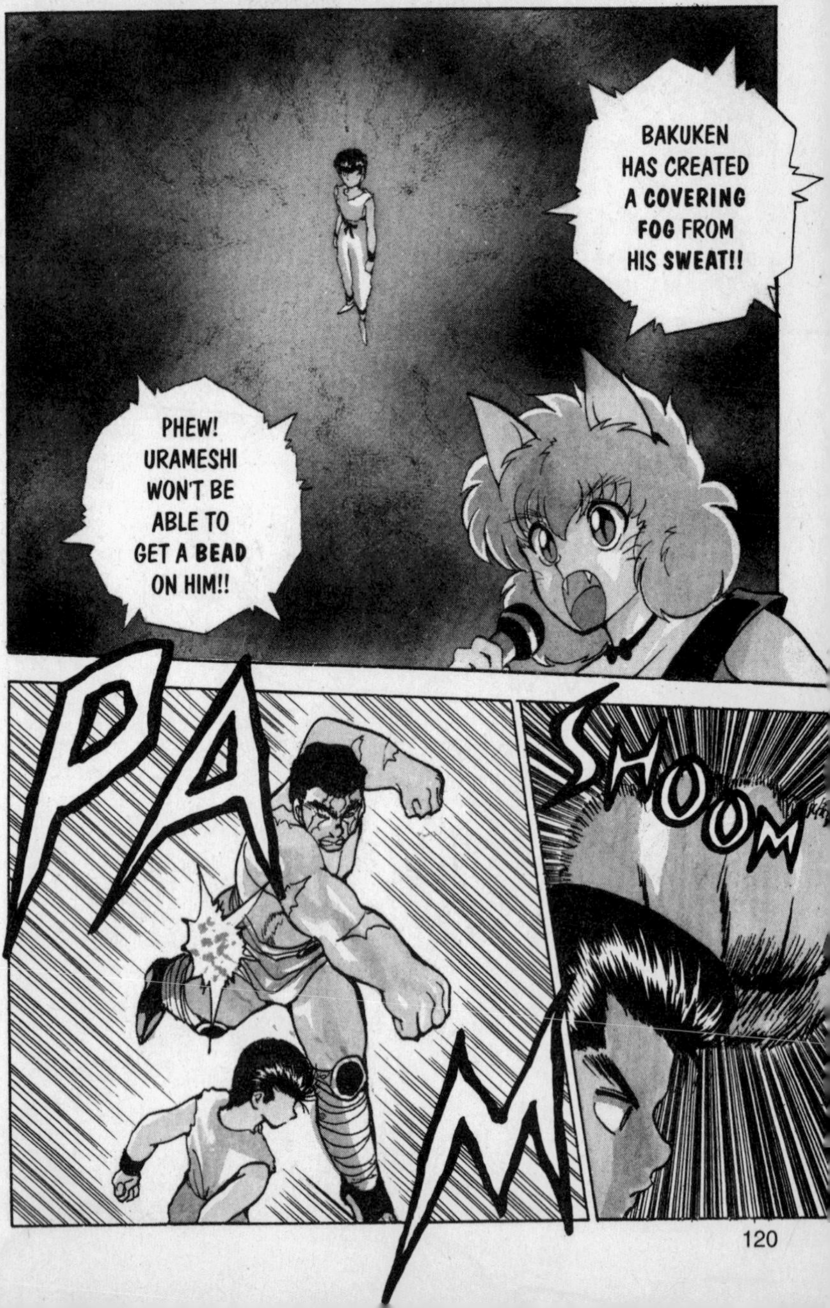
BAKUKEN HAS CREATED A COVERING FOG FROM HIS SWEAT!!
PHEW! URAMESHI WON'T BE ABLE TO GET A BEAD ON HIM!!
SHOOM
PAM

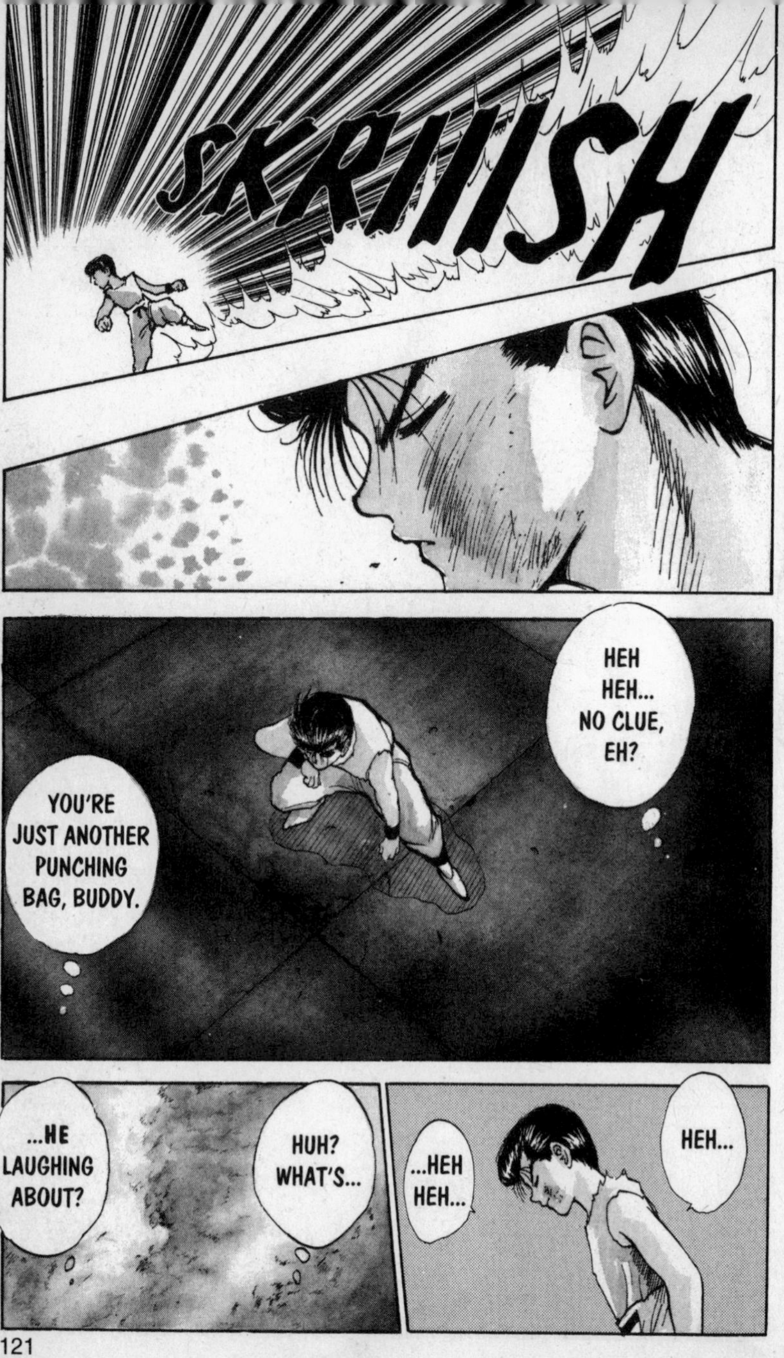
SKRIIISH
HEH HEH... NO CLUE, EH?
YOU'RE JUST ANOTHER PUNCHING BAG, BUDDY.
HEH...
...HEH HEH...
HUH? WHAT'S...
...HE LAUGHING ABOUT?

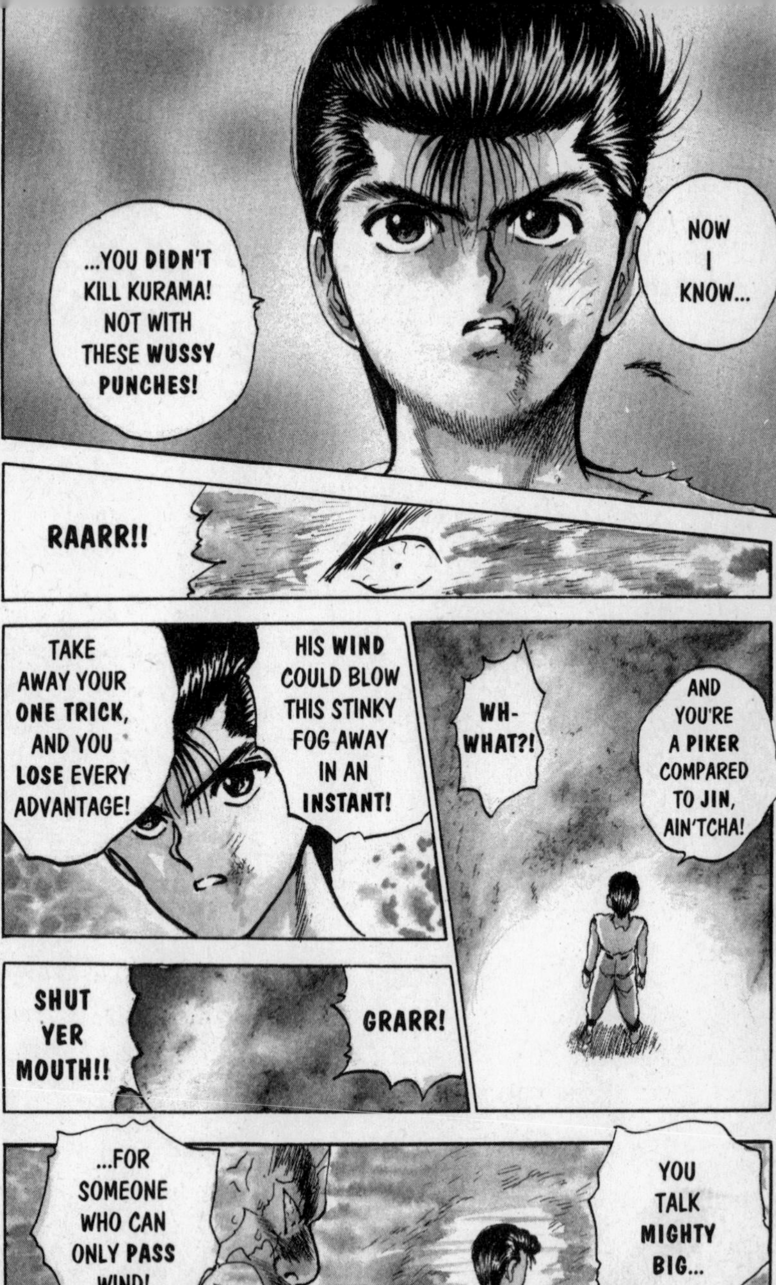
NOW I KNOW...
...YOU DIDN'T KILL KURAMA! NOT WITH THESE WUSSY PUNCHES!
RAARR!!
AND YOU'RE A PIKER COMPARED TO JIN, AIN'TCHA!
WH-WHAT?!
HIS WIND COULD BLOW THIS STINKY FOG AWAY IN AN INSTANT!
TAKE AWAY YOUR ONE TRICK, AND YOU LOSE EVERY ADVANTAGE!
GRARR!
SHUT YER MOUTH!!
YOU TALK MIGHTY BIG...
...FOR SOMEONE WHO CAN ONLY PASS WIND!

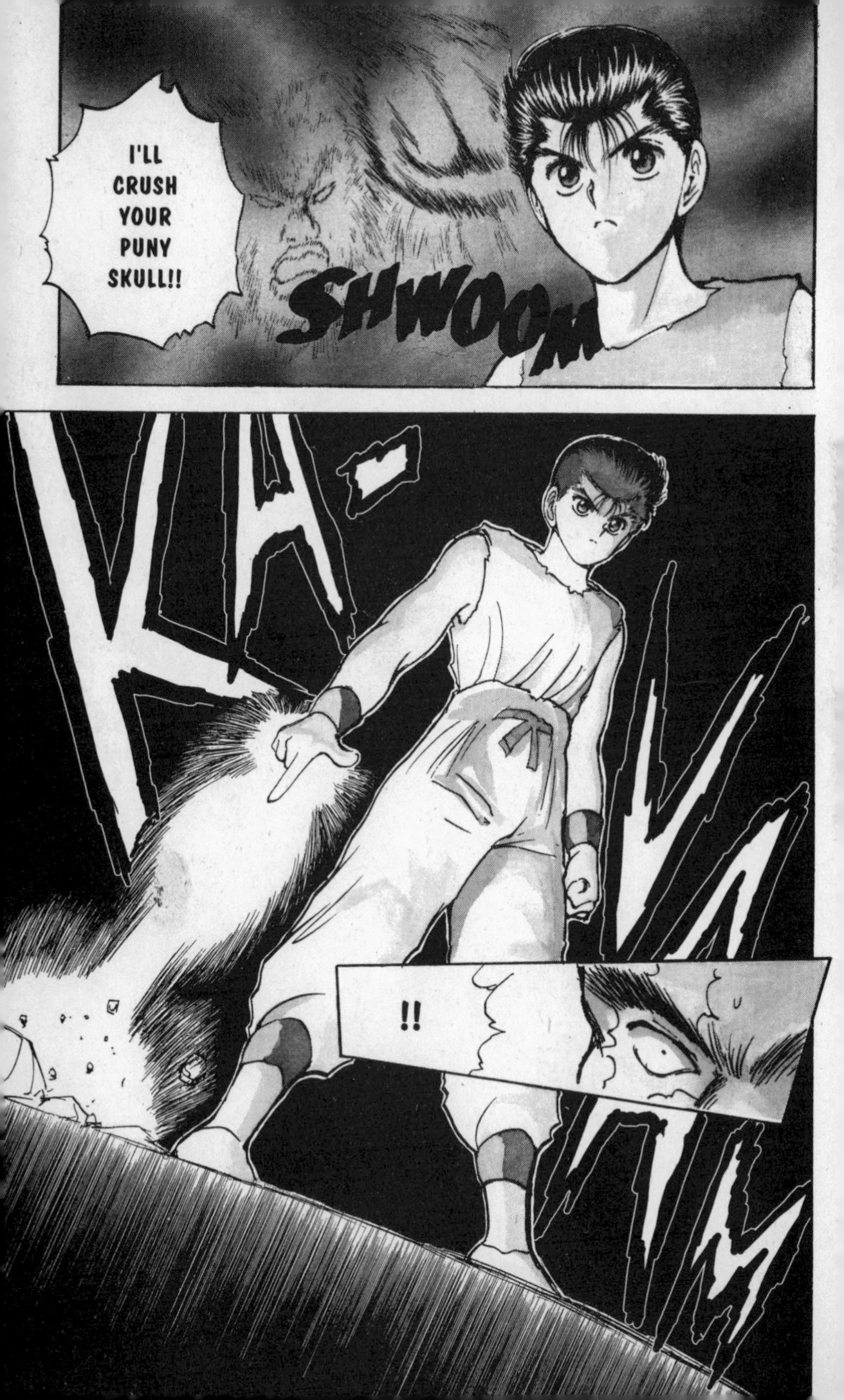
I'LL CRUSH YOUR PUNY SKULL!!
SHWOOM
!!

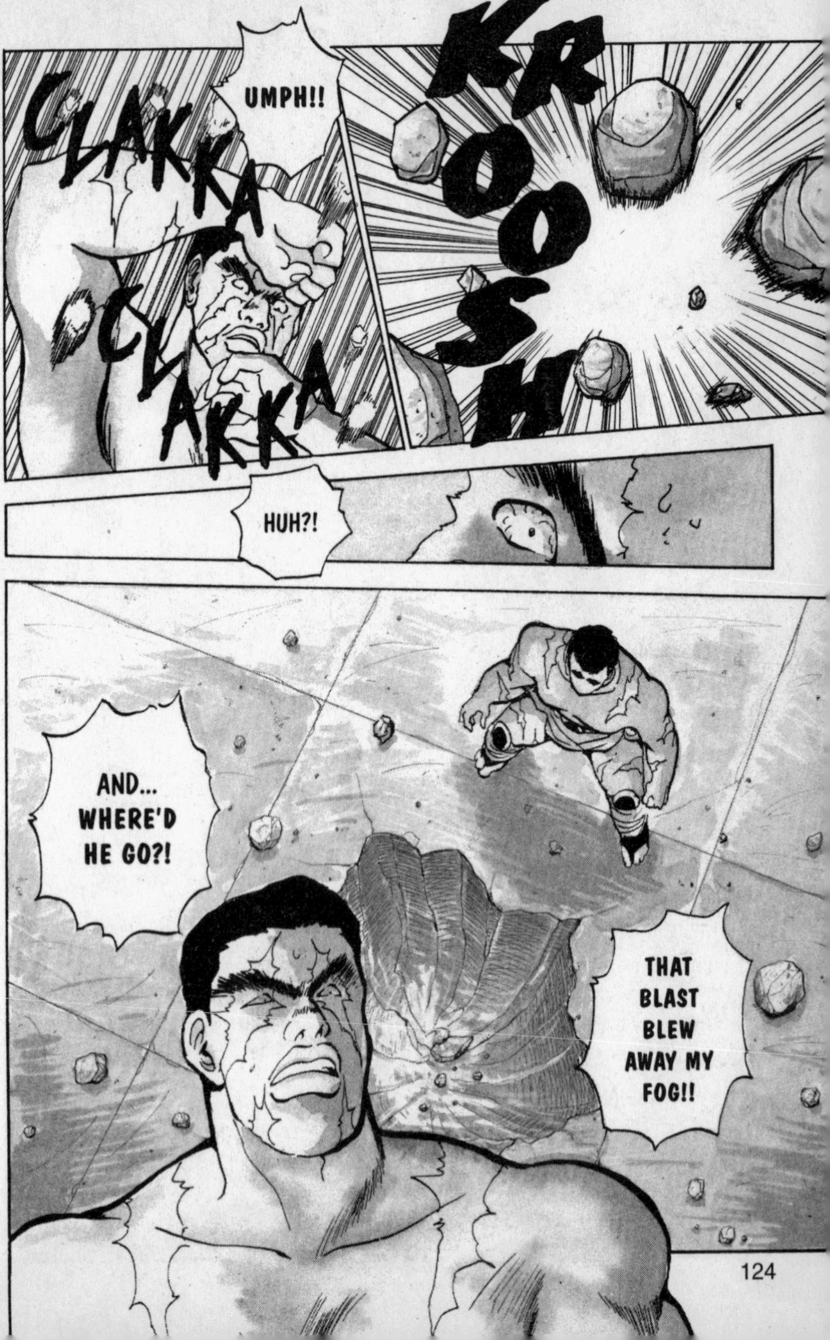
KROOOSH
CLAKKA CLAKKA CLAKKA
UMPH!!
HUH?!
THAT BLAST BLEW AWAY MY FOG!!
AND... WHERE'D HE GO?!

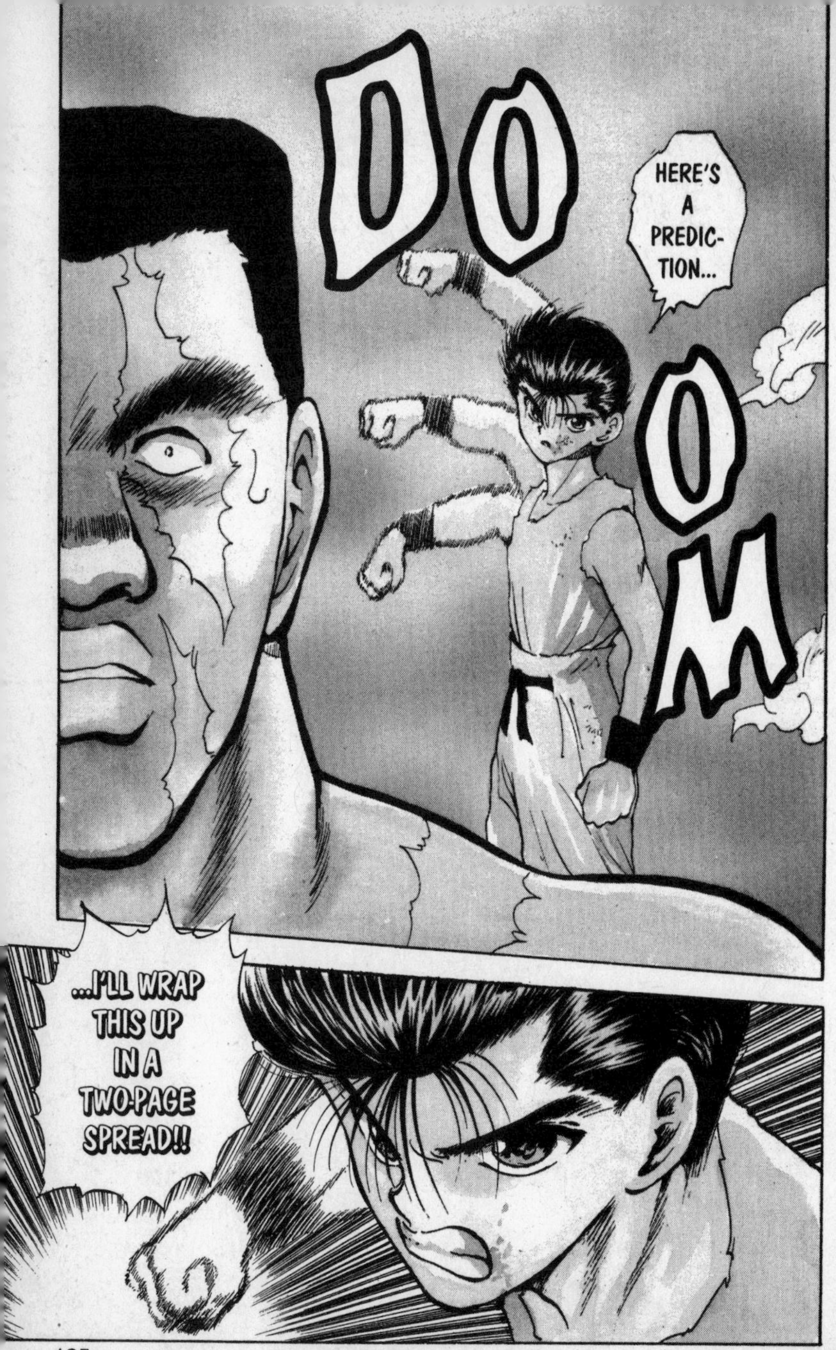
DOOOM
HERE'S A PREDICTION...
...I'LL WRAP THIS UP IN A TWO-PAGE SPREAD!!

1975

MY WORLD CONSISTED OF TV, BASEBALL, MANGA, AND SCHOOL. I THOUGHT I WAS PRETTY SMART. I NEVER IMAGINED THAT I WOULD GROW TO HATE SNOW.

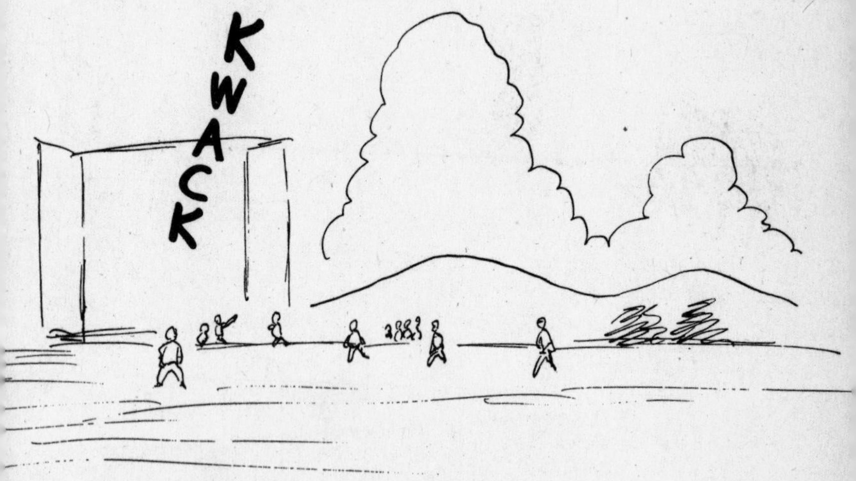
KWACK

FIST OF RAGE!!

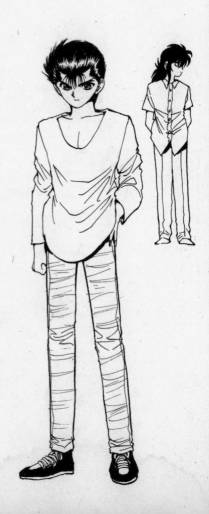

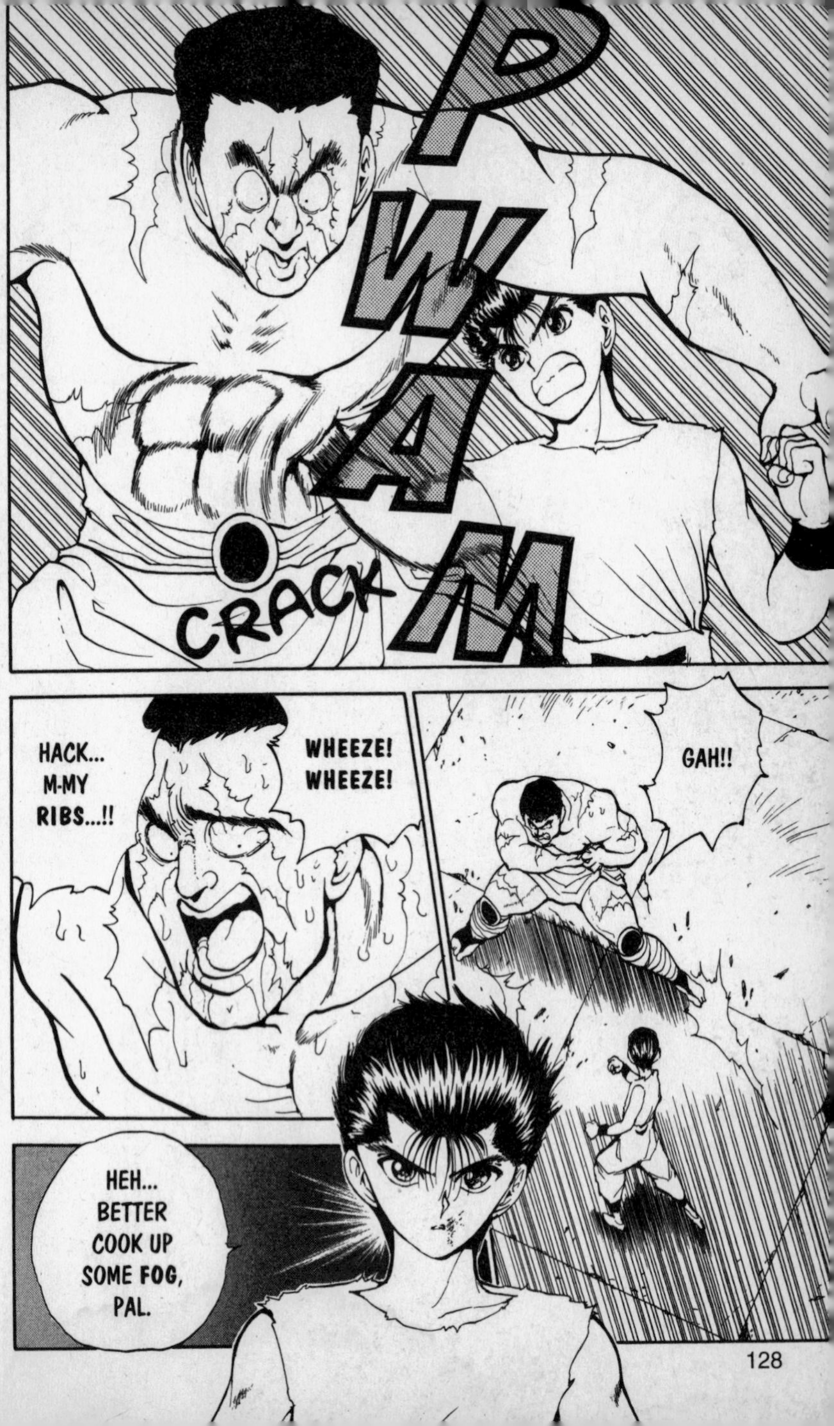
PWAM
CRACK
GAH!!
WHEEZE! WHEEZE!
HACK... M-MY RIBS...!!
HEH... BETTER COOK UP SOME FOG, PAL.

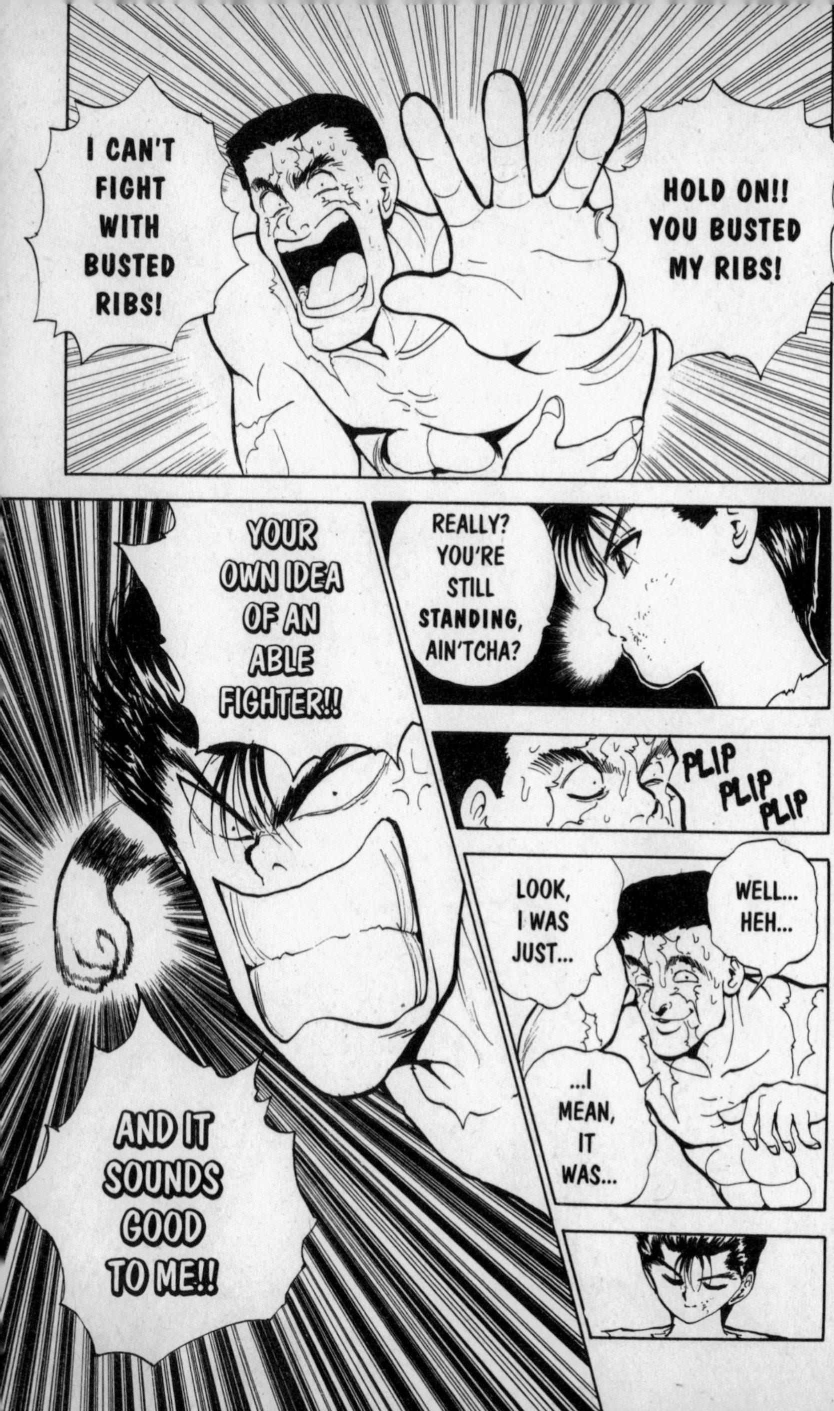
HOLD ON!! YOU BUSTED MY RIBS!
I CAN'T FIGHT WITH BUSTED RIBS!
REALLY? YOU'RE STILL STANDING, AIN'TCHA?
PLIP PLIP PLIP
WELL... HEH...
LOOK, I WAS JUST...
...I MEAN, IT WAS...
YOUR OWN IDEA OF AN ABLE FIGHTER!!
AND IT SOUNDS GOOD TO ME!!

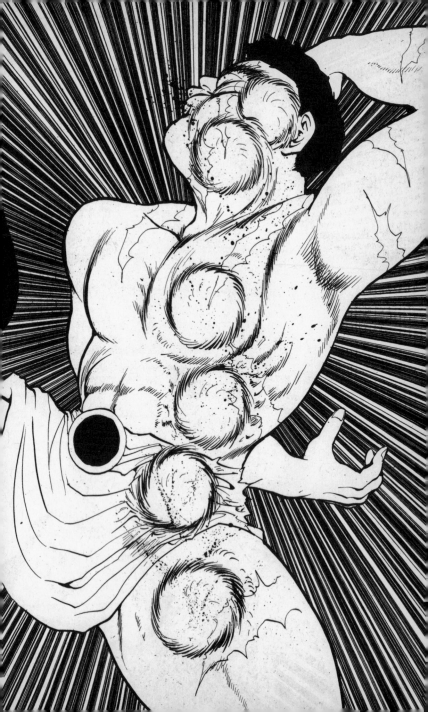

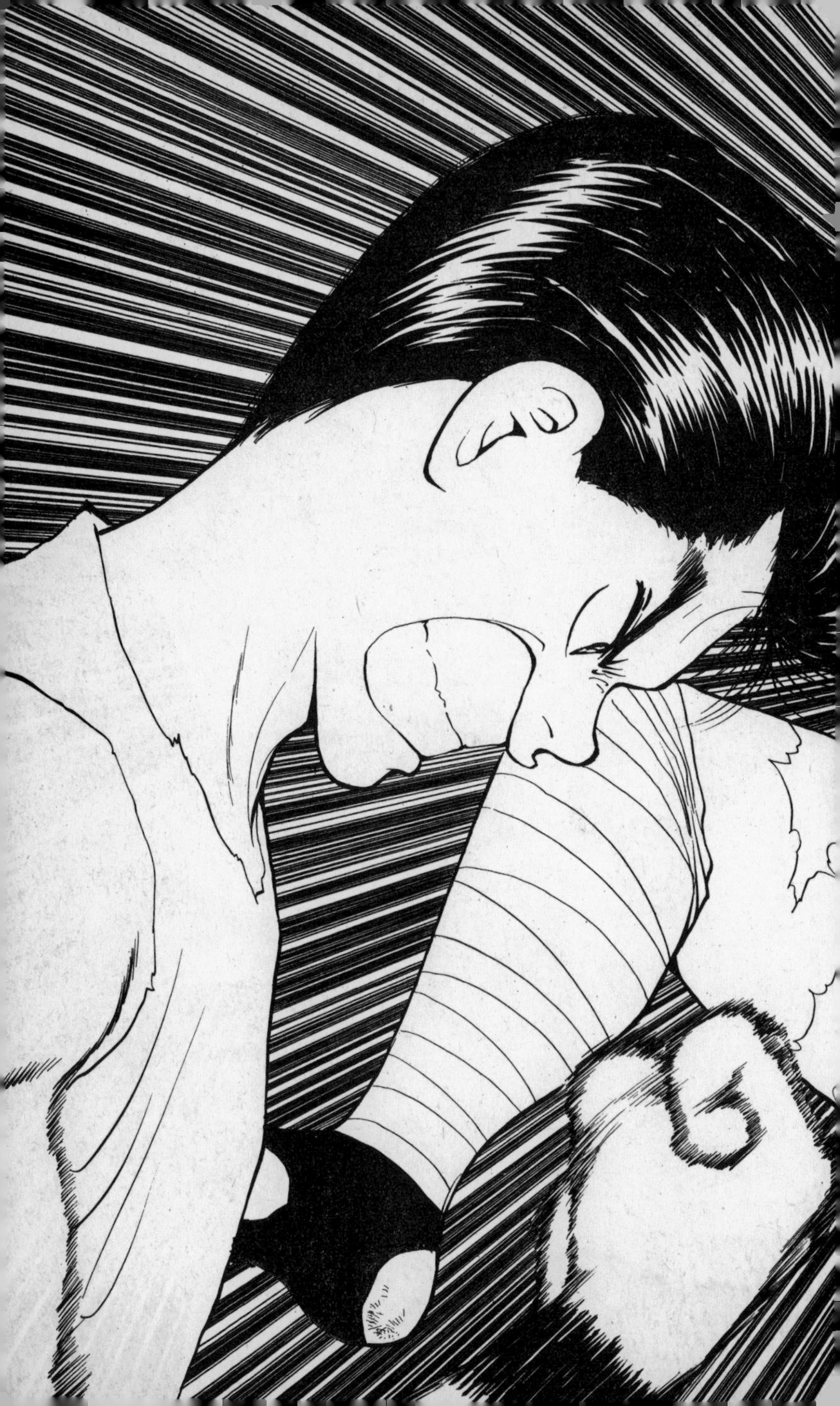

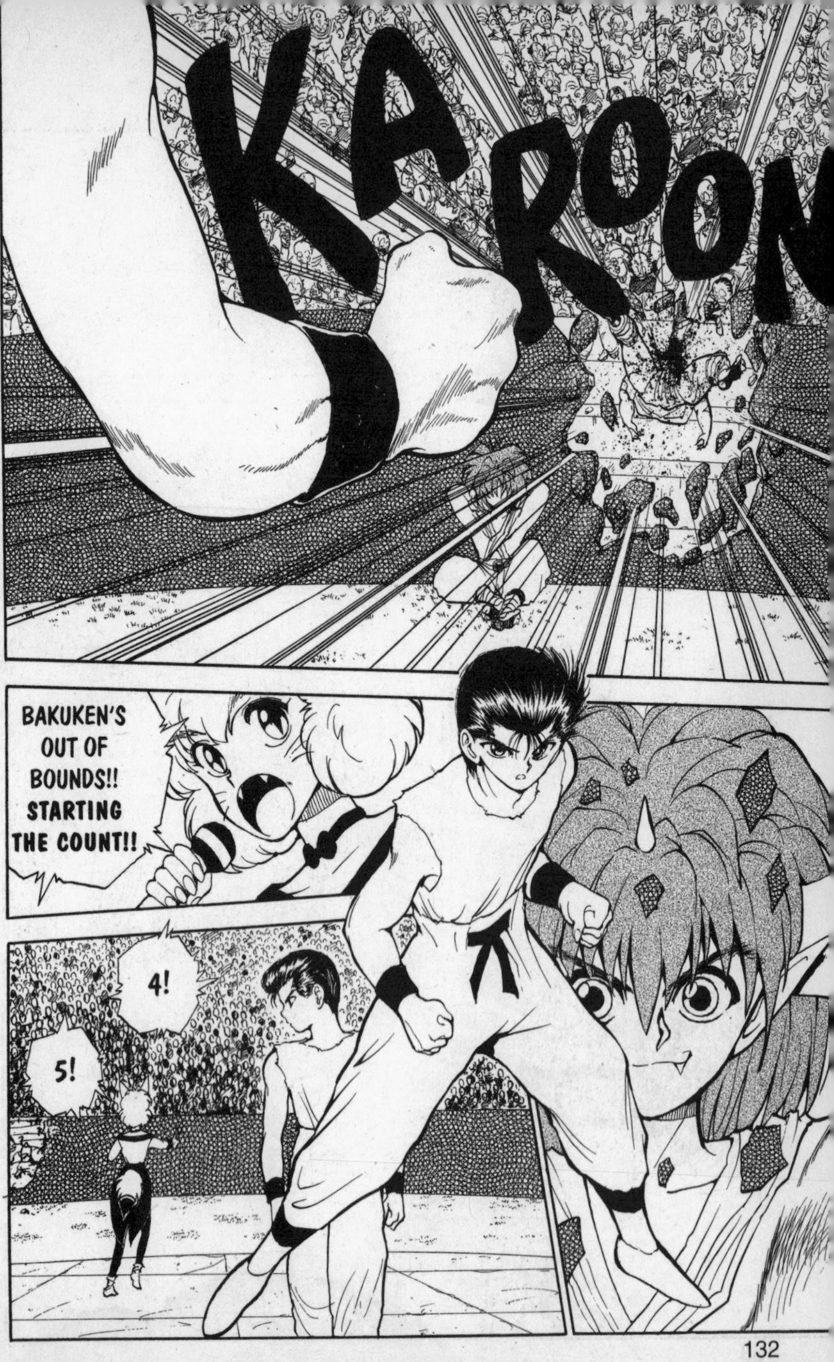
KAROO
BAKUKEN'S OUT OF BOUNDS!! STARTING THE COUNT!!
4!
5!

READ THIS WAY

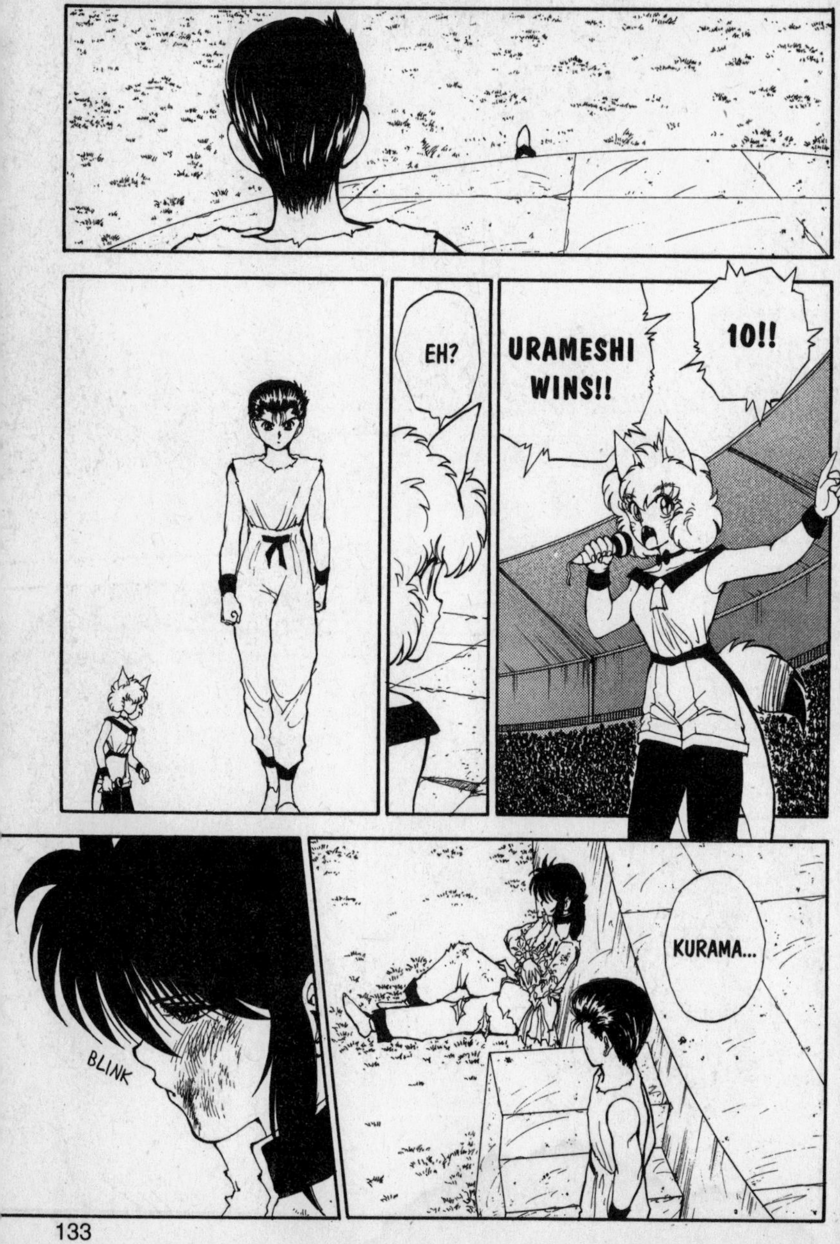
10!!
URAMESHI WINS!!
EH?
KURAMA...
BLINK

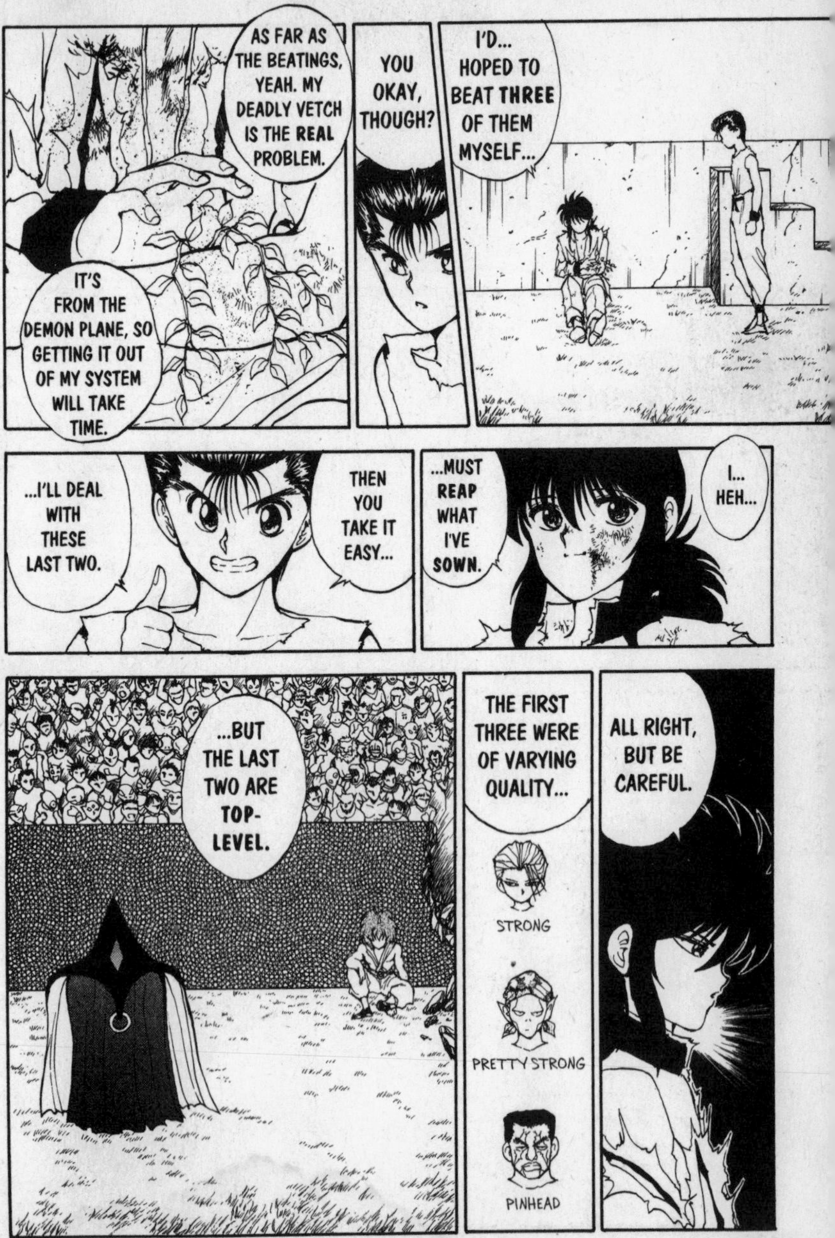
I'D... HOPED TO BEAT THREE OF THEM MYSELF...
YOU OKAY, THOUGH?
AS FAR AS THE BEATINGS, YEAH. MY DEADLY VETCH IS THE REAL PROBLEM.
IT'S FROM THE DEMON PLANE, SO GETTING IT OUT OF MY SYSTEM WILL TAKE TIME.
I... HEH...
...MUST REAP WHAT I'VE SOWN.
THEN YOU TAKE IT EASY...
...I'LL DEAL WITH THESE LAST TWO.
ALL RIGHT, BUT BE CAREFUL.
THE FIRST THREE WERE OF VARYING QUALITY...
STRONG
PRETTY STRONG
PINHEAD
...BUT THE LAST TWO ARE TOP-LEVEL.

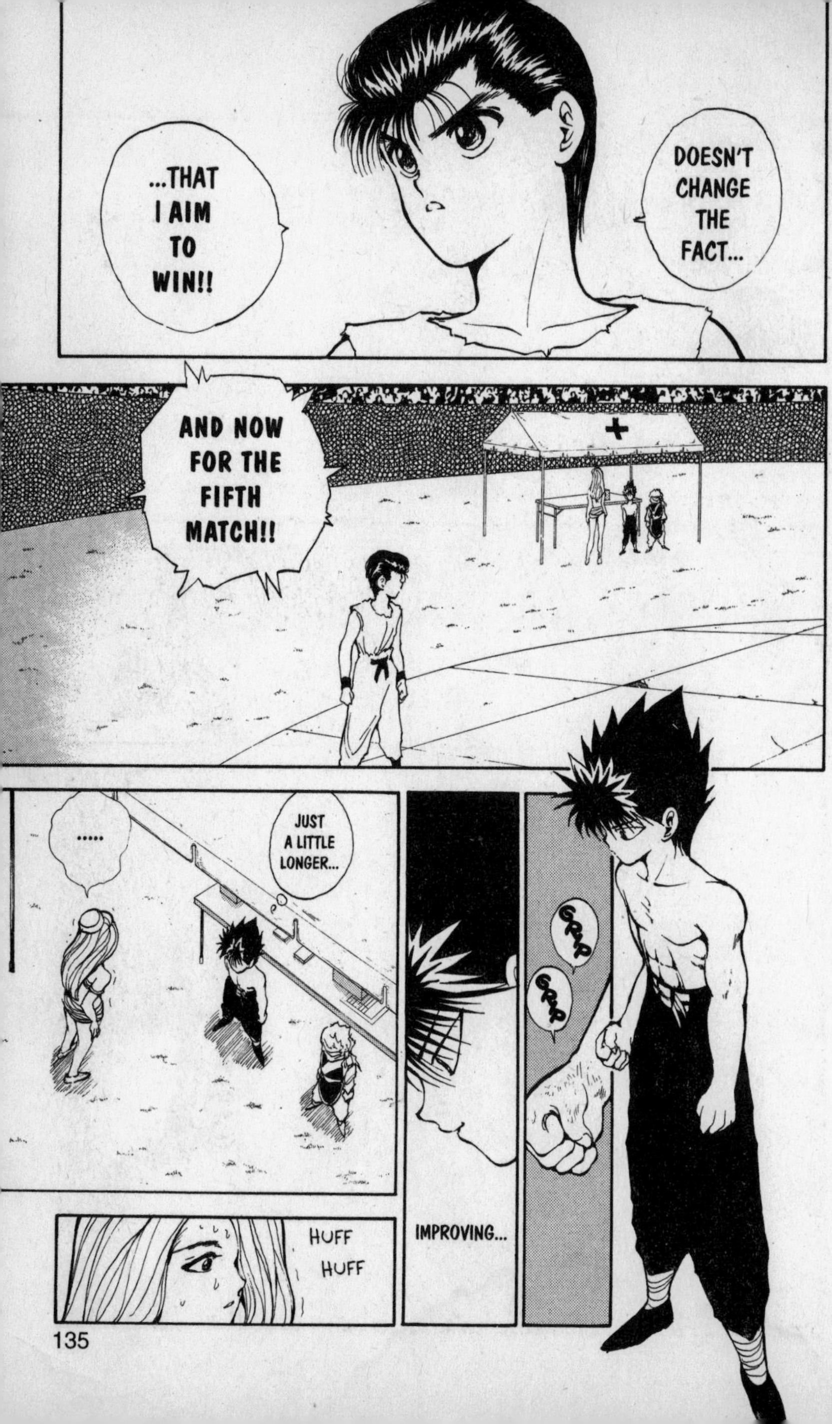
DOESN'T CHANGE THE FACT...
...THAT I AIM TO WIN!!
AND NOW FOR THE FIFTH MATCH!!
GRIP
GRIP
IMPROVING...
JUST A LITTLE LONGER...
.....
HUFF
HUFF

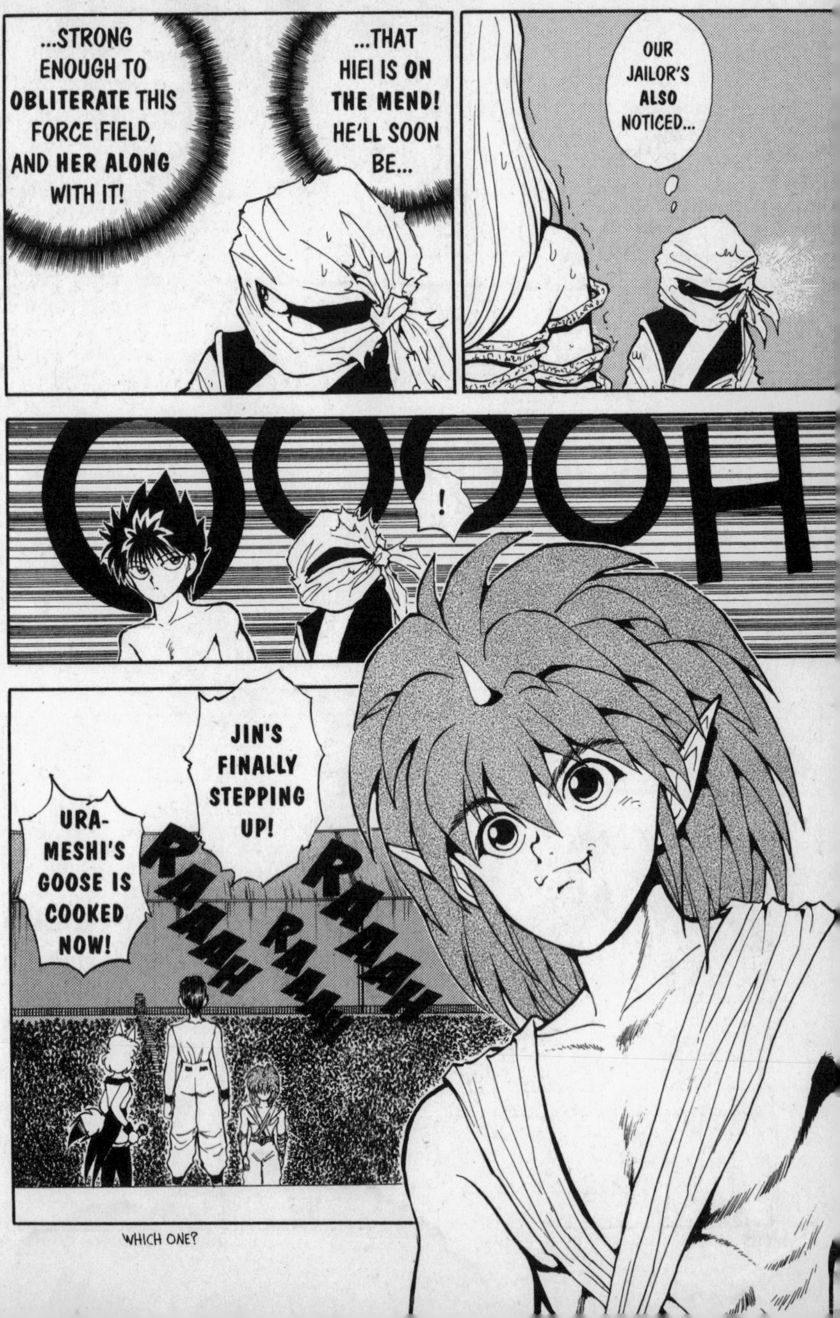
OUR JAILOR'S ALSO NOTICED...
...THAT HIEI IS ON THE MEND! HE'LL SOON BE...
...STRONG ENOUGH TO OBLITERATE THIS FORCE FIELD, AND HER ALONG WITH IT!
OOOOH
!
JIN'S FINALLY STEPPING UP!
URA-MESHI'S GOOSE IS COOKED NOW!
RAAAH
RAAAH
RAAAH

WHICH ONE?

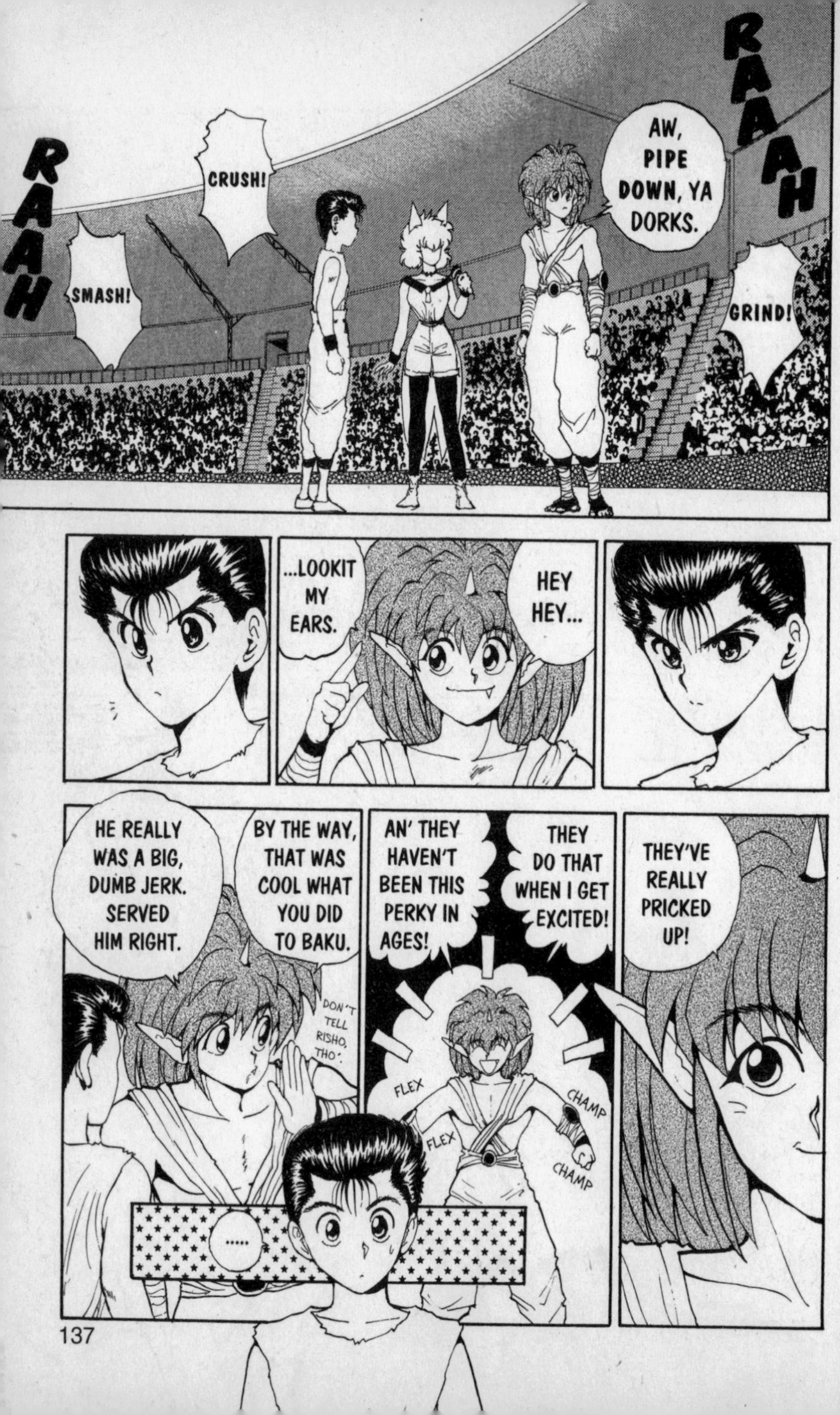
RAAAH
AW, PIPE DOWN, YA DORKS.
GRIND!
CRUSH!
RAAAH
SMASH!
HEY HEY...
...LOOKIT MY EARS.
THEY'VE REALLY PRICKED UP!
THEY DO THAT WHEN I GET EXCITED!
AN' THEY HAVEN'T BEEN THIS PERKY IN AGES!
CHAMP
CHAMP
FLEX
FLEX
BY THE WAY, THAT WAS COOL WHAT YOU DID TO BAKU.
HE REALLY WAS A BIG, DUMB JERK. SERVED HIM RIGHT.
DON'T TELL RISHO, THO'.
......

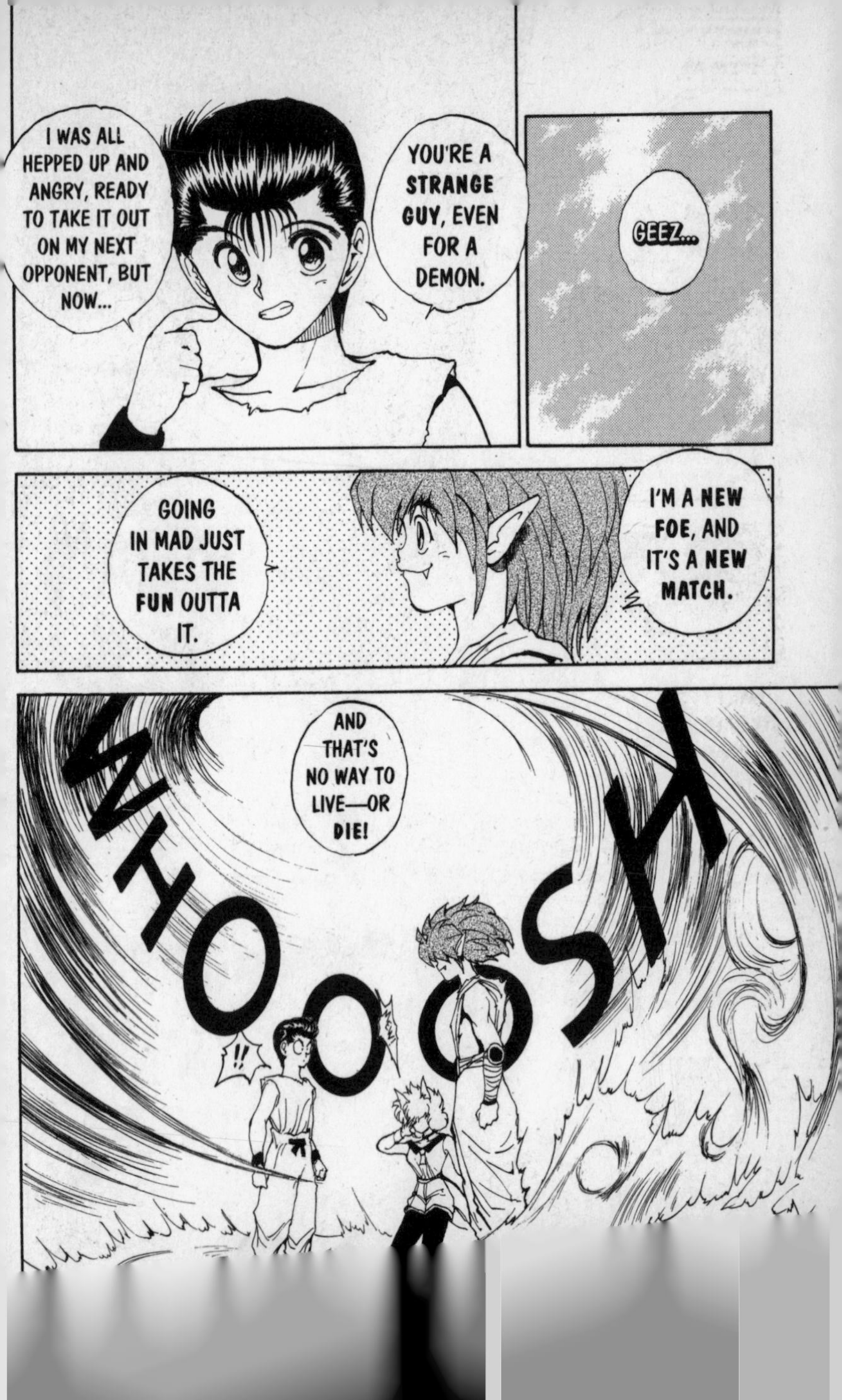
GEEZ...
YOU'RE A STRANGE GUY, EVEN FOR A DEMON.
I WAS ALL HEPPED UP AND ANGRY, READY TO TAKE IT OUT ON MY NEXT OPPONENT, BUT NOW...
I'M A NEW FOE, AND IT'S A NEW MATCH.
GOING IN MAD JUST TAKES THE FUN OUTTA IT.
AND THAT'S NO WAY TO LIVE—OR DIE!
WHOOOSH
!!

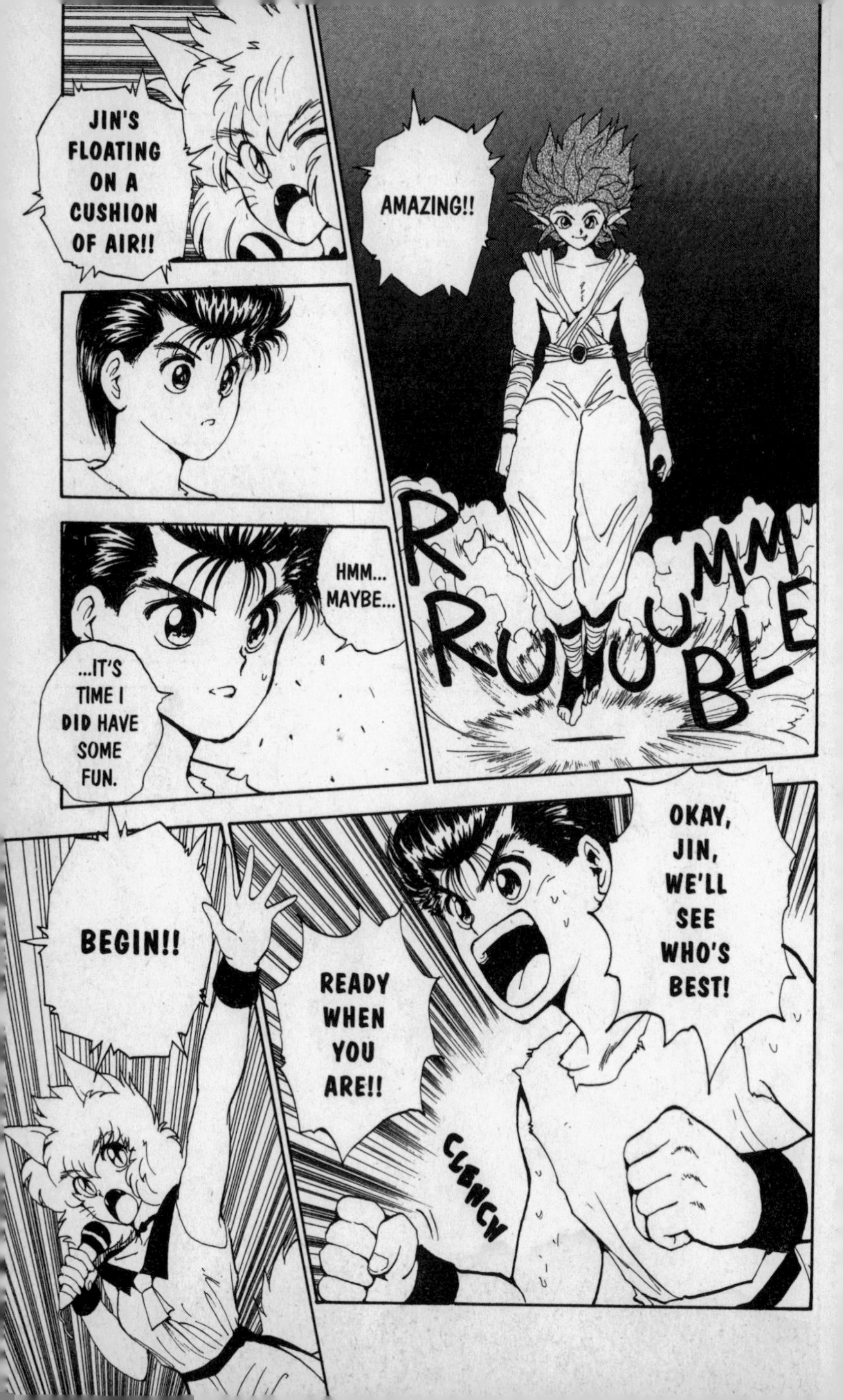
AMAZING!!
RMM
RUUUBLE
JIN'S FLOATING ON A CUSHION OF AIR!!
HMM... MAYBE...
...IT'S TIME I DID HAVE SOME FUN.
OKAY, JIN, WE'LL SEE WHO'S BEST!
READY WHEN YOU ARE!!
CLENCH
BEGIN!!

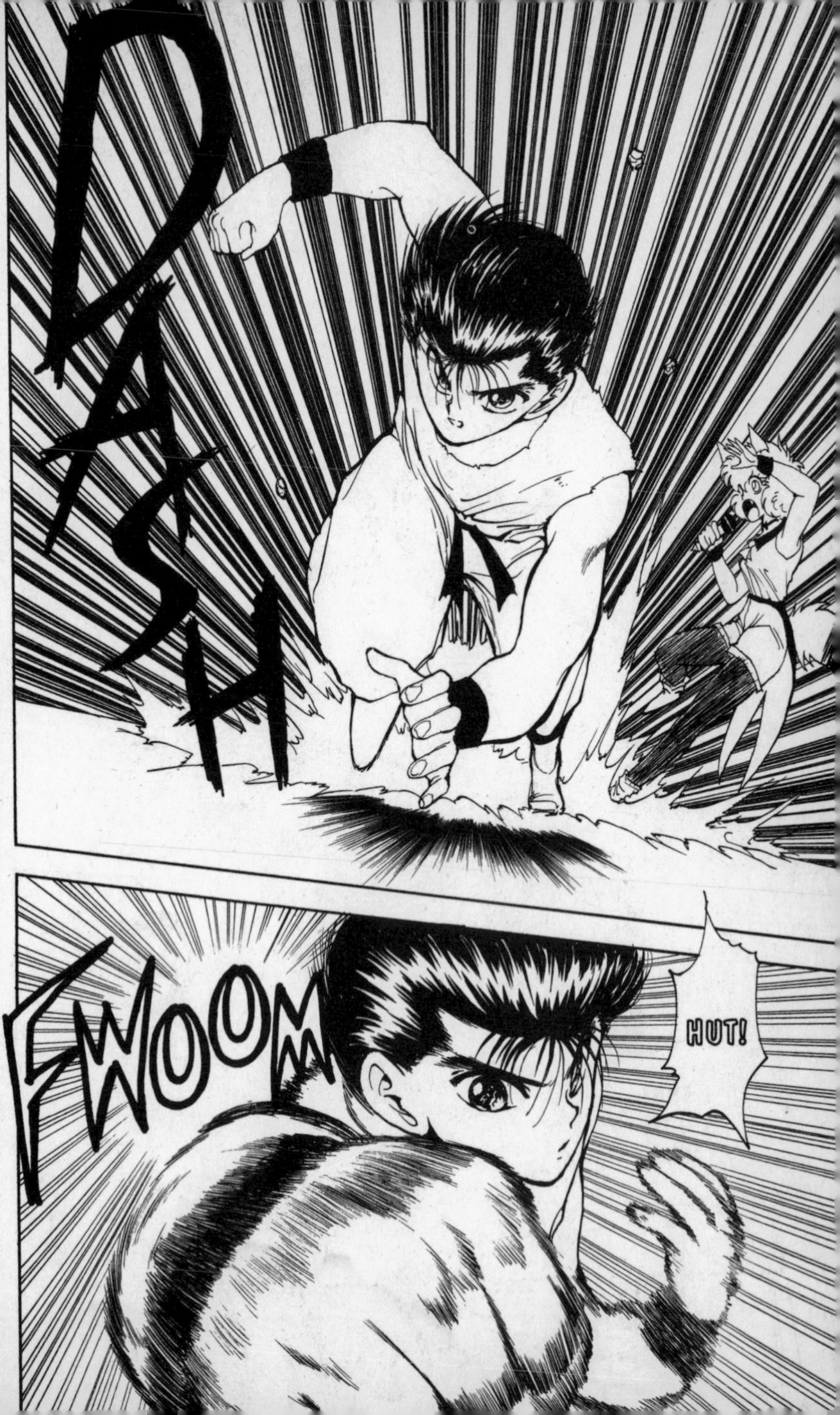
DASH
HUT!
FWOOM

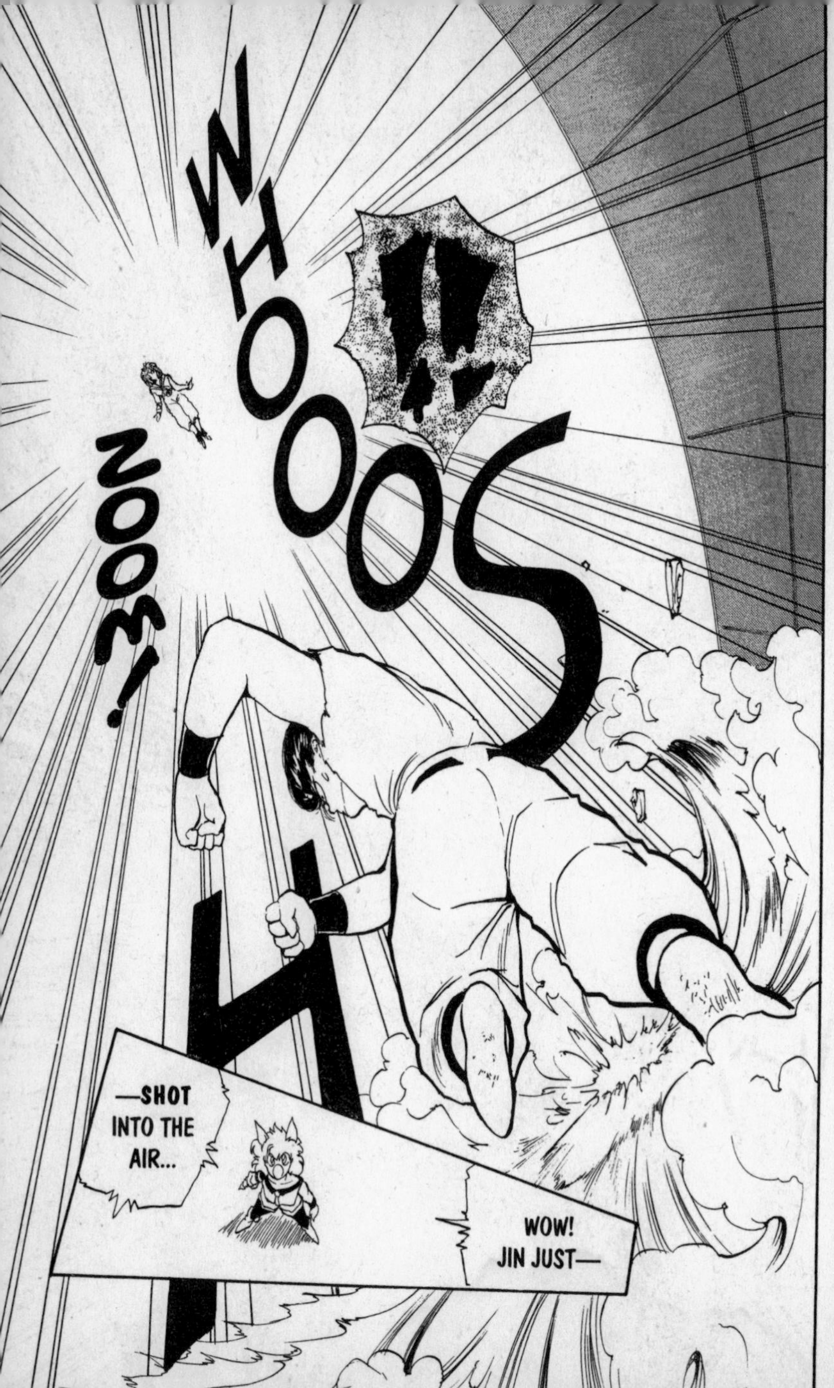
!!
WHOOOSH
ZOOM!
WOW! JIN JUST—
—SHOT INTO THE AIR...

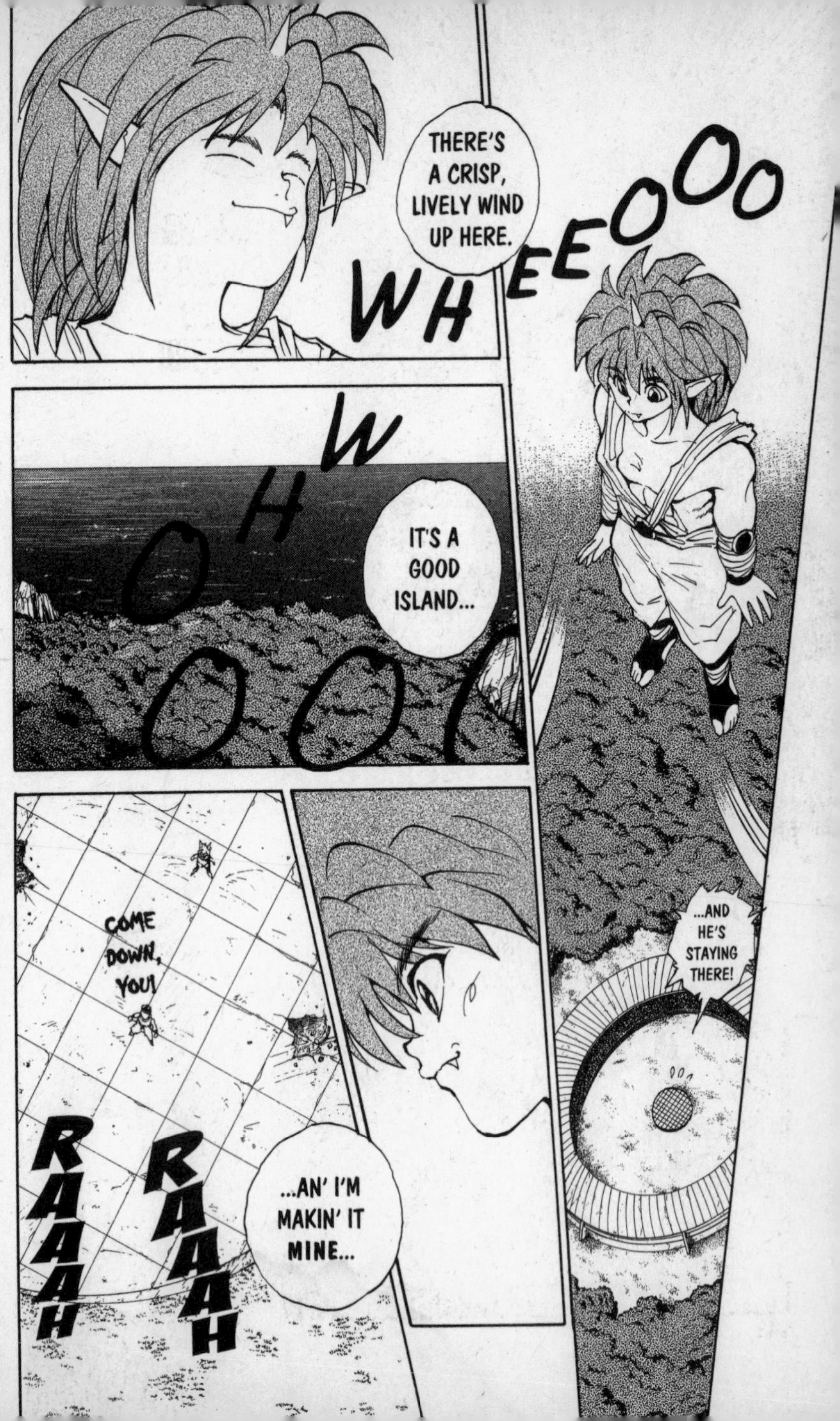
WHEEOOOO
...AND HE'S STAYING THERE!
THERE'S A CRISP, LIVELY WIND UP HERE.
WHOOOO
IT'S A GOOD ISLAND...
...AN' I'M MAKIN' IT MINE...
COME DOWN, YOU!
RAAAH
RAAAH

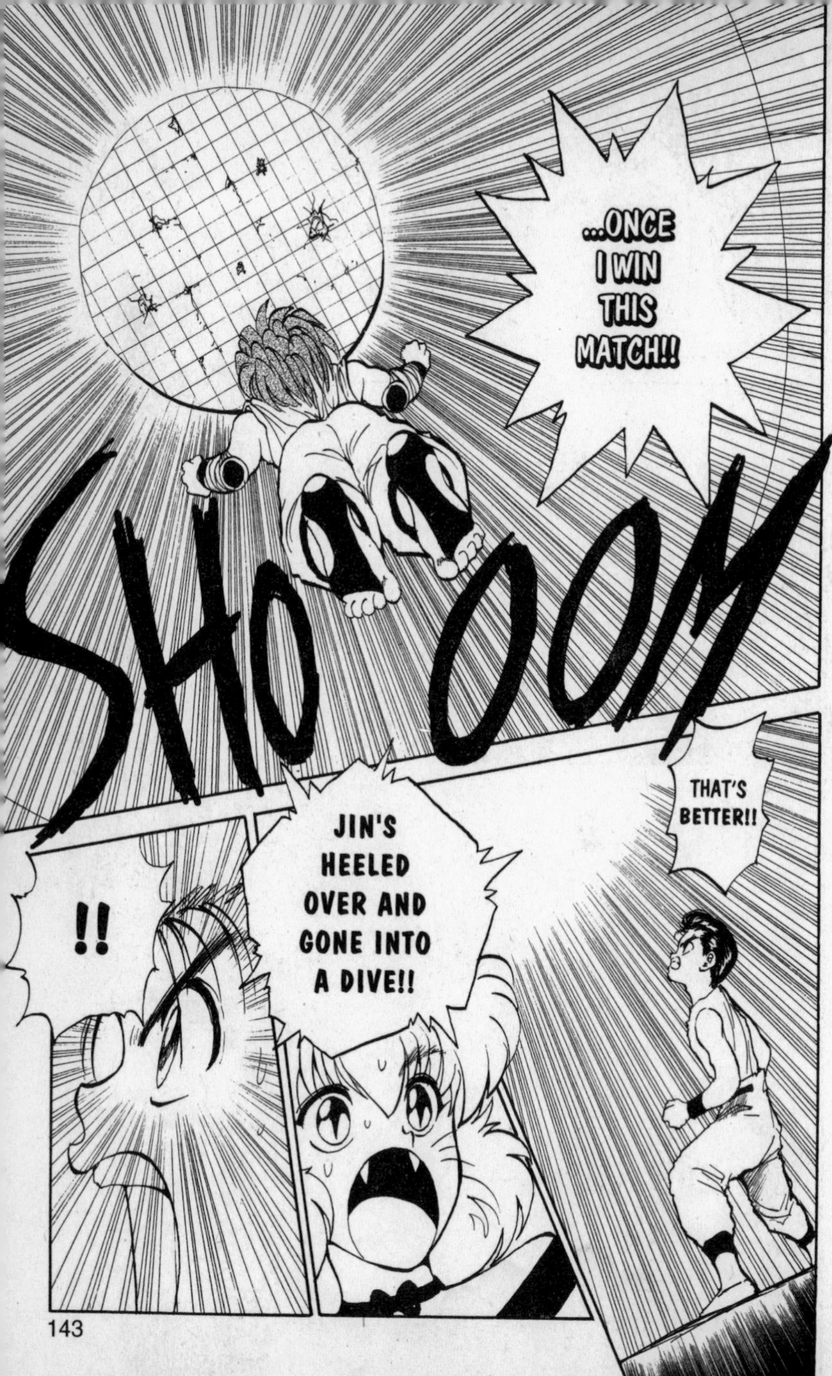
...ONCE I WIN THIS MATCH!!
SHOOOM
THAT'S BETTER!!
JIN'S HEELED OVER AND GONE INTO A DIVE!!
!!

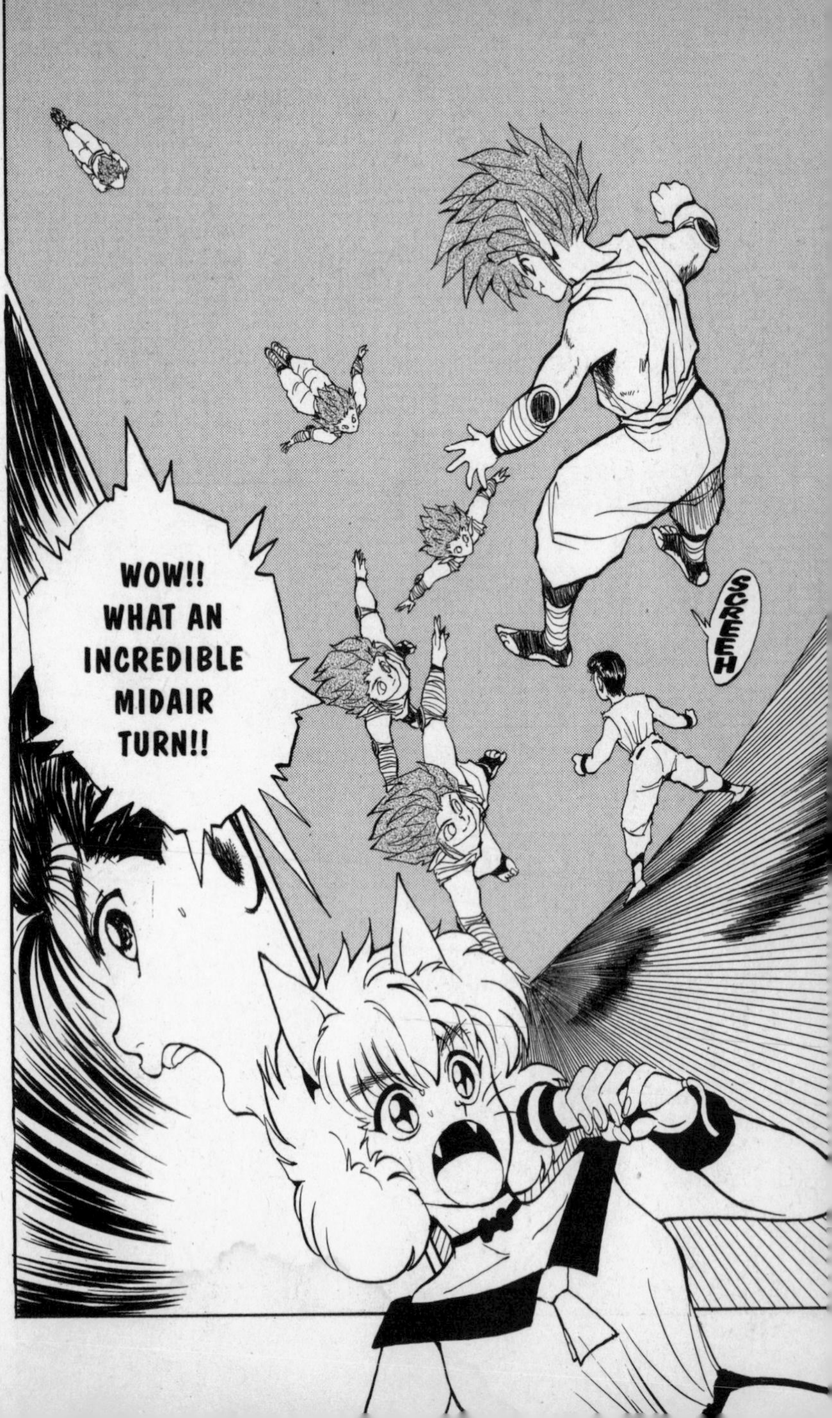
WOW!! WHAT AN INCREDIBLE MIDAIR TURN!!
SCREEEH

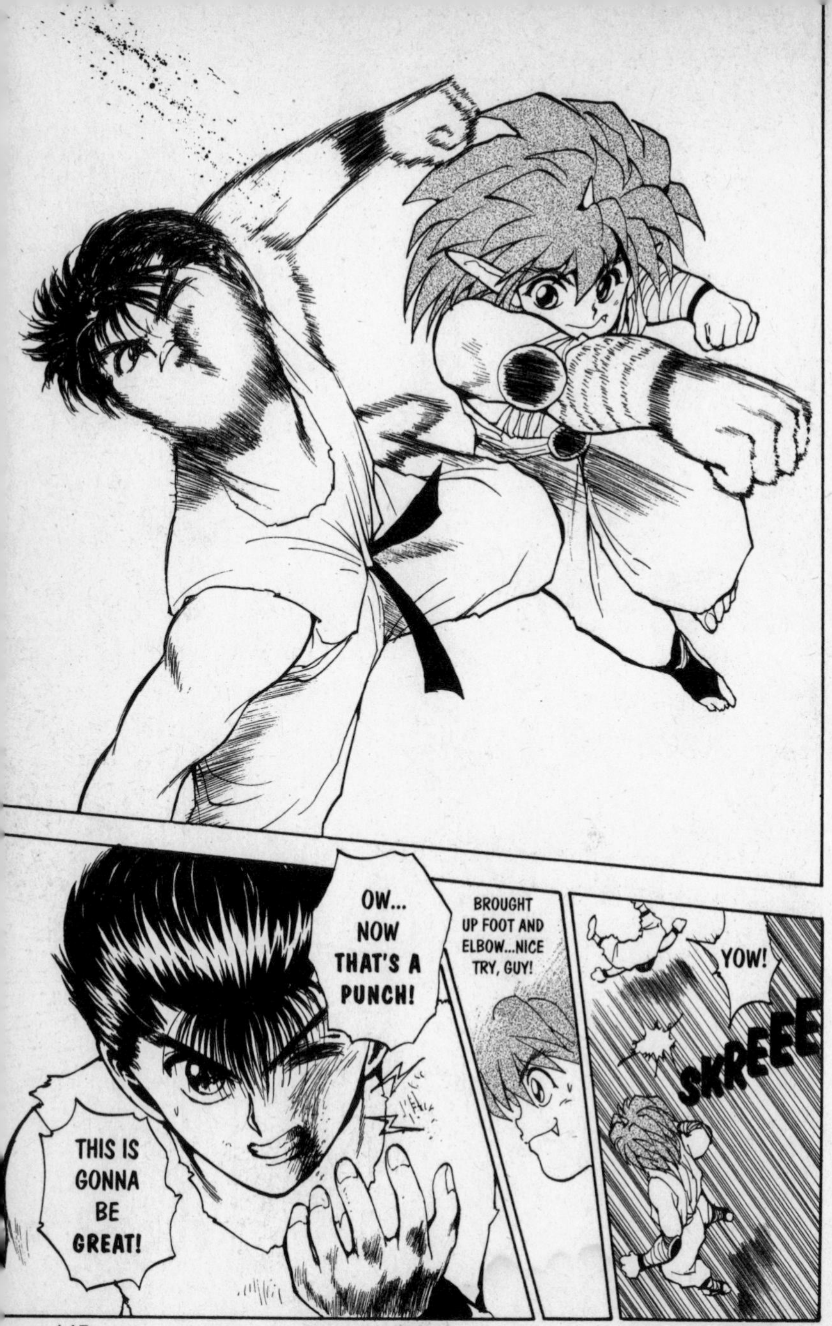
YOW!
SKREEE
BROUGHT UP FOOT AND ELBOW...NICE TRY, GUY!
OW... NOW THAT'S A PUNCH!
THIS IS GONNA BE GREAT!

1983

I WAS IN LOVE.
I COULD HIT THE HAY
WHENEVER I FELT LIKE IT.
I WANTED TO BE DOING
THE SAME THING
10 YEARS LATER.

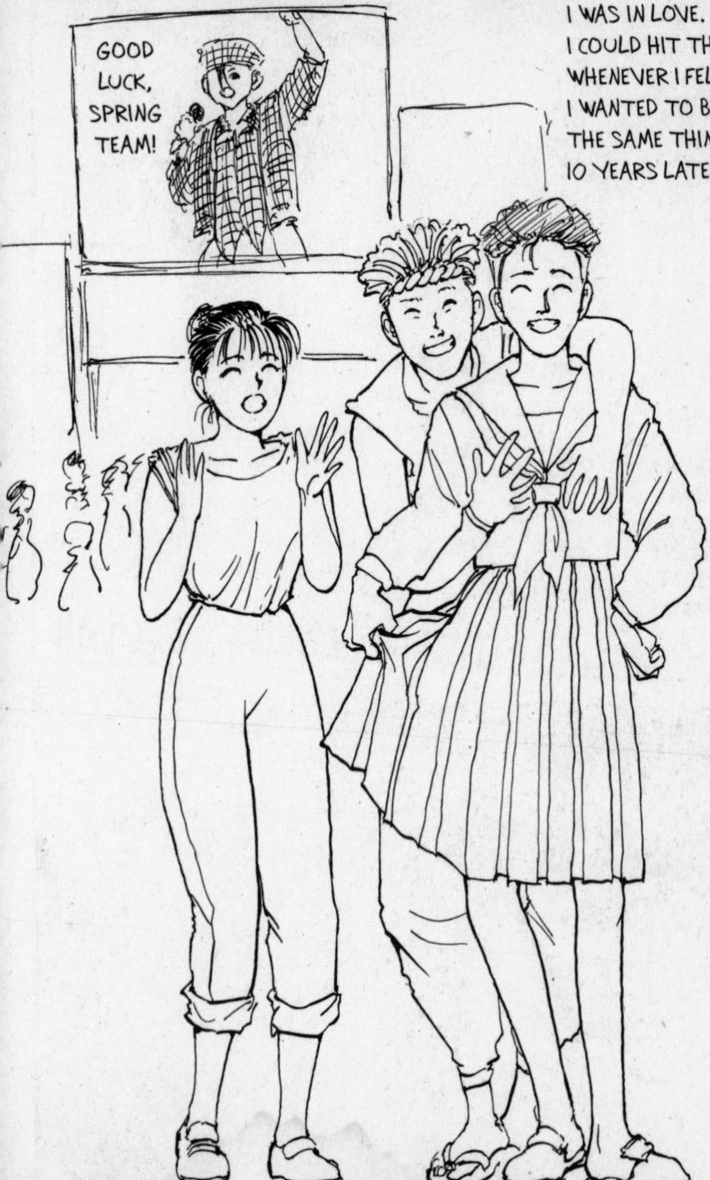
GOOD LUCK, SPRING TEAM!

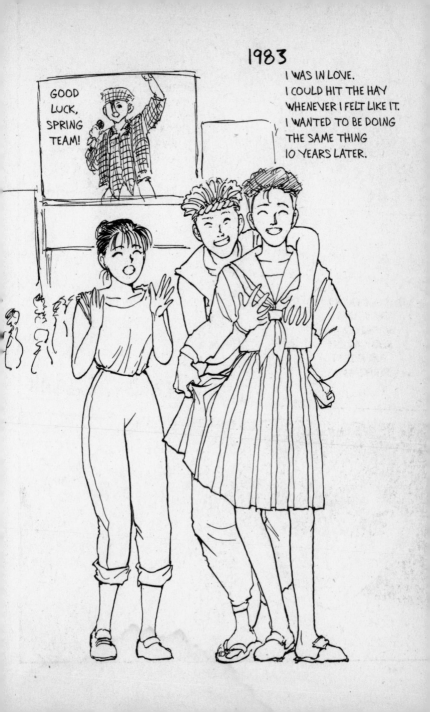

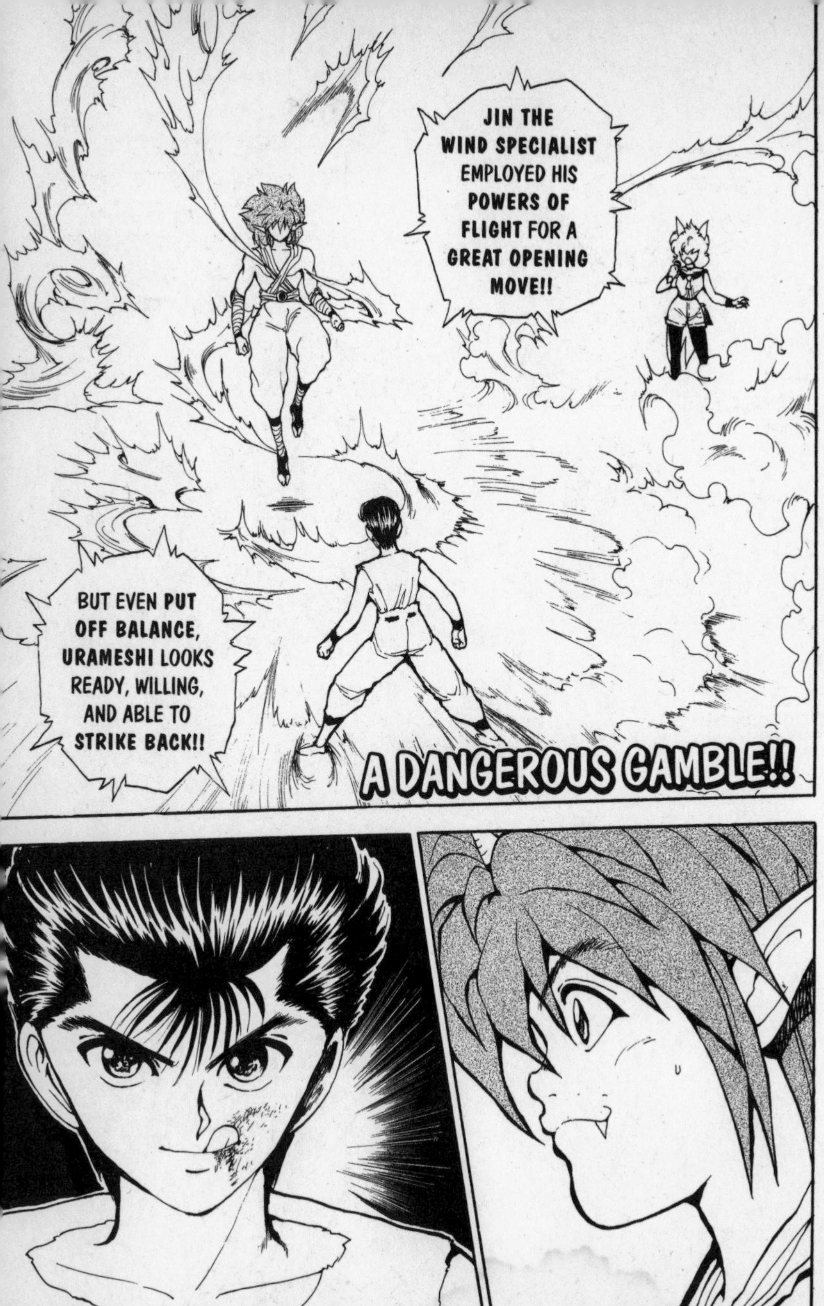
JIN THE WIND SPECIALIST EMPLOYED HIS POWERS OF FLIGHT FOR A GREAT OPENING MOVE!!
BUT EVEN PUT OFF BALANCE, URAMESHI LOOKS READY, WILLING, AND ABLE TO STRIKE BACK!!
A DANGEROUS GAMBLE!!

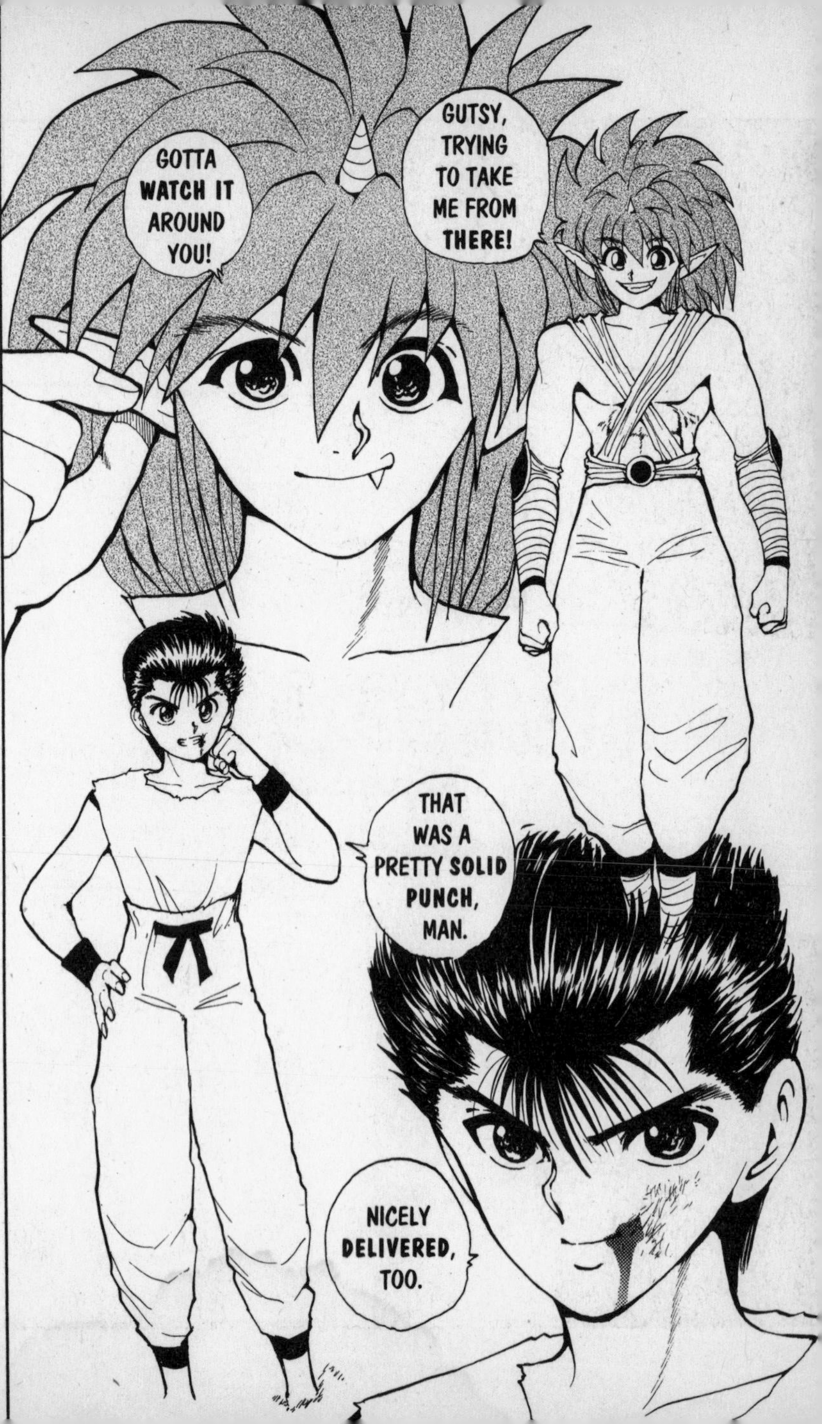
GUTSY, TRYING TO TAKE ME FROM THERE!
GOTTA WATCH IT AROUND YOU!
THAT WAS A PRETTY SOLID PUNCH, MAN.
NICELY DELIVERED, TOO.

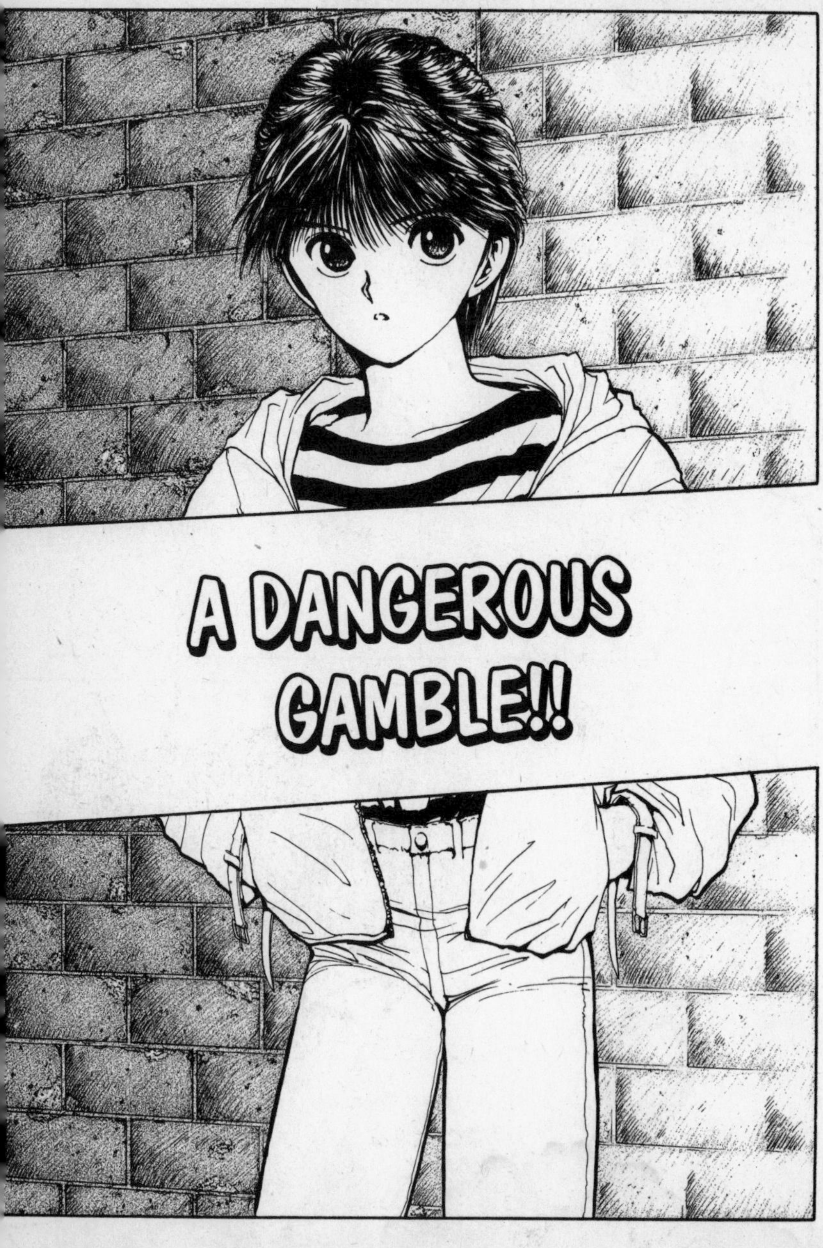
A DANGEROUS GAMBLE!!

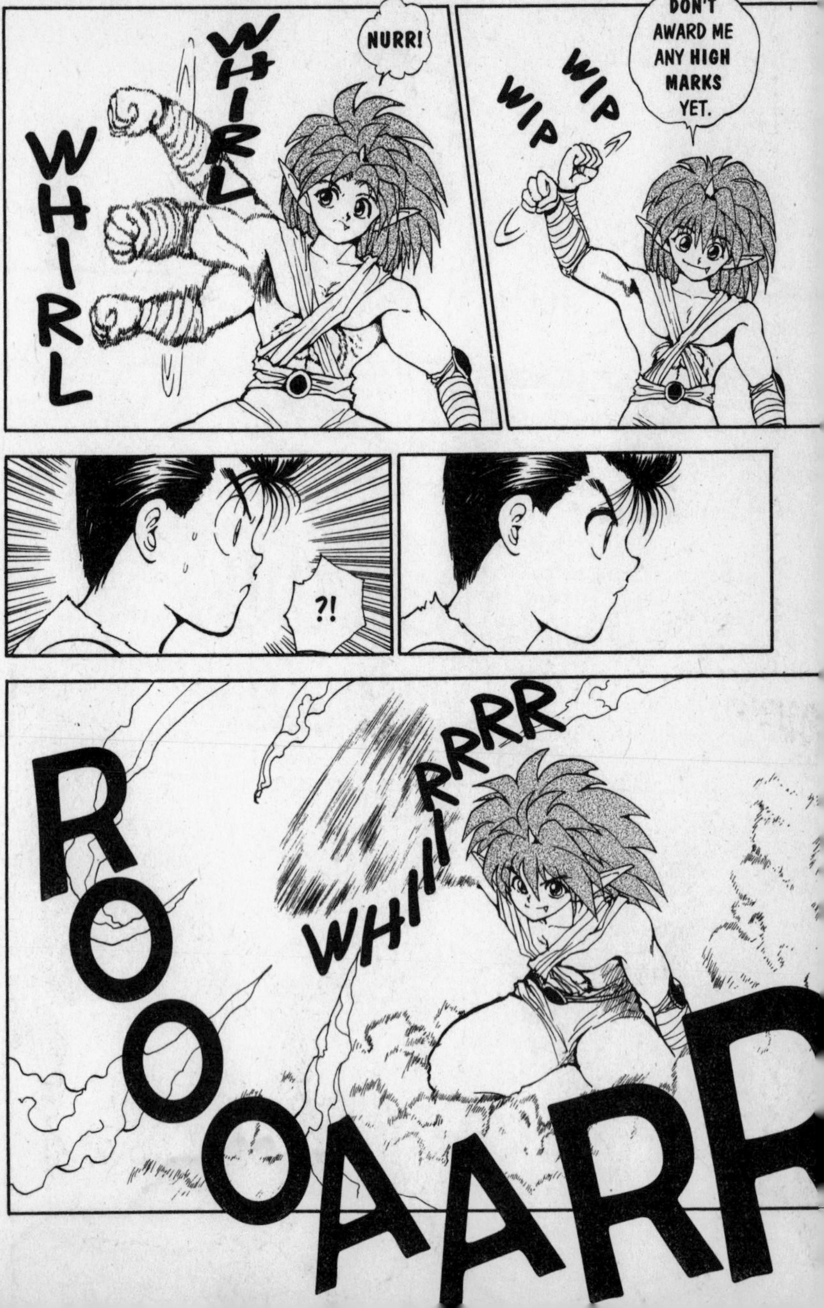
DON'T AWARD ME ANY HIGH MARKS YET.
WIP WIP
NURR!
WHIRL
WHIRL
?!
WHIIIRRRRR
ROOOAARR

READ THIS WAY

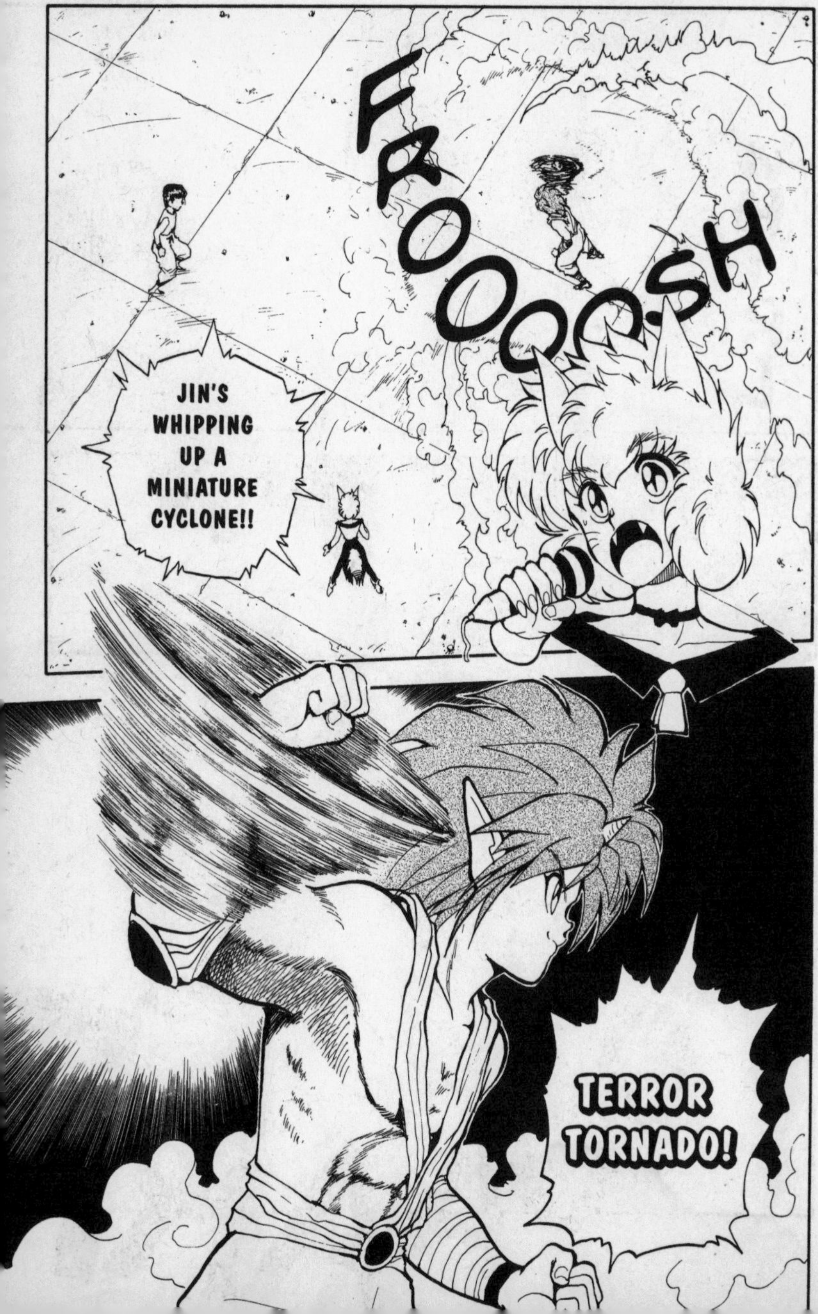
FROOOOSH
JIN'S WHIPPING UP A MINIATURE CYCLONE!!
TERROR TORNADO!

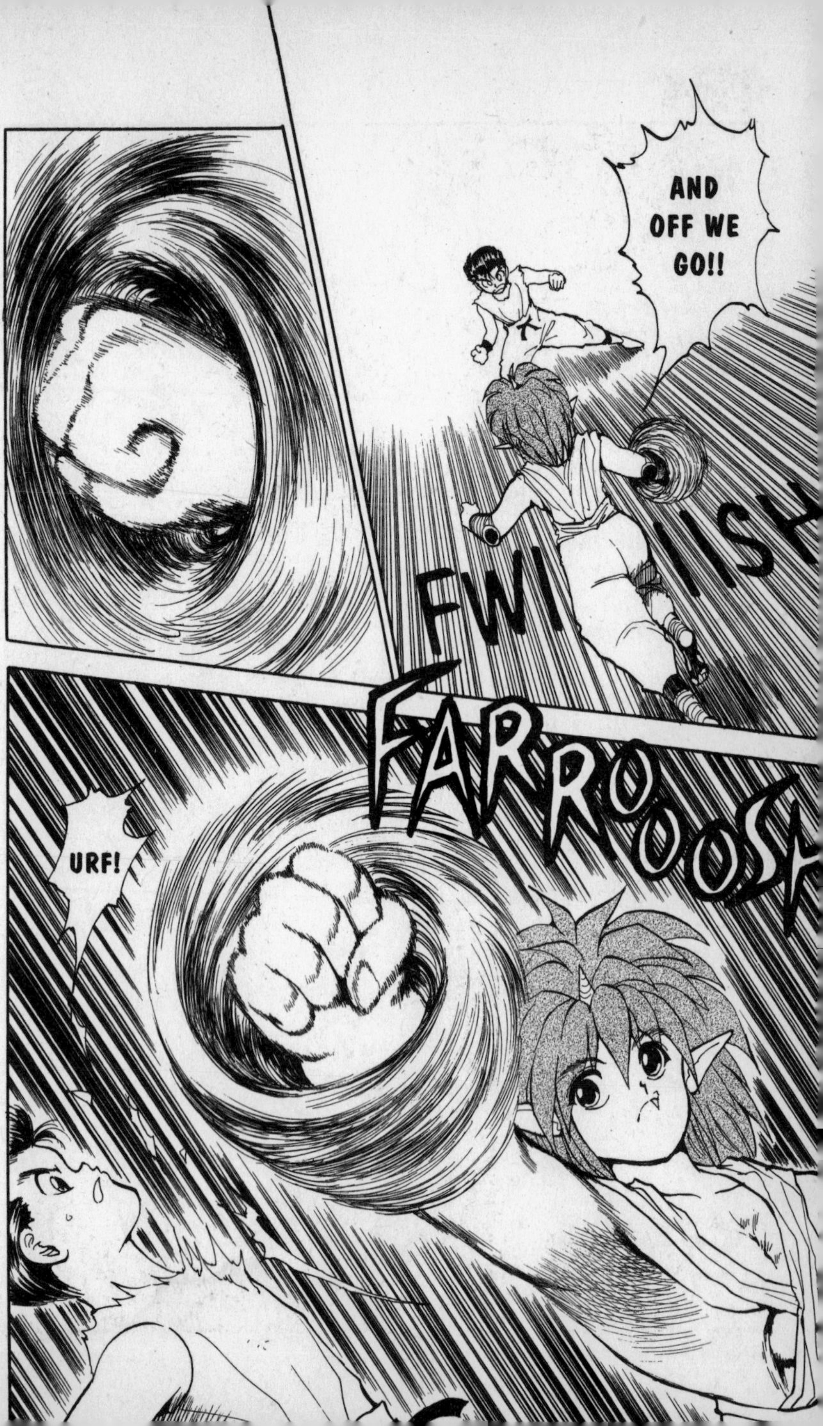
AND OFF WE GO!!
FWI ISH
FARROOOSH
URF!

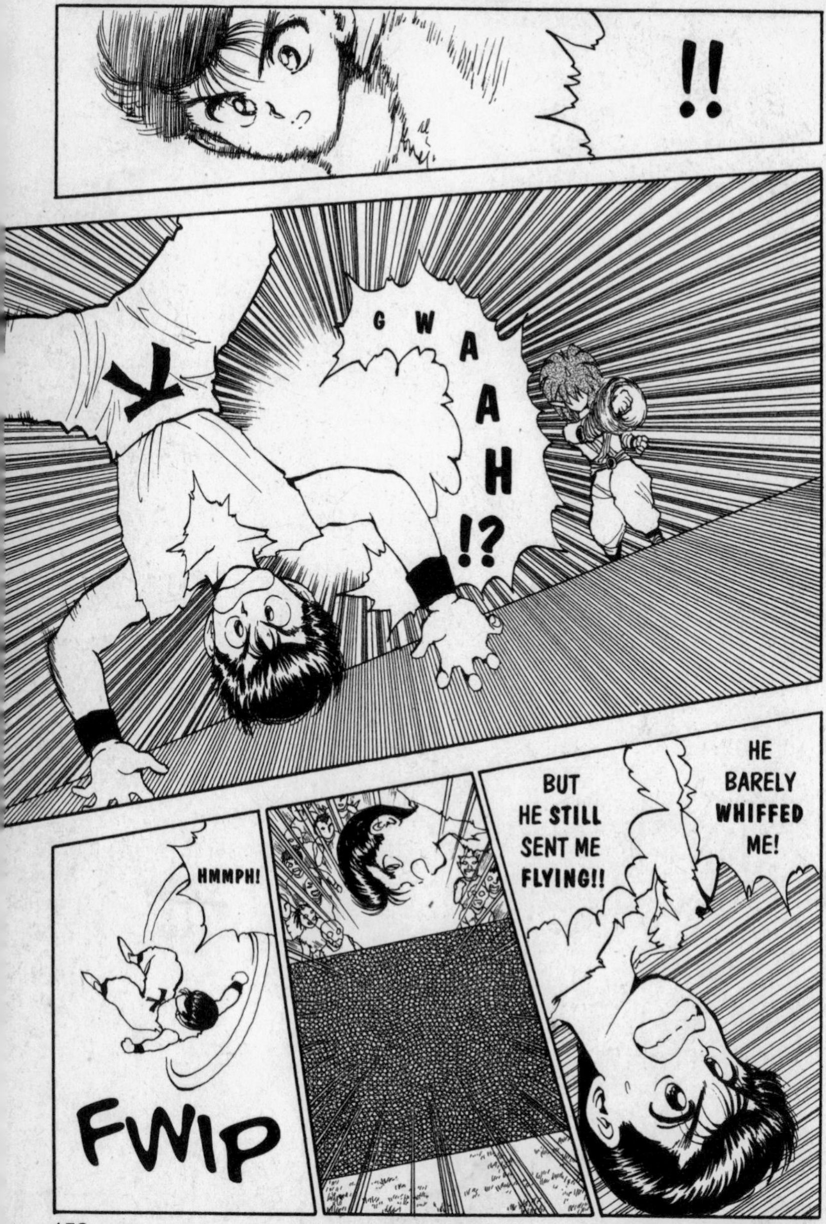
!!
GWAAH!?
HE BARELY WHIFFED ME!
BUT HE STILL SENT ME FLYING!!
HMMPH!
FWIP

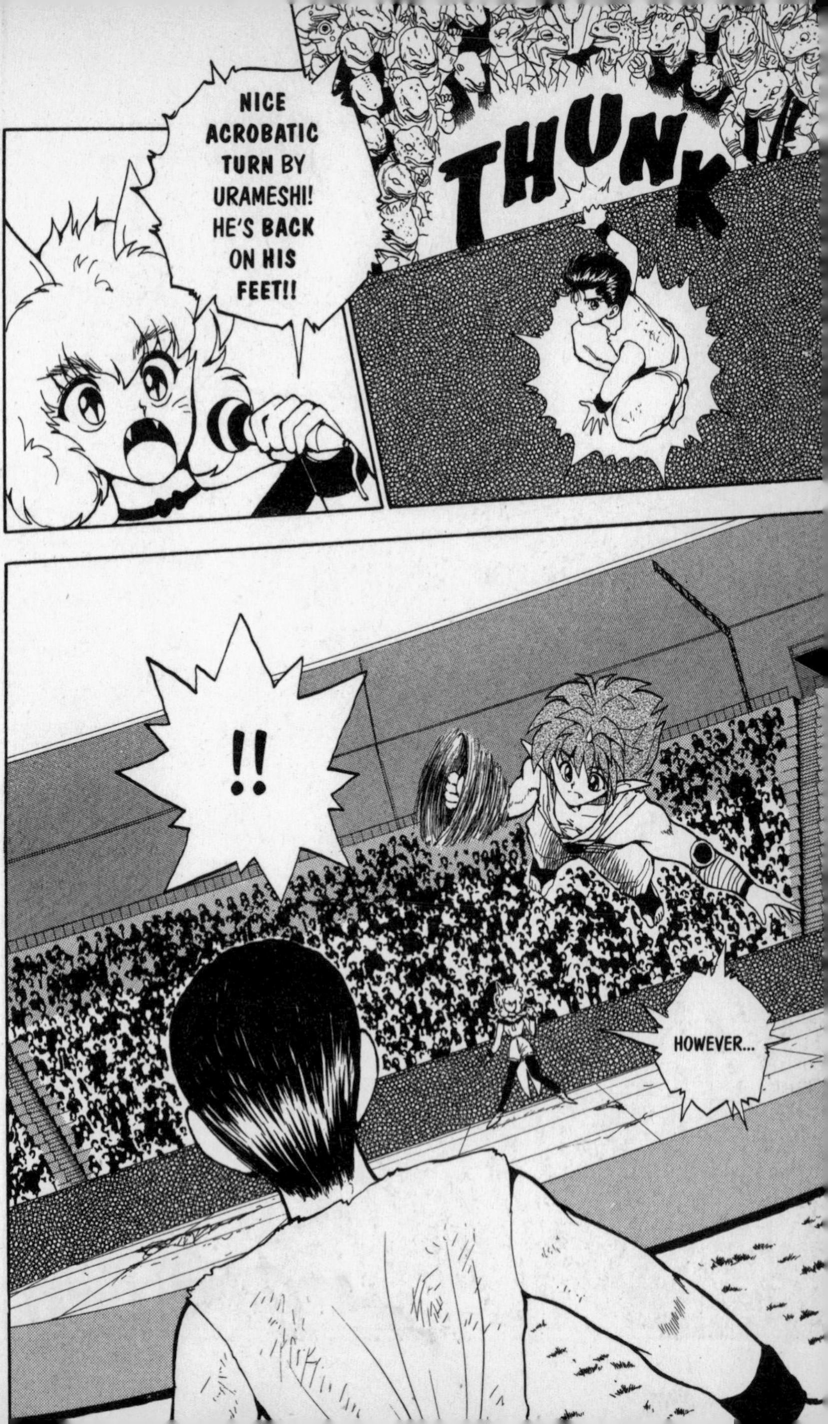
THUNK
NICE ACROBATIC TURN BY URAMESHI! HE'S BACK ON HIS FEET!!
!!
HOWEVER...

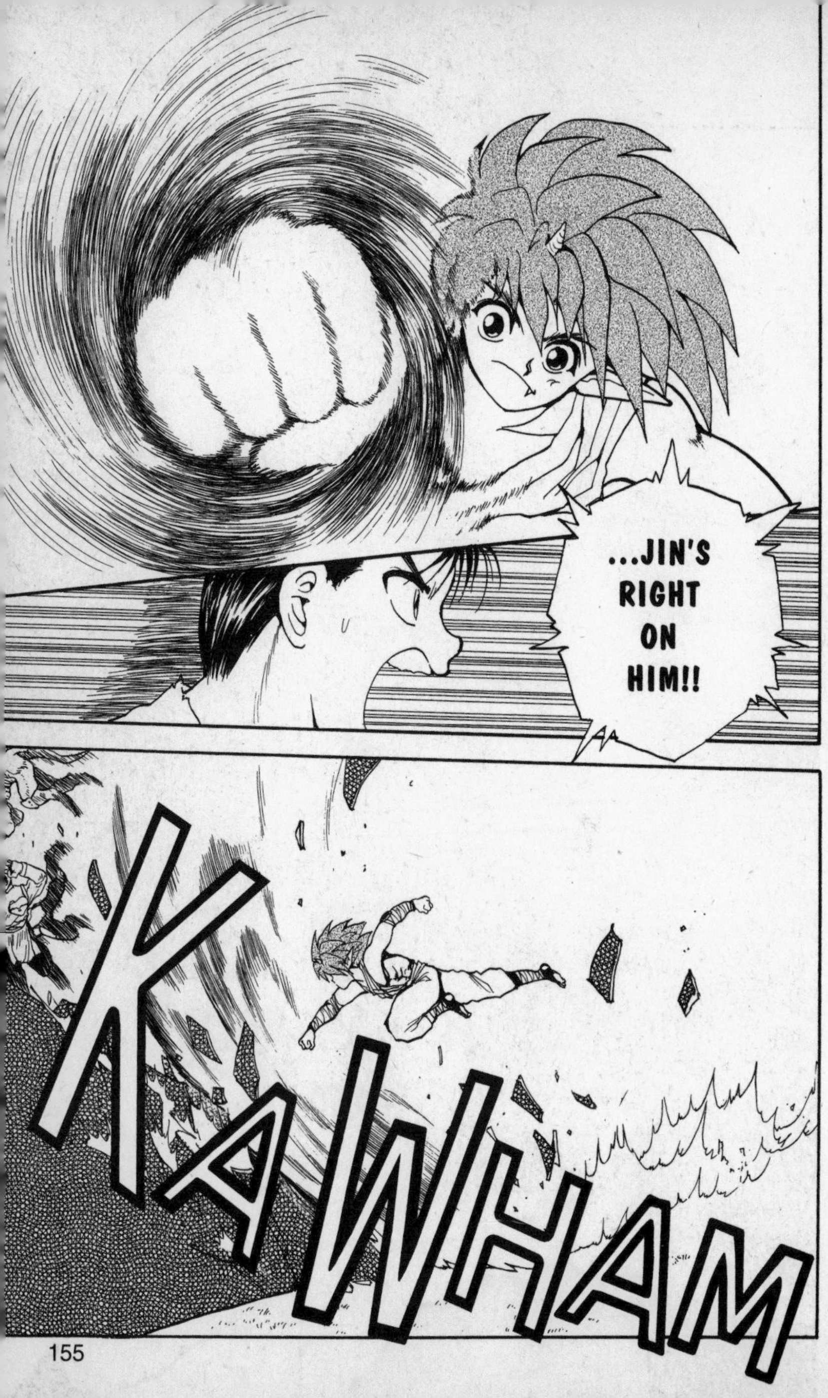
...JIN'S RIGHT ON HIM!!
KAWHAM

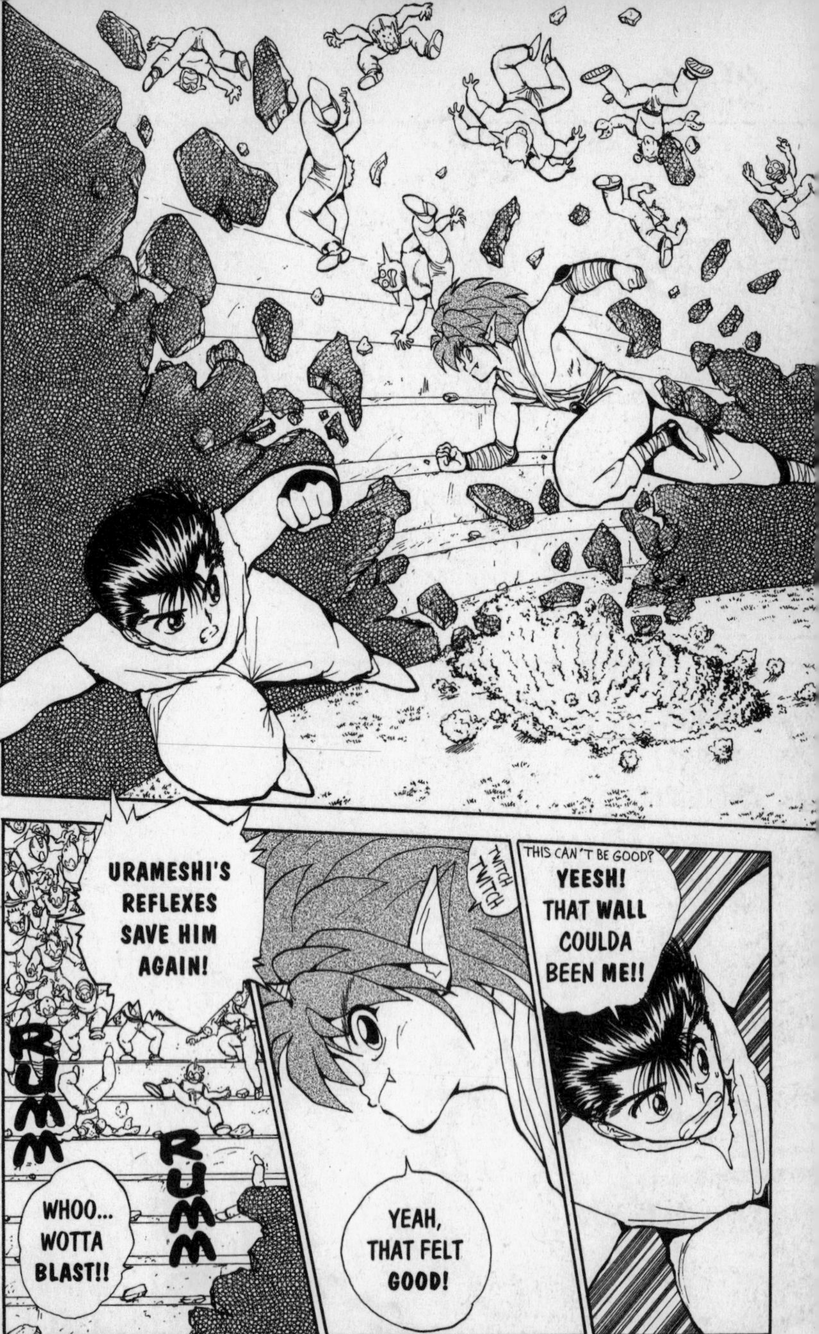
THIS CAN'T BE GOOD?
YEESH! THAT WALL COULDA BEEN ME!!
TWITCH TWITCH
YEAH, THAT FELT GOOD!
URAMESHI'S REFLEXES SAVE HIM AGAIN!
RUMM
RUMM
WHOO... WOTTA BLAST!!

READ THIS WAY

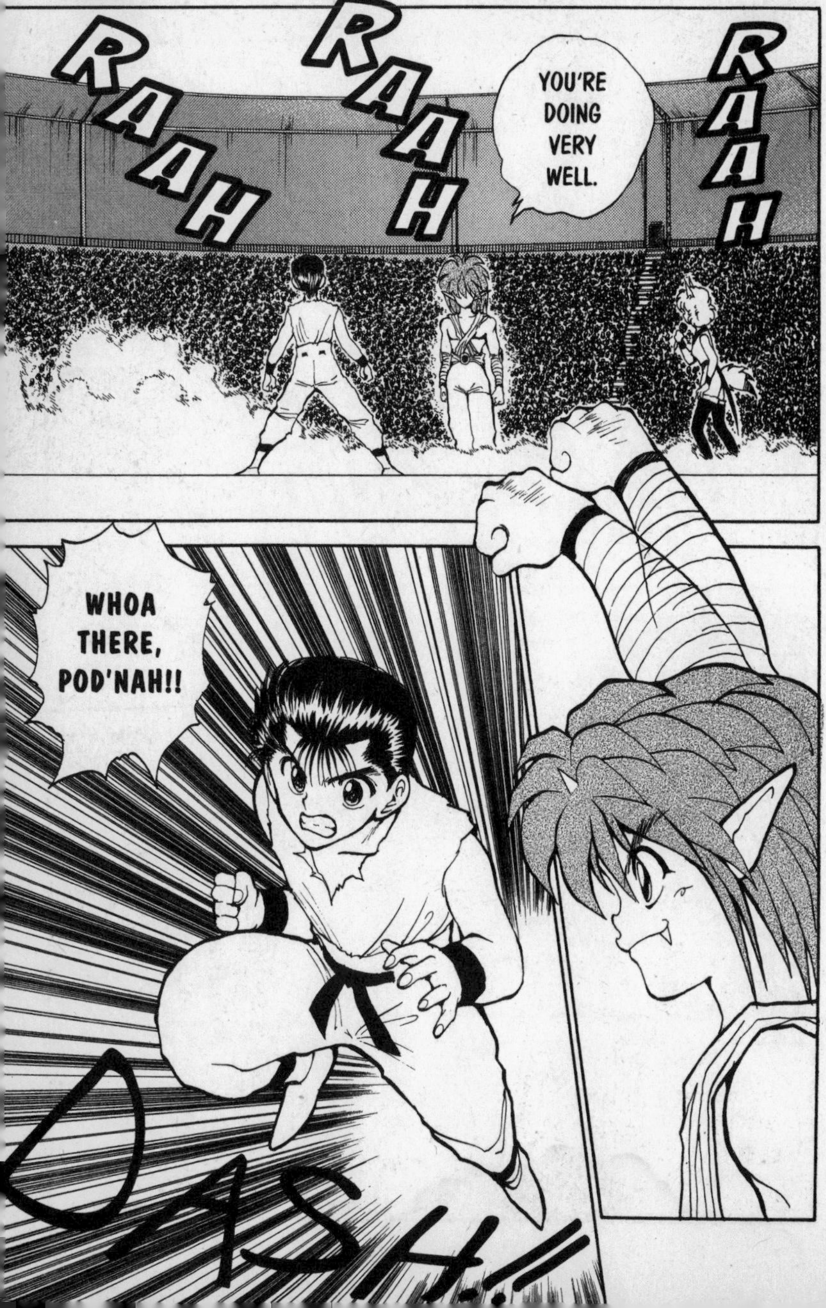
RAAAH
YOU'RE DOING VERY WELL.
RAAAH
RAAAH
WHOA THERE, POD'NAH!!
DASH!!

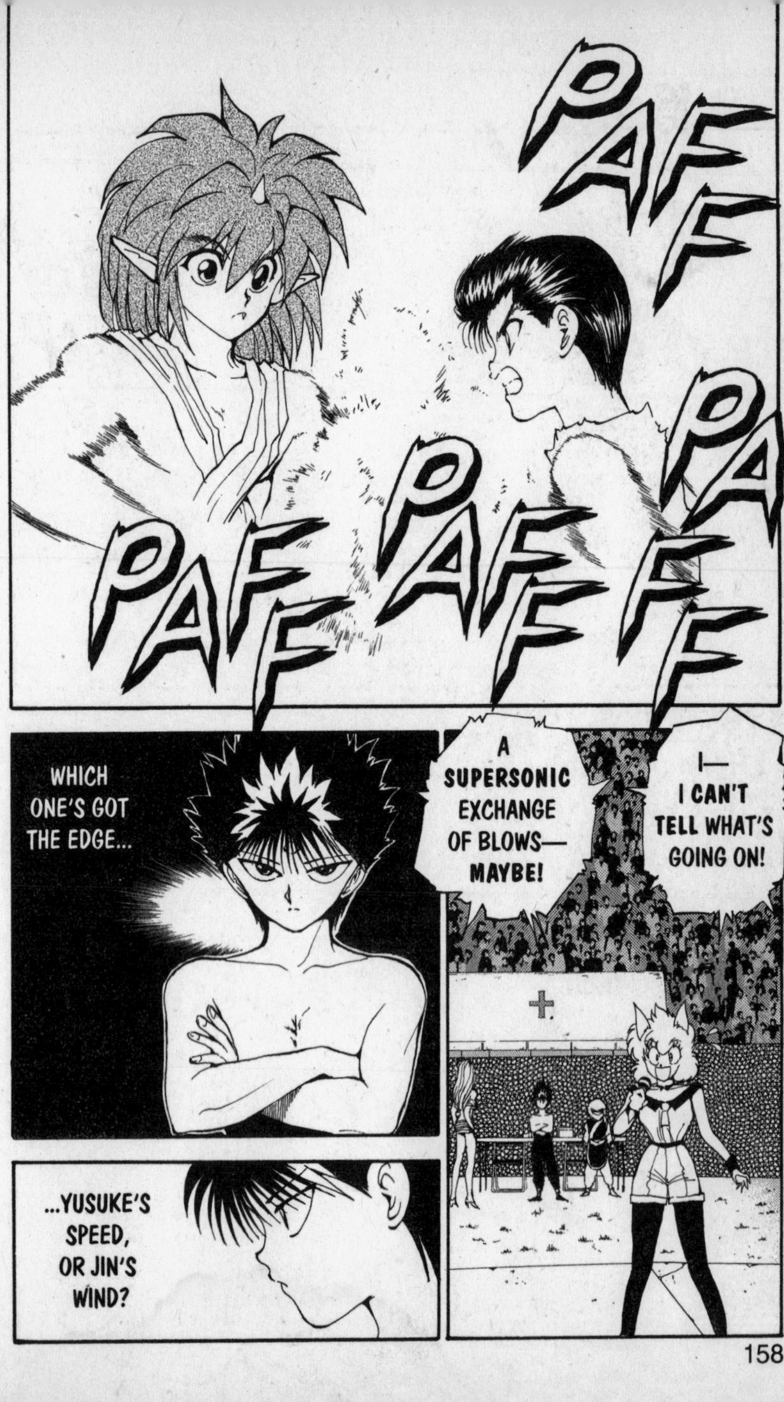
PAFF
PAFFF
PAFFF
PAFF
I— I CAN'T TELL WHAT'S GOING ON!
A SUPERSONIC EXCHANGE OF BLOWS— MAYBE!
WHICH ONE'S GOT THE EDGE...
...YUSUKE'S SPEED, OR JIN'S WIND?

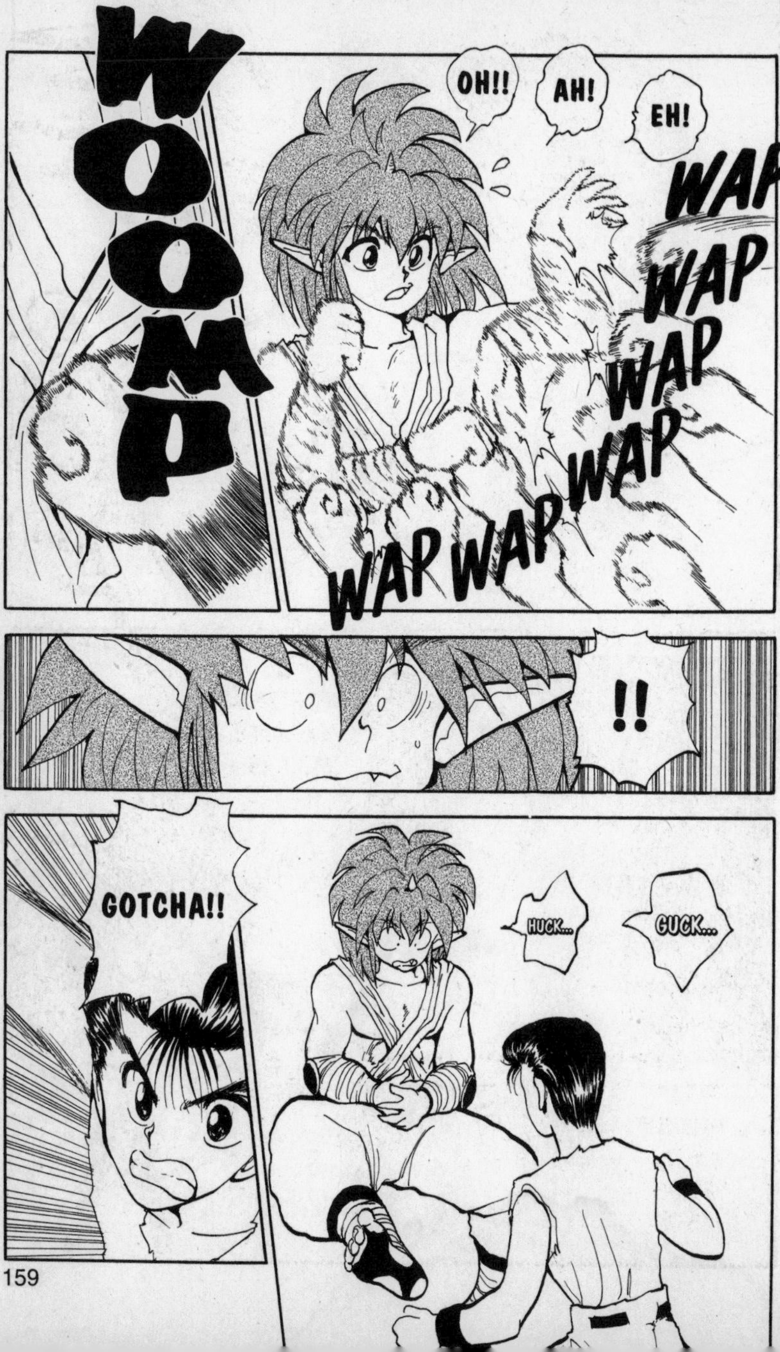
EH!
AH!
OH!!
WAP WAP WAP WAP WAP WAP
WOMP
!!
GUCK...
HUCK...
GOTCHA!!

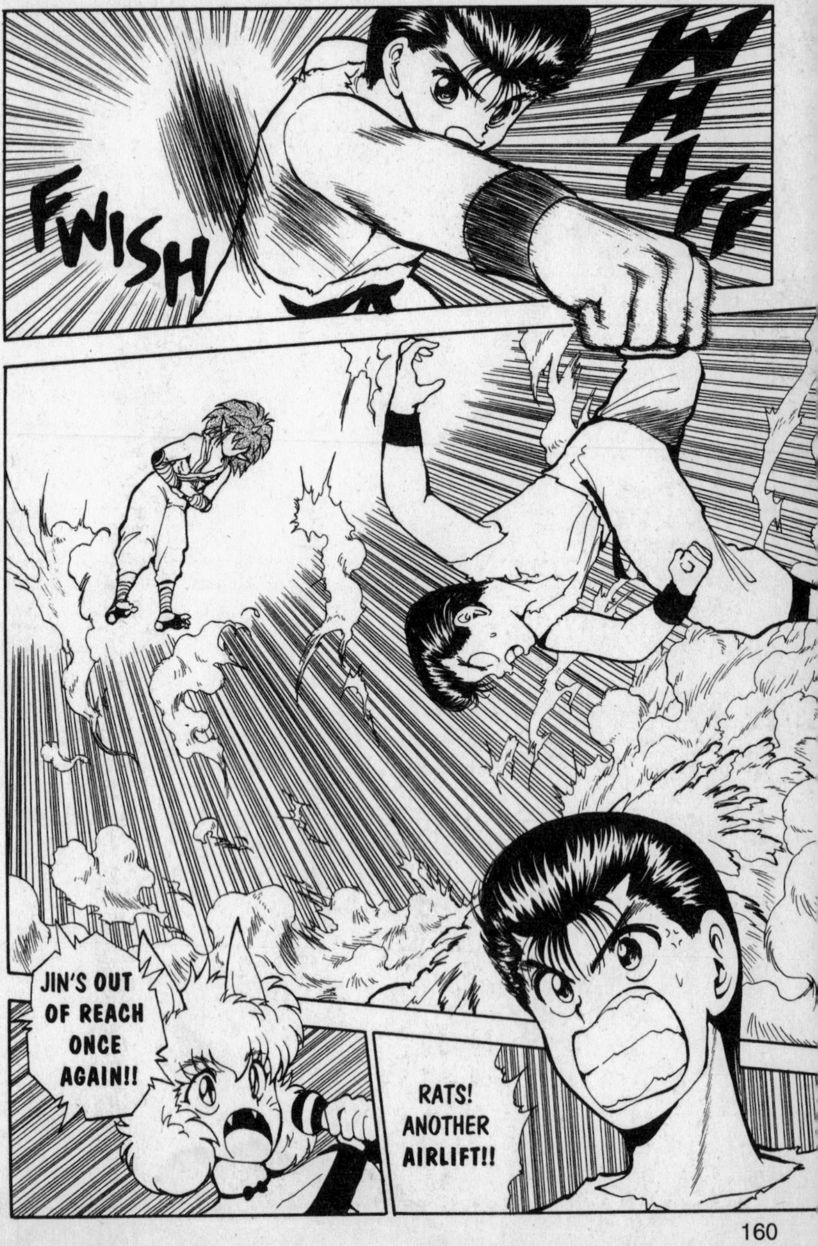
WHUFF
FWISH
RATS! ANOTHER AIRLIFT!!
JIN'S OUT OF REACH ONCE AGAIN!!

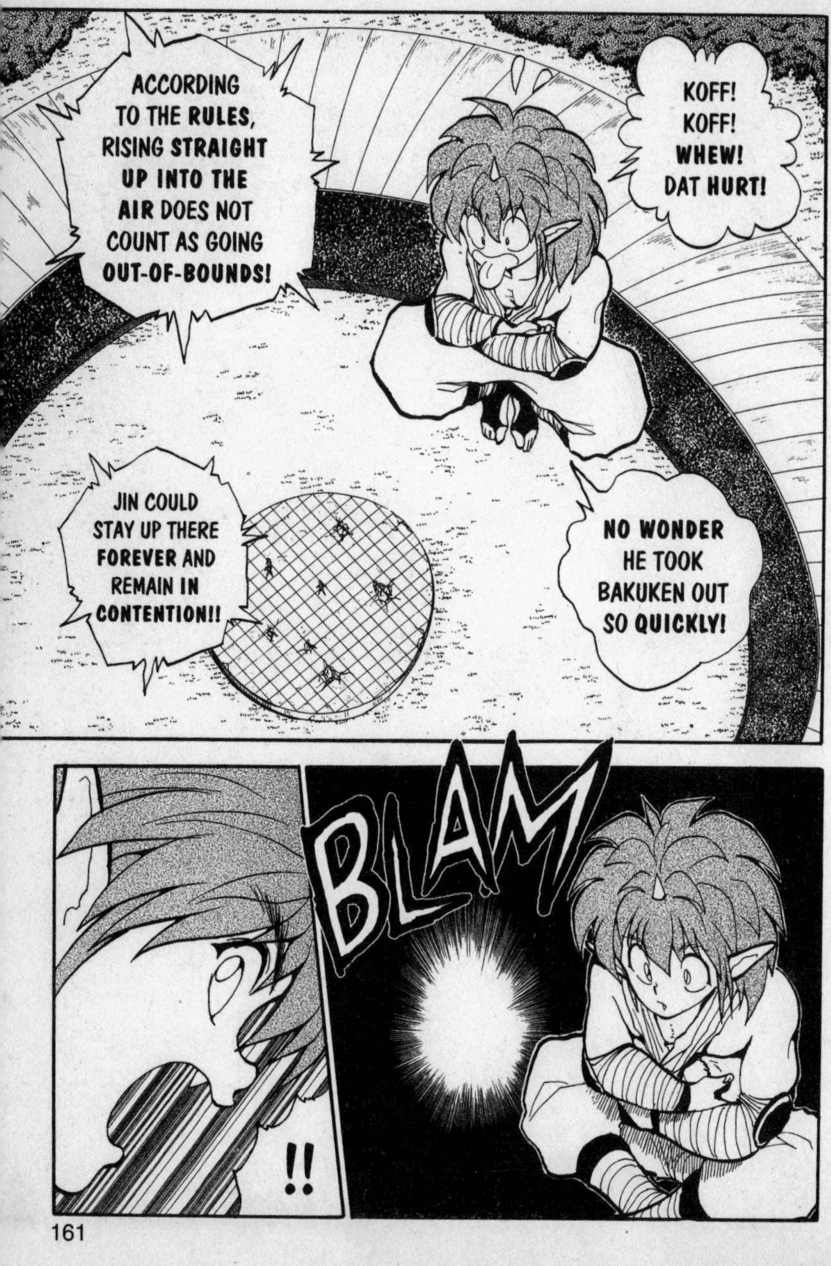
KOFF! KOFF! WHEW! DAT HURT!
ACCORDING TO THE RULES, RISING STRAIGHT UP INTO THE AIR DOES NOT COUNT AS GOING OUT-OF-BOUNDS!
JIN COULD STAY UP THERE FOREVER AND REMAIN IN CONTENTION!!
NO WONDER HE TOOK BAKUKEN OUT SO QUICKLY!
BLAM
!!

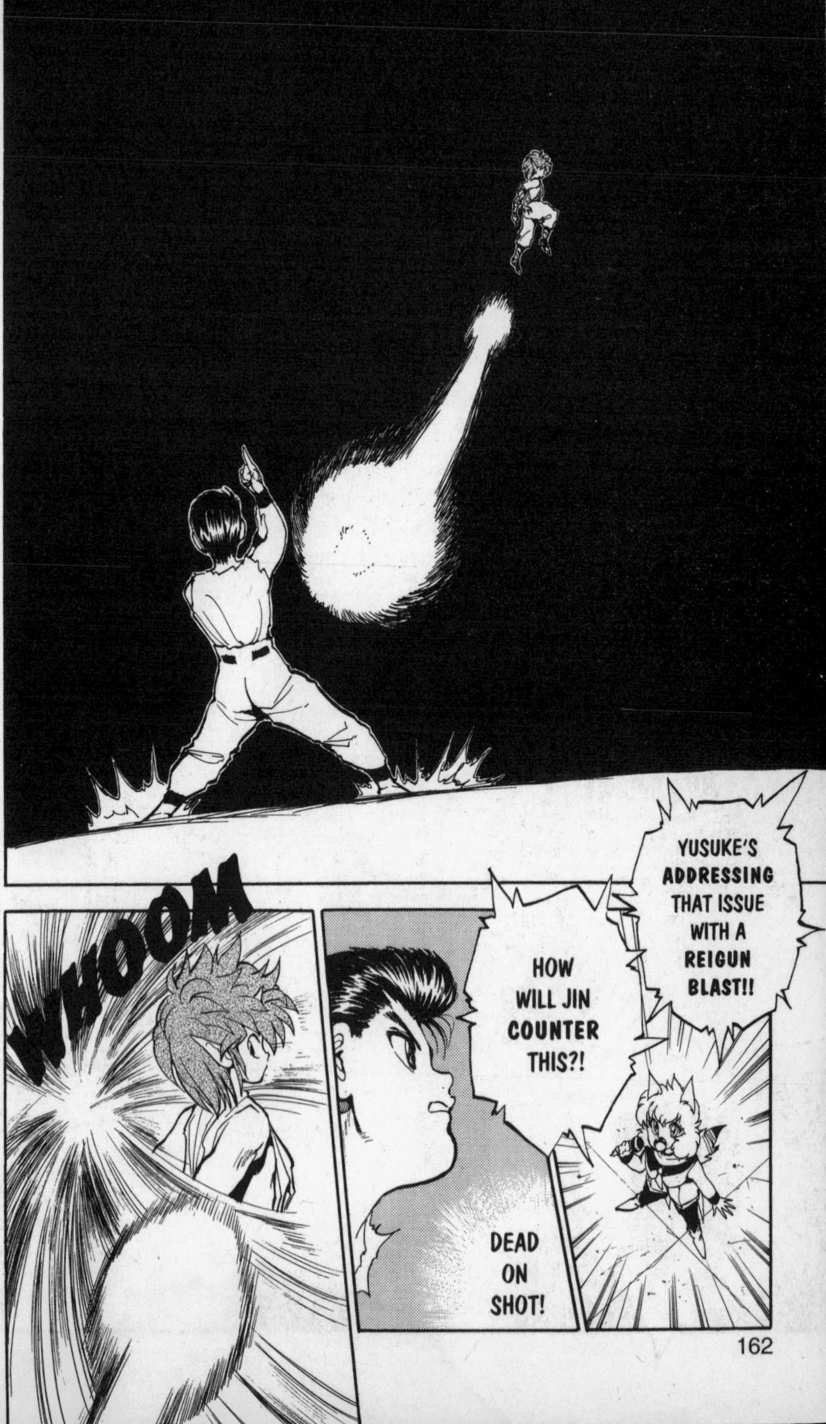

YUSUKE'S ADDRESSING THAT ISSUE WITH A REIGUN BLAST!!
HOW WILL JIN COUNTER THIS?!
DEAD ON SHOT!
WHOOM

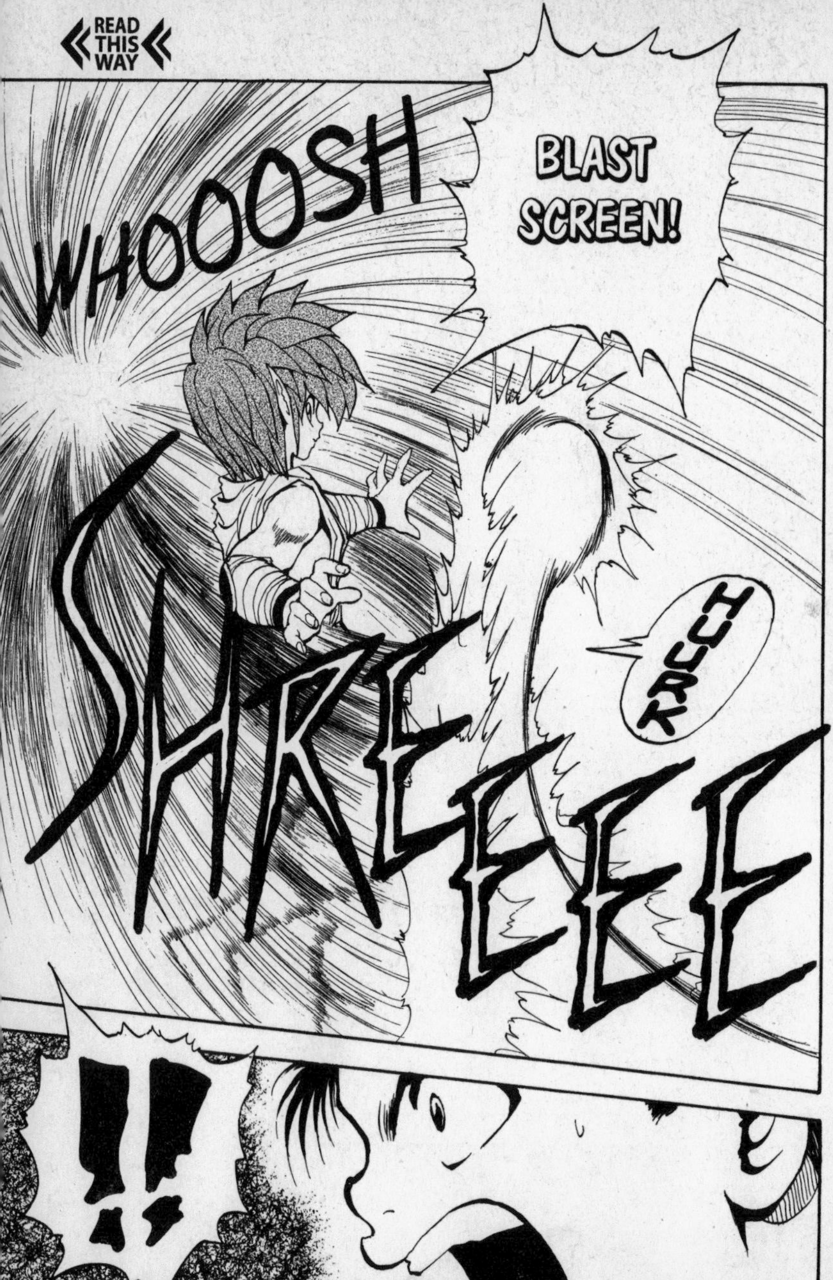
READ THIS WAY
BLAST SCREEN!
WHOOOSH
HURK
SHREEEE
!!

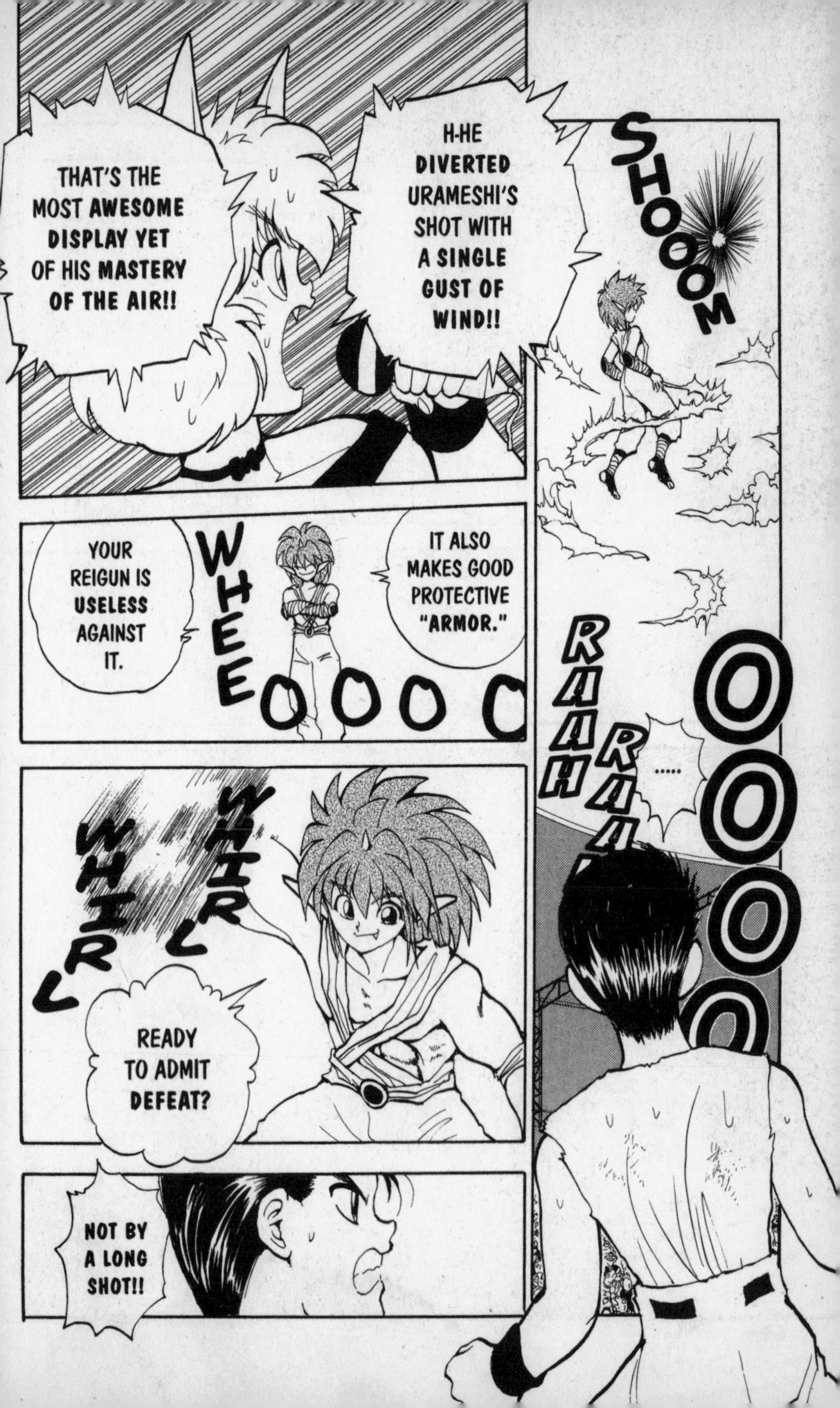
H-HE DIVERTED URAMESHI'S SHOT WITH A SINGLE GUST OF WIND!!
THAT'S THE MOST AWESOME DISPLAY YET OF HIS MASTERY OF THE AIR!!
SHOOOM
IT ALSO MAKES GOOD PROTECTIVE "ARMOR."
WHEEOOOO
YOUR REIGUN IS USELESS AGAINST IT.
RAAAH
RAAAA
OOOOO
.....
WHIRL
WHIRL
READY TO ADMIT DEFEAT?
NOT BY A LONG SHOT!!

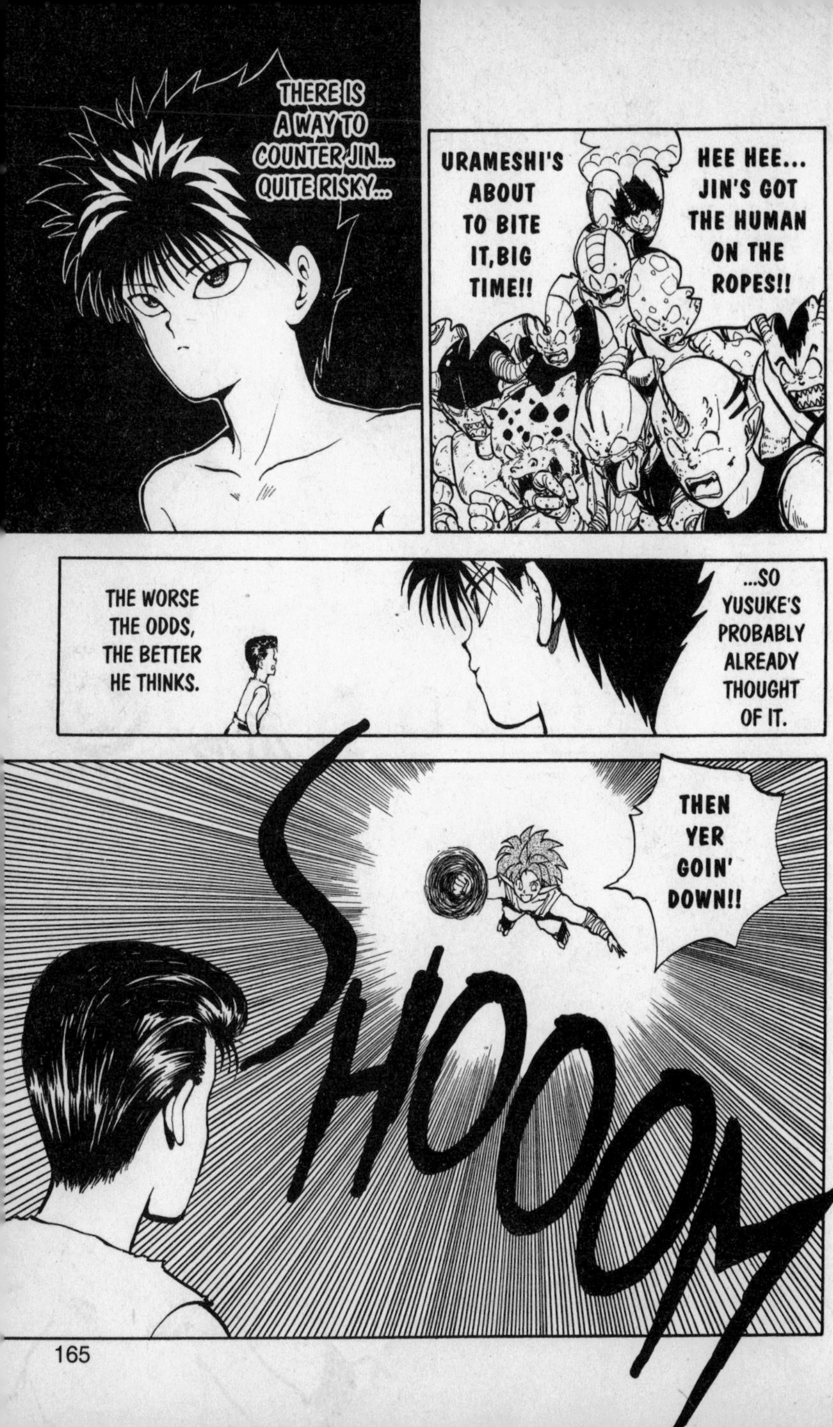

HEE HEE... JIN'S GOT THE HUMAN ON THE ROPES!!
URAMESHI'S ABOUT TO BITE IT, BIG TIME!!
THERE IS A WAY TO COUNTER JIN... QUITE RISKY...
...SO YUSUKE'S PROBABLY ALREADY THOUGHT OF IT.
THE WORSE THE ODDS, THE BETTER HE THINKS.
THEN YER GOIN' DOWN!!
SHOOOM

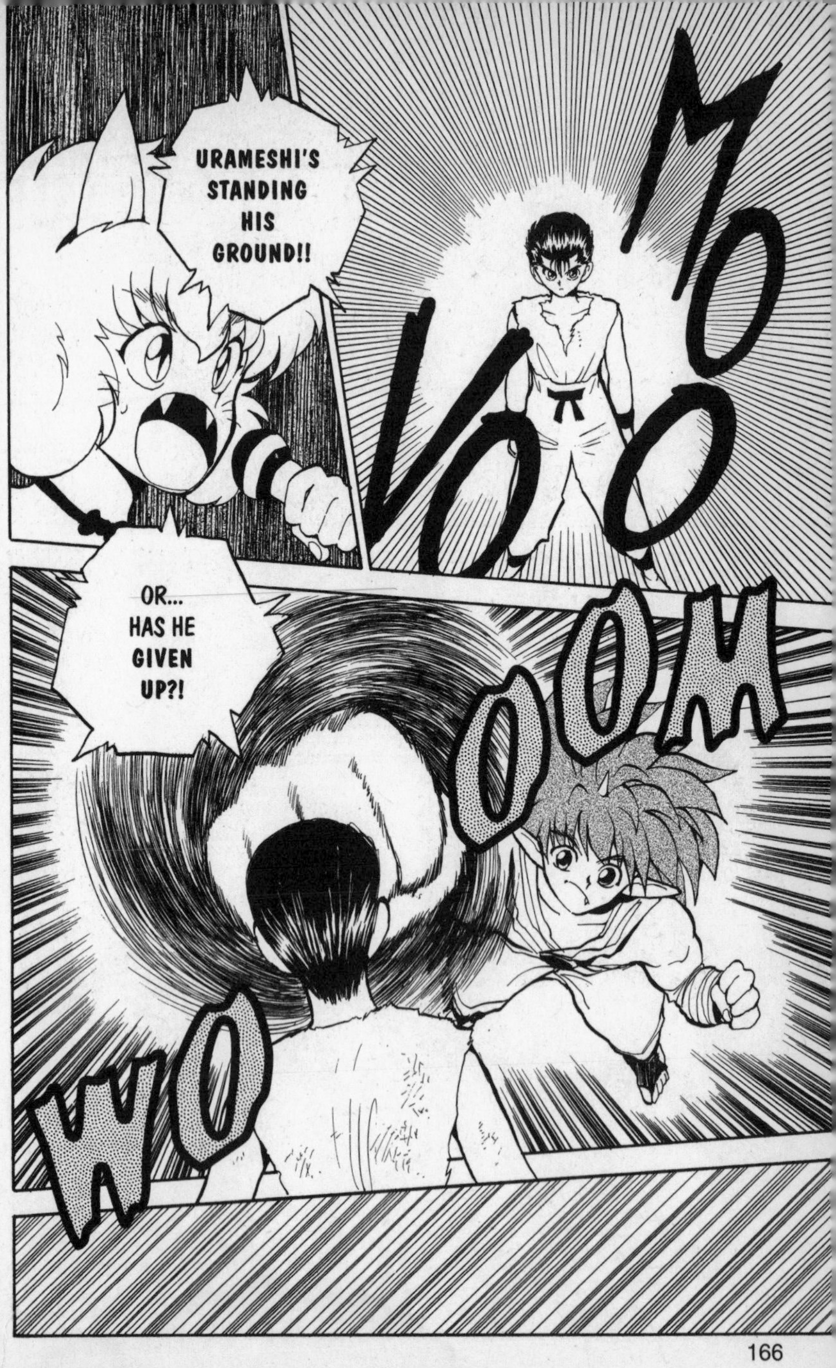
VOOOM
URAMESHI'S STANDING HIS GROUND!!
OR... HAS HE GIVEN UP?!
WOOOOM

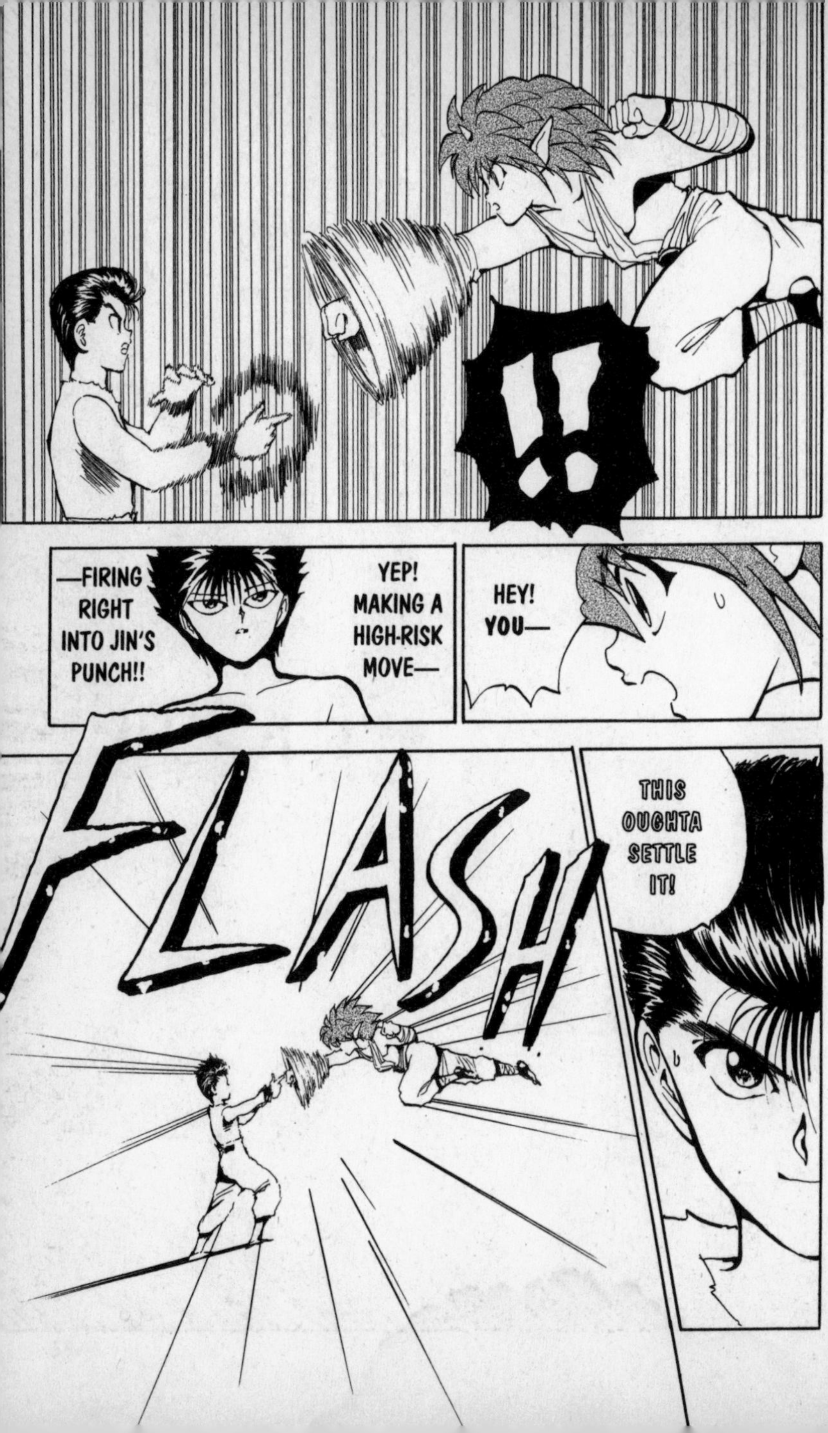
HEY! YOU—
YEP! MAKING A HIGH-RISK MOVE—
—FIRING RIGHT INTO JIN'S PUNCH!!
THIS OUGHTA SETTLE IT!
FLASH

1992 (PRESENT)

. . . . .

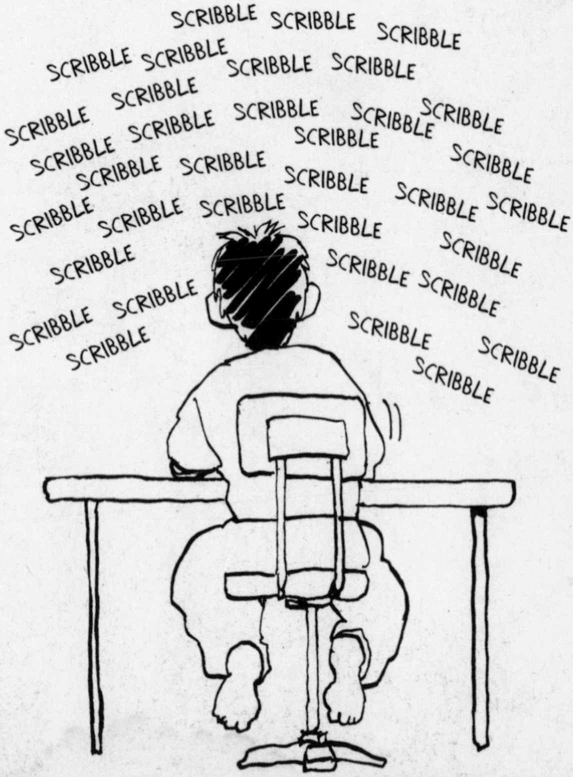
SCRIBBLE SCRIBBLE SCRIBBLE
SCRIBBLE SCRIBBLE SCRIBBLE SCRIBBLE
SCRIBBLE SCRIBBLE SCRIBBLE SCRIBBLE SCRIBBLE
SCRIBBLE SCRIBBLE SCRIBBLE
SCRIBBLE SCRIBBLE SCRIBBLE SCRIBBLE
SCRIBBLE SCRIBBLE SCRIBBLE SCRIBBLE SCRIBBLE SCRIBBLE
SCRIBBLE SCRIBBLE SCRIBBLE SCRIBBLE
SCRIBBLE SCRIBBLE SCRIBBLE SCRIBBLE SCRIBBLE SCRIBBLE

SURPASS THE REIGUN!!

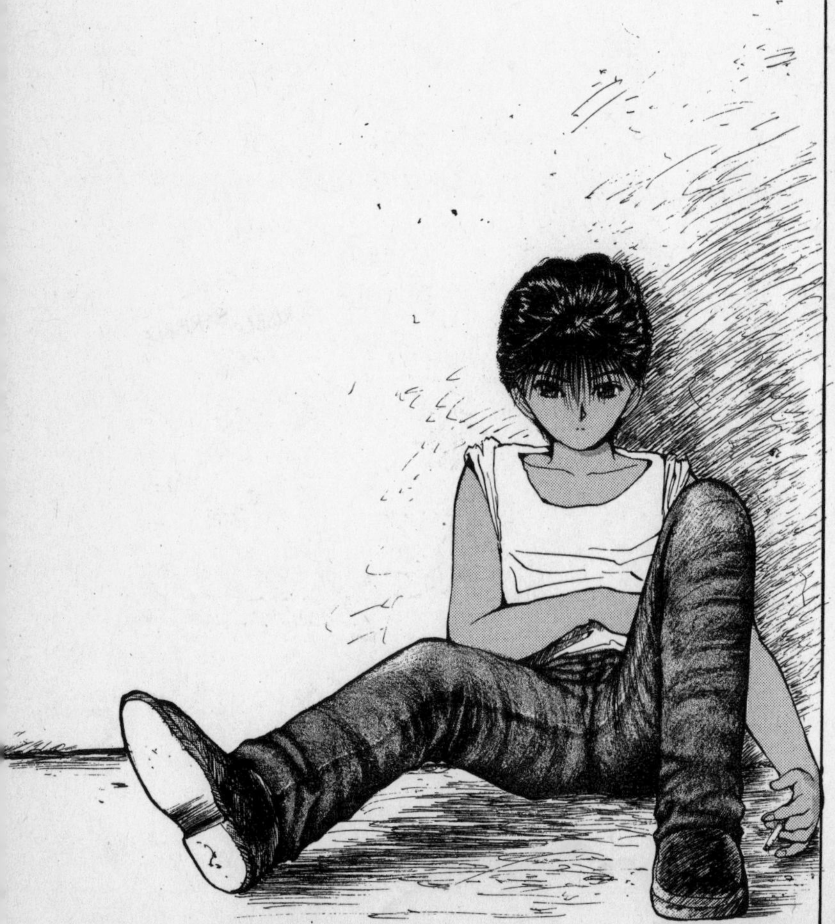

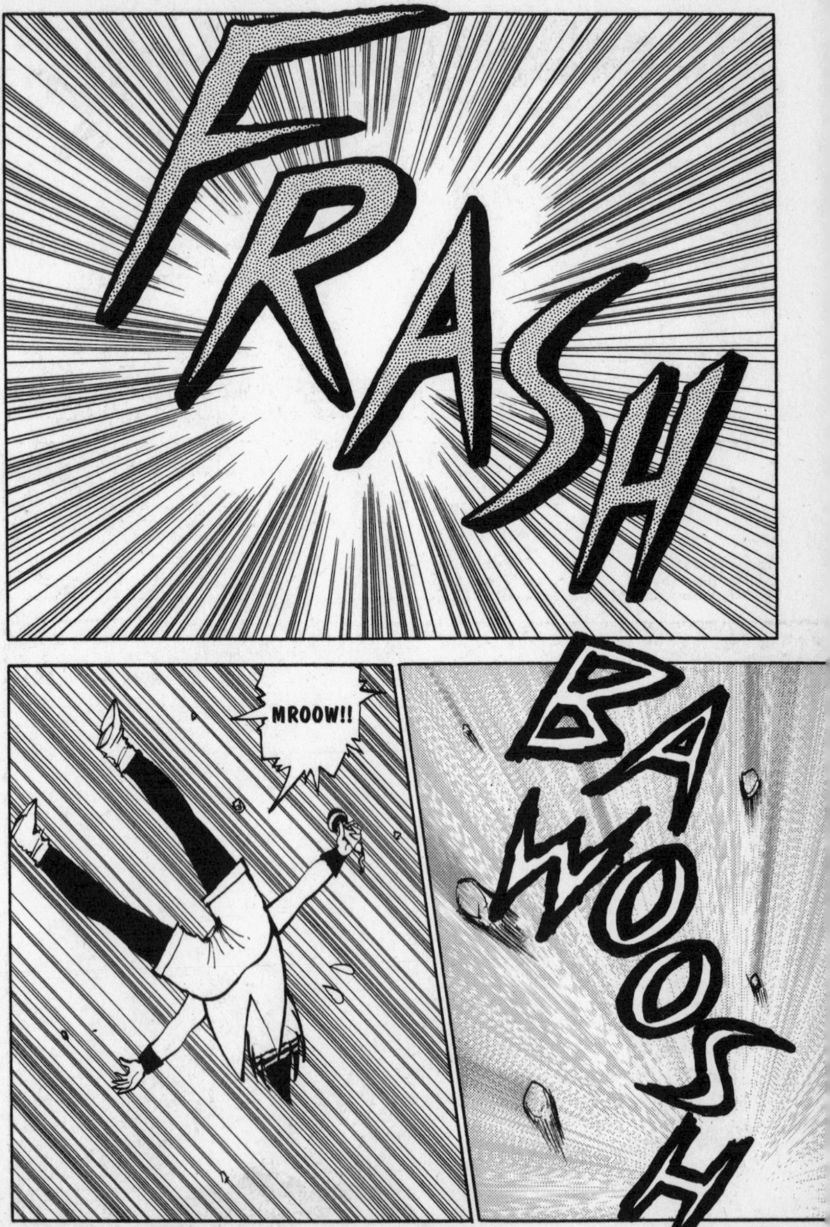
FRASH
BAWOOSH
MROOW!!

ZZIK

ZZIK

ZZAK

?!

WHOO!

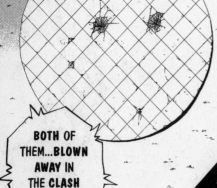

WHAT THE HEY?! THEY'RE GONE!!

BOTH OF THEM...BLOWN AWAY IN THE CLASH OF POWER!!

RAAAH

RAAAH

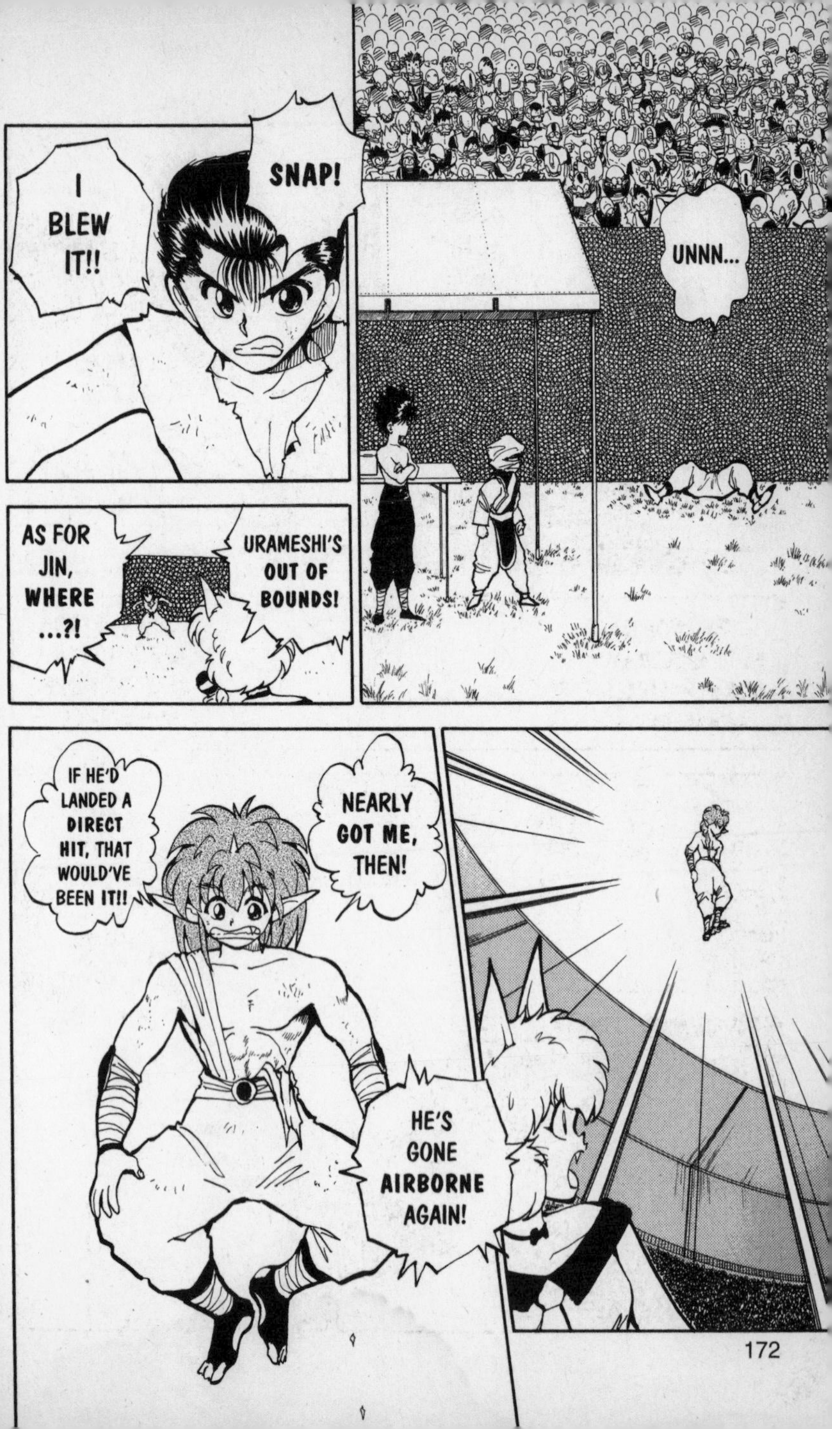
UNNN...
SNAP!
I BLEW IT!!
URAMESHI'S OUT OF BOUNDS!
AS FOR JIN, WHERE ...?!
HE'S GONE AIRBORNE AGAIN!
NEARLY GOT ME, THEN!
IF HE'D LANDED A DIRECT HIT, THAT WOULD'VE BEEN IT!!

READ THIS WAY

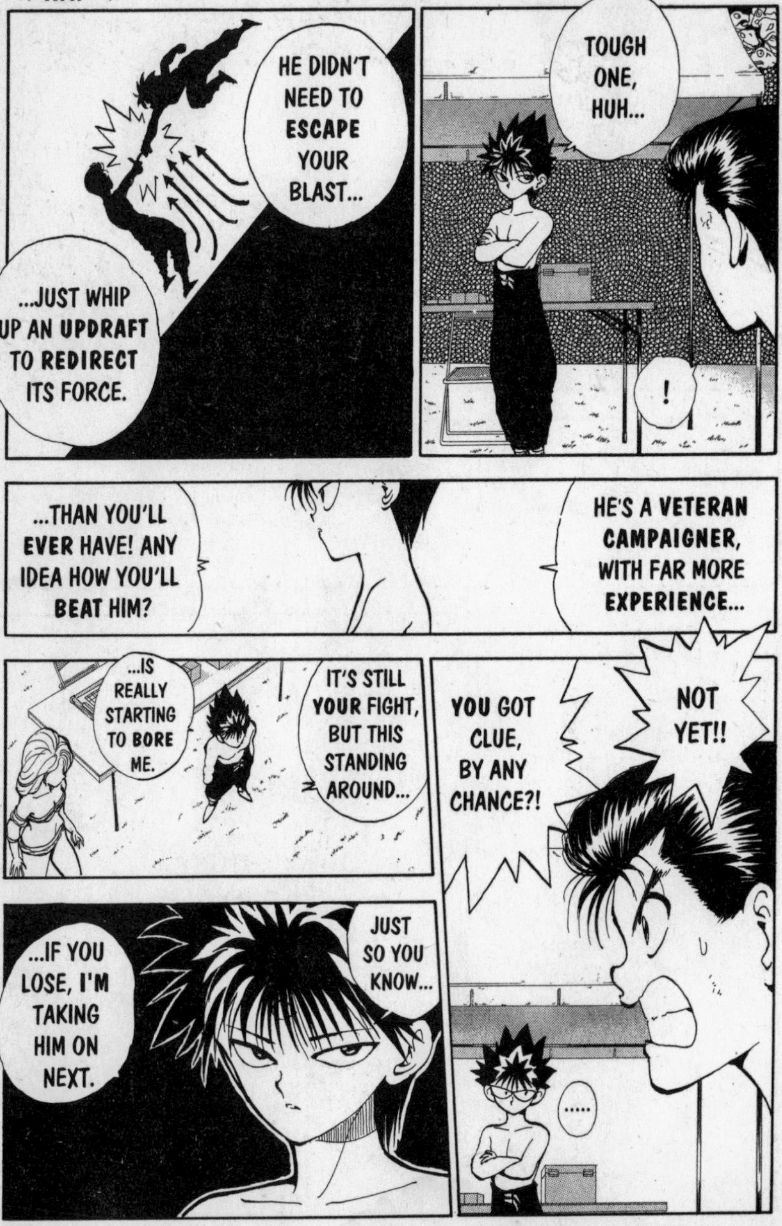
TOUGH ONE, HUH...
!
HE DIDN'T NEED TO ESCAPE YOUR BLAST...
...JUST WHIP UP AN UPDRAFT TO REDIRECT ITS FORCE.
HE'S A VETERAN CAMPAIGNER, WITH FAR MORE EXPERIENCE...
...THAN YOU'LL EVER HAVE! ANY IDEA HOW YOU'LL BEAT HIM?
NOT YET!!
YOU GOT CLUE, BY ANY CHANCE?!
.....
IT'S STILL YOUR FIGHT, BUT THIS STANDING AROUND...
...IS REALLY STARTING TO BORE ME.
JUST SO YOU KNOW...
...IF YOU LOSE, I'M TAKING HIM ON NEXT.

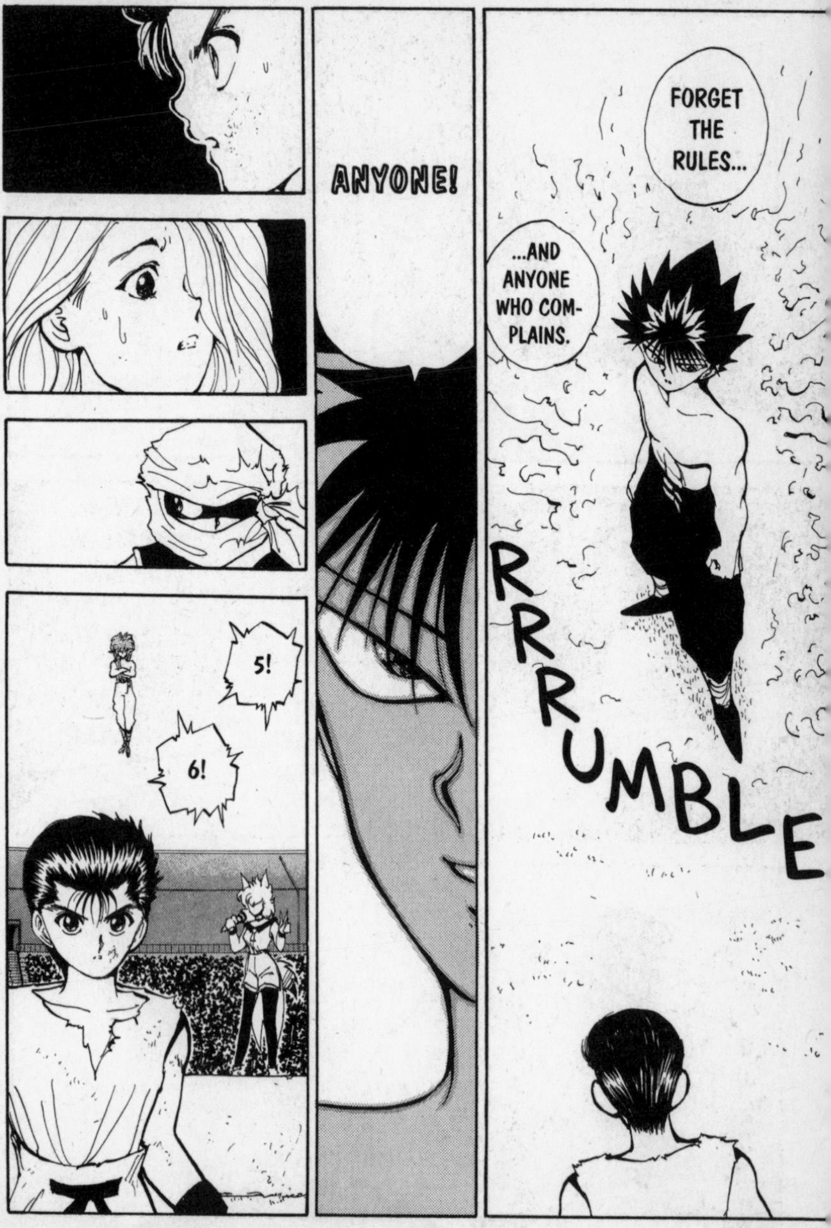
FORGET THE RULES...
...AND ANYONE WHO COM-PLAINS.
RRRUMBLE
ANYONE!
5!
6!

READ THIS WAY

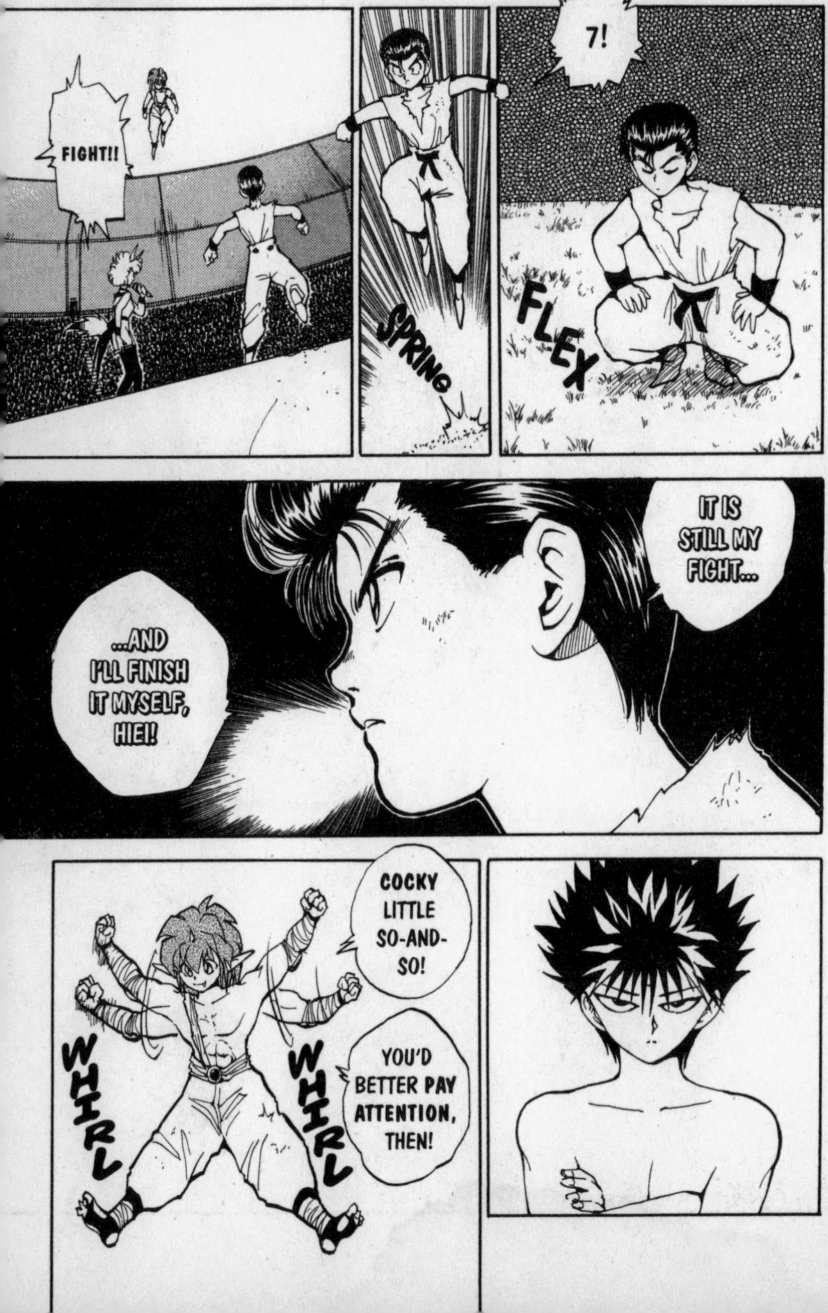
7!
FLEX
SPRING
FIGHT!!
IT IS STILL MY FIGHT...
...AND I'LL FINISH IT MYSELF, HIEI!
COCKY LITTLE SO-AND-SO!
YOU'D BETTER PAY ATTENTION, THEN!
WHIRL
WHIRL

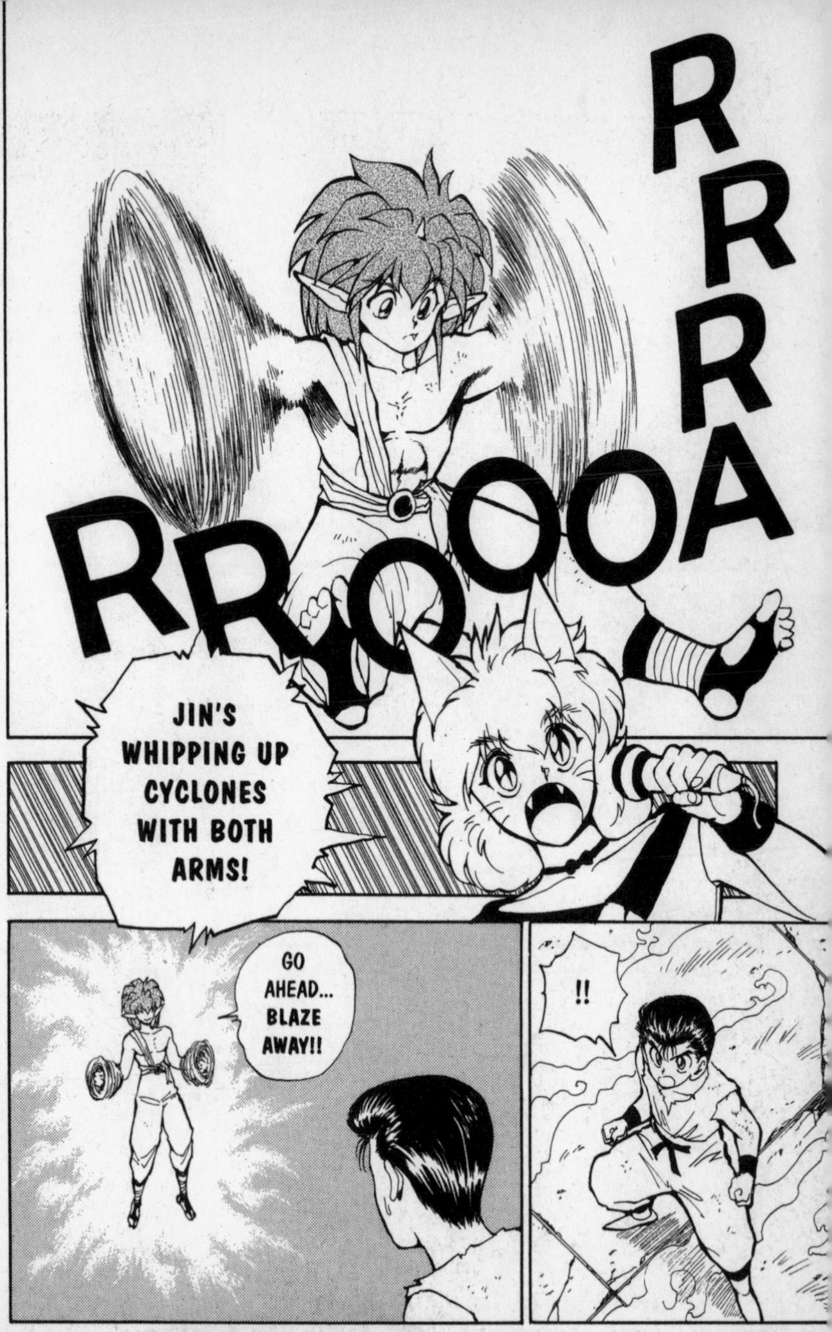
RRRA
RROOOA
JIN'S WHIPPING UP CYCLONES WITH BOTH ARMS!
!!
GO AHEAD... BLAZE AWAY!!

READ THIS WAY

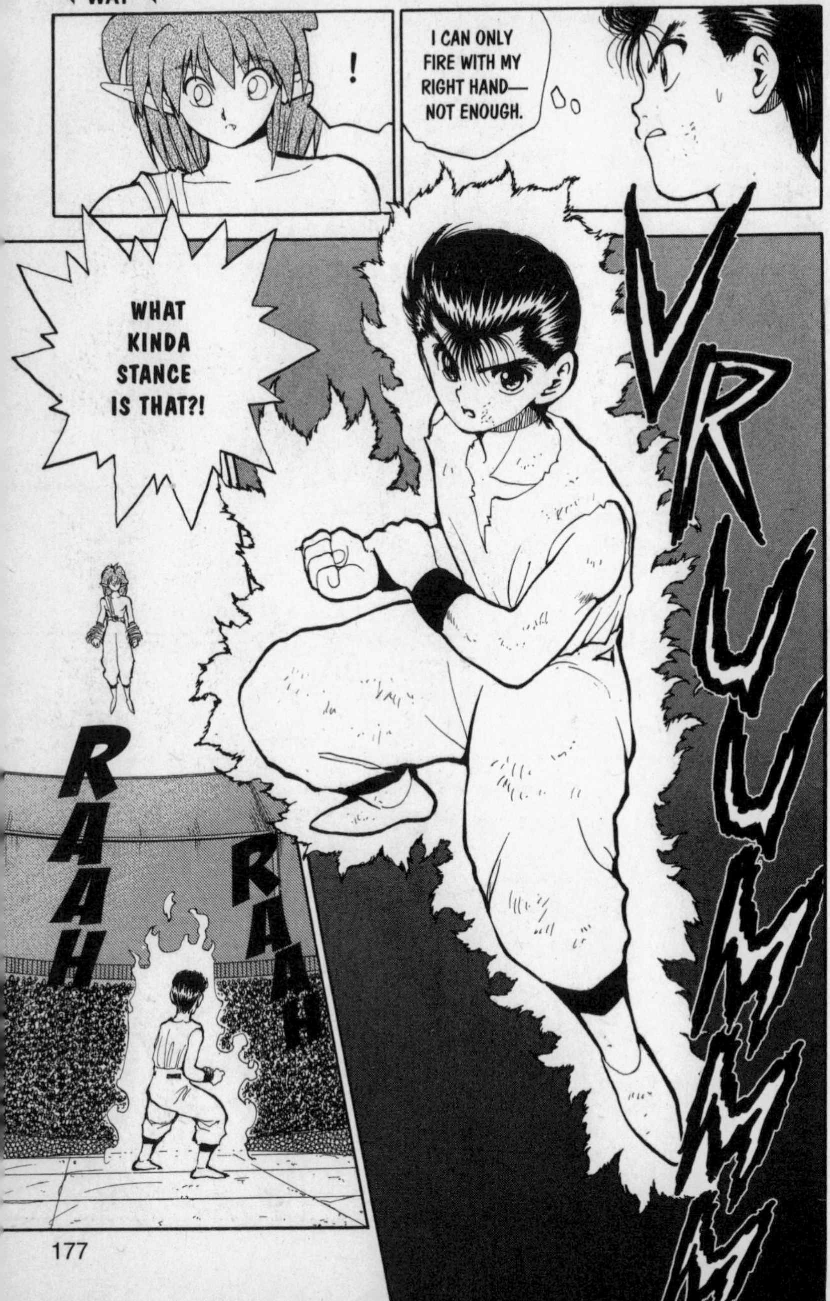

I CAN ONLY FIRE WITH MY RIGHT HAND— NOT ENOUGH.
!
VRUUMMMMM
WHAT KINDA STANCE IS THAT?!
RAAH
RAAH

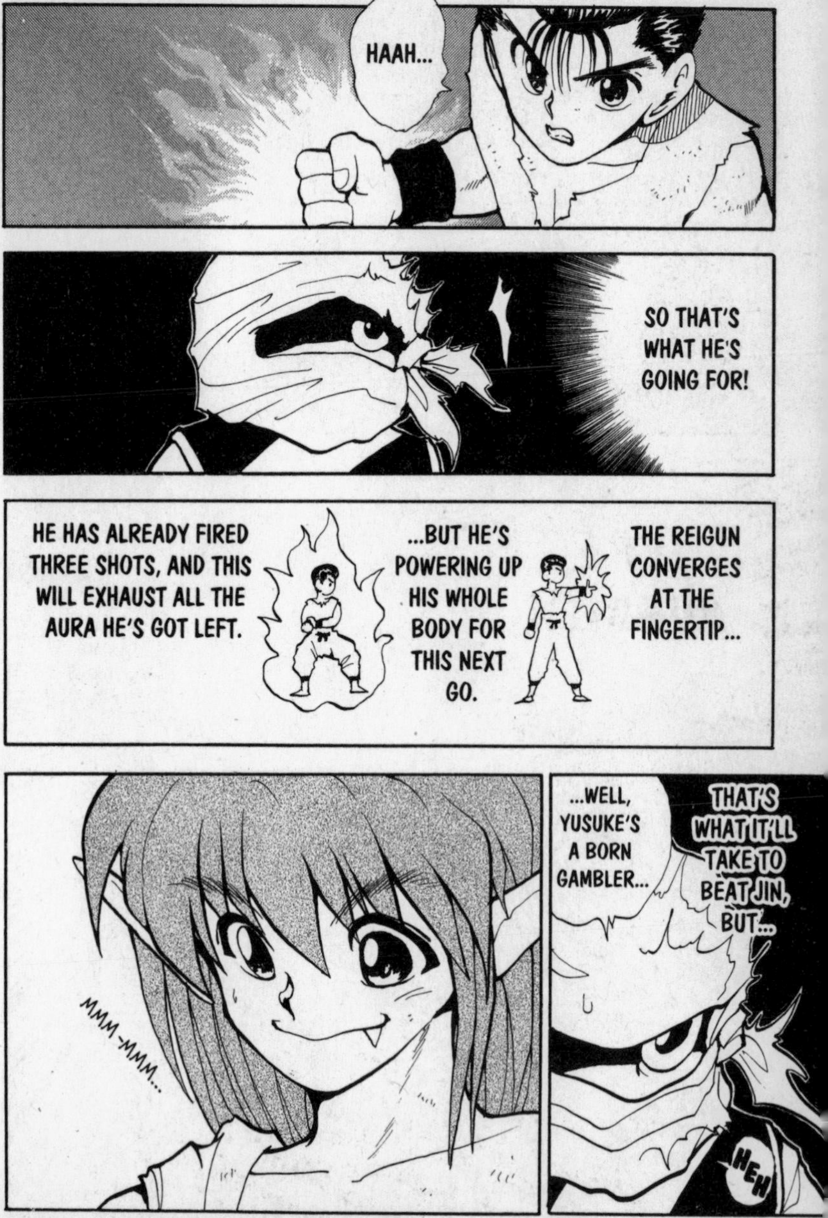
HAAH...
SO THAT'S WHAT HE'S GOING FOR!
THE REIGUN CONVERGES AT THE FINGERTIP...
...BUT HE'S POWERING UP HIS WHOLE BODY FOR THIS NEXT GO.
HE HAS ALREADY FIRED THREE SHOTS, AND THIS WILL EXHAUST ALL THE AURA HE'S GOT LEFT.
THAT'S WHAT IT'LL TAKE TO BEAT JIN, BUT...
...WELL, YUSUKE'S A BORN GAMBLER...
HEH
MMM-MMM...

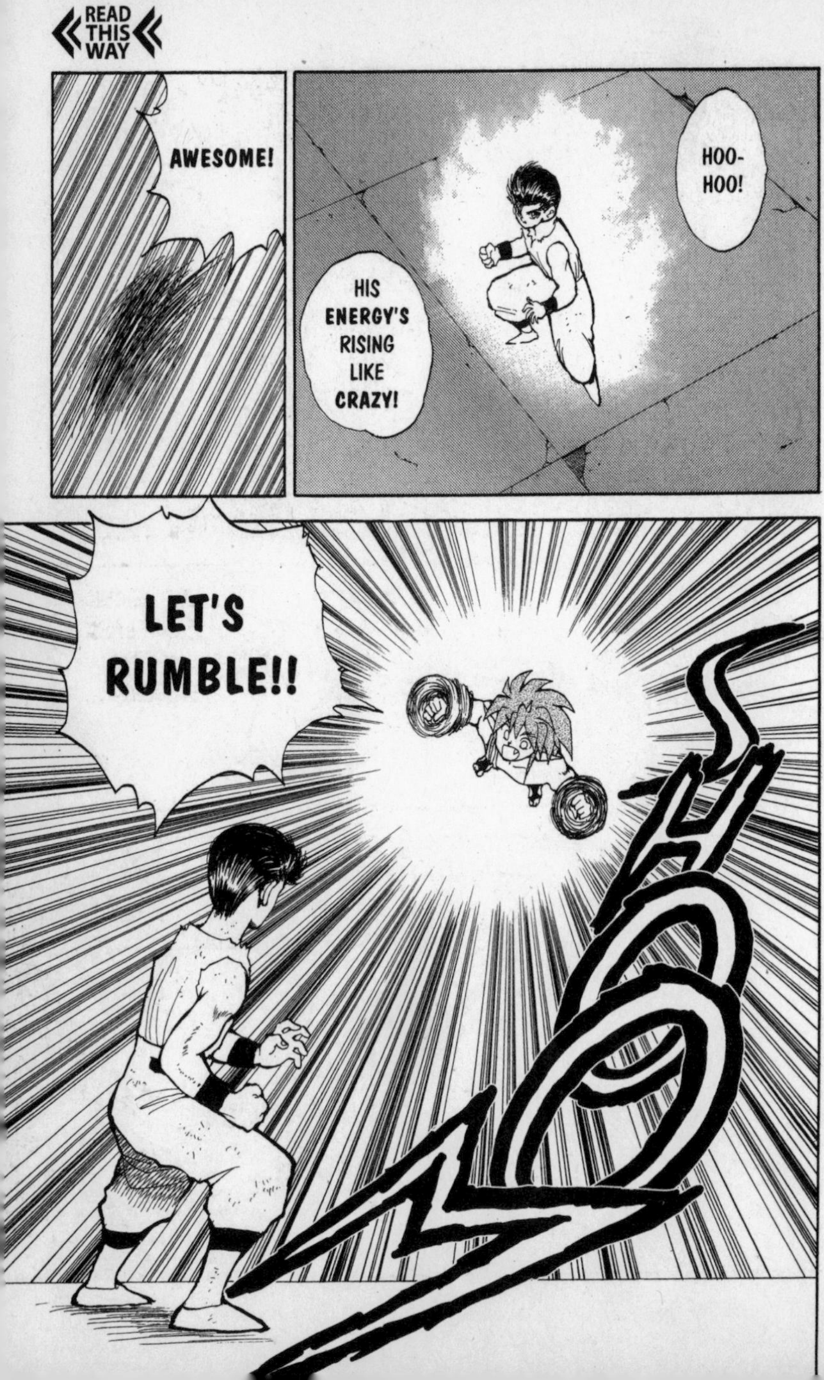
READ THIS WAY
HOO-HOO!
HIS ENERGY'S RISING LIKE CRAZY!
AWESOME!
LET'S RUMBLE!!

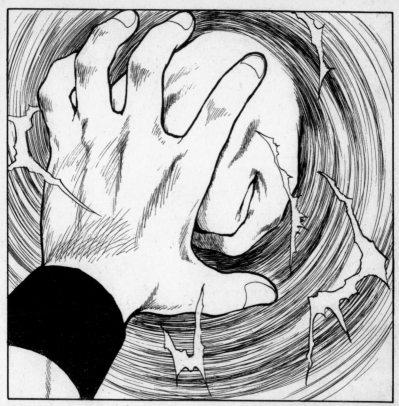

YIPES!!

READ THIS WAY

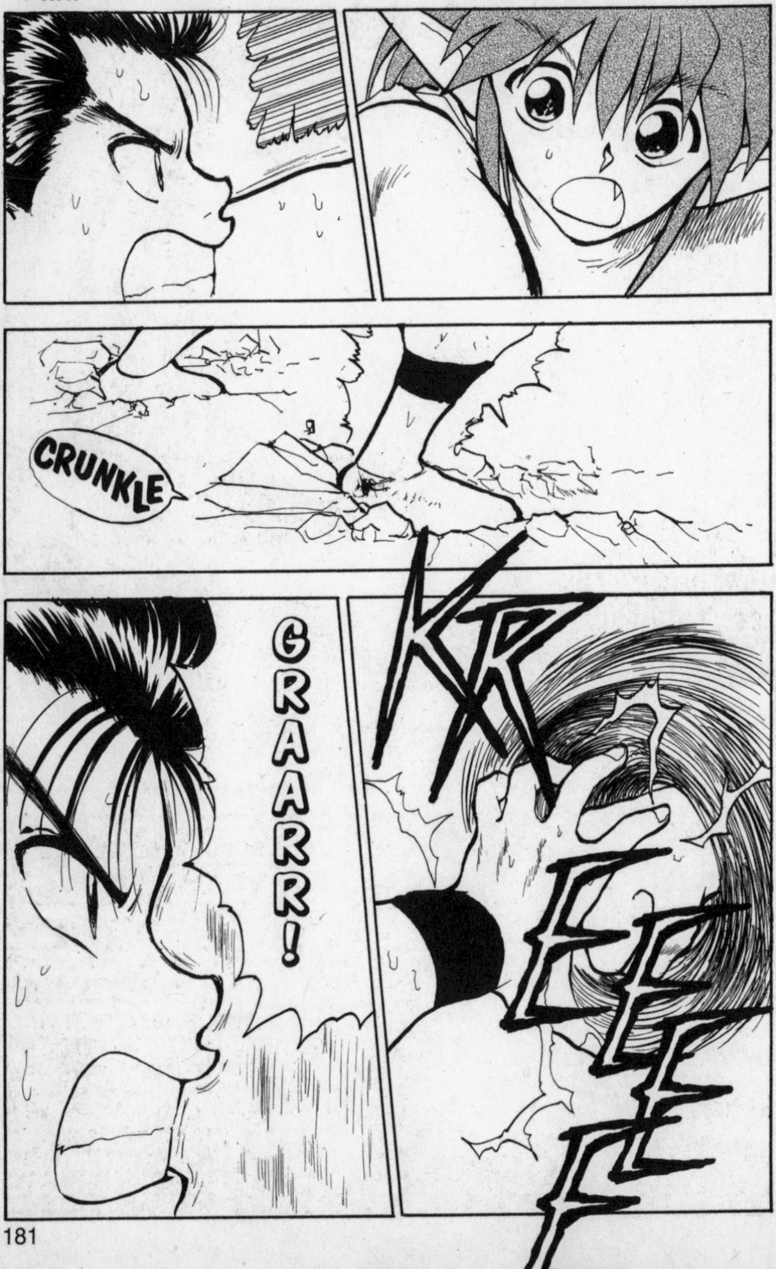
CRUNKLE
KREEEEE
GRAARRR!

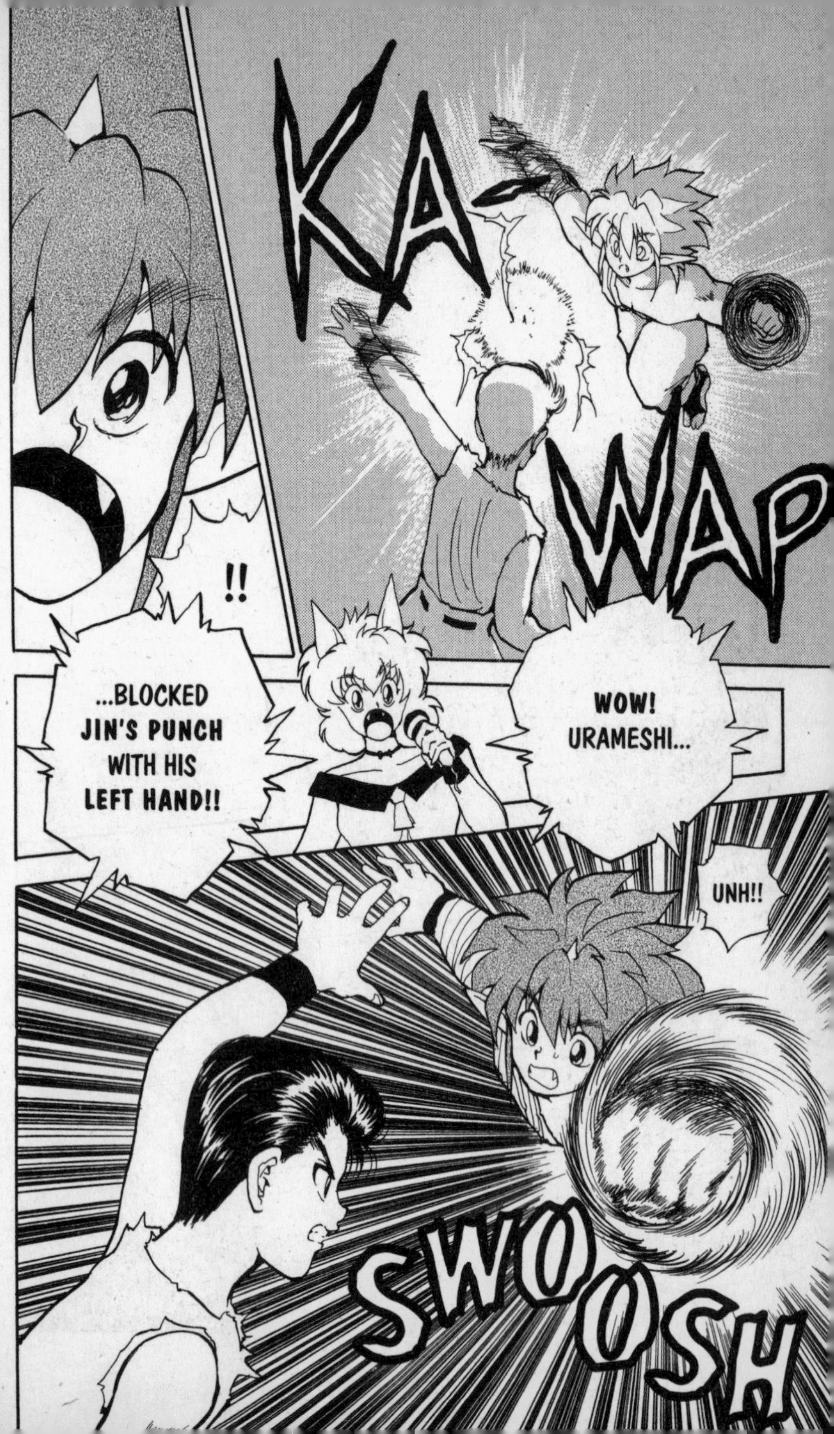
KA-WAP
!!
WOW! URAMESHI...
...BLOCKED JIN'S PUNCH WITH HIS LEFT HAND!!
UNH!!
SWOOSH

READ THIS WAY

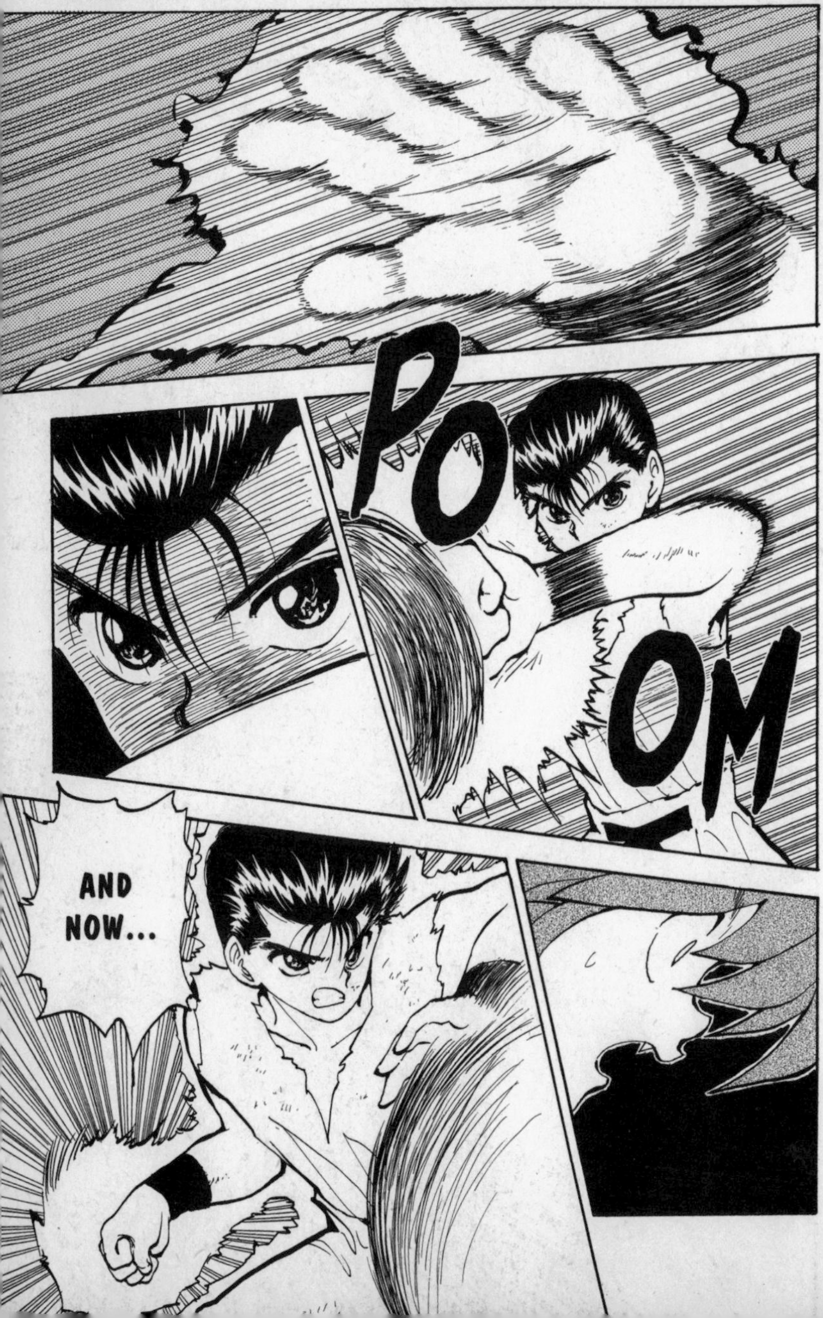
POOM
AND NOW...

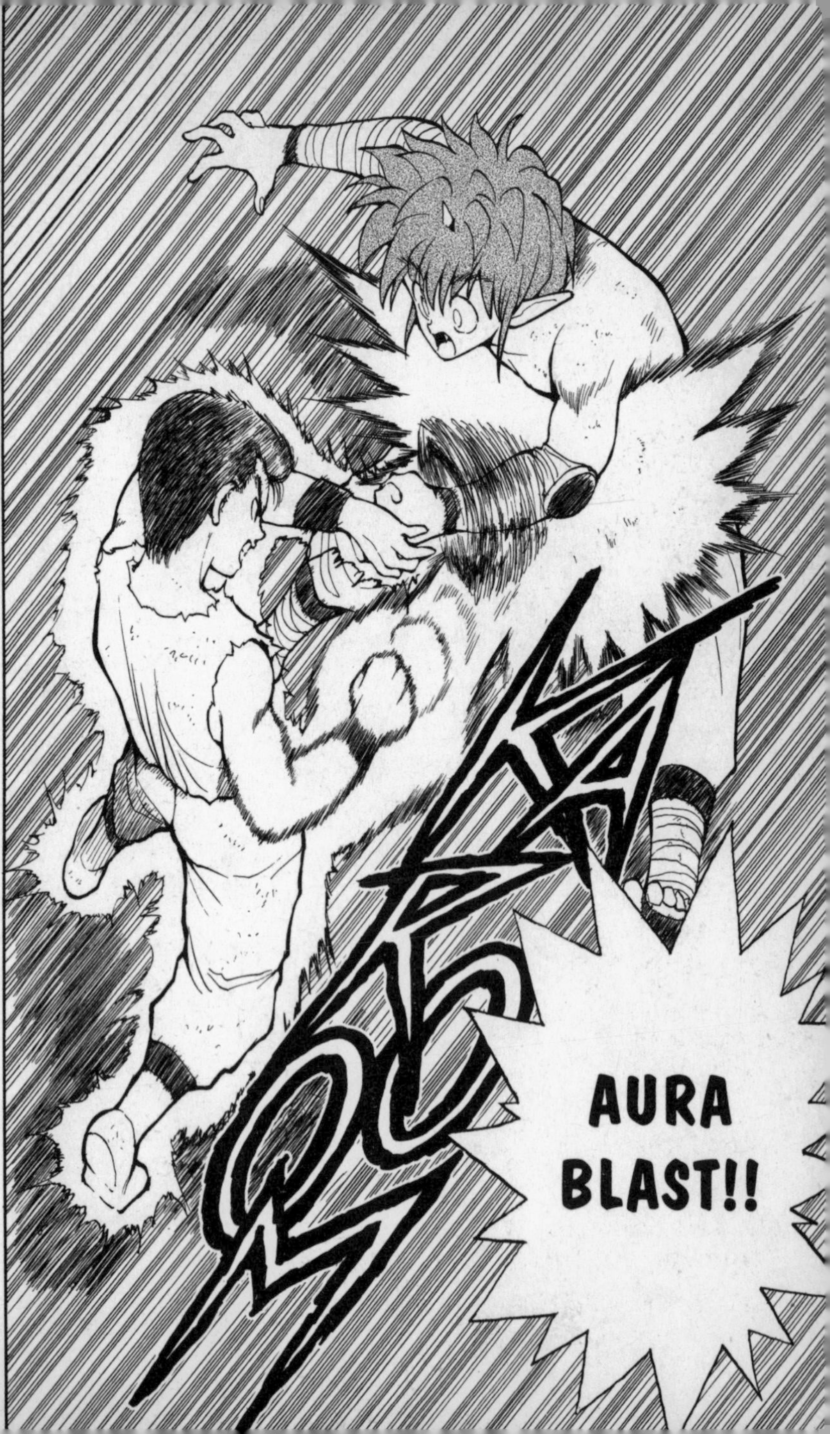
AURA
BLAST!!

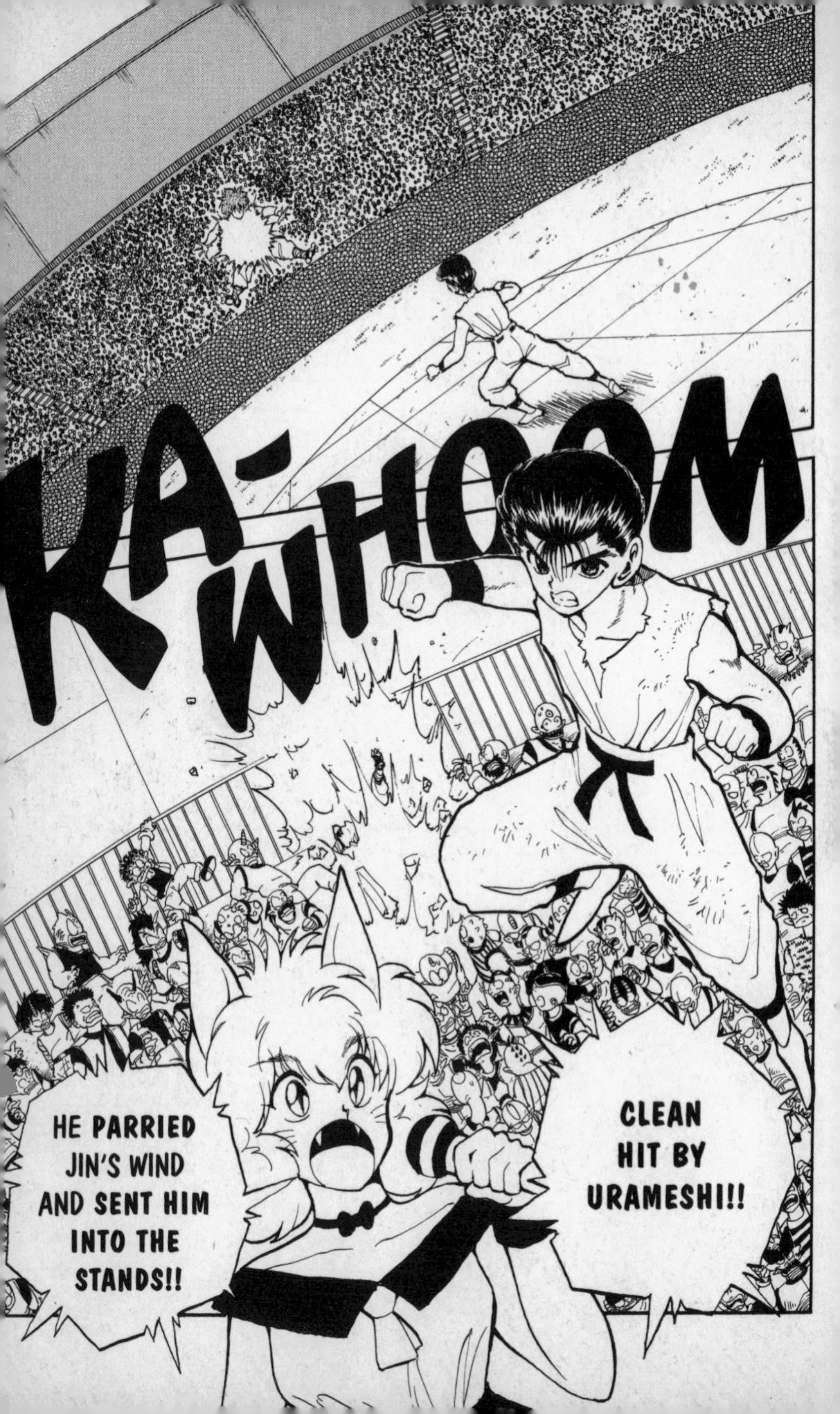
KA-WHOOM
CLEAN HIT BY URAMESHI!!
HE PARRIED JIN'S WIND AND SENT HIM INTO THE STANDS!!

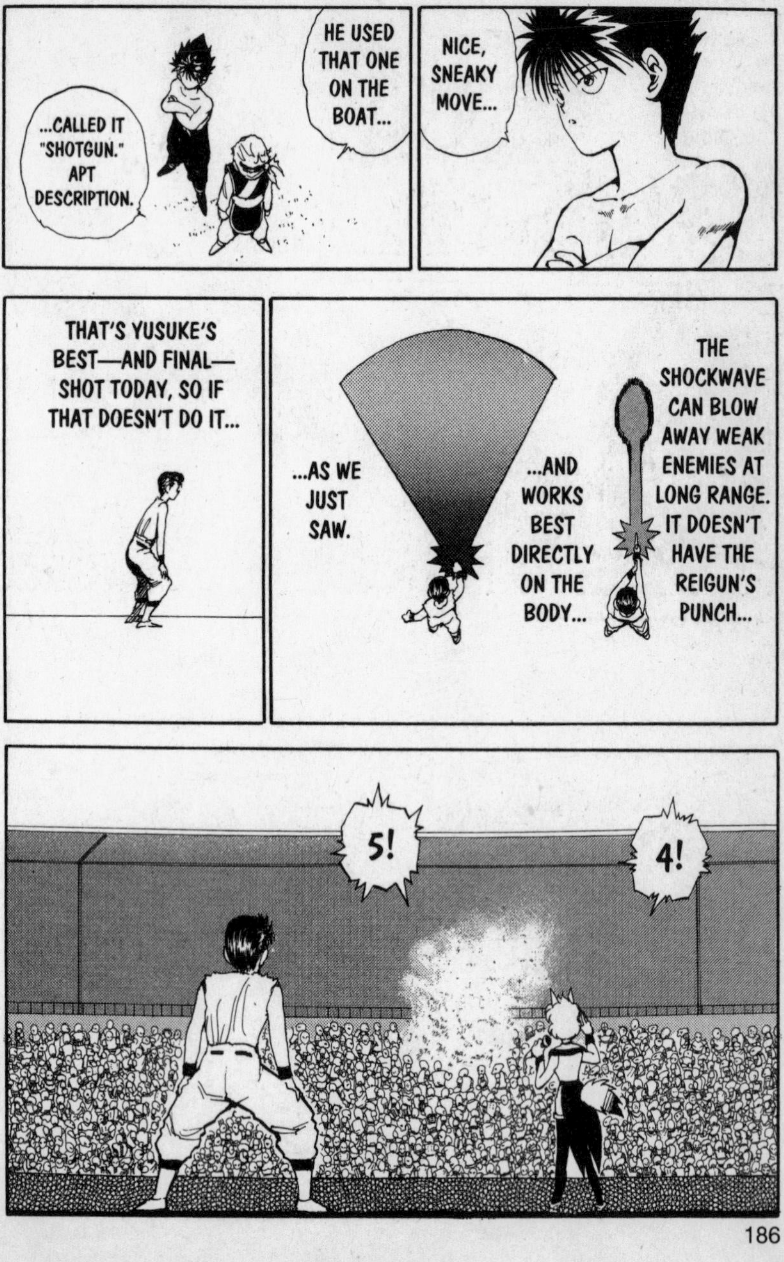

NICE, SNEAKY MOVE...
HE USED THAT ONE ON THE BOAT...
...CALLED IT "SHOTGUN." APT DESCRIPTION.
THE SHOCKWAVE CAN BLOW AWAY WEAK ENEMIES AT LONG RANGE. IT DOESN'T HAVE THE REIGUN'S PUNCH...
...AND WORKS BEST DIRECTLY ON THE BODY...
...AS WE JUST SAW.
THAT'S YUSUKE'S BEST—AND FINAL—SHOT TODAY, SO IF THAT DOESN'T DO IT...
4!
5!

READ THIS WAY

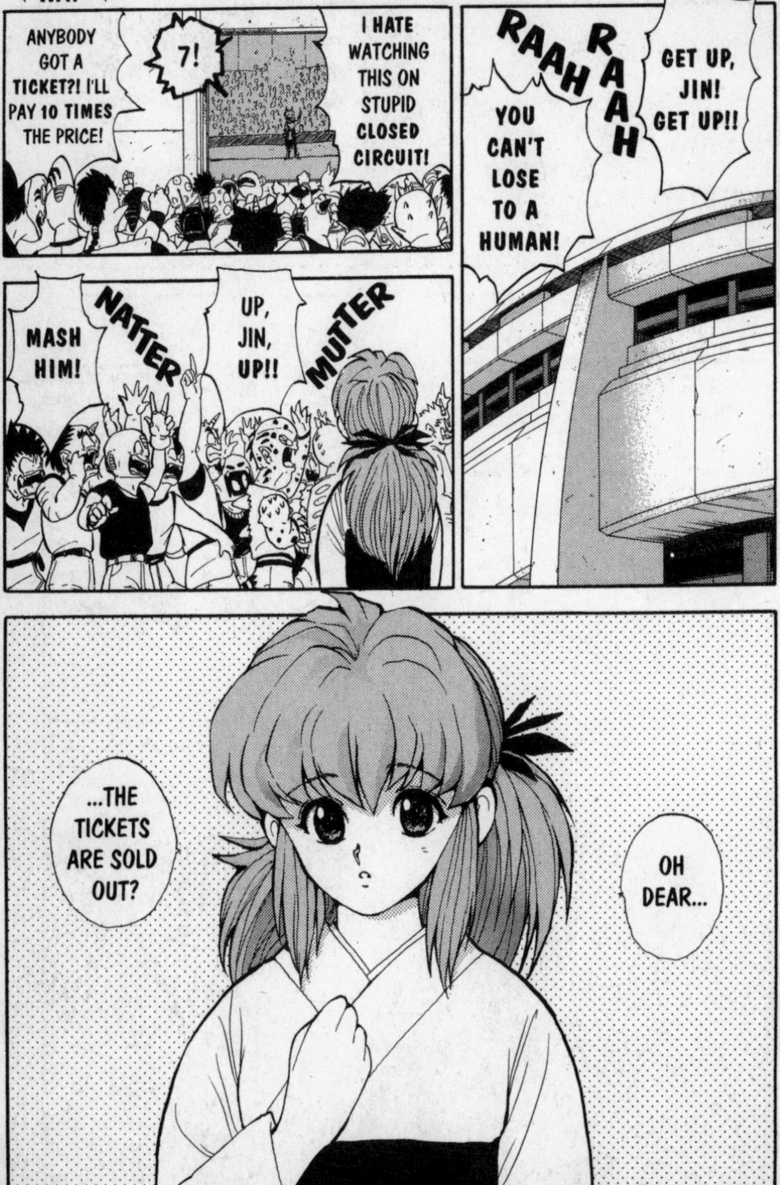

GET UP, JIN! GET UP!!
RAAH RAAH
YOU CAN'T LOSE TO A HUMAN!
I HATE WATCHING THIS ON STUPID CLOSED CIRCUIT!
7!
ANYBODY GOT A TICKET?! I'LL PAY 10 TIMES THE PRICE!
MUTTER
UP, JIN, UP!!
NATTER
MASH HIM!
OH DEAR...
...THE TICKETS ARE SOLD OUT?

COMING NEXT VOLUME...

Struggling to stay afloat—more like survive—in the Dark Tournament, Team Urameshi faces the Fractured Fairy Tales Team in the semifinals. With Team Urameshi missing Yusuke and Genkai, the match-ups are determined by rolling dice. But how can Yusuke's team remain on equal footing with their demon counterparts when there's nobody left to fight for their cause...?!

Coming April 2006

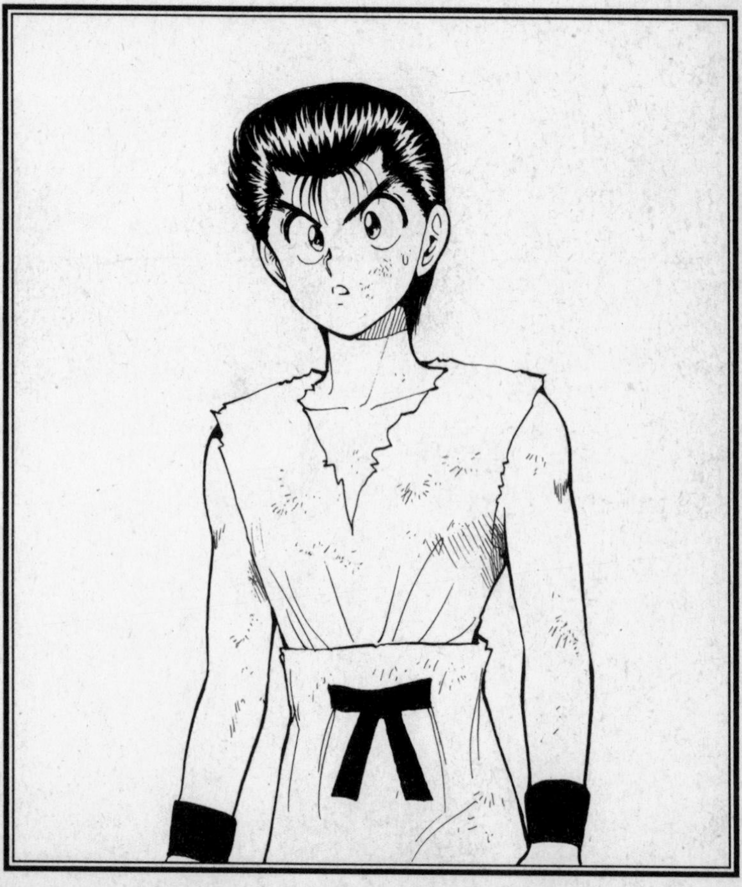

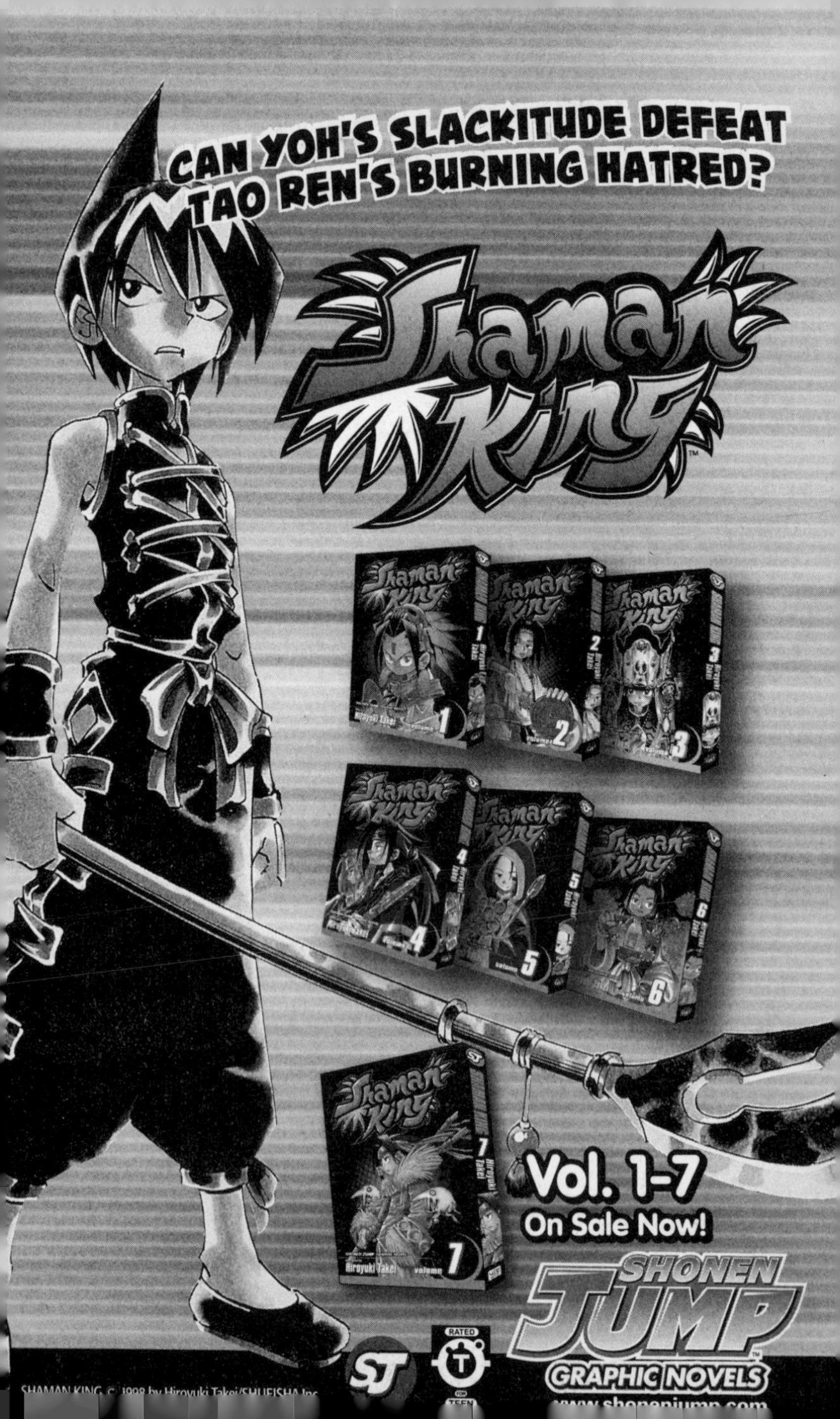

CAN YOH'S SLACKITUDE DEFEAT TAO REN'S BURNING HATRED?
Shaman King™
Vol. 1-7
On Sale Now!
SHONEN JUMP GRAPHIC NOVELS
RATED T FOR TEEN
www.shonenjump.com
SHAMAN KING © 1998 by Hiroyuki Takei/SHUEISHA Inc.

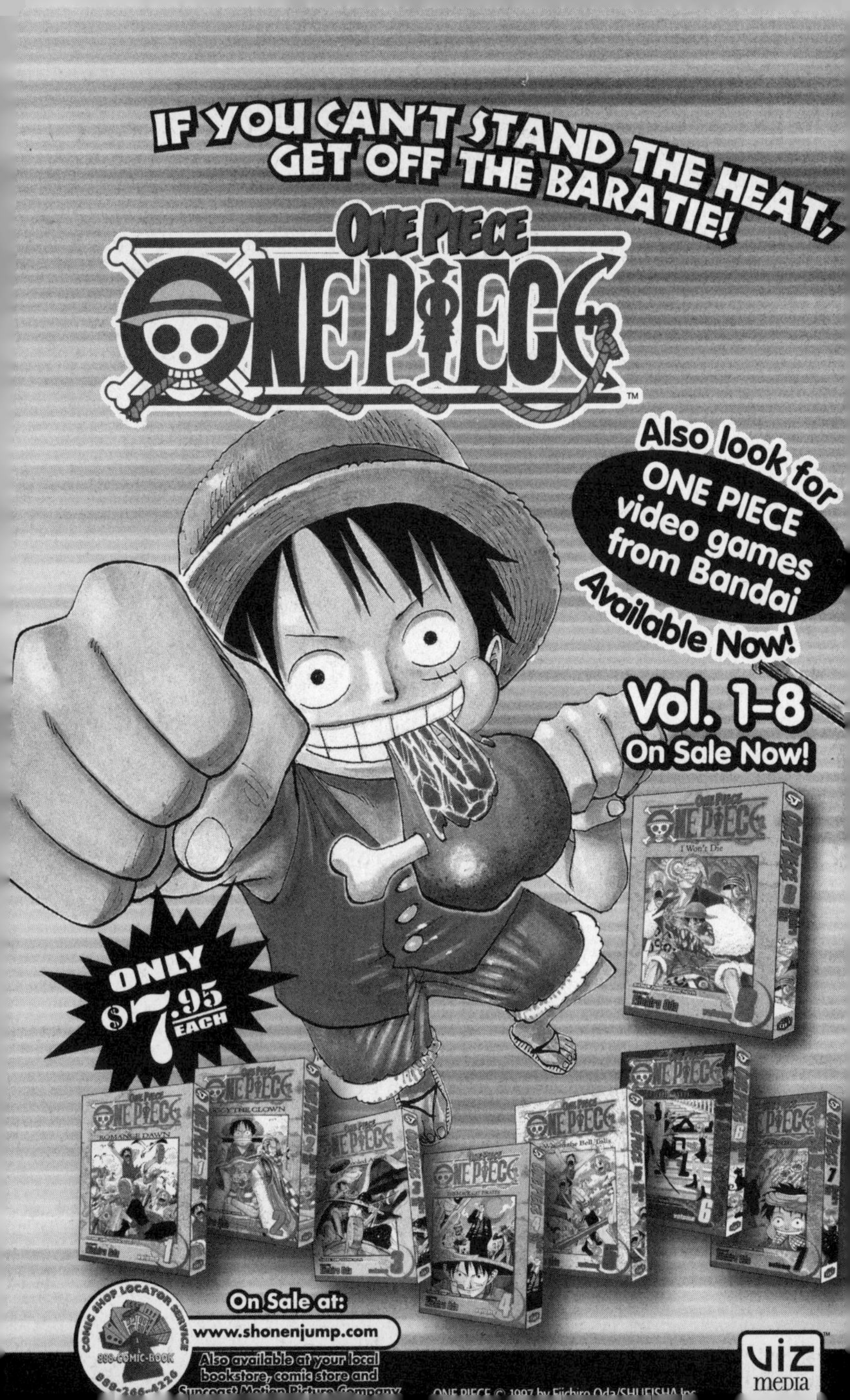
IF YOU CAN'T STAND THE HEAT, GET OFF THE BARATIE!
ONE PIECE
ONE PIECE
Also look for ONE PIECE video games from Bandai Available Now!
Vol. 1-8 On Sale Now!
ONLY $7.95 EACH
On Sale at:
www.shonenjump.com
Also available at your local bookstore, comic store and Suncoast Motion Picture Company.
COMIC SHOP LOCATOR SERVICE
888-COMIC-BOOK
888-266-4226
VIZ media
ONE PIECE © 1997 by Eiichiro Oda/SHUEISHA Inc.

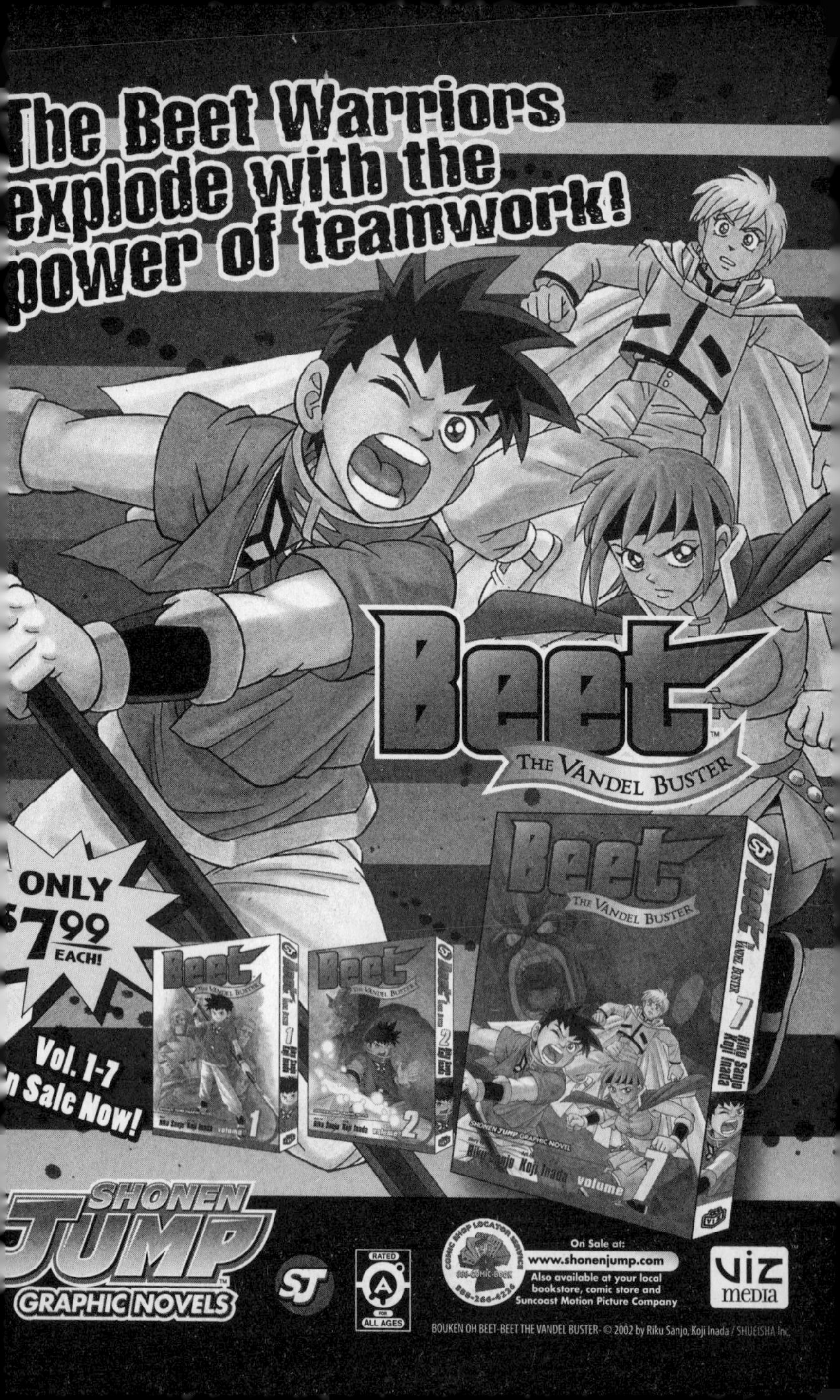

The Beet Warriors explode with the power of teamwork!
Beet THE VANDEL BUSTER™
ONLY $7.99 EACH!
Vol. 1-7 On Sale Now!
SHONEN JUMP GRAPHIC NOVELS
RATED A FOR ALL AGES
On Sale at:
www.shonenjump.com
Also available at your local bookstore, comic store and Suncoast Motion Picture Company
COMIC SHOP LOCATOR SERVICE 888-266-4226
viz media
BOUKEN OH BEET-BEET THE VANDEL BUSTER- © 2002 by Riku Sanjo, Koji Inada / SHUEISHA Inc.